RINGS OF SUPERSONIC STEEL

Nike Ajax site (*Golden Gate National Recreation Area Park Archives, SF Defense Site Photographic Collection, GOGA 17985.*)

Rings of Supersonic Steel:
Air Defenses of the United States Army 1950-1979

An Introductory History and Site Guide
Third Edition

By Mark L. Morgan and Mark A. Berhow

Hole in the Head Press
Bodega Bay, California

Revised Third Edition

For information on reprinting and purchasing contact:

Hole in the Head Press
Samuel E. Stokes, Publisher
P.O. Box 807, Bodega Bay, CA 94923
sestokes@sonic.net

1 2 3 4 5 6 7 8 9

ISBN: 978-0-9761494-0-8

Library of Congress Control Number
2010920593

Publisher: Samuel E. Stokes
Editor: Roxane Buck-Ezcurra
Design and production: Carole Thickstun
Illustrations and maps: Lawrence Ormsby

Photo credits—cover: Illustration by Lawrence Ormsby; back cover: Mark Berhow ©1998, Nike Site SF-88, Golden Gate National Recreation Area, Marin Headlands, California.

Printed in the USA by Wholesale Lithographers, Tucson, AZ

www.holeintheheadpress.com

Foreword . . . . *vii*

Acknowledgments . . . . *ix*

Introduction . . . . *xi*

List of Abbreviations . . . . *xii*

Part I **A SHORT HISTORY OF AMERICAN COLD WAR AIR DEFENSES**

      1.   U.S. Antiaircraft Artillery Service, 1917-1945 3

      2.   Postwar Developments 8

      3.   Army Antiaircraft Command 9

      4.   The Nike-Ajax Missile System 10

      5.   The Nike-Hercules Missile System 23

      6.   Nike Command Structure 45

      7.   US Air Force SAGE Combat/Direction Centers 46

      8.   Other American Surface-to-Air Missile Defense Systems 54

                  BOMARC (Air Force) 54

                  HAWK (Army) 56

                  Talos (Navy) 58

                  Ground-based Terrier (Navy) 58

      9.   US Army Antiballistic Missile Systems 62

                  Nike-Zeus 62

                  Nike-X 64

                  Sentinel 65

                  Safeguard 66

     10.   Inactivation of Nike and the Demise of ARADCOM 67

     11.   The Stanley R. Mickleson Safeguard Complex 69

     12.   Nike Missile Sites Today 75

Part II **UNITED STATES ARMY AIR DEFENSE SITE GUIDE**

    1.   Key to Nike Sites 80

    2.   AAA Gun Site Program 1951-59 204

    3.   Section A: The ARAACOM/ARADCOM Battalions 214

    4.   Section B: The ARADCOM CARS Battalions 272

Part III **NIKE UNIT DISTINCTIVE INSIGNIAS**

    Heraldry of the Air Defense Artillery 314

    Distinctive Insignia of the Army Antiaircraft Artillery/

    Air Defense Commands 316

Bibliography *328*

Internet Resource Sites *331*

Selected Nike-Ajax & Nike-Hercules Manuals *332*

Index *341*

Index of Sites *348*

Foreword

Rings of Supersonic Steel, Third Edition is a short history of the United States continental air defense missile network. The backbone of this defense, from 1954 to 1974, was the Army's Nike surface-to-air missile (SAM) system. This book provides a brief overview of the Army Air Defense Command and the major United States air defense systems—the Nike-Ajax and Nike-Hercules SAM systems of the US Army; the BOMARC interceptor missile system of the US Air Force; and the US Army Sentinel/Safeguard antiballistic missile systems. This publication contains a complete survey of all Nike, BOMARC, and Safeguard sites in the continental United States, Alaska, Hawaii, and Canada.

The illustrations for this third edition are substantially upgraded with a more extensive selection of photographs, including a full-color section of Nike unit distinctive insignias. We have redone many of the line drawings, especially the area defense maps. Both the introductory text and the site survey have been expanded upon and corrected with information from new resources cited in the bibliography and from fellow enthusiasts.

In 1994, when we began to revise Mark Morgan's "Nike Quick Look III" for publication as *Rings of Supersonic Steel*, reference material on the Nike system, and American missile air defenses in general, were hard to find. Little was published in the public sector and most of the Army materials were either published on a very limited scale or not available. Since that time, we have been delighted to find that a number of fine new publications and reports have been published, especially in the later part of the 1990s. Some of these have much more information than is provided here; we advise those who are interested in air defense systems to consult these sources.

Many document resources are now available directly via the Internet. A number of web sites are worth checking out; search for "Nike missile." A few key sites, with extensive links and/or documentation, are listed in the bibliography. Many of these sites offer online reprints of documents as viewable (and printable) html pages; others provide original reports as downloadable PDF files complete with illustrations.

Nike Hercules (left) and
Nike Ajax (US Army photo)

Acknowledgments

The authors and the publisher gratefully acknowledge the assistance of the following individuals in the preparation of this book:

Michael Baker, Michael Binder, Donald Bender, Buddy Blades, Charles Bogart, Commander Alvin H. Grobmeier, USN (Ret), Greg Hagge, Colonel Milton B. Halsey, USA (deceased), Colonel James Loop, USA (deceased), Tom Lundregan, Doyle Piland, Ron Plante, John McGrath, Scott Murdock, Patrick Murman, Thomas Page, Ed Thelen, Tim Tyler, and Tom Vaughn for providing material, references, illustrations and comments on the that have gone into the first two editions of this book as well as this third edition. Thank you for John R. Cauvel for the great Hawk image.

Project Editor Roxane Buck-Ezcurra for putting up with this ever changing project;
Frank Evans for his patient answering of many questions about his experiences as a Nike battery commander;

Ranger John Martini, National Park Service (Ret) for his meticulous proof reading of the manuscript;

Bob Capistrano; Dennis Covello; Ron Parshall, and Jim Rutherford for providing information on and access to their collections of distinctive insignias;

Robert Stewart of Art Seed Photography for his photographs of the distinctive insignias;

Carole Thickstun and Larry Ormsby for their fine graphics and layout of this new edition.

Not to be missed was the important assistance of Val Harvey; Marty Isham, USAF (Ret); Ralph Kroy; William C. Stark; Pat Rhodes; Gale L. Maxie; Amanda Williford for her assistance in obtaining photographs from the Golden Gate National Recreation Area archives, and Historian Stephen A. Haller, National Park Service. A special thanks to Matthew I. Bentley, Museum Operations Specialist, Atomic Testing Museum. Las Vegas, Nevada for his assistance in obtaining the images of the atomic tests.

The publisher is especially grateful to Mr. Eleanor Hansen for her permission to allow the extensive use of her late husband's material from "The Swords of Armageddon" version 2 in the warhead section of this edition.

Pushing a Nike-Hercules missile along the launcher rail (Signal Corps, U.S. Army)

Introduction

From the time of the first European settlements on the North American continent through World War II, artillery has provided the first line of defense against invasion for the nation. America's traditional enemies were overseas; to meet this threat, a series of powerful fortifications networks were erected on both coasts, from Canada to Mexico.

By the turn of the twentieth century the coastal areas and ports of the United States were secure behind these forts, armed with guns ranging in size from small calibers to sixteen inches. Despite the evolution of aircraft as modern weapons during World War I, the nation continued its reliance on Navy battleships and the big guns of the Coast Artillery Corps.

The rise of strategic air power and nuclear weapons during World War II brought the demise of both defensive systems. It became apparent early in the war that any future attack on the continental United States would first come not by sea but from the sky; the guns that protected the coastline from overseas armadas were not suitable against streams of enemy bombers. For the Army it meant the end of fixed seacoast fortifications. Thus, by 1950, the coastal defenses were inactivated and the big guns were scrapped.

A new defensive network, employing surface-to-air missiles, was developed and deployed. The Nike missile system was utilized under the same tactical considerations as the big seacoast guns had been during the previous century—as a deterrent against an attack by another nation.

The Nike system succeeded in this role for over two decades of the Cold War and paved the way for our modern Patriot missiles and other systems.

LIST OF ABBREVIATIONS

AA	antiaircraft
AAA	antiaircraft artillery
AAAMBn	anti-aircraft missile battalion
AADCP	Army Air Defense Command Post
AAF	Army Air Forces
ABAR	alternate battery acquisition radar
ABM	antiballistic missile
ABMA	Army Ballistic Missile Agency
ACQR	acquisition radar
ADA	Air Defense Artillery
ADB	Air Defense Board
ADC	Air Defense Command
ADCOM	Aerospace Defense Command
ADM	Atomic Demolition Munition
AEC	Atomic Energy Commission
AFB	Air Force base
AFS	Air Force station
AMSC	Army Missile Support Command
AN	Army/Navy
AOMC	Army Ordnance Missile Command
AOMSA	Army Ordnance Missile Support Agency
ARAACOM	Army Antiaircraft Command
ARADCOM	Army Air Defense Command
ARDC	Air Research and Development Command
ARGMA	Army Guided Missile Agency
ArNG	Army National Guard
ARPA	Advanced Research Projects Agency
ASP	annual service practice
AW	automatic weapons (battalions)
BIRDIE	battery integration and radar display equipment
BMDC	Ballistic Missile Defense Center
BMEWS	ballistic missile early warning system
Bn	battalion
BOMARC	missile developed by BO (Boeing Aircraft Company) + MARC (Michigan Aeronautical Research Center)
CC	combat center
CEBMCO	Corps of Engineers Ballistic Missile Construction Office
COBRA	Composite uranium-plutonium core
CONARC	Continental Army Command
CONAD	Continental Air Defense Command
CONUS	continental United States
DA	Department of the Army
DAR	defense acquisition radar
DC	defense center
DERP	Defense Environmental Restoration Program
DEW	distant early warning system
DMA	Director of Military Applications
DOD	Department of Defense
DPS	data processing system
DR	discrimination radar
D-T	Deuterium and Tritium
FAA	Federal Aviation Administration
FCC	fire coordination center
FOIA	Freedom of Information Act
FSN	Federal Stock Number
FUDS	formerly used defense site
GAPA	ground-to-air pilotless aircraft
GFE	government furnished equipment
GGNRA	Golden Gate National Recreation Area
GSA	General Services Administration

HABS	Historic American Building Survey		PPG	Pacific Proving Ground
HAER	Historic American Engineering Record		R&D	research and development
HAWK	homing-all-the-way killer		RAF	Royal Air Force
HE	high explosive		ROCC	regional operations control centers
HIPAR	high-power acquisition radar		ROTC	Reserve Officer's Training Corps
ICBM	intercontinental ballistic missile		RRIS	remote radar integration station
IFC	integrated fire control		RSL	remote Sprint launch (site)
IFI	in-flight insertion		SAC	Strategic Air Command
IRFNA	inhibited red fuming nitric acid		SAFSCOM	Safeguard Systems Command
JCS	Joint Chiefs of Staff		SAGE	Semi-automatic Ground Environment
LASL	Los Alamos Scientific Laboratories		SALT1	Strategic Arms Limitation Talks One
LOPAR	low-power acquisition radar		SAM	surface-to-air missile
MAB	missile assembly building		SDI	Strategic Defense Initiative
MAR	multifunction array radar		SENSCOM	US Sentinel Systems Command
MICOM	Army Missile Command		SHPO	State Historic Preservation Office
MLC	Military Liaison Committee		SLBM	submarine launch ballistic missile
MRV	multiple reentry vehicle		SMFU	secondary master fire unit
MSR	missile site radar		SMW	Strategic Missile Wing
MTR	missile-tracking radar		SNAP	short-notice annual practice
NASA	National Aeronautics and Space Administration		SRMSC	Stanley R. Mickleson Safeguard Complex
NATO	North Atlantic Treaty Organization		START	Strategic Arms Reduction Talks
NG	National Guard		TAC	Tactical Air Command
NORAD	North American Air/Aerospace Defense Command		TRR	target-ranging radar
			TTR	target-tracking radar
NSA	National Security Agency		USA	US Army
NSC	National Security Council		USAF	US Air Force
NTDC	Naval Training Device Center		USARAL	US Army Alaska
NTS	Nevada Test Site		USASDC	US Army Strategic Defense Command
Oralloy	Oak Ridge alloy (highly enriched uranium metal)		USN	US Navy
PAL	permissive action link		WSMR	White Sands Missile Range
PAR	perimeter acquisition radar		ZAR	Zeus acquisition radar

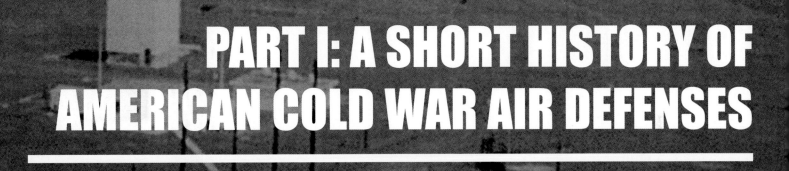

PART I: A SHORT HISTORY OF AMERICAN COLD WAR AIR DEFENSES

Antiaircraft Gun/Air Defense Missile Battalion Deployment
ARAACOM 1949-1957

Date deployed	Weapon type/Total battalions				
	40mm	75mm	90mm	120mm	Nike*
Dec. 1949	0	0	1	0	1
Apr. 1951	6	0	8	9	0
Dec. 1952	5	0	36	14	0
Dec. 1953	0	5	42	14	0
Dec. 1954	0	8	35	4	19
Dec. 1955	0	8	29	4	36
Jun. 1956	0	8	24	4	46
Dec. 1957	0	5	1	0	58

* Nike later designated Nike-Ajax   (Table compiled by James W. Loop)

75mm Skysweeper AA gun

1. U.S. Antiaircraft Artillery Service, 1917-1945

The conversion of coastal artillery to air defense artillery began with the lessons learned during World War I. The use of aircraft for observation and bombardment during that conflict showed its potential as a weapon. For the first time, both ground forces and cities came under threat of aerial attack.

The Army assigned the tactical development and deployment of antiaircraft weapons to the Coast Artillery Corps, as that branch was most familiar with the complicated mathematical formulas required for range finding and firing at moving targets. While an Antiaircraft Service was established in France and a number of antiaircraft (AA) units were outfitted by the coast artillery, little was done to integrate these units into an Army tactical command structure. The primary defense weapons remained with the service's harbor defenses. Airplanes were still considered to be a limited threat; the big guns of the battleship were still the primary weapon of a naval invasion force.

Tactical integration of American continental air defenses began during World War II. The emergence of the airplane as the ascendant offensive weapon, as demonstrated during the Spanish Civil War and first two years of World War II, forced corresponding changes in tactical considerations for the defense of the American continent. Interceptor commands, made up of units of the Army Air Forces (AAF), were established in late 1941 to react to the enemy air threat. In March 1942 the Army Antiaircraft Command was created; tactical control of all Coast Artillery AA units was integrated with that of the AAF's I and IV Interceptor Commands.

As the war widened, the need for antiaircraft units expanded. Antiaircraft artillery training centers were established at Fort Eustis, VA; Camp Davis, NC; Camp Stewart, GA; Fort Sheridan, IL; Camp Edwards, MA; Camp Haan, CA; Camp Callan, CA; Camp Irwin, CA; Fort Bliss, TX; and Camp Hulen, TX. The existing harbor defense units were stripped of personnel to man the growing number of AA units. Over time, as air defense came into its own, the responsibility for unit training and command was slowly removed from the Coast Artillery Corps.

New mobile AA weapons were developed and used during the war, including the M13 and M14 twin .50 half-track multiple gun

(left) 40mm Bofors AA gun, Rock Island Arsenal, IL, 2001. (Mark Berhow)

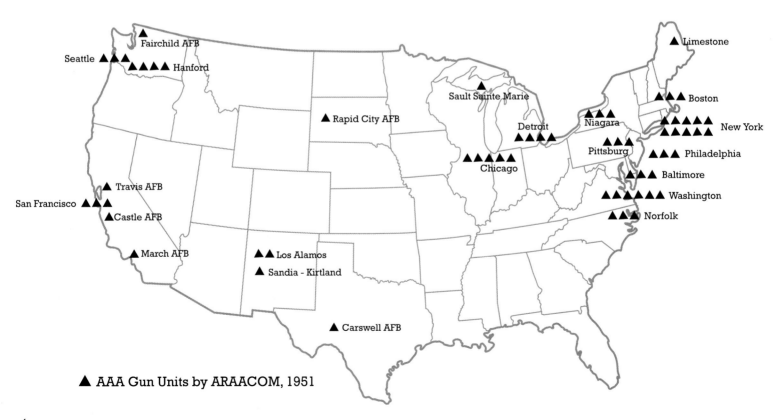

Fairchild AFB
Limestone
Seattle
Hanford
Sault Sainte Marie
Boston
Rapid City AFB
Niagara
New York
Detroit
Pittsburg
Philadelphia
Chicago
Baltimore
Travis AFB
Washington
San Francisco
Castle AFB
Norfolk
March AFB
Los Alamos
Sandia - Kirtland
Carswell AFB

▲ AAA Gun Units by ARAACOM, 1951

motor carriages; the M16 and M17 quad .50 half tracks; the M15 and M15A1 37mm/twin .50 half tracks; and the M19 twin 40mm tracked vehicle. Larger mobile weapons included the rapid fire M1/M2/M3 90mm and M1 120mm guns. Rockets and radar also emerged as effective new weapon technology. In August 1945 there were 331 active AA battalions with 246,000 troops scattered around the world.

One other Army antiaircraft development of World War II would have far-reaching postwar implications: Project "Nike."

The Army's first surface-to-air missile defense program was based on a 17 August 1944 memorandum written by 1st Lieutenant Jacob W. Schaefer, US Army (Ordnance), a former employee of Bell Telephone Laboratories (Bell Labs). Schaefer proposed the development of a radio-controlled antiaircraft rocket that could be used to protect large target areas from bomber attack. The proposal outlined the concept of command guidance: one radar tracking the target, a second radar tracking the projectile, with steering commands provided to the projectile by a computer to enable interception.

Copies of the memorandum were sent to the Radio Corporation of America and Bell Labs for their consideration and comments. In February 1945 the US Army Ordnance Corps and the Army Air Forces asked Bell Labs to explore the possibility of developing a new antiaircraft system based on Lieutenant Schaefer's memorandum.

In June 1945 Bell Labs and its manufacturing arm, Western Electric, began the development of the new system. Douglas Aircraft Company was selected as the major subcontractor to design and manufacture the missile, booster, and launcher equipment. The program was initiated by contract W-30-069-ORD-3182, negotiated and administered through the US Army New York Ordnance District. It was given the code name Project "Nike" after the winged goddess of victory in Greek mythology. Research and development of the Nike project continued through the bombing of Hiroshima and Nagasaki and the cessation of hostilities.

When the war ended on 15 August 1945, with the surrender of Japan, the Army began a general demobilization that included all of its units. During the rush, operational control of continental defense was treated as an afterthought. The Coast Artillery antiaircraft units were being demobilized with the rest of the wartime Army. Formal organization of the country's defense was limited

75mm Skysweeper AA gun and mount, Rock Island Arsenal, IL (Mark Berhow 2001)

90mm M2 gun on AA mount M2A1, Aberdeen Proving Grounds, MD *(Mark Berhow 1996)*

105mm M1 gun on M1 gun mount M1, Aberdeen Proving Grounds, MD (Mark Berhow 1996)

Guns Utilized by Army Air Defense Units 1950-58

- 40-mm automatic gun M1 (AA) on gun carriage M2A1
- 75-mm automatic gun M35 on AA gun mount M85 (Gun, AAA, towed, 75-mm system M-51)
- 90-mm gun M1 (M1A1) on AA gun mount M1A1 (gun, AAA, towed, 90-mm, M117)
- 90-mm gun M2A1 (M2A2) on AA gun mount M2A1 (gun, AAA, towed, 90-mm, M118)
- 120-mm gun M1 (M1A1) on AA gun mount M1 (M1A1) (M1A2)

WEAPON/MODEL	40m M1	75m M35	90m M1	90m M2A1	120m M1
caliber	L 60	L 50	L 50	L 50	L 60
length of gun w/breech	8' 5"	15' 3.12"	15' 6"	16' 9"	24' 3"
weight of gun on carriage	5,850 lb	19,285 lb	19,000 lb	32,300 lb	61,500 lb
length, travel	18' 9.5"	26' 5"	20' 10"	29' 6"	30' 9"
width, travel	6' 0"	8' 6"	8' 5"	8' 7"	10' 3.5"
height, travel	6' 7.5"	7' 1"	9' 4"	10' 1"	10' 4"
ground clearance	14.12"	15"	12"	15.62"	15"
# of axles/tires	2/4	2/4	1/4	2/4	2/8
elevation on wheels	-6° to 90°	-6° to 85°	0° to 80°	-10° to 80°	-5° to 80°
elevation on jacks	-11° to 90°	-6° to 85°	-5° to 80°	-10°to 80°	-5° to 80°
traverse	360°	360°	360°	360°	360°
breechblock	vert. slid.	vert. slid.	vert. slid.	vert. slid.	vert. slid.
muzzle velocity	2,870 f/s	2,800 f/s	2,700 f/s	2,700 f/s	3,100 f/s
effective altitude	9,000 ft	18,600 ft	33,800 ft	33,800 ft	48,000 ft
max horizontal range (45°)	12,600 yds	14,415 yds	19,560 yds	19,560 yds	28,250 yds
ammo configuration	fixed	fixed	fixed	fixed	separate
weight projectile	2.06 lb	15 lb	23.4 lb	23.4 lb	49.74 lb
max. rate of fire/sust.	120/120 rpm	55/45 rpm	22/22 rpm	28/23 rpm	12/10 rpm
prime mover	2.5 ton	M8A1 tractor	M4 18 ton tractor	M4 18 ton tractor	M6 36 ton tractor
Fire Control	M-5 director	M-4 radar/M-33A/B radar	M-33 AIC/BIC/C radar	M-33 AIC/BIC/C radar	M-33D radar; SCR-584 w/M1A1

(Table compiled by James W. Loop)

to a few Army Air Force fighter groups and fewer undermanned Coast Artillery units controlling the remaining forts.

In March 1946 the wartime Prime Minister of England, Winston Spencer Churchill, gave an address at Westminster College in Fulton, MO. In his speech, Churchill stated that "from Stettin in the Baltic to Trieste in the Adriatic, an Iron Curtain has descended across Europe." The stage was set for the Cold War.

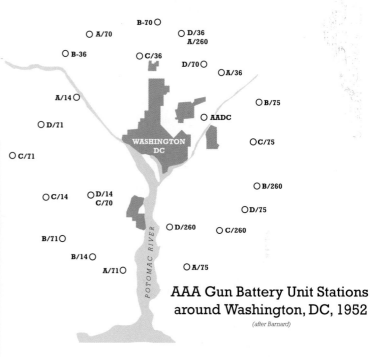

AAA Gun Battery Unit Stations around Washington, DC, 1952

(after Barnard)

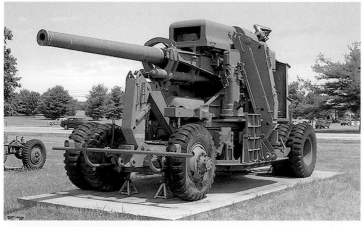

120mm gun (Mark Berhow 1996)

120 mm gun position at Wolf Ridge, Fort Cronkhite, CA (photo courtesy of the Golden Gate National Recreation Area)

2. Postwar Developments

Immediately after the war, American military debate centered on which service should achieve primacy as the defender of the nation. The Army Air Forces (created as an independent service, the USAF, on 18 September 1947) argued that its Strategic Air Command, equipped with B-29s and nuclear bombs, could defend the country. The Navy responded that carrier air power had won the war and would continue to serve the nation best in the future. There was a subdebate over who should have operational control over ground-based air defense units manning weapons in the United States, the Army or Air Force.

The National Security Act, passed on 26 Jul 1947, created the "Armed Forces of the United States" and integrated the Army, Navy, and Air Force under the Department of Defense (DOD). The intent, at least on paper, was to foster better inter-service cooperation. In practice, inter-service squabbling continued. Effectively, tactical command of antiaircraft units in the United States was assigned to the Air Force, while the Army would be responsible for manning, training, and equipping the units. All this was simply a matter of debate, as by 1949 there was only one Regular Army antiaircraft unit in active service: a training battalion at the Antiaircraft Artillery School at Fort Bliss, TX. Three events helped push the question of continental air defense to the forefront, and forced a decision on which service would supply what. On 23 October 1947 American observers noted the existence of forty-eight Tu-4 "Bull" aircraft in service with the Soviet Union. The Tu-4 was a reverse-engineered copy of the Boeing B-29, a few of which had landed in the Far East during World War II. These bombers gave the Soviets the range to blast targets in the United States.

On 1 April 1948 the Soviet Union closed off all land approaches to the Allied sectors of Berlin, Germany. The Berlin Blockade would last until 30 September 1949. More importantly, all friendly US-USSR interrelations effectively ended.

On 23 September 1949 President Harry Truman announced the detection of a Soviet nuclear weapon detonation, which had occurred between August 26 and 29. The United States' monopoly on nuclear weapons had ended. The Cold War had begun.

The deteriorating international situation in Europe and Asia during the years 1948–49 prompted new concern over the state of continental defense. Obviously, the existing antiaircraft defenses needed to be upgraded. The Nike missile was still in the classified development stage; gun units would have to be used until the missiles could be deployed.

3. Army Antiaircraft Command

The outbreak of the Korean War on 25 June 1950 finally brought about the wholesale reorganization and rebuilding of the air defense infrastructure. On 1 July 1950 the Army Reorganization Act combined all of the Army's artillery units into a single combat arm (and, incidentally, marked the formal demise of the Coast Artillery). It also established the Army Antiaircraft Command (ARAACOM) as the single command responsible for manning, training, and equipping the Army's AA units. Operational control, however, would still rest with the Air Force, much to the Army's consternation.

ARAACOM was formed without having any antiaircraft artillery battalions or batteries assigned; the first units assigned, on 10 April 1951, were three Federalized Army National Guard battalions in Boston; Camp Roberts, CA; and Seattle. An additional nineteen battalions were assigned the following month. ARAACOM planners determined that the command would quickly require a total of sixty-six AA battalions to man gun defenses at twenty-three critical locations. Until Nike could be brought on line, 40mm (later replaced by 75mm "Skysweeper" guns), 90mm, and 120mm guns would have to suffice. Active Army gun battalions were quickly established; others started replacing the Army Guard units in late 1952. The continental United States was divided into initially two, but later three, sectors: the Eastern, Central, and Western Army Antiaircraft Commands. Air defense brigades were activated in the sectors to assume operational control over the battalions manning defenses around key locations; important industrial, transportation and shipping centers; Air Force bases; and Atomic Energy Commission research centers.

In 1954 Continental Air Defense Command (CONAD) was established at Ent AFB, Colorado Springs, CO, to integrate the activities of ARAACOM and the Air Force's Air Defense Command (ADC).

ARAACOM's gun laydown was completed by early 1956, when the final 75mm and 90mm battalions went into service at Carswell AFB, TX; Ellsworth AFB, SD; Loring AFB, ME; Philadelphia, PA; Pittsburgh, PA; Savannah River, SC; and Travis AFB, CA. By this time ARAACOM was divided into five regions, Regular Army transition to Nike-Ajax was well underway, and the Army Guard was reassuming the gun defense mission.

By 1957 many of the Army's AAA units had been converted to missile battalions, and, on 21 March 1957, ARAACOM was redesignated US Army Air Defense Command, or ARADCOM. From this point, Army air defenders would man missile systems. That same year, CONAD (ARADCOM, ADC, and Naval Forces CONAD) and Canadian Air Defence Command were merged to form North American Defense Command (NORAD).

Beginning in 1958 units of the National Guard would also retire their guns and adopt the Nike mission to accommodate manpower cuts in the Regular Army. The transfer of Nike sites from Regular Army units to National Guard battalions would continue through the Nike period.

> *Battery* = basic unit, one battery was assigned to one missile site with personnel for rotating shifts.
>
> 4 Batteries = *Battalion*
>
> 1-2 Battalions = *Group*
>
> 2-4 groups = *Brigade*
>
> 1-6 battalions = *Regiment* (admin only)
>
> 1 to 2 Brigades/Groups were assigned to a defense area.

4. The Nike-Ajax Missile System

The development of the Nike missile system had been slowed by cuts in the post–World War II defense budget. The program was brought back up to speed following the start of the Korean War. The first complete system test was conducted at White Sands Proving Ground, NM, on 15 November 1951; the first successful intercept of a drone aircraft by an unarmed Ajax came twelve days later.

Testing continued through spring 1952, with some twenty unarmed missiles being fired. A full-scale demonstration of the complete Nike missile system occurred on 24 April 1952, resulting in the spectacular destruction of a drone QB-17G drone.

The Army emplaced the first operational Nike-Ajax unit at a temporary site at Fort George G. Meade, MD—designated W-13T—in December 1953, under the auspices of Battery B, 36th AAA Missile Battalion (B/36th). The service formally announced the site's operational status as the first Nike installation on 30 May 1954. The first fixed magazine site built was W-64 at Lorton, VA.

Nike-Ajax launch at White Sands Missile Range (US Army, Redstone Arsenal Historical Information Office)

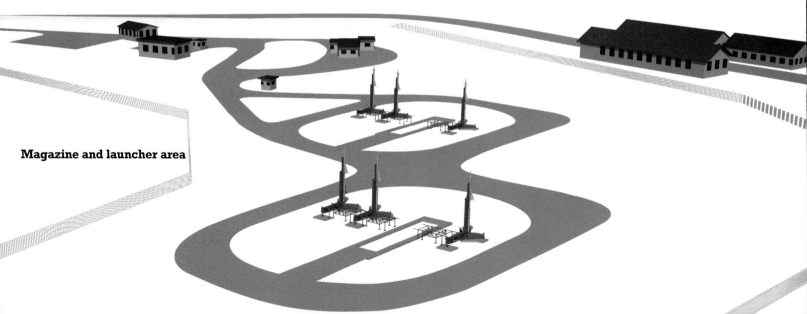

Magazine and launcher area

Nike-Ajax site

Nike-Ajax launch area W-25 Davidsonville, MD (US Army, courtesy Merle Cole)

Conversion of other gun battalions to Nike-Ajax rapidly followed; construction of Nike-Ajax equipped defense areas continued through 1957.

The Nike-Ajax (eventually designated MIM-3/3A) was the first supersonic surface-to-air missile system to become operational in the free world. It had a range of about thirty miles and could destroy targets at altitudes exceeding the operational ceilings of known threat aircraft. The missile had an all-weather capability, could attack from any direction, and was able to compensate for any evasive action taken by a target aircraft.

The two-stage Nike-Ajax weighed slightly more than one ton and was thirty-two feet, eight inches in length. It was powered to supersonic speed by a solid rocket booster with a liquid-fueled sustainer. The missile was designed to deliver three high-explosive (HE) warheads to the vicinity of the target aircraft and explode on command from the battery control site.

The Nike missiles were deployed at fixed sites in a circular pattern around key American government, industrial, transportation, and military locations; the larger the defended area, the more Ajax sites were constructed. For example, larger defenses such as Los Angeles or New York received sixteen and nineteen Ajax batteries respectively. Smaller defenses such as Ellsworth and Loring AFBs received four sites each.

Nike-Ajax in launch position (US Army, Redstone Arsenal Historical Information Office)

Typical Integrated Fire Control

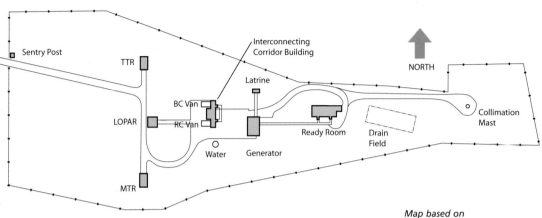

Sentry Post

TTR

Interconnecting
Corridor Building

Latrine

NORTH

BC Van

LOPAR

RC Van

Collimation
Mast

Ready Room

Drain
Field

Water   Generator

MTR

*Map based on
National Park Service
archives map by John
Martini.*

A typical Nike missile battery was divided into three major
areas: the Integrated Fire Control (IFC) area; the magazine and
Launcher area (L); and the Administration area (A). The three
components were often located on separate parcels of land,
although the most common configuration saw the IFC and
administrative sites co-located. The battery control installation
was at least 1,000 yards away from the launch area for missile
control and tracking reasons, but still in direct line of sight.

In practice, sites were constructed
with many variations depending on
the local conditions and geography.
Where possible, existing military
reservations were used, but in many
cases land for new sites had to be
purchased, leased, or borrowed from
other government agencies, local
governments, and private owners.

**Warrant Officer watching missile being
mated to its booster.** *Signal Corps
Photograph SC576508 - Circa 1960.
Washington D.C. Defense Area*

TTI

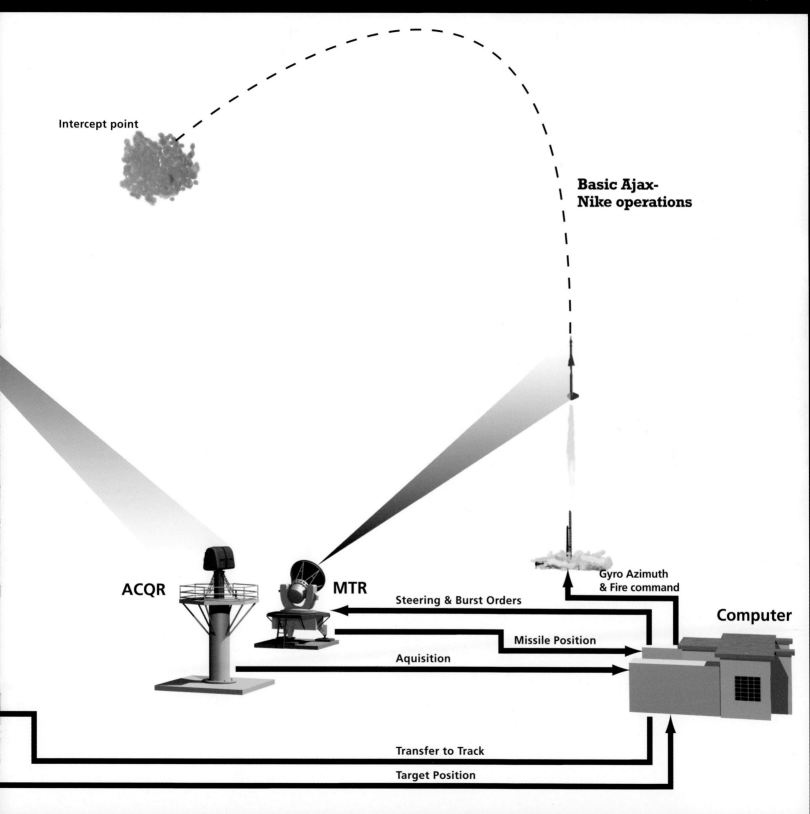

Intercept point

Basic Ajax-Nike operations

ACQR

MTR

Gyro Azimuth & Fire command

Computer

Steering & Burst Orders

Missile Position

Aquisition

Transfer to Track

Target Position

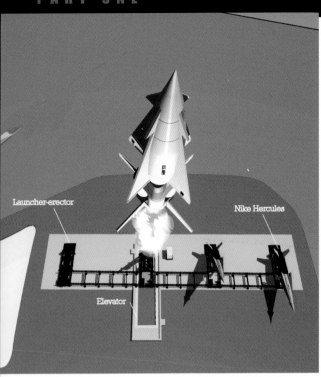

Launcher-erector

Nike Hercules

Elevator

Nike Battery Launch Facilities

The missile launch facility consisted of a self-contained installation with all of the capabilities for independent action. The normal launch area configuration incorporated two or three underground magazines—aka "pits"—each with an elevator for raising the missile to the surface for loading on the above-ground launch rails. In turn, the interior of each magazine included a missile storage bay with launcher loading, racks, crew shelter, launching section control panel, ventilation equipment, test equipment hydraulic controls and the elevator, which held launcher No. 1. The top, or "roof," of the magazine held the three other launchers and the rails used for sliding the missiles into position for elevating and firing.

The Army Corps of Engineers –through its contractors—constructed the Ajax magazines to one of two standard designs, known as Type A and Type B. The Type A was the initial magazine design for the Ajax missiles. In 1954 the planned introduction of Hercules resulted in the design and construction of a new magazine, the B-Mod/Ajax Universal type, which was also built during the deployment of the Ajax system. The two types differed primarily in dimensions with some minor differences in missile capacity:

Magazine Type	Elevator Width	Magazine Length	Magazine Width	Type Launchers	Missile Storage
A	8-ft 8-in	42-ft	63-ft	4 Ajax M28/M29	8 Ajax w/ fins or 4 w/ fins and 7 w/o fins
B	8-ft 8-in	49-ft	60-ft	4 Ajax M28/M29	8 Ajax w/ fins or 4 w/ fins and 6 w/o fins

The standard battery design of three magazines—usually in the 2A/1B configuration, although variations existed such as the 1-magazine configuration in some defenses with 10 launchers—conceivably stored anywhere from twenty-four built-up Ajax missiles to a mix of thirty-two missiles; however, the standard load was usually thirty missiles with and without fins attached.

Other launch area facilities generally consisted of the missile assembly and testing building, a liquid fueling area, a power generating facility, storage and repair buildings, sentry posts, and a nearby ready room for the men stationed there. The entire launch complex was surrounded by a security fence topped with barbed wire.

Battery personnel assembled, tested, and fueled the missiles at the above-ground facilities at the launch site, then stored the operational missiles underground in the magazine. Upon receipt of an alert order, they quickly attached the Ajax's guidance fins, moved the first three missiles to the surface, pushed them

FROM BELOW

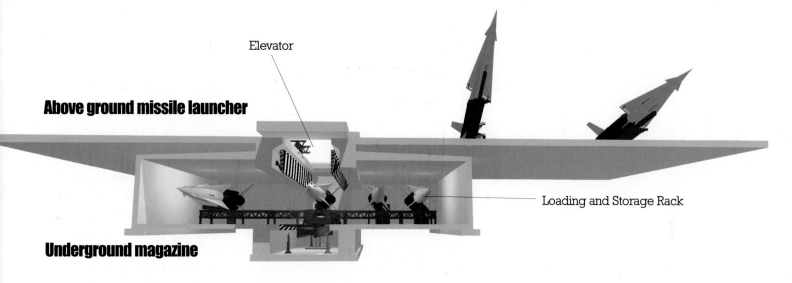

Elevator

Above ground missile launcher

Underground magazine

Loading and Storage Rack

FROM ABOVE

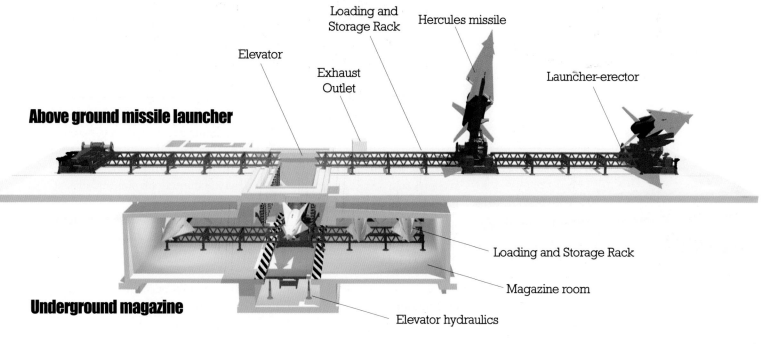

Loading and
Storage Rack

Hercules missile

Elevator

Exhaust
Outlet

Launcher-erector

Above ground missile launcher

Loading and Storage Rack

Magazine room

Underground magazine

Elevator hydraulics

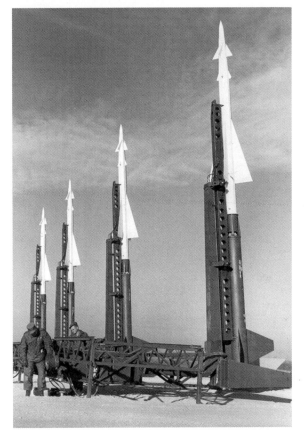

Nike-Ajax missiles in launch position (US Army Signal Corps)

Nike site SF-91, Angel Island, CA (US Army, Redstone Arsenal Historical Information Office)

Nike-Ajax launch site
(US Army, Redstone Arsenal Historical Information Office)

to the launchers and made the necessary electrical connections. The fourth missile came up on the elevator launcher and underwent similar preparation. With the completion of the pre-firing checklist, the battery then elevated the four missiles to an angle of about eighty-five degrees for firing. At that point the firing personnel returned to the crew shelter in the magazine; the firing section's first sergeant then pulled the safety and interlock pins and placed them on a labeled rack in the crew shelter.

The battery was now "hot" and ready to engage incoming targets. ARADCOM firing doctrine dictated that each magazine fired its elevator-mounted missile first and then quickly lowered the elevator, reloaded, elevated, and fired again; this sequence continued until the magazine was expended, at which point the remaining three missiles on launchers 2, 3, and 4 were fired if necessary.

Inside the Nike missile assembly building (US Army Signal Corps)

Nike-Ajax missile assembly building (Buddy Blades)

Control area layout

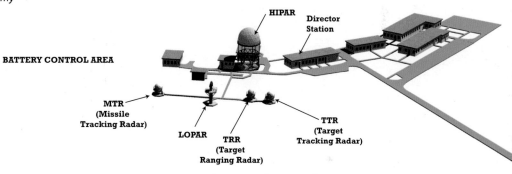

BATTERY CONTROL AREA

HIPAR

Director Station

MTR (Missile Tracking Radar)

LOPAR

TRR (Target Ranging Radar)

TTR (Target Tracking Radar)

Battery Control Area

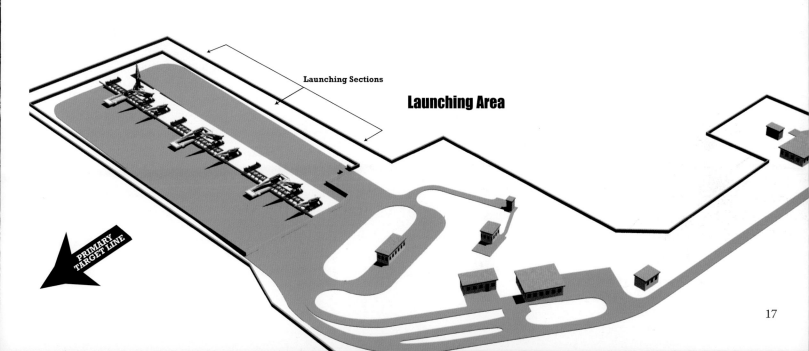

Launching Sections

Launching Area

PRIMARY TARGET LINE

Nike Battery Integrated Fire Control Facilities and Nike Administrative Facilities

The IFC, or Control site, contained the radars and radar equipment for acquiring and tracking the target and missile, the battery control assembly, the computer assembly, an early warning plotting board, an event recorder, and a switchboard cabinet.

Nike employed the command guidance system, in which the major control equipment was ground-based and not part of the expendable missile. Each battery had full operational control of the Nike-Ajax missile once it was launched.

The site's acquisition radar (ACQR) acquired the incoming target aircraft at long range and provided pointing data to the target-tracking radar (TTR), which locked on to the target. The site's missile-tracking radar (MTR) locked

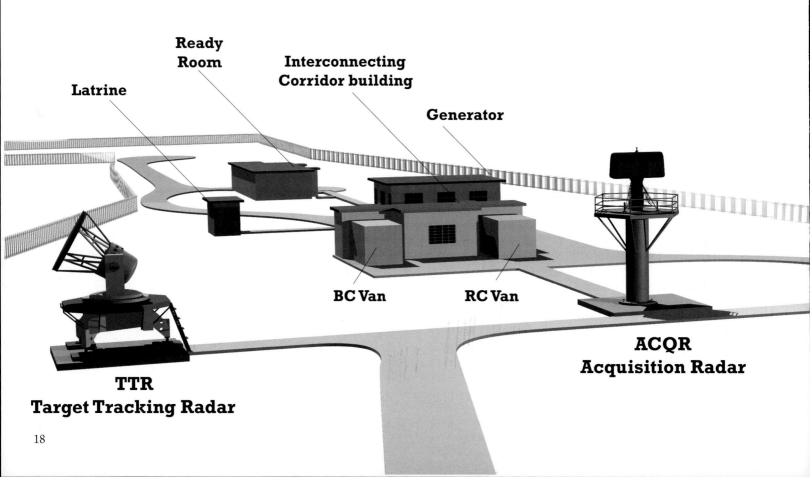

Latrine

Ready Room

Interconnecting Corridor building

Generator

BC Van

RC Van

TTR Target Tracking Radar

ACQR Acquisition Radar

Inside the battery control van, the Army National Guard battery commander and his crew go through a simulated fire attack exercise. CPT Bernard S. Rhees (center), CO, Btry A, 1st Missile Bn, 280th Arty, monitors the acquisition radar scope. Evaluating the Army National Guard unit is CPT Cyril G. Hess (Bellingham, WA) (standing) the Guided Missile Officer from the 19th Arty Gp. SFC Robert C. Brooks (right) acquisition radar operator, and SP4 Warren Wilson, computer operator, await instructions. 11 Apr 60. Photo by SP4 John B. Kelley, 19th Arty Group (Air Defense). Signal Corps Photograph SC571679. W-64 Lorton.

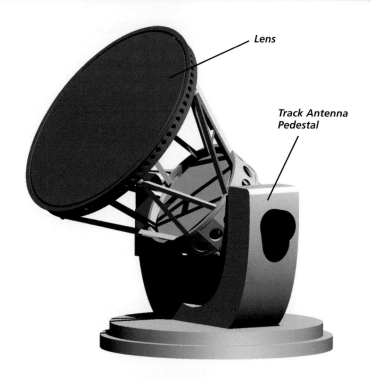

Lens

Track Antenna Pedestal

MTR
Missile Tracking Radar

on the missile prior to firing and tracked the outbound Nike-Ajax. Data from the radars was fed to the electronic data processing equipment, which compared the position of the target and the missile and fed guidance commands to the missile to enable
the intercept.

The IFC area also housed the electrical generating equipment which supplied 400-cycle power to operate the radars and consoles. The various components were interconnected via the Battery Control Area Cable System. The control site also had a maintenance facility, spare parts storage, and was secured by fencing.

The Administrative area contained the barracks, mess hall, recreational facilities, and administrative offices for the battery. In most cases, this area was located within walking distance of either the battery control area or the launch facility, as neither had provisions for housing the crews.

Nike-era buildings were built to standard Corps of Engineers design. They were usually constructed of cinderblock with flat roofs, although the designs varied depending upon the location. For example, some of the buildings in the Angeles Forest in the Los Angeles Defense Area had steep pitched snow roofs.

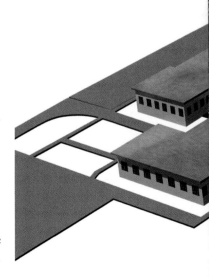

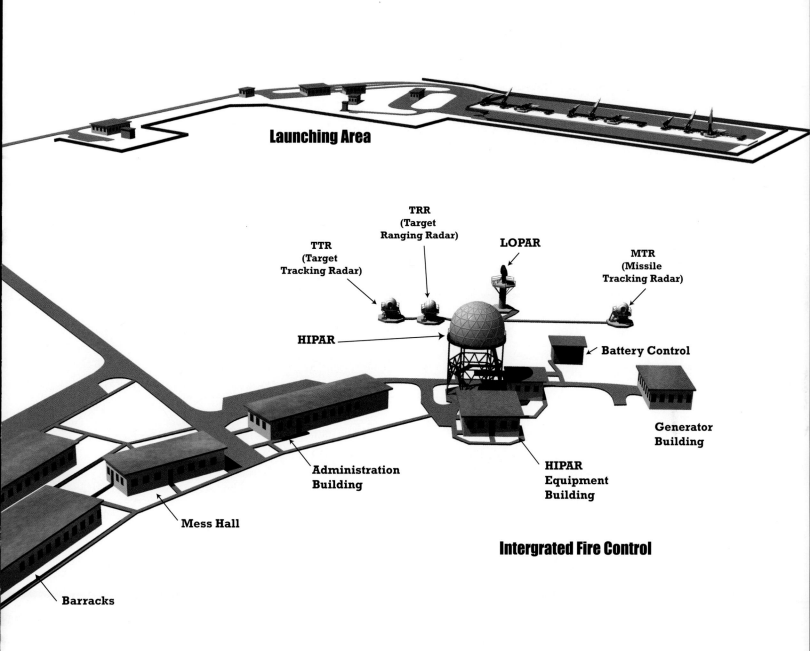

Launching Area

TRR
(Target
Ranging Radar)

TTR
(Target
Tracking Radar)

LOPAR

MTR
(Missile
Tracking Radar)

HIPAR

Battery Control

Generator
Building

Administration
Building

HIPAR
Equipment
Building

Mess Hall

Intergrated Fire Control

Barracks

NIKE MISSILE COMPARISON

	CHARACTERISTICS	AJAX	HERCULES
Designation		MIM-3A	MIM-14B
Weight (lbs)	gross	2,259	10,711
	sustainer	1,051	5,531
	booster	1,208	5,180
Length (in)	overall	392	478
	sustainer	251	322.5
	booster	158	170.8
Diam. (in)	sustainer	14.6	31.5
	booster	16.2	34.5
Span (in)	sustainer	50	90
	booster	76	138.2
Propellant	sustainer	liquid*	solid
	booster	solid	solid
Cost (1958)		$19,300	$55,200
Warheads		3 HE	1 HE or 1 Nuc
range (miles)		30.7	96.3
altitude (feet)		60,000	>100,000
Thrust (lbs)	sustainer	2,600	10,000
	booster	48,700	194,800
speed (Mach)		2.3	3.65
Flight time (min)		1	1-2
Rate of Fire (per min)**		1	2

*Liquid fuel consisted of a mixture of red fuming nitric acid, UDMH, and JP-4 jet fuel.
**only one missile per site could be guided to the target at a time.

(Table compiled by James W. Loop, illustrations by Larry Ormsby)

5. The Nike-Hercules Missile System

In 1953, prior to the deployment of the Nike-Ajax system, research and development began on a more capable, longer ranged missile. Originally designated Nike-B, it was later named Nike-Hercules (MIM-14/14A/14B).

Hercules was expected to mitigate several of the problems found with the Nike-Ajax. The Hercules booster was effectively four, strapped-together Ajax boosters; the sustainer was also solid-fueled, removing one major difficulty with Ajax. The larger Hercules would be able to carry a nuclear warhead, giving it the ability to knock out formations of bombers and not just individual aircraft. Finally, the new system would use as much as possible of the existing Ajax site components and support infrastructure, but still have room for modifications as the threat changed.

The missile was expected to have a maximum range of fifty miles and altitude capability of 70,000 feet at a speed in excess of Mach 1. The first test firing came at White Sands in 1955; further testing resulted in a missile with a range of over seventy-five miles, effective ceiling of over 100,000 feet, and a top speed of Mach 3. Development continued, leading to the conversion of the first Nike-Ajax site to Hercules on 30 June 1958. Battery A, 2nd Missile Battalion, 57th Artillery (the former A/485th), at site C-03 Montrose/Belmont in the Chicago Defense Area, had the honor.

As Nike-Hercules was fielded, Congress began to cut spending on the implementation of the Army's Nike and Air Force's BOMARC programs. Lack of Congressional support, mostly over the large manpower requirements of the Nike system, would plague the Nike program through its lifetime.

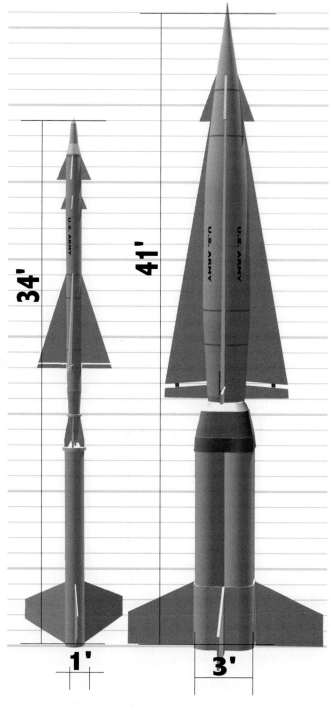

NIKE AJAX   **HERCULES**

Nike-Hercules outside an Alaskan site (US Army, Redstone Arsenal Historical Information Office)

(below)
Nike-Hercules at a Chicago site (US Army, Redstone Arsenal Historical Information Office)

Because the Army was already fielding Nike, the program was allowed to continue, but at a reduced level.

As the Hercules was more effective than Ajax—both in terms of range and destructive power—it was determined that each defense area only required about one-third to one-half of the number of sites. Conversion of the selected sites took place from 1958 to 1962. In addition, ARADCOM and the US Army Corps of Engineers embarked on a second round of construction, which added 15 new Hercules-only defense areas. The new defenses were two-battery above-ground complexes that guarded seven bases of Strategic Air Command; new four-battery complexes around Minneapolis-St Paul, Kansas City, Cincinnati-Dayton, St Louis, and Dallas-Fort Worth; as well as new battery complexes in Alaska (two battalions which covered

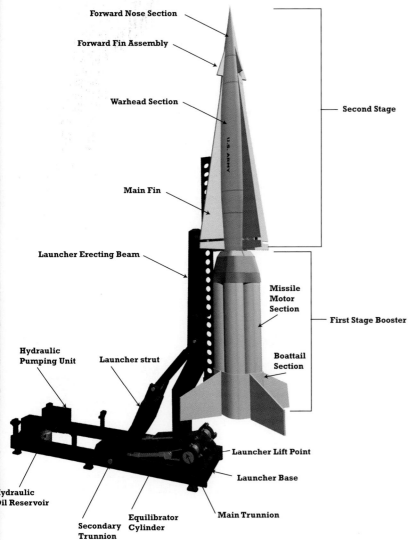

Forward Nose Section

Forward Fin Assembly

Warhead Section

Second Stage

Main Fin

Launcher Erecting Beam

Missile Motor Section

First Stage Booster

Hydraulic Pumping Unit

Launcher strut

Boattail Section

Hydraulic Oil Reservoir

Launcher Lift Point

Launcher Base

Secondary Trunnion

Equilibrator Cylinder

Main Trunnion

Nike-Hercules launch at White Sands Missile Range (US Army, Redstone Arsenal Historical Information Office)

Anchorage/Elmendorf AFB area and Fairbanks-/Eielson AFB area); on Oahu, Hawaii; and at Thule, Greenland.

Regular Army Nike-Ajax batteries were either converted to Hercules or inactivated, leading to the disestablishment of several missile battalions. The Army National Guard continued to operate the Nike-Ajax through 18 November 1964, by which time it was acquiring Nike-Hercules.

Hercules Battery Modifications

The introduction of the newer missiles resulted in changes to the design of the two major components, the battery launch facility and the IFC. The new defense area construction brought four new magazine designs: the Type B "Rising Star;" the Type D; the above ground "SAC"-type; and the "Alaska"-type.

Magazine Type	Elevator Width	Magazine Length	Magazine Width	Type Launchers	Missile Storage
B (Universal)	8-ft 8-in	49-ft	60-ft	4 Hercules/ Universal M-36	6 Hercules
B Rising Star	8-ft 8-in	49-ft	123-ft	2 Hercules M-36	10 Hercules
C (A-Mod)	8-ft 8-in	42-ft	63-ft	4 Hercules M-36	6 Hercules
D	8-ft 8-in	62-ft	68-ft	Hercules M-36	6 Hercules
"SAC" Type (AG)	n/a	xxx	xxx	4 Hercules M-36	4 Hercules (open storage)
"Alaska" Type (AK)	n/a	xxx	xxx	2 Hercules M-36	4 Hercules

Nicknamed the "Universal," the Type B magazine was designed from the start to initially operate Ajax and then undergo conversion for Hercules; as a result, the majority of the converted sites in ARADCOM's defense areas were already of this specification. The Corps of Engineers developed the Type B "Rising Star" specifically to address the incredibly harsh conditions found in Greenland. Built to a modified B design, they featured two elevators with launchers and no remote launcher rails.

According to ARADCOM records, the Type C magazines were modified Type A magazines to accept Hercules missiles. The modified magazines generally had only three remote launchers with no elevator launcher.

Type D magazines were of a wholly new design specifically for Hercules operations.

The magazines built specifically for the SAC bases and in Alaska were of two totally different designs. They were never formally named, but are identified in this work as "AG" and "AK" types for clarity.

The above-ground "AG" SAC and the above-ground Hawaiian Nike site "magazines" were basically earthen revetments divided into two segments. Each segment incorporated two missiles and an emergency crew bunker countersunk into the exterior wall away from the threat axis and direction of fire; none of the sites had a reload capability. The Army and its contractors developed an air supported tent—in military-speak, "Shelter, Guided Missile, Launcher"—to provide some measure of protection for the valuable missiles and their warheads. In theory, upon the receipt of an alert order, the battery personnel would deflate and remove the shelter prior to elevating the missiles; in reality, they proved a constant maintenance problem. During winter the missile boosters and sustainers received heater blankets to mitigate the impact of low temperatures on the propellants.

The Alaskan "AK" sites, which ringed Anchorage and Fairbanks, had above-ground reinforced concrete magazines, each with two roller doors. They normally stored four Hercules missiles on carts, which the crews rolled out to the launchers, two at a time, during alerts. Again, the environmental conditions played a major role in the development of the unique design; along the same lines, special clamshell shelters normally encapsulated the IFC radars at the Alaskan sites.

In addition, Hercules sites received a warhead building where the nuclear warheads were mated to the missiles on site. Hercules sites also received a double fence system for the guard dog runs and an exclusion area with the large sentry building where soldiers turned in their blue restricted area badge for the red exclusion area badge.

NIKE-Hercules Warhead Systems

NOTE: *Much of the following material comes from the work of the late Chuck Hansen and is presented in this form for the first time by special permission. Chuck Hansen spent several decades filing FOIA (Freedom of Information Act) requests for material relating to nuclear weapons testing. Over time, Mr. Hansen accumulated some 50,000 documents on the subject of nuclear weapons development, testing, and effects. The publisher and authors thank Mrs. Eleanor Hansen for her kind permission to use her late husband's material.*

One of the achievements of the early nuclear weapons engineers and designers was their success in turning virtually undeliverable atomic devices—weighing thousands of pounds and requiring all manner of ancillary equipment—into serviceable weapons that could be fit into artillery shells, rockets, depth charges, demolition devices, and small bomb casings. In addition to reducing the size of the device, the early designers devised ways to utilize very expensive and scarce fissionable material in the most efficient manner possible.

The need for an improved air defense weapon became apparent early in 1952, during the final development of the Nike-Ajax missile system. The problem stemmed from the Ajax radar system and its limitations in dealing effectively with bomber formations, the units of which were too closely packed for individual resolution by the Nike radar. The spacing between the aircraft was larger than the lethal radius of the Nike's conventional warhead, making its limitations particularly severe. In recognition of these shortcomings, the Special Assistant for Mobilization Production Office, Chief of Ordnance, suggested on 11 March 1952 that a study be made to determine the feasibility of providing the Nike missile with an atomic warhead.

Early planners considered mating the existing XW-9 gun-type nuclear warhead to the Nike-Ajax. (The XW-9 had been used in the 280mm atomic cannon.) It was found that extensive redesign of the missile would be required and that the XW-9 was inefficient in its use of fissionable materials. In addition, a gun-type weapon was unsuitable in an air defense missile because of its single-point detonation system. In the end, the Military Liaison Committee (MLC) decided on a new, larger missile— the Nike-Hercules. The Hercules was designed to carry the 30-inch W-7 warhead and fit the yet-to-be-developed XW-31/XW-37 warheads to the new missile.

Early Nike-Hercules planners envisioned simultaneous development of new 30-inch warheads (the XW-31 and XW-37) and a new missile system utilizing the existing Nike-Ajax launch facilities and radars as much as possible. A new warhead was required, one that would be safer and employ scarce fissionable material in a more efficient manner. It was predicted that the new missile and the new warheads would become available at the same time. Various delays caused the missile to be ready before the warheads. The result of these delays was that the Nike-Hercules initially deployed with the existing "universal" W-7-X2 warhead. The Nike-Hercules could also be fitted with the T-45 blast-fragmentation warhead. (See "Fragmentation Warheads" for more information about the T-45 and T-46 warheads.)

The W-7 Nuclear Warhead

By the 1950s, weapon designers had sufficiently reduced the size of nuclear weapons to fit them into small cylindrical cases, about 30 inches in diameter. The W-7 was the lightest and most compact implosion bomb design yet developed. In fact, its implosion system was used as a primary in several thermonuclear devices. The W-7 became the closest thing to a "universal" warhead in the stockpile; it was fitted to bombs, rockets, depth charges and an Atomic Demolition Munition (ADM). However, the W-7 design did not use the fissionable material economically and technical details of the W-7's safety systems raised concerns, especially in a widely deployed role, such as air defense.

In March 1952, the Army's Office of the Chief of Ordnance undertook a study to determine the feasibility of mating a nuclear warhead to the Nike-Ajax. This study revealed two possible paths to a nuclear Nike. One option was to use the W-9 warhead on the Nike-Ajax; the second alternative would be to design an entirely new missile that would carry the W-7 warhead without any special modifications. The path the Army chose was really two paths: use the "universal" W-7 until a new 30-inch warhead and missile could be developed. At the time, it was estimated that a new missile could be ready in three years.

The MK-7 Nike-Hercules warhead installation design was released in November 1956, but issues with the missile delayed the program. The MLC accepted the design on 6 May 1957. The final design was essentially a "kit" that allowed the "universal" MK-7 warhead to be mated with the Nike-Hercules. The MK-7 Nike-Hercules installation was retired in May 1967.

Nuclear Safety Concerns

The plutonium in the early air-defense warheads was an expensive and dangerous contaminant. Designers considered the contamination problem so serious that, on 15 October 1956, they commissioned Sandia National Laboratories to study the idea of using parachutes to recover aborted air-defense warheads. The report concluded that the recovery of warheads by parachute appeared feasible; however, the desirability of this approach was never considered.

In the air defense role, these atomic warheads would be shipped, deployed, and handled at numerous sites within the continental United States. Such widespread deployment concerned the Atomic Energy Commission (AEC), that and the possibility the W-7's self-destruct device (designed to initiate a one-point warhead detonation if the missile missed its target) might either malfunction or function too well, causing a significant nuclear yield if the weapon's capsule were inserted into the high explosive assembly.

Fishbowl Tightrope *detonation*

The W-7 warhead (specifically, the W-7-X2) utilized an automatic internal mechanism called an IFI (in-flight insertion). The IFI used an electric motor-driven gear mechanism to insert the fissionable material into the core while the weapon was in flight. The IFI was part of the safety system designed to keep the fissionable material out of the core until the last moment. Although the W-7 was designed as a universal warhead, early designers did not foresee its use on a supersonic air defense missile. The IFI operated much too slowly for the Nike. Using the W-7-X2 in the Nike-Hercules meant that there was a good possibility that the IFI would not have armed the warhead in time to engage the target, especially a low altitude target.

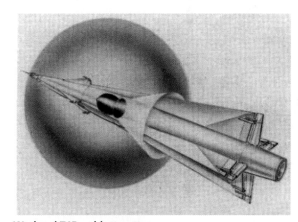

Warhead T45 — blast pattern

By the end of July 1955, the engineers went to work on the W-7-X3 with a faster IFI. Just one team was developing the Nike-B warhead at Sandia/LASL (Los Alamos Scientific Laboratories), and giving them the added responsibility of designing a new version of the W-7—with a faster acting IFI—would compete with the design of the new W-31/37 warheads. In addition, at the end of 1955, Douglas had problems with the liquid-fueled sustainer motor, which delayed delivery of the 40 missiles for the flight-test program. Redesigning the W-7 would also compete with flight time on the scarce test missiles.

A memorandum dated 12 March 1956 from Brigadier General (BG) A.D. Starbird, USA, Director of Military Application (DMA), to the Chairman of the MLC stated: "The XW-7-X2 can be used with the Nike-B instead of the XW-7-X3 with certain compromises:

1. The [deleted] retraction time of the XW-7-X2 IFI limits the low-altitude intercept capability of the missile system [deleted].

2. If this is not acceptable, use of one-point destruct for 'clean up' removes the limitation, but at the cost of possible degradation in civilian safety."

The referral to "… possible degradation in civilian safety" meant an increase in the possibility of a "radiological incident" involving radioactive contamination from a W-7 warhead if it were to malfunction over a large urban area. Ultimately, all work on both the W-7-X3 and the W-37 warhead was canceled. The W-37 became the W-31Y3—the high yield warhead eventually used on the Honest John and Corporal missiles.

When the Nike-Hercules was first deployed, they were mated with the W-7-X2 warhead. The military thought the risk of delayed deployment of the nuclear warheads outweighed the risk from the decreased performance at low altitudes and of an accident. The accident risk was reduced by a new self-destruct system that minimized the requirement for a fast-reacting IFI and removed the premature explosion hazard by permitting high-altitude arming. In any case, it was anticipated that this situation would last only three to six months until development of the XW-31-Y1 and XW31-Y2 warheads were completed.

XW-7 Warhead Tests

The XW-7 warhead in its various configurations was tested at the Nevada Test Site (NTS), the Pacific Proving Grounds (PPG), and in the Pacific Ocean off San Diego starting in the early 1950s. The following is a chronological list of those tests.

5 November 1951 (NTS) *Buster*
Shot Easy, in the Buster series of Buster-Jangle, was the TX-7E in the bomb configuration and the first drop of a "live" nuclear bomb from a jet aircraft.

1 May 1952 (NTS) *Snapper*
Shot Dog was a test of a modified TX-7 bomb weapon (previously tested in Buster Easy). The device tested the usefulness of deuterium gas fusion boosting (not deuterium-tritium boosting). The effects of the terrain on blast phenomena were studied to determine the optimum height-of-burst. This is an example of a combination weapon development and weapon effects test. Shot Dog was dropped from a B-45 bomber. The height of burst was 1,040 feet.

4 June 1953 (PPG) *Upshot-Knothole*
Shot Climax was a weapon test of the composite COBRA = Composite uranium-plutonium core in Type D pit. This was a 30-inch W-7 in a bomb configuration dropped from a B-36.

15 April 1955 (NTS) *Teapot*
Shot Met was a military effects test. The same device used in Shot Easy was detonated on a tower. This was the first daytime tower shot at NTS.

Shot Easy in the Buster series, November 5, 1951

15 May 1955 (Approx. 400 miles southwest of San Diego) *Wigwam*

Wigwam was a test of the MK-7 depth charge to determine the lethal range of a deeply detonated atomic weapon on a submarine. A 4/5-scale model of a Tang-class submarine was used as a target.

16 May 1958 (PPG) *Hardtack I*

Shot Wahoo was a MK-7 shot using a Wigwam-type pressure vessel. The MK-7 was used in an atomic depth charge. This test used an automatic IFI system and was detonated in 3,200 feet of water.

9 June 1958 (PPG) *Hardtack I*

Shot Umbrella was another underwater burst in a pressure vessel similar to the one used during Wigwam. The yield was about 8 kilotons.

18 October 1958 (NTS) *Hardtack II*

Shot Rio Arriba was a low-yield MK-7 weapons test detonated from a wooden tower.

15 February 1962 (NTS) *Nougat*

Shot Hardhat was the detonation of an MK-7 warhead 943 feet below the ground in a test of "hardening" underground structures.

18 December 1964 (NTS) *Whetstone*

Shot Sulky was a weapon effects test using an MK-

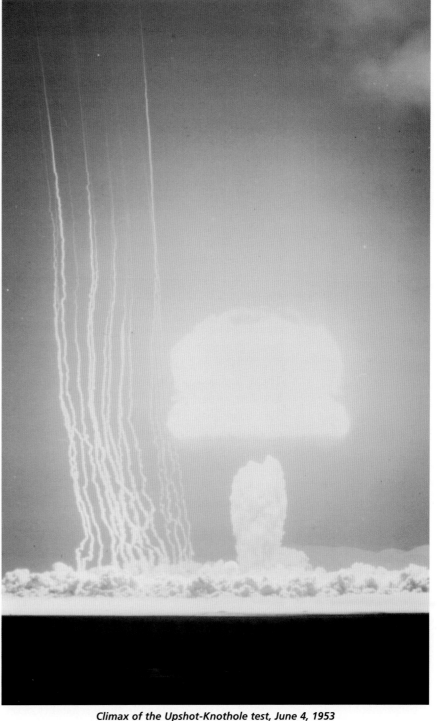

Climax of the Upshot-Knothole test, June 4, 1953

7 device to study cratering mechanics in hard, dry rock. In addition, the test studied the dispersion patterns of airborne radionuclides. The test was conducted 90 feet underground.

Operation *Snodgrass*

Operation *Snodgrass* deserves special mention as the W-7 nuclear warhead test that didn't happen. The Snodgrass saga also provides a peek into some of the early problems the Army experienced with the Nike-Hercules system. During the 1950s, the Defense Department lobbied the AEC for full-scale nuclear weapon tests in Nevada or over the Gulf of Mexico. The AEC denied these repeated requests due to safety concerns about an atomic blast outside of the test area, or a missile or drone running wild and going "off the reservation."

As originally planned, *Snodgrass* (named for Brigadier General (BG) John T. Snodgrass) was to have been a full-scale Nike-Hercules test conducted at the NTS in the spring of 1959. The plan was to detonate nuclear warheads against formations of target drones to study the ability of the missiles to operate in electromagnetic pulse, blast, and heat from nuclear detonations. In addition, Snodgrass would study the damage inflicted on the drone aircraft and the effects of nuclear explosions on the operation of ground radar systems. In April 1958, the original plan was scrapped and *Snodgrass* became a "crash" program to be completed by 1 September 1958 at a location other than NTS. This sense of urgency was created by the pending nuclear test moratorium agreed upon by the United States in the summer of 1958.

The new plan would be a joint Army–Air Force defense test conducted at Eglin Air Force Base, Florida. The Army's portion would be conducted in four phases by a Continental Army Command (CONARC) Task Force headed by BG J.T. Snodgrass, with Army Ordnance Missile Command (AOMC) furnishing coordination and support for Ordnance. Two units were selected for Operation *Snodgrass*: (1) Nike-Hercules system number 1009 from the Air Defense Board (ADB) at Fort Bliss, Texas was assigned the role of warhead firing battery, under the command of Capt. R.L. Klenik, and (2) system number 1060 from Battery C, 738th Guided Missile Battalion, of the Philadelphia Defense Area (Lumberton) was assigned the role of instrumented missile firing battery, under the command of Capt. F.E. Newland.

Phase 1 (1 May to 15 June) would involve organizing and training the Task Force at Fort Bliss, Texas. During Phase 2 (16 June to 5 July) the Task Force would move to Eglin Air Force Base and set up their batteries and equipment. Phase 3 would consist of final on-site training and six dress rehearsal flight tests (from 6 July to 31 July). Phase 4 (1 August - 31 August) would include four full-scale nuclear firings over the Gulf of Mexico.

During Phase 1 of the operation, the ADB warhead battery fired five practice rounds at White Sands Missile Range, and the instrumentation missile battery fired two rounds at McGregor Range. All seven of these practice firings were unsuccessful. This should not have been a surprise to anybody because an earlier WSMR (White Sands Missile Range) study showed that firings of the Nike-Hercules through May 1958 revealed an overall system in-flight reliability of only 25 percent. Most of the problems were attributed to failure or malfunction of the missile guidance package beacon, auxiliary power supply, and circuitry leading to the W-7 warhead. When subsequent test firings, through mid-June 1958, failed to show any improvement in reliability, Major General John B. Madaris, Commander of AOMC, urged the Chief of Ordnance to cancel Operation *Snodgrass* and Project *AMMO*, a public showing of the Nike-Hercules at WSMR scheduled for 30 June and 1 July 1958.

On 14 June 1958, the Department of the Army suspended the movement to Eglin for one week and also suspended shipment of missiles and W-7 warheads to operational sites as it was discovered that the warheads developed a pressure problem. By late June 1958, and after some seventeen modification work orders, kits to address the problems were sent by air freight to the launch sites. These measures apparently worked, as all firings in Project *AMMO* and the six Phase 3 *Snodgrass* firings were successful. The Department of the Army cancelled the Phase 4 firings of the W-7 warheads. There were no nuclear detonations over the Gulf of Mexico.

The W-31 Nuclear Warhead

The XW-31 warhead arose from fundamental concepts that weapon designers had been working on since the beginning of the nuclear weapons program. Tests in 1951 confirmed the theoretical concept of a boosted fission implosion design conceived in the late 1940s. Further tests confirmed core design and fusing technology. Still further tests refined safety features of a 30-inch sealed-pit, gas-boosted implosion device.

By 1954, small, tactical, nuclear weapons in the 15-inch to 30-inch range were under development, such as the 15-inch device for an air-to-air rocket warhead and the 22-inch device for the TALOS-W surface-to-air missile. True to the concept of the time—using the same device in multiple weapons—this device was also under development for a potential tactical bomb. The exact military

Buster Dog

characteristics of the 30-inch weapon had not been established, nor had the military made any firm requests for a 30-inch nuclear warhead.

In January 1955, the DMA (Director of Military Applications) authorized the development of a 30-inch warhead for the Nike missile; and in March 1955, the AEC's Santa Fe Operations Office issued a scope of work covering the design of adoption kits for the XW-7 warhead and 30-inch warheads for the Nike-B program. In mid-September 1955, Sandia and LASL presented the formal design of the XW-31. The design was still evolving and had a lower yield than the proposed design released in the previous March. By fall 1956, the XW-31 warhead was far enough along for the army to propose a full-scale test of the Nike and its nuclear warhead against high-altitude bombers during Operation *Hardtack*. These tests never occurred, however.

Sandia released the final design of the XW-31 in mid-September 1957. Since the W-31 was to be used on other missiles, an adaption kit (which eventually became designated XM75E1), designed to mate the XW-31 to the Nike-Hercules, was released in June 1958. The W-31 Mod 0 became operationally available on October 1958. The adapter kit included a cartridge assembly with two baroswitches, a self-aligning static tube adapter ring, and a "stovepipe" or "mushroom" guidance package. The "mushroom" guidance package, with its more modern components, eventually replaced the troublesome "stovepipe" package. Also included were a one-point self-destruct system and a mechanical combination lock PAL (permissive action link).

The U.S. Army's Picatinny Arsenal designed the warhead sections, including the M-22, M-22C, M-22D, M-22F, M-23, M-23C, M-97, M-97D, and the M-97F. The warhead section on the missile was 62.5 inches long, of which the warhead occupied 48.5 inches. The warhead section contained the warhead, adoption kit, warhead body section, and safety and arming devices, including a fail-safe device, sequential timer, and M-30A1 safing-arming devices. Total weight was 1,123 pounds.

The warhead body assemblies, produced by Douglas Aircraft/Charlotte Ordnance Missile Plant, were delivered to the Ramon Engineering Company as government furnished equipment (GFE) for assembly with the loaded warhead.

Production of the W-31 began in 1959, with the last versions phased out in 1989. The W-31 was also used on the *Honest John*, the *Corporal*, and the ADM. Some 2,500 W-31 warheads were produced for the Nike-Hercules missiles.

The W-31 was a boosted fission nuclear device, meaning that the yield could be enhanced by the introduction of deuterium and tritium (D-T) gas into the core of the weapon in exactly the right amount and at the exactly correct time. The W-31 used the COBRA core and a Type D pit. This type of fission device was also used as the "primary" in later thermonuclear weapons.

Unlike the W-7, the W-31 was a "sealed pit" type weapon and did not use an automatic IFI. The W-31 was designed in such a way that in the unlikely event that the high explosives surrounding the nuclear material were to detonate at only one point, as might happen in a missile accident, there would be practically no nuclear yield. This was a major advantage over the W-7 and allowed the W-31 to be stored and transported in a ready condition with a greater margin of safety.

Several modifications were made to the W-31 over the life of the Nike system, the W-31, Mod 2, for example, had improved electrical and safety devices. The two warhead sections on the Nike-Hercules were located directly behind the forward fin assembly, starting at station 87.500. The forward warhead section extended to section 136.000 and the rear warhead section ran to section 150.000. (Sections represent measurements in inches, starting from the nose of the missile.)

Identifying and Maintaining Nuclear Warheads

A Nike-Hercules equipped with a nuclear warhead could be identified by a colored stripe on the outside of the forward missile body. If the stripe was yellow, it was carrying a 2-kiloton warhead; green meant 20 kilotons; and red designated 40 kilotons. No colored stripe meant the missile had a conventional blast-fragmentation warhead. The other external feature indicating the presence of a nuclear warhead was the barometric probe on the nose of the missile. The probe was usually seen covering a small, red "dog house."

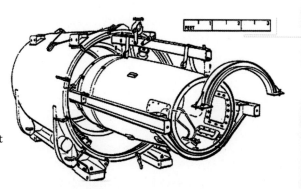

Warhead body section M-409 container

Although the W-31 warhead was designed to produce three different yields, the exact yields of each of the different warheads was determined by higher authority and varied from defense to defense. This fact may help explain the variation in yield numbers among various sources. Each launching section was supplied with warheads of appropriate yield for their particular missions.

Each section in a battery had missiles equipped with warheads of various yields. The battery commander would select a section with a missile of the appropriate yield based upon the fire mission. The various panels and consoles in the battery had switches that were set to the proper positions (Y-1, Y-2, etc.) depending on the missile selected. The panel switches did not set the yield of the missile, but were set according to the yield of the missile selected. It is the authors best guess that the actual yield of the missile was determined by which warhead section (M-22, M-23, M-97, etc.) was attached to the missile. Since the Nike-Hercules W-31 warhead was a boosted fission device, it is logical to believe that the various warhead sections provided different amounts of D-T gas into the core of the warhead, along with varying the internal timing of the fusing system.

The warhead was delivered to the site in the M-409 container. The M-409 container was a round, steel container equipped with a removable cover on the front. The warhead section was supported inside the container on a set of rails that allowed it to be removed and lifted by means of the overhead crane in the warhead building. The M-409 container was airtight and packaged with desiccant to maintain a moisture-free weapon.

The maintenance of the Nike-Hercules nuclear warhead required periodic wipe tests to detect any radioactive leaks. The wipes were disposed of in a facility that conformed to AEC standards. A common facility was a lead-lined drum kept in a secure location. Defective electron tubes containing radioactive isotopes were also disposed of in these facilities. A 1984 report by the US Army Toxic and Hazardous Material Agency stated that no radioactive leaks were detected from these facilities.

Arming the W-31 Warhead

The W-31 warhead arming sequence was a three-step process. The first step was the physical replacement of the safe plug with the arm plug on the body of the missile. This was done by manually opening a small access door on the body of the missile. The second step began after the missile was launched. The missile was required to be subjected to a predetermined set of maneuvers for a preset amount of time for the second arming device to release. The third step in arming the warhead was based on altitude. When the missile reached a preset altitude, as detected by a barometric probe on the nose of the missile, the last arming device was cleared and the warhead could be detonated by a "burst command" sent to the guidance system from the director's trailer in the IFC area. The "burst command" was actually a series of invalid navigation commands sent to the missile guidance system through the MTR. This command consisted of five simultaneous invalid steering orders for pitch and yaw. These commands were interpreted by the guidance system as a command to initiate the fusing mechanism on the warhead.

The M-74 Training Device

The M-74 Warhead Section Trainer was developed for the Army by the Naval Training Device Center (NTDC). NTDC originally procured 225 of the M-74 warhead trainers and spares from the Bendix Aviation Corporation, which operated an AEC component manufacturing facility in Kansas City. The M-74 was used to train personnel in war heading procedures. The T-4014 Tester was used to set the baroswitches. Other test equipment included: T-4016 (used at depot level to test and calibrate the baroswitches and other circuitry); T-4115 (used to test the warhead arming, plug, PAL and other circuitry); and T-4046 (used to actually test the warhead detonators through the SA/SS plug connector).

WX-31 Warhead Tests

Testing of the engineering concepts of the XW-31 warhead began with Shot Item during the Operation *Greenhouse* series tests on Eniwetok Atoll at the PPG in 1951. Shot Item confirmed that a small, gas boosted, fission warhead was feasible, although the device tested was far from a usable weapon.

In 1954, the AEC advised the Military Liaison Committee (MLC) that boosted air defense warheads would be developed. In July 1954. the design characteristics of a 22-inch and a 30-inch diameter warhead were issued. It was estimated that the Nike-B 30-inch warhead would be operational by early 1957, in tandem with the missile.

The summer of 1955 test program proposed safety experiments on the XW-31 warhead as well as others that were to be produced in large numbers for air defense and anti-submarine weapons. The military was concerned with the testing schedule, in particular that safety and operational testing of the warhead were very close together. However, in August 1955, the XW-31 and XW-34 warheads were deleted from these tests because their designs were still evolving.

Greenhouse test, May 25, 1951

Sandia's testing of the W-31 continued into the fall of 1955 with a static load test simulating Nike thrust and maneuvering loads on the W-31 warhead. In these tests, the warhead withstood combined longitudinal and lateral loads of up to 150 percent of the design limit without apparent damage. At the end of October 1956, a Nike-Hercules carrying a simulated atomic warhead successfully intercepted a drone aircraft.

There were several different kinds of tests carried out during the development of the XW-31 warhead. Four of the most important were weapon development tests, weapon proof tests, safety tests, and weapon effect tests. Some tests were combined tests.

25 May 1951 - *Greenhouse* (PPG)
Shot Item was a weapon development test to verify the concept of a small, fusion, D-T gas boosted all-Oralloy core device.

1 July 1957 - *Plumbob* (NTS)
Shot Coulomb-A was a one-point safety test of the XW-31/ COBRA warhead.

9 September 1957 - *Plumbob* (NTS)
Shot Coulomb-B was another one-point safety test of the XW-31/COBRA warhead.

21 May 1958 - *Hardtack* (PPG)
Shot Holly was a weapon proof test of the XW-31-Y3 warhead.

27 May 1958 - *Hardtack I* (PPG)
Shot Magnolia was a weapon proof test of the XW-31 warhead.

4 November 1962 - *Dominic I* (PPG)
Shot Tightrope was the first and only time a W-31 warhead was tested on a Hercules missile.

November 1962 – *Fishbowl*, a subset of high-altitude tests (Pacific Test Range)
Shot Fishbowl Tightrope was a Department of Defense sponsored live launch of a Nike-Hercules missile with W31 nuclear warhead. The warhead detonated at 69,000 feet, approximately two miles South–South West of Johnston Island. The yield of this test is not in the public literature, but the W31 could be set to yield a range from 1 to 40 kilotons. (Some references indicate a yield from 2 to 40 kilotons.)

The air burst created an intense white flash (as seen on Johnston Island) too bright to view through high-density goggles. A strong heat pulse accompanied the detonation. A yellow-orange disk formed, slowly changing to a purple toroid that faded from view after several minutes. This shot is usually regarded as the last US atmospheric test. The later zero yield atmospheric plutonium dispersal tests conducted in Operation *Roller Coaster* are however listed as nuclear tests by the US government and counted as part of the total of US nuclear tests. Furthermore, several later Plowshare nuclear tests (Cabriolet, Palanquin,

Buggy, and Schooner) were surface cratering shots in which the explosions intentionally broke through the surface, venting a substantial fraction of the radioactivity produced.

27 May 1966 - *Flintlock* (NTS)
Shot Discus Thrower was a W-31 weapon effects/stockpile assurance test. This was conducted underground test.

Fragmentation Warheads

The T-45 Warhead
The first drone kill using the T-45 warhead on a Nike-Hercules was on 25 April 1957. Warhead T-45 consisted of approximately 20,000, 140-grain-cubical-shaped steel fragments arranged in single and double layers around a 625-pound explosive charge and warhead booster. The M-17 (T-45) blast-fragmentation warhead metal parts were loaded at the Iowa Ordnance Plant, installed in the warhead body assembly, and shipped to Ordnance depots for issue to the users.

A burst pulse from the missile guidance set initiated detonation of the warhead. The burst pulse ignited a small explosive charge in two safety and arming devices, M-30A1. These charges ignited two explosive harnesses, M-38. The explosive harnesses detonated the warhead booster that in turn detonated the warhead charge. The safety and arming devices could not be fired until armed by the force of acceleration, during the boost period. The fragment distribution (blast pattern) of warhead T-45 was approximately spherical with a conical dead zone to the rear.

The T-46 Warhead

In the early phase of the R&D program, primary emphasis was placed on development of the T-45 blast-fragmentation warhead as the interim armament for both the Ajax and Hercules, pending availability of the T-46 cluster warhead. The latter warhead, however, offered the Hercules missile system two major advantages: 1) it would provide a greater kill probability against targets at all ranges and altitudes, particularly in the low-altitude region; and, 2) in comparison with the nuclear warhead, it would not contaminate or damage the territory below its bursting point, permitting firings over friendly territory.

Although a significant improvement over the basic T-46 design, the T-46E1 was expensive warhead system and still lacked the desired effectiveness. The Chief of R&D, DA, therefore requested that necessary action be taken to complete the development and test effort and to effect an orderly termination of the program. The Secretary of the Army approved the formal termination of the T-46 project on 21 September 1961.

The R&D contract cost of conventional warheads for the Hercules missile totaled $3,679,985. Of this amount, $260,430 went for development of the M-17 (T-45) fragmentation warhead and the remaining $3,419,555 for development of the T-46 cluster warhead.

Hercules Operations and Command & Control

The Hercules received an upgraded version of the Ajax ACQR and an additional target-ranging radar (TRR) along with the MTR and the TTR. Eventually, the Army upgraded the Basic Nike-Hercules to the Improved Nike-Hercules. This program introduced new radars and electronics at several sites. The most effective (and costly) addition was the high-power acquisition radar (HIPAR), which was able to detect targets at the longer ranges attainable with Hercules. Instead of HIPAR, several Hercules IFCs received alternate battery acquisition radars (ABAR), usually the AN/FPS-69, FPS-71, or FPS-75. As part of the conversion from Ajax to Hercules, the original Hercules acquisition radar became the low-power acquisition radar (LOPAR).

The new Nike-Hercules systems also brought changes in command and control of the firing batteries. With Nike-Ajax,

INTERCEPT POINT

TARGET

TARGET

TARGET

HIPAR/ ABAR System

LOPAR System

Target Ranging Radar System

Missile Tracking Radar System

Computer System

Missile position data

Antenna positioning data

Steering and burst orders

Designated target azimuth and range data from HIPAR or LOPAR

Designated target position data

Gyro azimuth preset da

Improved Nike-Hercules operations (illustration based on FM 44-1-2 ADM Reference Handbook, US Army)

operational combat control ultimately rested on the individual battery; for the longer range Hercules, a new system was devised to coordinate the efforts of multiple batteries.

Development of an automated command and control system for Nike had commenced in the early 1950s; until 1957 all Army Air Defense Command Post (AADCP) operations were performed manually, utilizing plotting boards. The first integrated electronic air defense system developed to replace manual operations was the AN/FSG-1 Missile Master, designed by the Martin Company of Orlando, FL. The system featured its own radars, multiple computers, and electronic plotting devices that enabled the coordination of target acquisition, tracking, and battery firing. Missile Master was housed in a semi-hardened concrete blockhouse and could monitor twenty-four missile sites against fifty individual targets. The first to go on line was at Fort Meade in 1957; the last of ten installations was at Fort MacArthur in the Los Angeles Defense Area on 14 December 1960.

A less complicated (and less capable) system was the AN/GSG-5(V) BIRDIE, designed to handle four to sixteen fire units. BIRDIE (battery integrated radar display equipment) was designed specifically for the smaller defense areas; some single battalion defenses received AN/GSG-5(V) installations during 1961 and 1962.

The final addition to the command and control suite saw the

Launcher

nch

LOPAR radar

Auxiliary antenna

Acquisition antenna

Lifting handle

Hydraulic control unit

Acquisition antenna pedestal

Acquisition modulator

Acquisition receiver-transmitter

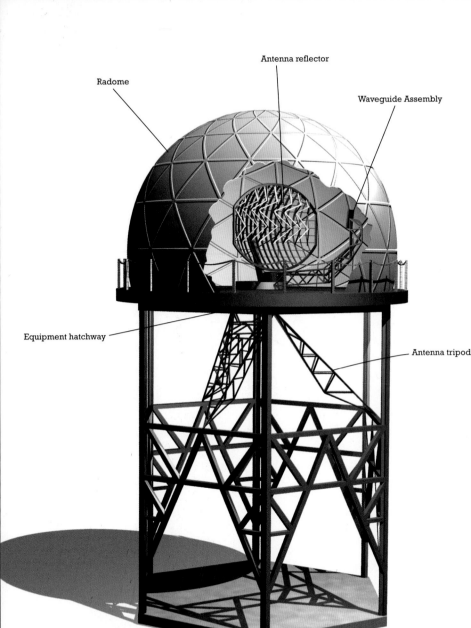

Radome

Antenna reflector

Waveguide Assembly

Equipment hatchway

Antenna tripod

HIPAR radar

development and deployment of defense acquisition radars (DAR) at the battalion/AADCP level or higher. The types included the AN/TPS-1D, TPS-1G, FPS-36, FPS-56, and FPS-61. The latter variants featured improved range and altitude capabilities as well as a reasonably high rate of effectiveness in an electronic countermeasures/counter-counter-measures environment.

Administrative changes continued following the retirement of the Army Guard Ajax sites: the Seattle Defense Area was downgraded from Missile Master to BIRDIE; two BIRDIE defense areas, Homestead-Miami and Providence (New England), were upgraded from BIRDIE to the new Hughes AN/TSQ-51 Missile Mentor command and control system during the mid-1960s. Missile Mentor featured all solid-state construction and could control twenty-four firing batteries; it replaced seven Missile Master installations by the end of 1967.

Many defense areas also had a secondary master fire unit (SMFU) and one or more remote radar integration stations (RRIS). The SMFU installation served as an alternate command post in the event the AADCP was destroyed or otherwise incapacitated; the RRISs were used to provide radar coverage to any part of the defense area that was not adequately covered by the AADCP radars.

These defense area systems operated under the overall tactical command of the Air Force's Semi-automatic Ground Environment (SAGE) system, through the NORAD sector and region direction centers (SDC/RDC). These centers received automatic detection and tracking data from a ground-based air search radar network, height-finding radars, gap-filler radars, and air and seaborne early warning assets. Information from these sources

Nike Hercules on launcher at White Sands test range circa 1970, US Army photo

was received by telephone, radio, teletype, and direct data links and programmed into a large main-frame computer. The analyzed data was then transmitted to Air Force missiles and interceptor aircraft by data link.

Digital data transmissions were also passed on to the ARADCOM AADCPs for engagement by Nike missiles. Selected data was also transmitted automatically to adjacent direction centers and ADC Region/Sector combat command posts. Additional information was passed by telephone, teletype, and/or radio to civil defense agencies, Strategic Air Command, and other combat units.

The SAGE system was the centralized control network for all defensive assets. Through Missile Master, BIRDIE and Missile Mentor, each ARADCOM battery was effectively linked with the entire North American air defense system through NORAD's central coordinating center.

Life at the stations was fairly routine; maintenance, cleaning, and practice duties filled the time. Live firings were never performed at sites in the continental United States; once a year each unit would travel to a firing range facility (initially Red Canyon Range, then McGregor Range) for their annual practice firings. Designated short-notice annual practice (SNAP) after 1961, these were not scheduled in advance; any unit could be called on forty-eight hours notice, ordered to Fort Bliss, and dispatched to the range for live firing practice.

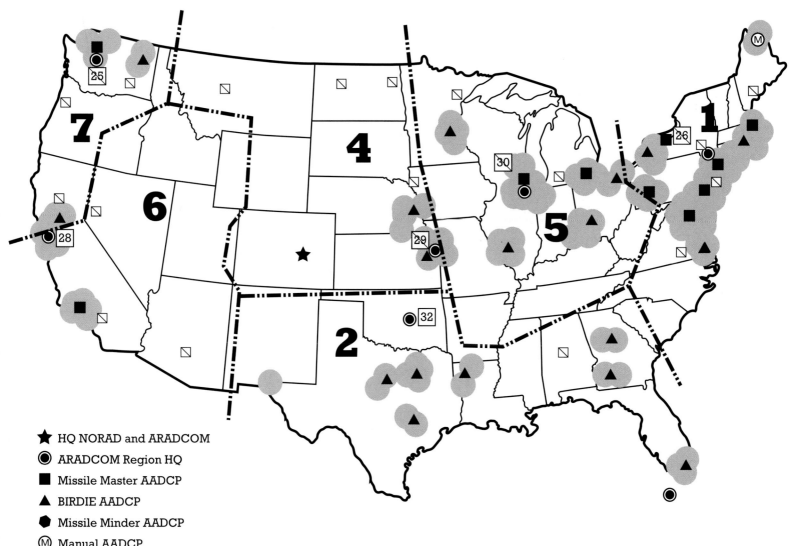

★ HQ NORAD and ARADCOM
◎ ARADCOM Region HQ
■ Missile Master AADCP
▲ BIRDIE AADCP
⬢ Missile Minder AADCP
Ⓜ Manual AADCP
☐ NORAD Region HQ
◨ NORAD SAGE CP

Aradcom Organization - July 1963

6. Nike Command Structure

The Nike missile firing batteries were linked by a command structure outlined below.

ARADCOM REGIONS—the ARADCOM regions were established to provide intermediate command and control between HQ ARADCOM and the defense areas. The first three regions were activated in 1951; two additional regions were activated in 1955 and a sixth region was activated in 1960. Inactivation of regions commenced in 1963; after 1971 the First and Sixth ARADCOM regions controlled all remaining operations in the United States.

DEFENSE AREA—defense areas were initially named after the cities or Air Force base of their assignment. Each area consisted of a brigade, group, or defense command element controlling the missile battalions. In the early 1960s, ARADCOM began a process of merging defense areas.

BRIGADES—artillery brigades (air defense artillery brigades after 1972) were activated as the controlling agency for major city defense areas, reporting directly to the ARADCOM region. Normally each brigade had multiple groups assigned. As ARADCOM contracted during the 1960s, brigade designations were inactivated and/or transferred among the defense areas. In several instances brigades were inactivated and replaced by group-level organizations.

GROUPS—artillery groups were activated to control single or multiple battalions; the early tendency was to activate a group-level unit for each single-battalion defense and one group per each two battalions in the larger defenses. As with brigades, there were multiple activations and inactivations.

DEFENSE COMMAND ELEMENTS—in the absence of a brigade or group, Defense Command Elements were designated as the senior air defense unit in each defense area.

BATTALIONS—missile battalions were the actual operational units of ARADCOM, manning the individual sites through a battery organization. As Nike-Ajax came on line, several antiaircraft artillery battalions were redesignated as antiaircraft artillery missile battalions (AAAMBn) or missile battalions (MBn) (Nike-Ajax). Each battalion consisted of a Headquarters & Headquarters Battery (HHB) and normally four firing batteries.

On 1 September 1958 Regular Army missile battalions were inactivated and replaced by missile battalions assigned to regiments (the units were actually redesignated in place). For example, the former Battery A, 11th Missile Battalion (A/11th), site HA-08, East Windsor, CT, became Battery A, 2nd Missile Battalion, 55th Artillery Regiment (A/2/55th). This was done as part of the Army's Combat Arms Regimental System, for unifying units along mission, historical, and regimental lines. The Army National Guard missile battalions followed along the same lines during 1959.

Units active on 20 December 1965 were redesignated as battalions assigned to regiments, such as the 3rd

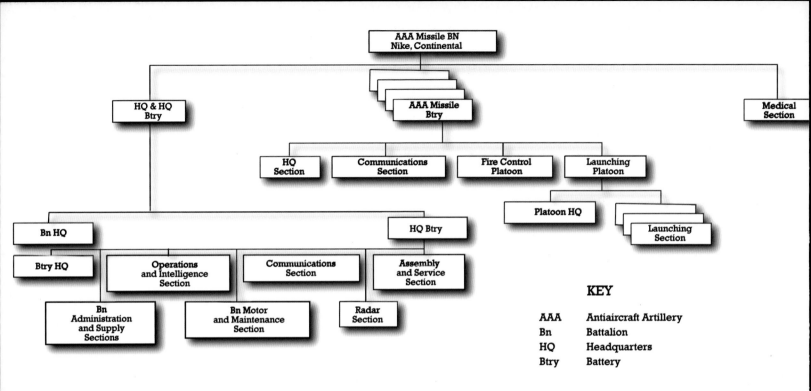

Battalion, 43rd Artillery. In recognition of the division of field and air defense artillery into two separate combat arms, units active on 1 September 1971 were redesignated as battalions assigned to air defense artillery regiments, such as the 4th Battalion, 60th Air Defense Artillery.

On 13 September 1972 several of the remaining ADA battalions were redesignated by the Army in order to preserve the lineage of older units. Examples include the 2nd/3rd in the Detroit Defense Area, which replaced the 3/517th; the 2/65th in Los Angeles, which replaced the 4/65th; and the 1/4th in Seattle, which replaced the 4/5th.

7. US Air Force SAGE Combat/Direction Centers

ARADCOM's Army Air Defense Command Posts—whether equipped with Missile Master, Missile Mentor, or BIRDIE—relied on long-range command and control (C2) data from the NORAD, CONAD, and the US Air Force's ADC.

The initial system of providing the warfare information was strictly manual, just like the Army's early antiaircraft and air defense missile command and control "systems." The Air Force's long-range radar sites and civilian Ground Observers Corps scanned the skies for unknown aircraft and relayed the contact information via phone line to a manual direction center. Air Force personnel plotted the suspected threat aircraft on a large Plexiglas board, which depicted the geographic operations area; the primary information included the "bogie's" altitude, airspeed, and direction of flight. Other watch personnel then compared the threat's track to known high-value targets—such as cities, industrial complexes, and military installations—and then determined which air defense asset could best respond. At that point more phone calls went out, to ADC's fighter interceptor units, which received the scramble orders, and to the local Army defenses. For the Army, the incoming alert phone call provided guidance on the probable threat and the direction in which to start radiating.

Not surprisingly, the manual system—which had proven valuable during World War II—was slow, ponderous, and unable to keep up with high-speed jet aircraft coming in at high altitude. Worse, large numbers of aircraft could easily overcome the manual system. As a result, during the early 1950s the Air Force, the Massachusetts Institute of Technology (MIT), and IBM developed a new, computerized system. It became known as SAGE.

The system combined large computers with electronic data transfer systems (primarily via phone line and microwave) automated analysis and determination of the level of the threat, and selection of the best defensive systems to handle the threat. The "semi" part of the title came into play when Air Force personnel manually designated targets of interest with light guns while concurrently alerting the defenses. Then the automated portion of the system came back into play, forwarding the target data to the interceptor aircraft, back to the long-range radar sites that provided ground-controlled intercept services to the fighters, and to the Army Air Defense Command Posts.

SAGE radar in Bath, ME, includes AN/FPS-31 experimental long-range search radar and AN/FPS-6 height finder radar. (Ref. BB01, Picture used with the permission of The MITRE Corporation. Copyright © The MITRE Corporation. All rights reserved.)

Operator uses special light gun to target potential intercept coordinates. (Ref. BB10, Picture used with the permission of The MITRE Corporation. Copyright © The MITRE Corporation. All rights reserved.)

SAGE building at McGuire Air Force Base. First SAGE air defense center to go operational. (Reg. M0-183, Picture used with the permission of The MITRE Corporation. Copyright © The MITRE Corporation. All rights reserved.)

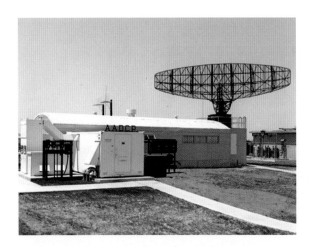

Battery A, 4/7, Site BG-40, Bergstrom AFB, Texas, 13 September 1962. Shown is the Army Air Defense Command Post (ADCAP),the Alternate Battery Acquisition Radar, (ABAR), the Fire Unit Integration Facility (FUIF), and behind the building, two antennas for the AN/TRC-47 intrabattery communications VHF radio. (U.S. Army SC598141)

Three series of tests validated the effectiveness of the original computer (nicknamed *Whirlwind I*) and its associated communications, command and control systems. During 1953 and 1954 MIT's Lincoln Laboratories operated the Cape Cod interim systems, which tied together the long-range radar site at North Truro, MA with several gap-filler radars and validated the direction center's operational concepts. An experimental SAGE sub-sector at MIT's Lincoln Laboratory in Lexington, MA went into operation in 1955 and tested the prototype XD-1 direction center computer; this system later became the AN/FSQ-7, the heart of SAGE.

Operational Deployment

The system passed its tests and entered service on 28 June 1958 with the formal activation of ADC's New York Defense Sector at McGuire AFB, NJ. Upon activation the sector assumed responsibility for the air defense of eastern New York—including New York City and Long Island—eastern Pennsylvania, Maryland, Delaware, and New Jersey. From that small beginning the SAGE network expanded to incorporate twenty-two direction centers in the continental United States; the last one, at Sioux City Air Base, IA (DC-22), went operational in April 1961.

As designed, the DCs housed the AN/FSQ-7 in large, three- or four-story windowless, semi-hardened buildings packed full of the computer, electronics, communications systems, displays, and offices. The computer itself weighed 250 tons, employed over 49,000 vacuum tubes and required a 3000-kilowatt power supply. In each center several hundred joint-service personnel—primarily US Air Force, but also Canadian, US Navy, and US Army—operated 24-hours per day, 365-days per year to coordinate air defense operations. When an Air Force long-range radar site or airborne radar (or one of the Navy's seaborne or airborne radars, for that matter) detected a possible intruder, the information was automatically relayed by the SAGE system to the nearest direction center. There, personnel analyzed the tracking data, processed it, and compared it to known flight plans and military/civilian aircraft tracks. If it remained an unknown, the direction center dispatched interceptor aircraft to locate and identify the intruder or intruders. If the unknowns turned out to be hostile—or if additional targets popped up with obvious hostile intent—the entire sector and region went on war footing and started designating targets electronically, while concurrently providing track data to adjacent sectors.

During this process ADC's control centers (later renamed combat centers) came into action, employing the AN/FSQ-8 computer and a similar but smaller staff. Collocated with specific direction centers in adjacent buildings, the

CCs ran the regional battles for CONAD and NORAD, tying in the inputs of multiple DCs and maintaining the "big picture." Through 1966 the SAGE combat centers at Hancock Field, NY; Truax Field, WI; and McChord AFB, WA directed the regional operations in the eastern, central, and western United States respectively.

Generally, the hierarchy for engagement called for employment of the 250- to 400-mile BOMARC first (but only in the northeastern United States and Canada), interceptor aircraft second, and ARADCOM's Nikes third, to handle any aircraft that penetrated the outer defensive ring. As the battle proceeded, the SAGE DCs and CCs continued to provide tracking data to ADC, RCAF, and ARADCOM assets, and designated fighter squadrons and Nike defense areas for each target.

At the Army Air Defense Command Post level, the AADCP commander took the tracking and battle information from the SAGE network and then designated specific batteries for engagement. SAGE proved particularly valuable in providing long-range early-warning information to the individual defense areas, improving response time while enabling the individual battery IFCs to search, track, and acquire within a specific threat arc. This substantially improved the effectiveness of the Nike system as a whole.

The Inactivation of SAGE

ADC's original plans from 1954 called for as many as thirty-three SAGE direction centers and eight combat centers to blanket the entire United States. In the end, budget constraints—in particular, the incredible cost of the phone service linking the proposed system together, even at government rates—and the high manpower requirements limited deployment to twenty-two direction centers, three combat centers, two remote combat centers, and two manual-direction centers in the Lower 48 and Canadian Maritimes with two additional SAGE DCs emplaced at North Bay, Ontario. The manual DC at Oklahoma City AFS, just east of Tinker AFB, covered the SAGE system's gaps in the south-central United States while the second manual center at Goose AB, Labrador handled the extreme northeastern approaches to North America. As for the combat centers, the Air Force went to the trouble of constructing a fourth one but it never went into operation and all SAGE FSQ-8 systems were cancelled.

Within a year of full activation of the network Air Defense Command started shutting down brand new SAGE facilities. Again, the problem was budget and manpower constraints; to that end, the subsequent twenty years of NORAD and CONAD force structure reductions mirrored what happened to ARADCOM and the Nike missile system. The network and the nation's air defense systems steadily declined. Plans to develop a "Super SAGE" system of buried, nuclear-hardened direction and combat centers around the country also went by the boards; an initial proposed facility outside of Cornwall, NY never got beyond the planning stage.

The first to go was DC-8 on 1 January 1962, when the Kansas City ADS at Richards-Gebaur AFB inactivated; however, the installation lived on as a SAGE combat center. By the end of 1963 the Air Force shut down an additional six direction centers at Beale, Minot, Larson, Hancock, Grand Forks, and KI Sawyer. Officially all closed for the same reason: their proximity to primary targets, i.e., SAC bomber and missile installations. A massive reorganization of Air Defense Command and the NORAD/CONAD regions on 1 April 1966 resulted in the closure of the three combat centers and direction centers at Stewart, Norton, and Stead, leaving thirteen operational SAGE DCs under direct assignment to numbered air divisions. Notably, DC-3 at Hancock Field, NY, initially inactivated on 4 September 1963, went back into operation under the 35th AD. Concurrently, the former SAGE DC at Stewart assumed regional C2 duties, along with the center at Richards-Gebaur AFB and the former remote combat center at Hamilton AFB, CA. The Stewart and Richards-Gebaur facilities continued to operate their AN/FSQ-7 computers while Hamilton upgraded from a manual combat center using three AN/GSA-51 computers, the same type used at SAGE Backup Interceptor Control (BUIC-II) facilities. The manual combat center at Oklahoma AFS was likewise slated to for an upgrade to an SCC, but funding shortages force cancellation; all three SCC's were deactivated by the end of 1969.

Even this major rearrangement of air defense command and control facilities didn't remain intact for long. Between 31 December 1967 and 31 December 1969 NORAD lost the seven direction centers at McGuire, Truax, Sioux City, Adair, Topsham, Gunter, and Custer, again under the guise of budget constraints and the proverbial "improved capability through new technology," also termed as "doing more with less." In order to provide command and control redundancy for the surviving DCs, Air Defense Command stood up "mini-SAGE" centers at twelve long-range radar sites under the Backup Interceptor Control, or BUIC III, program which followed the BUIC I and II deployments. The only one to remain in operation beyond 1 January 1974 was the 678th Air Defense Group facility at Tyndall AFB, FL, partly to augment the 20th Air Division SAGE DC at Fort Lee AFS, VA (the FSQ-7 couldn't process all of the radar inputs in the 20th AD's large geographic area) and partly to keep an eye on the Caribbean and Cuba. The others inactivated for budget reasons.

That left six direction centers at McChord, Fort Lee, Malmstrom, Hancock, Duluth, and Luke AFBs. They exercised operational control over a steadily dwindling number of Air Force-manned radar sites and fighter interceptor squadrons into the early 1980s. The end came between 1981 and 1983 with the introduction of the new joint Federal Aviation Administration (FAA)–Air Force radar and C2 network appropriately titled the "JSS" for Joint Surveillance System. The FAA assumed full responsibility for radar operations in the continental United States—albeit with small Air Force detachments handling height-finder radar activities until newer three-dimensional air route surveillance radar systems could come on line—while NORAD stood up four regional operations control centers (ROCCs) at McChord; March AFB, CA; Griffiss AFB, NY; and Tyndall AFB, FL.

On 23 December 1983 the Air Force pulled the plug on the last operational AN/FYQ-7 —like all of the Q-7s nicknamed "Clyde"—at Luke AFB, AZ. The new Southwest ROCC at March AFB then fully assumed command and control responsibilities for the southwestern quarter of the United States, under the 26th Air Division. Thus ended the SAGE era of continental air defense history.

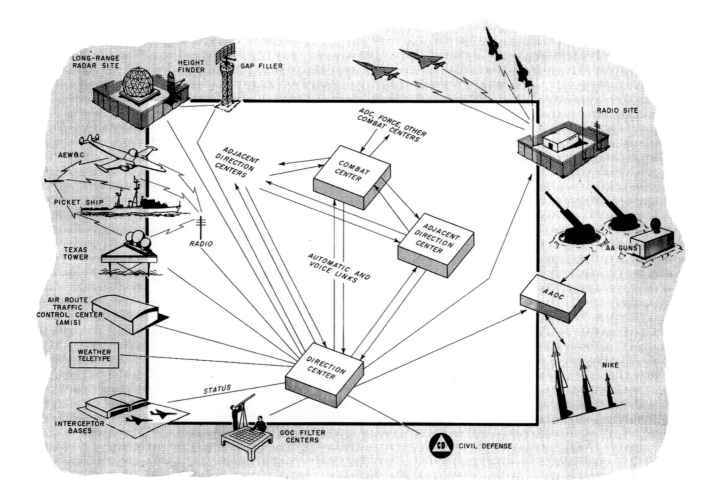

LONG-RANGE
RADAR SITE
HEIGHT
FINDER
GAP FILLER
RADIO SITE
ADC, FORCE, OTHER
COMBAT CENTERS
AEW&C
ADJACENT
DIRECTION
CENTERS
COMBAT
CENTER
PICKET SHIP
ADJACENT
DIRECTION
CENTER
AA GUNS
RADIO
TEXAS
TOWER
AUTOMATIC AND
VOICE LINKS
AIR ROUTE
TRAFFIC
CONTROL CENTER
(AMIS)
AAOC
WEATHER
TELETYPE
DIRECTION
CENTER
NIKE
STATUS
INTERCEPTOR
BASES
GOC FILTER
CENTERS
CD CIVIL DEFENSE

Was SAGE successful? Undoubtedly! Despite the expense and complexity of the system, it served effectively and faithfully for twenty-five years and was a remarkable example of first-generation computer technology. Notably, most of the laptop and handheld computers that an individual can buy today are faster and more capable than SAGE, but the precepts and systems established by SAGE continue to live on in a several guises including today's highly capable and mobile command and control systems. The famous MITRE Corporation, formed in 1958 from MIT's Lincoln Laboratory, remains a leader in research and technology. Finally, every time you make an airline reservation you're using SABER (semi-automatic business environment research) system, developed by IBM as another outgrowth of SAGE.

AAOC	*Anti-aircraft Operations Center*
ADC	*Adjacent Direction Center*
AEW&C	*Airborne Early Warning and Control*
AMIS	*Air Movements Information Service*
GOC	*Ground Observer Corps*

Air Defense diagram showing relationship of SAGE to national air defense system. (Ref. RB-04, Picture used with the permission of The MITRE Corporation. Copyright © The MITRE Corporation. All rights reserved.)

The following is a list of SAGE DCs and CCs, with associated ARADCOM defense areas, as of September 1, 1961.

Desig	Location	Air Division/Sector	Sector AADCP	ARADCOM Def Areas
DC-1	McGuire AFB, NJ	26th AD/New York ADS	NH-55DC	New York
			PH-64DC	Philadelphia
DC-2	Stewart AFB, NY (SCC-4)	26th AD/Boston ADS	PR-69DC	New England
DC-3	Hancock Field, NY	26th AD/Syracuse ADS	NF-17DC	Buffalo-Niagara Falls
			PI-70DC	Pittsburgh
DC-4	Fort Lee AFS, VA	26th AD/Washington ADS	W-13DC	Washington-Baltimore
			NF-55DC	Norfolk
DC-5	Topsham AFS, ME	26th AD/Bangor ADS	(manual)	Loring AFB
DC-6	Custer AFS, MI	30th AD/Detroit ADS	D-15DC	Detroit
			CD-27DC	Cincinnati-Dayton
			CL-34DC	Cleveland
DC-7	Truax Field, WI	30th AD/Chicago ADS	C-80DC	Chicago-Gary
			C-80DC	Milwaukee
DC-8	Richards-Gebaur AFB, MO	29th AD/Kansas City ADS	KC-65DC	Kansas City
			SL-47DC	St Louis
DC-9	Gunter AFB, MO	32nd AD/Montgomery ADS	HM-01DC	Homestead-Miami
			KS-19DC	Key West
			R-44DC	Robins AFB
			TU-01DC	Turner AFB
DC-10	Duluth AB, MN	30th AD/Duluth ADS	MS-48DC	Minneapolis-St Paul
DC-11	Grand Forks AFB, ND	29th AD/Grand Forks ADS		
DC-12	McChord AFB, WA	25th AD/Seattle ADS	S-90DC	Seattle

Desig	Location	Air Division/Sector	Sector AADCP	ARADCOM Def Areas
DC-13	Adair AFS, OR	25th AD/Portland ADS		
DC-14	KI Sawyer AFB, MI	30th AD/Sault Ste Marie ADS		
DC-15	Larson AFB, WA	25th AD/Spokane ADS	Geiger Field	Fairchild AFB
DC-16	Stead AFB, NV	28th AD/Reno ADS		
DC-17	Norton AFB, CA	28th AD/Los Angeles ADS	LA-45DC	Los Angeles
DC-18	Beale AFB, CA	28th AD/San Francisco ADS	SF-90DC	San Francisco
			Travis AFB	Travis AFB
DC-19	Minot AFB, ND	29th AD/Minot ADS		
DC-20	Malmstrom AFB, MT	29th AD/Great Falls ADS		
DC-21	Luke AFB, AZ	28th AD/Phoenix ADS		
DC-22	Sioux City AB, IA	29th AD/Sioux City ADS	Omaha AFS	Lincoln AFB
				Offutt AFB
SAGE Combat Centers				
CC-1	Hancock Field, NY		HQ Eastern NORAD Region/HQ 26th AD	
CC-2	Truax Field, WI		HQ Central NORAD Region/HQ 30th AD	
CC-3	McChord AFB, WA		HQ 25th AD	
CC-4	Minot AFB, ND		(not operational)	
Remote Combat Centers				
RCC	Richards-Gebaur AFB, MO (SCC-6) HQ 29th AD			
RCC	Hamilton AFB, CA (SCC-5) HQ Western NORAD Region/HQ 28th AD			
Manual Direction Centers				
Goose AB, LB		64th AD/Goose ADS	Thule AB	Thule AB
Oklahoma City AFS, OK		32nd AD/Oklahoma City ADS	LAAP	Barksdale AFB
			Bergstrom AFB	Bergstrom AFB
			DF-30DC	Dallas-Fort Worth
			Sweetwater AFS	Dyess AFB

8. Other American Surface-to-Air Missile Defense Systems

During the years following World War II, several other SAM designs were developed by the Army, Air Force, and Navy. Many different proposals were considered and several research efforts were funded during the 1940s and 1950s; each service pushed its particular program at the expense of the others.

Congressional debate over these different systems came to a head between 1957 and 1959, as both the Army and the Air Force worked for acceptance and full-scale development of their particular programs. Congress failed to come to a decision on which SAM system to use in 1959, but did decide to cut spending on both programs. Hence, the Army's Nike-Hercules and Air Force's BOMARC systems were allowed to proceed, albeit at a reduced level. Several other programs were left hanging; their disposition would not be fully resolved for another ten years.

BOMARC being assembled at Boeing plant (from Chan)

BOMARC (Air Force)

In January 1946 the Boeing Aircraft Company began a research program to design and construct a ground-to-air pilotless aircraft (GAPA). The lessons learned from this research led Boeing to propose building a pilot-less interceptor missile to the USAF. A contract to develop the IM-99 interceptor from the experimental XF-99 was established between Boeing and the USAF in 1949. Two months later the Michigan Aeronautical Research Center was added as a participant in the research. The resulting missile was named BOMARC using the initials from these two organizations. A long and difficult testing period followed, during which the Air Force was competing with the Army over which system, BOMARC or Nike, would be used as the US air defense system. Even though BOMARC prototypes were still imperfect, the Air Force established a contract for its production with Boeing in November 1957.

The resulting production missile was the IM-99A, which could contain either a conventional or a nuclear warhead. It was launched vertically and quickly rose to 60,000 feet using a liquid-fueled rocket engine. Once it achieved the cruise altitude it then flew like a plane using liquid-fueled ramjets with a range of 230 nautical miles. It was guided to its target area by the SAGE center system using information gathered by the ADC air search radar network. Once within ten miles of the target, the internal homing radar took over and guided the missile to intercept.

In 1958 the Air Force established a testing and training facility for its BOMARC program at Hurlbert AFB in Florida and built the first dedicated BOMARC launch facility on nearby Santa Rosa Island. Work here and at other sites resulted in the development of the Model II launch facility for BOMARC, a reinforced concrete garage-like structure in which the missile was stored horizontally. The launcher had a split roof, which was raised after the two-minute fueling process was completed, allowing the missile to be raised by an elevator arm to firing position. The mechanical and electrical components to operate this procedure were located in an adjacent room.

Initial plans in 1952 were for fifty-two air defense missile sites each basing 120 missiles. This was soon scaled back to forty sites, then to twenty-nine sites with sixty missiles each by 1959. As the result of the intense congressional debate in the 1959, it was decided to deploy both the Air Force BOMARC system and the Army Nike system in more scaled back versions than proposed. The Air Force would get eighteen BOMARC sites with twenty-eight missiles each. In March 1960, it was decided only to deploy BOMARC at eight US sites and two Canadian sites.

The first BOMARC A site became operational at McGuire AFB, NJ, on 19 September 1959, followed by sites at Suffolk County, NY; Langley AFB, VA; Otis AFB, MA; and Dow AFB, ME by December 1960.

BOMARC A was dogged by the same problems of all liquid-fueled rockets—the corrosive fuel could not be stored in the rocket itself, it had to be mixed and loaded just before launch, and it was dangerously explosive. This was graphically demonstrated on 7 June 1960, when a nuclear-armed BOMARC A burst into flames at McGuire AFB, NJ, after its fuel tank ruptured. The resulting fire melted the nuclear warhead spilling radioactive plutonium. The fire was quickly controlled and the radioactively contaminated areas were encased under asphalt and concrete.

The Air Force was developing solid fuels for their ICBM programs; this and other improvements were incorporated into the BOMARC system during 1959 and 1960, resulting in the IM-99B. The solid-fueled BOMARC B had a longer range—440 nautical miles—and could be launched in thirty seconds. A new streamlined launch facility, the Model IV with underground mechanical and electrical services, was deployed with the new missile. In June 1961 the first BOMARC B site became operational at Kincheloe AFB, MI; followed by sites at Duluth, MN; Niagara Falls, NY; and the two Canadian sites at North Bay, Ontario; and La Macaza, Quebec. BOMARC B missiles replaced the BOMARC A missiles at Langley AFB, McGuire AFB, and Otis AFB (the Suffolk County and Dow AFB sites were not upgraded to B). The Air Force's answer to Nike went in service at the following sites on the dates indicated in table on following page. The appropriate air defense missile squadrons are listed as are the eight cancelled sites; notably, the Paine Field site in Everett, WA was nearly 100 percent complete at the time of its shutdown and scrapping. The Air Force performed all training and test activities at Hurlburt Field, FL with operational firing from a facility on Santa Rosa Island.

Top and bottom images both are BOMARC missiles on display at the Air Force Museum, Dayton, OH (Ron Plante, AF Museum, Dayton OH)

Once these deployments were completed in fall 1964, it was realized that BOMARC (as well as Nike-Hercules) could not be used effectively in an ABM role. The Air Force began to shut down some of the Niagara launchers, all operations ended there by late 1969. In 1972 as the

6th ADMS	Suffolk County AFB, NY	56	BOMARC A	12/59-12/64
22nd ADMS	Langley AFB, VA	56	BOMARC A/B	9/58-10/72
26th ADMS	Otis AFB, MA	56	BOMARC A/B	3/59-4/72
28th ADMS	Paine Field, WA	28	BOMARC B	cancelled
30th ADMS	Dow AFB, ME	28	BOMARC A	6/59-12/64
35th ADMS	Niagara Falls A/P, NY	56	BOMARC B	6/60-12/69
37th ADMS	Kincheloe AFB, MI	28	BOMARC B	3/60-10/72
46th ADMS	McGuire AFB, NJ	84	BOMARC A/B	1/59-10/72
74th ADMS	Duluth AB, MN	28	BOMARC B	4/60-4/72
————————	Adair AFS, OR	28	BOMARC B	cancelled
————————	Travis AFB, CA	28	BOMARC B	cancelled
————————	Vandenberg AFB, CA	28	BOMARC B	cancelled
————————	Malmstrom AFB, MT	28	BOMARC B	cancelled
————————	Minot AFB, ND	28	BOMARC B	cancelled
————————	Glasgow AFB, MT	28	BOMARC B	cancelled
————————	Charleston AFB, SC	28	BOMARC B	cancelled
4751st ADS (Missile)	Hurlburt Field, FL		multiple launchers	training facility
446 (SAM) Squadron, RCAF	CFB North Bay, ON	28	BOMARC B	12/61-4/72
447 (SAM) Squadron, RCAF	CFB La Macaza, QC	28	BOMARC B	9/62-4/72

Army was closing out its Nike-Hercules sites, the Air Force closed down its BOMARC sites, the final one being the McGuire AFB site in late 1972.

The sixty-acre McGuire Air Defense Missile Site retains nearly all its of structures and is the only unaltered BOMARC site remaining today. It has been nominated to the National Register of Historic sites as a Historical District.

HAWK (Army)

In 1954 the Army began research and development on a smaller, low-to-medium altitude missile system that would be deployed in a supporting role to Nike-Hercules. Designated the MIM-23 HAWK (homing-all-the-way killer), the system featured a sixteen-foot long solid-fueled missile with a range of twenty-two miles at Mach 2.5. All radars and missile launchers were trailer mounted for mobility. HAWK became operational in 1959, with the Army deploying thirteen battalions, primarily as forward frontier area coverage.

HAWK

HAWK firing (John R. Cauvel)

ARADCOM actually performed site surveys for its proposed HAWK units, but deployment under the command was limited to two battalions emplaced in Homestead-Miami and Key West, FL, in response to the Cuban Missile Crisis. These units passed to US Army Forces Command following ARADCOM's demise in 1974, and were inactivated in 1979.

The Regular Army retired HAWK on 1 April 1994 with the inactivation of the 2/1st ADA at Fort Bliss. It left service with the US Marine Corps and the Army National Guard shortly afterward. The last HAWK battalion in the Army National Guard was 2/174th ADA, OHArNG, which retired its HAWKs for Avenger in 1997. In the US Marine Corps, the 1st Low Altitude Air Defense Battalion, 1st Marine Air Wing, converted to a Stinger battery on 14 May 1993 while the 2nd LAADB, 2nd Marine Air Wing, transitioned to a mix of Stingers and Avenger. The Marine Corps Reserve's 4th LAADB at Pasadena, CA, converted to the Avenger weapon system in 1995.

The MIM-23B Improved HAWK continues in service with several foreign nations. Notably, the most recent combat use of the system came on 2 August 1990 when Kuwaiti HAWK batteries managed to shoot down over twenty Iraqi aircraft during the latter nation's invasion of Kuwait.

Talos (Navy)

In 1955 the Air Force was assigned responsibility for the evaluation of the Navy's Talos (SAM-N-6/RIM-8) shipboard air defense missile system for possible use as a land-based SAM. The intent was to provide Strategic Air Command bomber bases and Atomic Energy Commission installations with a capable point-defense system.

Development of the Talos program commenced during World War II and led to the missile's deployment to the fleet in 1957. The missile utilized beam-riding guidance with semi-active terminal homing; propulsion was via a solid-fuel booster with ramjet sustainer. Talos was fitted with either a 300-pound high-explosive or nuclear warhead.

The Air Force, concerned with the idea of relying on Nike-Ajax for the protection of its installations, decided to proceed with the ground-based variant of Talos. In 1956 the service requested funding for site surveys and actually had the survey teams ready to go; instead, the DOD ordered the program transferred to the Army.

After a period of testing, the Army decided to proceed with its Nike-Hercules program, and the ground-based Talos program came to an end. The missile served successfully with the Navy through 1979 on several guided missile cruisers.

Ground-based Terrier (Navy)

During the mid-1950s, the Army participated in the development of the Navy's Terrier (SAM-N-7/RIM-2) shipboard air defense missile system, to the extent of ordering twenty-five for test purposes. In 1952 ARADCOM proposed the deployment of two battalions of ground-based Terriers as a defense for the Hanford Atomic Works.

The solid-fueled Terrier was slightly over twenty-seven feet long and was equipped with a 218-pound HE warhead (later versions had nuclear warheads). The missile had a maximum speed of Mach 1.8, range of 12 nautical miles, and maximum effective altitude of 40,000 feet. The system employed beam-riding guidance; the missile flew up the center of the tracking radar's signal, using minor course corrections to remain within the beam.

The first evaluation missile was test fired from the Naval Ordnance Test Station Inyokern, CA, on 15 February 1950. The first successful shipboard launch was accomplished in September 1951; in May 1952 Terriers successfully shot down two F6F-5D Hellcat drones. Operational Evaluation commenced in July 1954.

However, by that time the commanding general of ARADCOM had had second thoughts about Terrier

TALOS

Terrier BW-1 guided missile just after leaving the USS Bainbridge's *after launcher, and just prior to boost phase blast, during an anti-submarine warfare-fire power demonstration on 15 August 1963. The missile made a direct hit on the drone target seconds after this picture was taken.(Official US Navy Photograph, from the Collections of the Naval Historical Center)*

and, on 25 April 1953, declared that the system would not be acquired by the Army. The official reason given was poor test results. The US Marine Corps did acquire the ground-based Terrier system and operated two battalions of the missile from 1954 through 1960.

The Navy operationally deployed Terrier in 1956; the conventional warhead variants were replaced by the RIM-67 Standard Missile (Extended Range) in the early 1980s. The nuclear warhead version, sub-designated the BTN (Beam-riding Terrier, Nuclear), remained in fleet service through 1989.

TERRIER

Comparison of other American Surface to Air Missiles

		HAWK	Talos	Terrier	Nike-Zeus B	Spartan	Sprint
Designation		**MIM-23**	**RIM-8A**	**RIM-2A**	**XLIM-49A**	**LIM-49A**	
Weight (lbs) gross		1,295	7,000	2,350	40,000	22,800	29,000
	sustainer	1,295	2,700	1,060	-	-	
	booster	-	4,300	1,290	-	-	
length (in)	overall	198	330	325	580	662	323
	sustainer	-	-	-	-	206	191
	booster	-	-	-	-	211	132
	booster	-	-	-	-	245	-
Diameter (in) sustainer		14	28	14	-	29	31
	booster	-	-	-	36	43	53
	booster	-	-	-	-	43	-
span (in)	sustainer	48	84	47	96	117.6	53
warhead		con rod	HE/nuke	HE	nuke	nuke 5mt	nuke 20kt
range (miles)		22	50	10	250	460	25
altitude (miles)		7.7	11.4	7.6	200	342	15.6
thrust (lbs)	sustainer	-	-	-	450,000	500,000	300,000
	booster	-	-	-	-	360,000	-
	booster	-	-	-	-	450,000	-
speed (mach)		2.5	1.6	1.8	-	8.61	10+
flight time		-	-	-	-	-	51 sec

(Table prepared by James D. Loop)

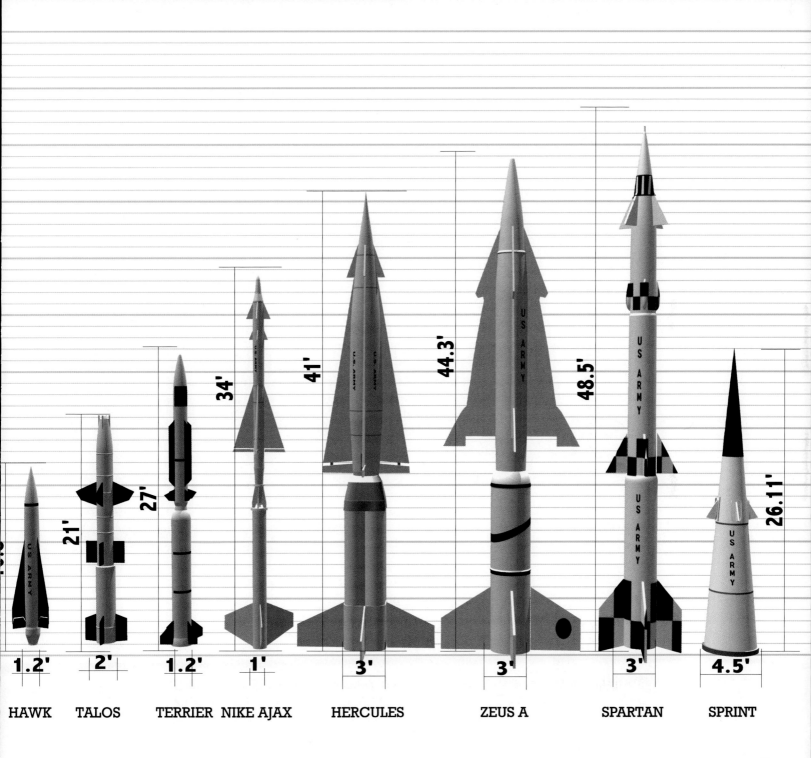

HAWK TALOS TERRIER NIKE AJAX HERCULES ZEUS A SPARTAN SPRINT

1.2' 2' 1.2' 1' 3' 3' 3' 4.5'

21' 27' 34' 41' 44.3' 48.5' 26.11'

61

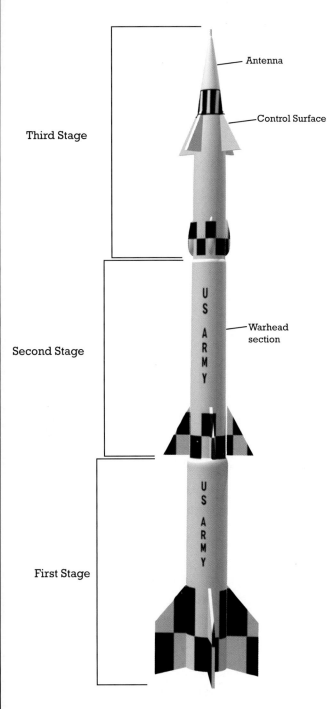

Third Stage

Antenna

Control Surface

Second Stage

Warhead
section

First Stage

SPARTAN

9. US Army Antiballistic Missile Systems

The genesis of the U.S. ABM programs had its beginnings in 1945 as the War Department began to look for ways to defend against rocket attacks like that of the German V-2s on Great Britain. A May 1946 report recommended a defense by "guided interceptor missiles dispatched in accordance with electronically computed data obtained from radar detection stations." As the Cold War participants turned to the development of ICBMs in the mid-1950s, the DOD began looking for measures to defend against such attacks. The Air Force had been studying the problem since the end of the war with Project Wizard and other R&D programs. The Air Force argued that the Army's Nike systems were unfit to guard the nation against such a threat. The Army countered that they could improve on the already existing technology of the Nike program and modify it for use in an ABM role.

In February 1955 Bell Labs and the Douglas Aircraft Company contracted with the Army to study a follow on to the Nike-B/Hercules, nicknamed Nike-II. The Army system was expected to counter the projected threats of the next decade—including postulated advanced air breather weapons and Soviet ICBMs. The US was working on its own ICBM systems, which would lead to the eventual development and deployment of the nuclear-tipped SM-65 Atlas and SM-68 Titan. Both sides relied on German scientists captured at the end of World War II; the Americans fully knew the Soviets had their own program underway, which would put North America at risk.

Nike-Zeus

In 1958—right about the time the Soviets made their first successful test of the 6,214-mile range SS-6 Sapwood—the Secretary of Defense assigned the Army the lead role in ABM development based on the progress they had made with Nike-II. Bell Labs and Western Electric were assigned responsibility for full-system development of the Nike-II as a functional ABM system. The new system, named Nike-Zeus, was designed to go higher, faster, and carry a bigger nuclear warhead than its Nike-Hercules sibling.

The initial design, Nike-Zeus A, the DM-15 (Douglas Missile-15), was a scaled-up, two-stage version of the Hercules. The second design, Nike-Zeus B, DM-15S, was released in spring 1960 and was designated XLIM-49A. The weapon was 48 feet, 3 inches long and weighed about 22,800 pounds. Like Hercules, it featured solid-fueled boosters—a unique tandem design in this case, capable of generating 450,000 pounds of thrust—and a sustainer for a

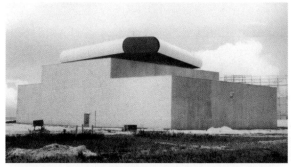

ZAR radar transmitter (left) and ZAR radar receiver antenna complex (right) on Klajawan Island (Thompson, Erwin N., Pacific Ocean Engineers: History of the U.S. Army Corps of Engineers in the Pacific 1905-1980, USACE Office of History, GPO, Washington, DC, 1982.)

(right, both photos) Nike Zeus B being launched. (US Army, Redstone Arsenal Historical Information Office)

maximum range of over 250 miles at 200 miles of altitude. Nike-Zeus B carried a 400-kiloton W-50 warhead, powered by its own third-stage motor.

Guidance was by the command method, using four radars. The MTR and TTR (RV, or reentry vehicle) were both designed to be effective at suborbital ranges. Added to the electronics suite were the Zeus acquisition radar (ZAR), which could detect objects as they came over the horizon, and a discrimination radar (DR), for separating actual warheads from decoys and booster debris. The first successful launch of the XLIM-49 Nike-Zeus occurred at White Sands Missile Range in October 1959. On 14 December 1961 the Army fired a Nike-Zeus from its newly dedicated test facility on Kwajalein Atoll in the southwest Pacific.

However, the outgoing Eisenhower Administration made the decision not to deploy the missile for technology reasons. The ZAR had difficulty breaking out multiple targets, partly due to its mechanical beam steering.

On 24 May 1963, a Zeus test vehicle successfully intercepted an incoming Atlas RV. Further testing indicated the system would in fact work as advertised and—in addition—had a demonstrated antisatellite (ASAT) capability.

Despite the string of successes, the Cabinet members of the new Kennedy Administration did not believe the Nike-Zeus system could defend against an attack by Soviet ICBMs. Secretary of Defense Robert S. McNamara thought the system could be overwhelmed and could not discriminate between real and decoy warheads. The system was maintained on Kwajalein through the end of the year for ASAT test purposes. Notably, following the cancellation of deployment, the ZAR successfully steered ten Nike-Zeus intercepts out of fourteen attempts during its final months.

Nike-X

Rather than cancel the ABM program, McNamara directed the Army to field a more advanced ABM system. To replace Zeus, a new, higher acceleration missile system was substituted. The new system was announced on 30 January 1964, under the temporary designation of "Nike-X."

The new system was to be a layered system with the first layer being a reconfigured Zeus missile that would intercept incoming warheads at an altitude of seventy to one hundred miles. The second layer would be a new short-range high-speed missile that would intercept the warheads missed at an altitude of twenty to thirty miles. The key difference over the old Zeus system was the use of phased-array radars pioneered under the DOD's Advanced Research Projects Agency (ARPA). The phased-array radars could track several targets and direct several missile intercepts simultaneously, unlike the single target and missile engagement of the previous Nike programs. The improved radars, computers, and missiles were designed to be a complete antibomber, antifighter, and antimissile system. With the completion of full-system design in October 1965, the Army presented a program that incorporated two nuclear-tipped missiles, the XLIM-49A Spartan (formerly the Zeus DM-15S2) and Sprint; the phased-array perimeter acquisition radar (PAR); and the multifunction array radar (MAR).

The McDonnell Douglas Astronautics Spartan was the long-range interceptor missile and obvious successor to Nike-Zeus, measuring just over fifty-five feet in length. The missile had three solid-fuel stages good for about 465 miles at over 300-miles altitude. Once launched, Spartan would fly to the target at approximately Mach 9 and then detonate its five-megaton W-71 warhead via computer command, like the earlier Nike systems.

To handle "leakers," the system relied on the short—twenty-seven foot—extremely high-speed Sprint missile, which never gained a military designator. Developed by Martin Marietta/Orlando, Sprint was designed to accelerate to reportedly Mach 17 and hit targets at about twenty-five miles within a few seconds of launch. The warhead was a W-66, rated in the "low kiloton" range.

As for the radars, both employed electronically steered beams, overcoming the major shortcoming of the predecessor ZAR. The PAR was designed for housing in a reinforced concrete operations building approximately 130-feet tall. Once the PAR detected incoming warheads, at approximately 1,000 miles (or greater), it handed off the data to the Raytheon missile site radar (MSR)—which had replaced the MAR—which then tracked the incoming targets while guiding in the Spartans and Sprints. As with the PAR, the majority of the supporting equipment for the MSR was underground. Tying everything together was the data processing system, or DPS, that handled all digital data processing, weapons controlling, and powered the tactical displays at the Ballistic Missile Defense Center (BMDC) and Fire Coordination Center (FCC).

The Army's original intent was to deploy the Spartan/Sprint system in the existing ARADCOM defense areas and, to that end, performed several site studies. However, problems with the war effort (which also affected the staffing and deployment of the existing Nike-Hercules program), and objections raised by scientists, researchers, and members of Congress, kept the project from receiving full funding.

A small but influential group of senators on the Armed Services Committee, worried about Soviet ABM development, had regularly pressed the Johnson Administration through the 1960s. This group maintained a strong interest in promoting Sentinel, an ABM system. In opposition were several liberal senators, who brought a general skepticism to defense spending, stimulated by opposition to the Vietnam War. In April 1968, they were joined by some conservatives and by the summer of 1968 had organized opposition to Sentinel deployment. The Johnson Administration fought these efforts and was generally successful.

Events overseas helped drive the program back into national priority. The Chinese had exploded a nuclear bomb in 1964, and by 1967 had successfully tested a missile delivery system. This meant that another nation, in addition to the USSR, posed a potential ICBM treat. Furthermore, the Soviets were beginning to develop their own ABM system.

Sentinel

On 18 September 1967 McNamara announced a major drawdown of ARADCOM's Nike-Hercules strength. Concurrently, he announced the austere deployment of the Sentinel system, which was to include a mix of existing and new locations. Notably, the stated purpose of the system was not to protect the United States from Soviet ICBMs, but instead from Chinese ICBMs.

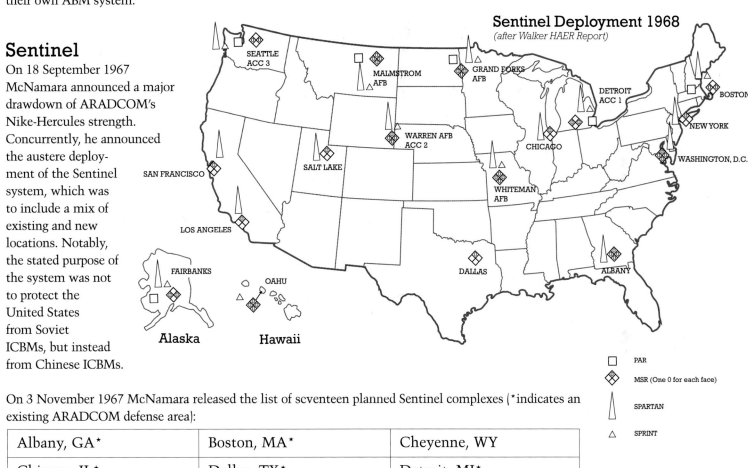

Sentinel Deployment 1968
(after Walker HAER Report)

PAR		
MSR (One 0 for each face)		
SPARTAN		
SPRINT		

On 3 November 1967 McNamara released the list of seventeen planned Sentinel complexes (*indicates an existing ARADCOM defense area):

Albany, GA*	Boston, MA*	Cheyenne, WY
Chicago, IL*	Dallas, TX*	Detroit, MI*
Grand Forks, ND	Great Falls, MT	Los Angeles, CA*
New York, NY*	Oahu, HI*	Salt Lake City, UT
San Francisco, CA*	Seattle, WA*	Sedalia, MO
Anchorage, AK*	Washington, DC*	

*Seventeen Planned
Sentinel Complexes*

Public concern, quiescent until 1968, became widespread as it was revealed that the first phase of Sentinel—a population defense system—would involve missile deployments near major cities, including Boston and Chicago. When the 1969 ABM funding of $1.2 billion was approved in October 1968, the public took to the streets in various cities. The major demonstrations of the period persuaded even sympathetic senators that Sentinel could become a serious political liability. One of the earliest public groups to be formed against Sentinel was the WSCSG (West Suburban Concerned Scientists Group). Five members of the Federation of American Scientists organized WSCSG in late 1968 to work against the Chicago installation. The scientists managed to get a lot of press attention and drew public debate around ABM deployment. Public opinion, vocal and primarily negative, snowballed. The Army held public meetings in the Boston area that were marked with great hostility towards the air defenders. As with the ICBM debates, protestors against Sentinel came from all over the country. The main point of contention was that ABM was a destabilizing influence that would force the Soviet Union to either build a lot more ICBMs, and/or attempt a first strike against the United States.

Despite widespread opposition, the Army completed its initial site studies at the proposed Boston-area installation in July 1968. Initial construction began following the contract award on 22 January 1969.

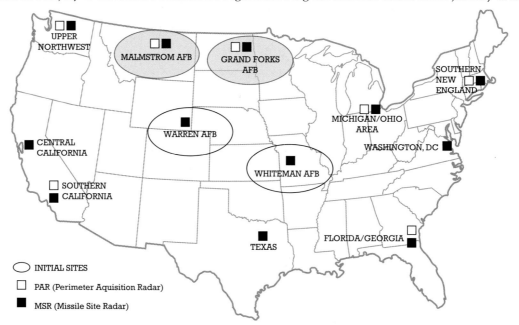

Proposed Safeguard deployment 1969
(after Walker HAER Report)

Safeguard

The Nixon Administration took office in January 1968. Among the issues the new administration tackled was the deployment of *Sentinel*. As could be expected for the times, the outburst of public and political opposition to any sort of ABM system—which included protests and an occupation of the early *Sentinel* site near Boston—played a part in the new administration's assessment. The decision was soon made to halt the work on the Boston site and to relocate the ABM system away from population centers to new sites near Strategic Air Command bases.

Officially, though, the shift was made in response to the slow rate of ICBM development in the People's Republic of China, and the continued deployment of newer, more capable Soviet missiles. One new generation Soviet ICBM, the SS-9 Scarp, absolutely terrified people; the Mod 2 variant had a range of nearly 7,500 miles and was capable of delivering a 25-megaton warhead. Later variants carried multiple reentry vehicles, or MRVs.

On 14 March 1969, *Sentinel* was renamed *Safeguard* and formally given the task of protecting America's land-based nuclear deterrent forces. Eroding political and public support resulted in a smaller planned deployment pattern of twelve locations, with an initial deployment at two locations near the Minuteman II/III ICBM fields at Grand Forks AFB, ND (321st Strategic Missile Wing (SMW)); and Malmstrom AFB, MT (341st SMW). In 1970 funding was approved for the development of two more Safeguard sites to defend the ICBMs stationed near Whiteman AFB, MO (351st SMW); and Francis E. Warren AFB, WY (90th SMW).

Construction started at both Grand Forks and Malmstrom, although due to the design requirements for the Safeguard system, the actual ABM and radar sites were many miles removed from their respective Air Force bases. Initial site surveys commenced at the same time near Whiteman and Francis E. Warren AFBs.

In 1972 the United States and the Soviet Union signed the Anti-Ballistic Missile Treaty at the Moscow Summit meeting. The treaty permitted the United States and the Soviet Union to retain two ABM facilities—one near each nation's capital and one protecting an ICBM field. Since labor problems had hampered the work on the Malstrom site (which was then only 10 percent completed), it was decided to retain the nearly complete Grand Forks site as the single US ABM defense for a ICBM field. The construction programs at Malstrom, Whiteman, and F.E. Warren AFBs were halted; the ABM site for Washington, DC was never started.

10. Inactivation of Nike and the Demise of ARADCOM

The peak year for ARADCOM came in 1963, when the command fielded 134 Nike-Hercules, 77 Army National Guard Nike-Ajax, and 8 HAWK batteries in defense of the United States. Five years later, Regular Army Hercules began inactivating, beginning a process that would be concluded in 1974.

The Nike-Hercules was designed for defense against high-altitude formations of bombers. As the perceived threat changed from bombers to ICBMs, the usefulness of Nike-Hercules diminished. Nike-Zeus was designed to fulfill the antimissile defense role and be used in conjunction with Hercules, but it was

Retiring regimental colors, site W25 Davidsonville, 1974
(US Army, courtesy Merle Cole)

found to be unsatisfactory. Finally, the large manpower requirements of ARADCOM worked against it in the face of the expanding Vietnam War.

ARADCOM's size and its apparent inability to defend against ICBMs spelled the end of all fixed land-based SAM programs in the United States, including Nike. A gradual decrease in Nike deployment began in 1967, with the first batteries inactivating in November 1968. By the end of 1969, several ARADCOM units had inactivated; in several defense areas, Army Guard units actually manned the majority of the surviving sites. Additional cutbacks occurred in 1971.

The new strategic defensive thought was that air defense of North America could be better served by an effective ABM defense and American naval might abroad. SAMs were more effective in the defense of warships, and defense money better spent on space-defense and space-based systems (leading to the Strategic Defense Initiative, or "Star Wars," of the Reagan Presidency). For CONUS SAM systems like Nike-Hercules, it was just too little too late in the day of global defense considerations.

On 8 November 1973 ARADCOM was directed by the Army to inactivate all remaining firing batteries, with the exception of the Hercules and HAWK defenses in Florida and the single battalion in Alaska. The surviving batteries in the remaining eight defense areas (Seattle, San Francisco, Los Angeles, Pittsburgh, Washington-Baltimore-Norfolk, Chicago-Detroit, New York–Philadelphia, and New England) were to be shut down by the end of May 1974. All group, regional Headquarters, and Headquarters & Headquarters Batteries were to be inactivated by 1 October 1974. The last to go were the 1st ARADCOM Region, 16th ADA Group (New York–Philadelphia Defense Area), and 24th ADA Group (New England Defense Area). On 30 June 1975 ARADCOM itself inactivated.

The last Nike-Hercules unit in the continental United States assigned the air defense mission was the 2nd Battalion, 52nd Air Defense Artillery at Homestead AFB, FL. In 1975 the battalion was still assigned to the 31st Air Defense Brigade with the 3/68th (HAWK) and 1/65th (HAWK-Key West).

In June 1979 the 2/52nd transferred to Fort Bliss, replaced the 4/62nd ADA, and assumed the Nike-Hercules training function in support of the last four battalions in Germany. Also transferred to Fort Bliss were the 31st ADA Brigade and 1/65th ADA Battalion (HAWK). The other surviving Nike-Hercules battalion with an air defense mission in North America, the 1/43rd at Fort Richardson, AK, was also inactivated during this period. On 15 March 1983 the 2/52nd inactivated at Fort Bliss, ending employment of the Nike air defense missile system in North America.

US Army Nike-Hercules units were deployed overseas, to Taiwan, Okinawa, South Korea, and West Germany. The Nike-Hercules system was also sold to various allied nations; their military units were trained in its use by US Army personnel. By 1979 the majority of the units had transferred their equipment to their host countries and inactivated. The last Nike-Hercules unit in the United States Army was the 3rd Battalion, 71st Air Defense Artillery, which inactivated in West Germany in 1984.

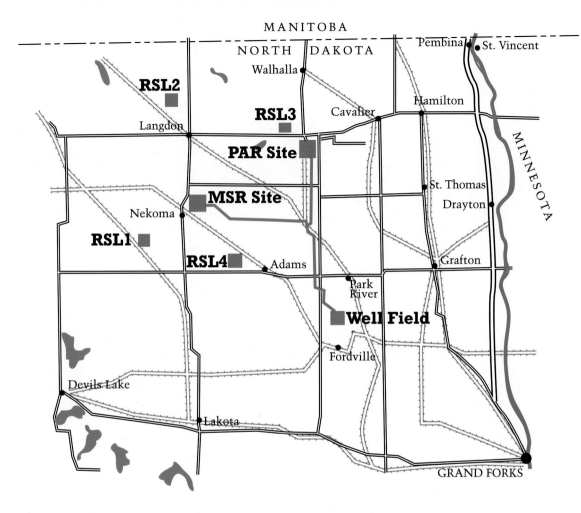

Map shows locations of Safeguard Sites around Grand Fork, North Dakota (after Walker HAER Report)

11. The Stanley R. Mickleson Safeguard Complex

The only Safeguard ABM facility completed by the United States was located near Langdon, ND. The basic hardware components of the Safeguard system consisted of two radars—the PAR and the MSR; two missiles—Spartan and Sprint, and the data processing system (DPS) that controlled the entire system.

The 400-acre MSR site, located next to Nekoma, ND, had a phased-array radar designed to track incoming targets at ranges up to several hundred miles. In addition to tracking enemy ICBM's and SLBM's (submarine launch ballistic missile), the MSR also launched and command guided the Spartan and Sprint missiles to intercept incoming targets. The MSR site consisted of the missile site control building (MSRB), the largest structure on the site, which housed the radar and the

Inside the MSR

MSR building in distance

computer elements and served as the command and control center for the site; an underground power plant adjacent to the missile site control building; a missile launch field containing both Spartan and Sprint missiles; a missile handling building; and warhead handling building. The major portion of the MSRB structure was underground, with only the radar faces and necessary electronic equipment above ground, resulting in an exposed concrete pyramid at a height of approximately seventy-seven feet. The MSR was to have four radar faces to facilitate 360-degree coverage. The only visible evidence of the underground power plant was a series of exhaust stacks and air intake structures, which served as the breathers for the power generation units. The units operated on diesel fuel or natural gas, or a combination of those fuels. Within the missile field, both Spartan and Sprint were stored in underground cells from which they were to be launched.

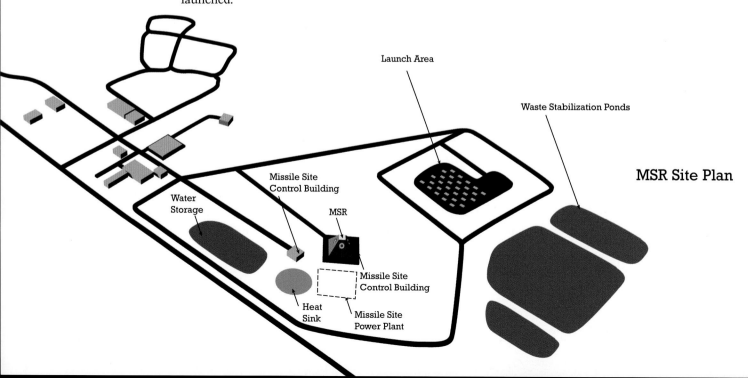

Launch Area

Waste Stabilization Ponds

MSR Site Plan

Missile Site
Control Building

Water
Storage

MSR

Missile Site
Control Building

Heat
Sink

Missile Site
Power Plant

MSR Cross-section

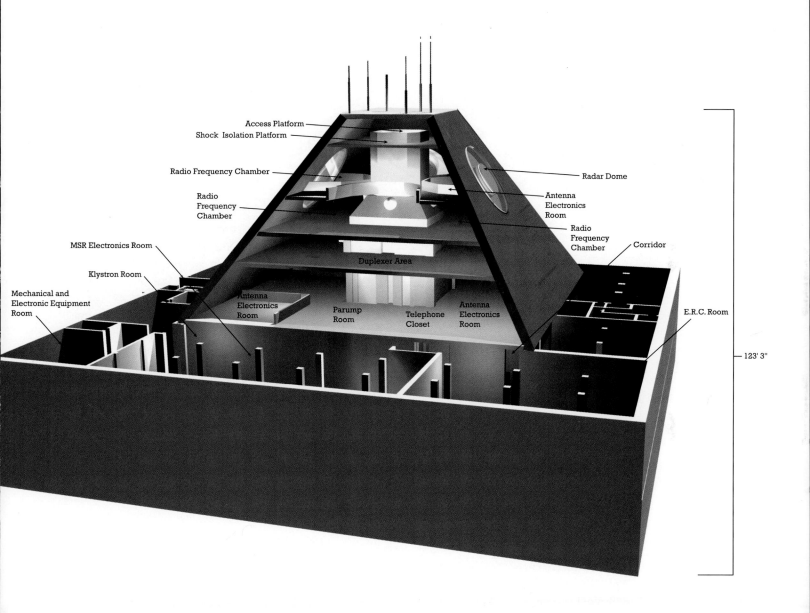

Access Platform

Shock Isolation Platform

Radio Frequency Chamber

Radio Frequency Chamber

Radar Dome

Antenna Electronics Room

Radio Frequency Chamber

MSR Electronics Room

Corridor

Duplexer Area

Klystron Room

Mechanical and Electronic Equipment Room

Antenna Electronics Room

Parump Room

Telephone Closet

Antenna Electronics Room

E.R.C. Room

123' 3"

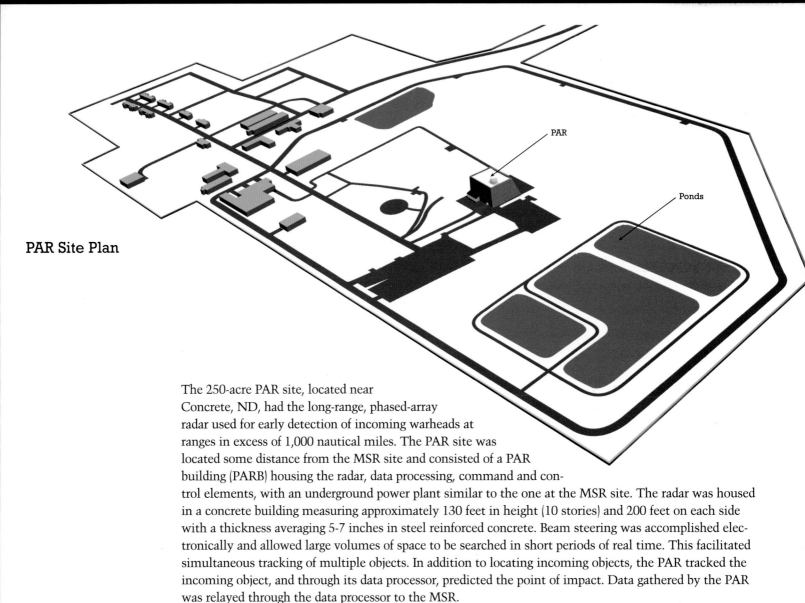

PAR

Ponds

PAR Site Plan

The 250-acre PAR site, located near
Concrete, ND, had the long-range, phased-array
radar used for early detection of incoming warheads at
ranges in excess of 1,000 nautical miles. The PAR site was
located some distance from the MSR site and consisted of a PAR
building (PARB) housing the radar, data processing, command and con-
trol elements, with an underground power plant similar to the one at the MSR site. The radar was housed
in a concrete building measuring approximately 130 feet in height (10 stories) and 200 feet on each side
with a thickness averaging 5-7 inches in steel reinforced concrete. Beam steering was accomplished electronically and allowed large volumes of space to be searched in short periods of real time. This facilitated
simultaneous tracking of multiple objects. In addition to locating incoming objects, the PAR tracked the
incoming object, and through its data processor, predicted the point of impact. Data gathered by the PAR
was relayed through the data processor to the MSR.

The data processing system (DPS) performed the control digital data processing, and display functions.
The DPS consisted of both the computer hardware and software programs required to control the
Safeguard system in accordance with defense objectives and components were located as required. The
Safeguard DPS also interfaced with all the major subsystems, such as PAR, MSR, FCC, BMDC, and the
Spartan and Sprint missiles.

The nontactical support facilities included an administrative building, an industrial building, a community center, chapel, dispensary, and BOQ (bachelor officers' quarters). Family housing areas of two-, three-, and four-bedroom duplexes were to be provided in sufficient numbers to accommodate married military personnel and essential civilians. Both the MSR and PAR sites had these facilities with the PAR site facilities being somewhat smaller because fewer personnel were required to man the site.

The four remote Sprint launch (RSL) sites contained twelve to sixteen Sprint missiles installed in underground cells next to a remote launch operations building. The Grand Forks sites were located north of Langdon; northeast of Olga; northeast of Hampden; and west of Adams, each totaling about fifty acres. Support facilities were not built at these sites.

PAR building (PARB) housing the radar, data processing, command and control elements (Mark Berhow 2001)

Construction was completed on 21 August 1972; the MSR facility was completed and formally turned over to the US Army Safeguard Systems Command (SAFSCOM) Site Activation Team, followed by the PAR facility on 3 January 1973. SAFSCOM acquired the fourth and final remote Sprint site on 5 November 1972.

The complex was named the Stanley R. Mickelson Safeguard Complex (SRMSC) on 21 June 1974. General Mickelson had commanded ARADCOM during the late 1950s, and his command's early efforts toward ballistic missile defense had started during his tour. The entire complex was turned over to US Army Safeguard Command (SAFECOM), a wholly separate organization from ARADCOM, on 3 September 1974. The Spartan and Sprint missiles were emplaced in their hardened vertical launch structures the following spring, leading to a declaration of Initial Operating Capability for the complex. Finally, SAFECOM formally declared the Mickelson complex fully operational on 1 October 1975.

In 1974, subsequent ABM treaty protocol agreement eliminated the planned Washington, DC deployment, leaving the Grand Forks site to be the only Safeguard ABM site to be completed by the United States. That year, Congress decided to cancel the entire Safeguard program while allowing the work on the Grand Forks site to continue. The Congressional decision to terminate the operation of the SRMSC complex came anyway on 2 October 1975, the day after the site had become fully operational. The missile site radar was permanently turned off in February 1976, and the MSR complex was placed in a mothball status. All electronics and mission specific equipment were placed in secure storage, while the Spartan and Sprint warheads were sent to Sierra Army Depot in Northern California for storage. Later, the interior of the MSRB was salvaged for scrap.

PAR Cross-section

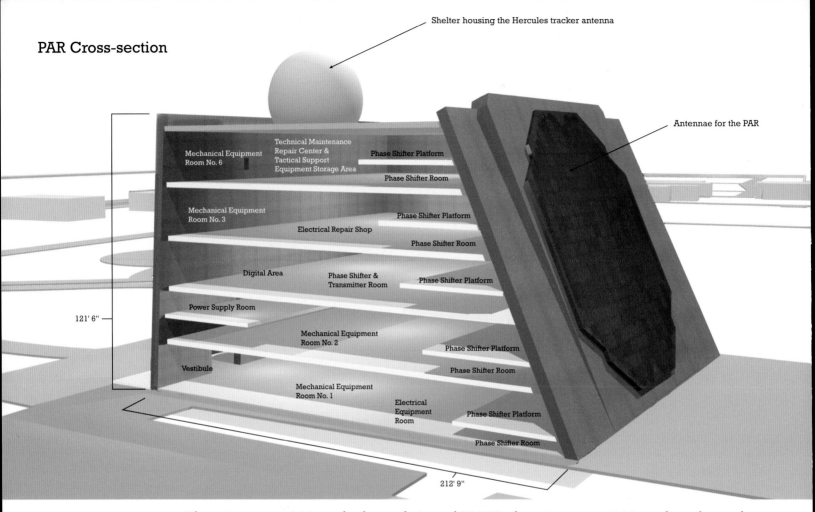

Shelter housing the Hercules tracker antenna

Technical Maintenance Repair Center & Tactical Support Equipment Storage Area

Mechanical Equipment Room No. 6

Phase Shifter Platform

Phase Shifter Room

Antennae for the PAR

Mechanical Equipment Room No. 3

Phase Shifter Platform

Electrical Repair Shop

Phase Shifter Room

Digital Area

Phase Shifter & Transmitter Room

Phase Shifter Platform

Power Supply Room

121' 6"

Mechanical Equipment Room No. 2

Phase Shifter Platform

Vestibule

Phase Shifter Room

Mechanical Equipment Room No. 1

Electrical Equipment Room

Phase Shifter Platform

Phase Shifter Room

212' 9"

The perimeter acquisition radar, later redesignated PARCS—for perimeter acquisition radar and control system—was loaned to the Air Force in October 1977 for missile early warning purposes. Designated Cavalier Air Station, the site remains in operation, the only surviving operational component of Safeguard. It is possibly the most powerful single radar facility in the world today.

Even with the 1989 demise of the Cold War, just about anything remains possible on the plains of North Dakota. The MSR site and the four remote Sprint sites were salvaged for all other useful equipment and parts. Several of the support buildings at the MSR site have been destroyed, and all of the housing facilities have been moved to other locations. US Army Space and Missile Command maintain the MSR and RSL sites in the event an ABM system may be redeployed. The Reagan, Bush, and Clinton Administrations all considered the introduction of new antiballistic missile systems—nowadays for protection against missiles from "rogue states," such as North Korea. The Grand Forks complex is usually one of the first places identified for possible deployment, mainly due to the ABM treaty considerations. The United States Defense Department began to deploy a new ABM system in 2005, so the fixed defense saga is not over yet.

12. Nike Missile Sites Today

Generally, as ARADCOM vacated the missile sites in the CONUS, they were turned over to the General Services Administration for disposition. Some, particularly the housing areas, were retained for further use by other services, the Army National Guard, and the Army Reserve. (A substantial portion of the base closings submitted in 1989 were Nike housing). A large number of the sites were then sold to private owners and local governments.

Many Nike sites have been destroyed over the past twenty-five years; the buildings razed, the magazines destroyed or filled in and covered, leaving the odd chunk of foundation concrete to hint at prior usage. The structures at other sites have been modified and converted to serve in new roles. A few sites have become public parks, but have been essentially destroyed for safety or political reasons.

A major role in determining the disposition and current condition of former Nike sites is the result of the Superfund clean-up project. Most Nike sites have had to be cleaned up as the Army often dumped acid, fuel, and other chemicals into sumps on the sites. Under the Defense Environmental Restoration Project for formerly used defense sites (DERP-FUDS), all of the properties have to be certified clean of contaminants. The process is ongoing under the auspices of the Army Corps of Engineers.

There are a few other sites located in public parks that are relatively intact, but most are secured from entry. Sites contained in the National Park System or in county/city parks include SF-51, SF-59, SF-87, SF-88, and SF-89 in the Golden Gate National Recreation Area (GGNRA); sites NY-49 and NY-56 in the Gateway National Recreation Area; and site LA-43 at White Point and Angels Gate Parks, San Pedro, CA.

Site LA-43, White Point and Angels Gate Park, San Pedro, CA, in disrepair. (Photo by publisher)

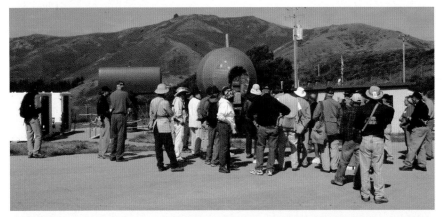

Top: Launchers and missiles at site SF 88 (Mark Berhow 2006)
Middle: Radars at site SF-88 (Mark Berhow 2006)
Bottom: Launchers and missiles at site SF-88 (Mark Berhow, 1994)

Site SF-88L—the Last Nike Site

All CONUS Nike missile sites were de-commissioned after 1974—except for site SF-88L given to the National Park Service intact to be the Nike museum. That site remained in caretaker status—except for the effect of the elements and vandals—for about ten years.

In 1984 the Military Vehicle Collectors Club began the difficult task of restoring the site. In 1990 retired US Army Colonel Milton B. "Bud" Halsey took over the restoration process. Over the next ten years under his guidance the site has acquired enough equipment to outfit a complete missile site. Equipment came from bases all over the country such as Fort Bliss in Texas; Letterkenny Army Depot in Pennsylvania; Pueblo Army Depot in Colorado; Tooele Army Depot in Utah; Edwards Air Force Base, China Lake Naval Air/Weapons Station, NASA Ames at Crows Landing, and Mare Island Naval Ship Yard, all in California. The National Park Service provides funding for special restoration projects and pays for the electricity and water. Funding also comes from a grant from the Friends of the National Parks and from private donations.

Over the years Bud and his team of volunteers have restored almost 70 percent of the original configuration. Eighteen missiles have been brought to the site, the buildings have been restored, water and electrical service have been returned, all fences and gates were repaired, the radar vans have been refurbished, the dog kennel area has been completely rebuilt, a target drone was restored, a motor generator restored, launchers restored to fully functional working status, and a radar park created complete with operations trailers and LOPAR and MTR radars. Bud Halsey passed away in 2000, but his efforts remain today for all to enjoy. Site SF-88L is now an important part of the GGNRA.

SF-88 missile and launcher being raised (Mark Berhow, 2006)

PART II: UNITED STATES ARMY AIR DEFENSE SITE GUIDE

The following list is a summary of known permanent ARADCOM Nike-Ajax, Nike-Hercules, HAWK, and Safeguard sites in the United States and Greenland, and the non-ARADCOM sites in Alaska and Hawaii. The sites are listed alphabetically by defense area; temporary or tactical sites are listed where known.

Key to Tabular Information

Site Designations and Locations
Each CONUS and Hawaiian site was designated utilizing a 1-100 "compass," with the center of the defense area as the reference point. For example, WA-74 in the Washington-Baltimore Defense Area was due west of the Washington Monument. There were exceptions, with sites numbered apparently out of sequence, and some sites were renumbered during their service careers.

Nearby towns are listed; the sites were popularly known by name over number, such as Cougar Mountain (S-20), and Hagerman (W-50). Each site designation number was followed by a letter or letters indicating its mission or use:

A	Admin facility
C	Control/IFC (integrated fire control)
DC	Direction Center
H	Housing
L	Launch facility
R	Radar facility

Location—the location (LOC) and current status (CUR) of the IFC and launch sites are given where known. Current disposition is indicated by:

(I) Intact; buildings, launch pads and possibly radar towers in place

(P) Partial; some modifications or dismantling of buildings and launch facilities

(O) Obliterated; all traces removed

Site Equipment
RADARS—all Nike-Ajax sites were equipped with an acquisition radar (AQCR), a missile-tracking radar (MTR), and a target- tracking radar (TTR). Nike-Hercules specific radars and equipment are identified as follows:

LOPAR	low-power acquisition radar
HIPAR	high-power acquisition radar
ABAR	alternate battery acquisition radar; either an AN/FPS-69, -71 or -75. Listed as ABAR/#.
RRIS	remote radar integration station
SMFU	secondary master fire unit
TTR	target-ranging radar

HAWK batteries were equipped with the AN/MPQ-35 pulse acquisition radar (PAR); AN/MPQ-34 improved continuous wave radar (ICWAR); AN/MPQ-33/39 high-power illuminator (HIPIR); and the AN/MPQ-37 range-only radar (ROR).

COMMAND & CONTROL—Army Air Defense Command Post (AADCP) command and control equipment is identified by name and designation.

BIRDIE	AN/GSG-5
Missile Master	AN/FSG-1
Missile Mentor	AN/TSQ-51
Missile Minder	AN/TSQ-38 (Key West only)

Co-located US Air Force and/or Federal Aviation Administration radars are listed where applicable. Sites equipped with the defense acquisition radar system (DAR), in lieu of an Air Force radar installation, are indicated by the radar types: AN/FPS-69 and AN/FPA-15.

MISSILES/STORAGE— the first listing indicates the number of missile magazines at the site, by type:

A The original unmodified design for Ajax (3 satellite launchers, 1 launcher on elevator, 42 feet x 63 feet).

B Ajax/Hercules universal magazine design for both types of missiles (3 satellite launchers, 1 launcher on elevator, 49 feet x 63 feet)

C Original Ajax magazines converted for Hercules use—modifications were made for the elevator to handle the increased weight of the Hercules missile and launcher (3 satellite launchers, no launcher on elevator, 42 feet x 63 feet).

D Post-1958 new universal Nike magazine, with increased magazine space (3 satellite launchers and 1 launcher on elevator, 62 feet x 68 feet)

AG Above-ground embankments; SAC installations (missiles stored on launchers covered with tents, 2 launchers per segment, 2 segments per launch section) and Homestead-Miami (Modified US Army–Europe types, with missiles in "Butler Type" building and 3 launchers outside)

RS Rising Star (two-elevators with launchers), Greenland only

AK Above-ground reinforced concrete blockhouses (2 satellite launchers, two launchers at entrance to storage blockhouses); Alaskan sites

The magazine type normally determined the number of stored missiles, presented by # of Ajax or # of Hercules, for example 20A/8H (Note: Ajax and Hercules were never stored in the same pit—this entry would show # of Ajax stored when site was Ajax, then # of Hercules stored when site was used

for Hercules). Magazine/elevators/launch structures were as follows:

A	Ajax launch site
AA	Two Ajax launch sites co-located
H	New Hercules launch site
U	Universal: Ajax launch site later converted to Hercules launch site
UA	1/2 Universal: 1/2 Ajax
UU	Double Universal

At several sites, one magazine was used with only two launchers ("1/2 launcher"), resulting in non-standard combinations such as ten launchers at a battery instead of eight or twelve; this is noted where applicable. Not all launchers were converted to Hercules capability; the number of operational Hercules launchers following conversion is given in parenthesis (8L-H).

It was fairly common to co-locate two sites during Ajax battery construction, resulting in large twenty or twenty-four launcher sites. Each group of twelve was usually manned by a separate battery and each had a separate control site. Examples of this practice were Site LA-70/73, Playa del Rey, CA; and Site S-32/33, Lake Youngs, WA. Conversely, some sites, such as Site S-13, Redmond, WA, had twenty-four launchers and only one control site. In most cases additional radars were installed to enable the control of two missiles at once.

Nike-Hercules Conversion (N/H)—dates when the site or a portion was converted from Nike-Ajax to Nike-Hercules.

While the information in the following list is incomplete, we hope enough is presented to assist the Nike hunter in the field. Future editions of this publication will provide updated material.

ANCHORAGE DEFENSE AREA

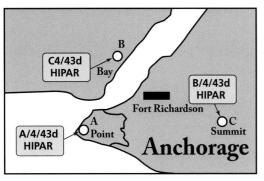

Anchorage was the southern component of the two Alaskan defense areas, under the operational command of US Army Alaska (USARAL) Air Defense Artillery Group. The city served as the primary commerce and transportation center for the state.

The AADCP was co-located with an Air Force radar station on Fire Island in Cook Inlet. The HQ and HHB were located at Fort Richardson, north of Anchorage. Elmendorf Air Force Base, adjacent to Fort Richardson, hosted the Alaskan Air Command (AAC) air defense units of the Nike period. AAC units assigned included the 10th Air Division, the 5020th Air Defense Group, and the 317th FIS. The Strategic Air Command used Elmendorf as a bomber forward operating base under the 4168th Strategic Wing.

Annual service practice by the three Anchorage Nike-Hercules batteries was performed at Site Summit. Site Point was a dual site, with four magazines and sixteen launchers. One site was damaged during the 1964 Alaskan Earthquake and not returned to service.

Site Location	Radars	Magazines, Missiles, LaunchersConvert to Herc	Units (years)
POINT Site "A" Dual firing site	HIPAR	4AK 16L-H	A/4/43d (4/59-9/72) A/1/43d (9/72-5/79)
	LOC: CUR:	10 SW Anchorage, near Anchorage Int. Airport C - (O) foundations only L - (P?) Kincaid Park, cross country ski area	
Fire Island AFS	AADCP LOC:	15 WSW Anchorage	1959-1969
King Salmon AFS (F-3)	AADCP		1969-1979
BAY Site "C"	HIPAR	2AK 8L-H	C/4/43d (3/59-9/72) C/1/43d (9/72-5/79)
	LOC: CUR: NOTE:	20 NW Anchorage, Goose Bay C - (I) State of Alaska correctional center L - (I) State of Alaska First operational Nike-Hercules site in Alaska, 20 Mar 59	
Fort Richardson			HHB/4/43d (9/58-9/72) HHB/1/43d (9/72-5/79)
	LOC: NW Anchorage CUR: HQ US Army Alaska		
SUMMIT Site "B"	HIPAR	2AK 8L-H	B/4/43d (5/59-9/72) B/1/43d (9/72-5/79)
	LOC: CUR:	25 E Anchorage, Chugach Mountains C - (I) US Army, Chugach State Park; Nominated to the National Register. L - (I) US Army, Chugach State Park, Mt Gordon Lyon; Listed on the	

National Register of Historic Places on 11 July 1996.

BALTIMORE DEFENSE AREA

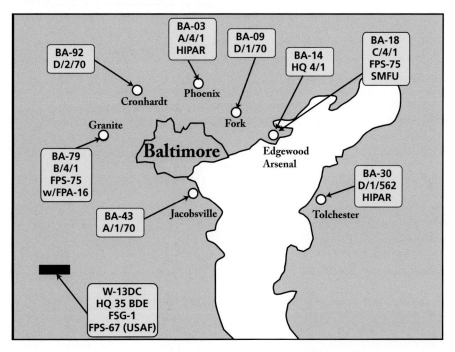

The Washington/Baltimore Defense Area was activated 28 March 1956. The northern end of the defense perimeter protected the government, business, and industrial concerns around the Middle and Patapsco Rivers, which included several shipyards, steel mills on Sparrows Point, the Martin Airplane Company plant east of Baltimore, and the Army's substantial chemical and ordnance facilities at Aberdeen and Edgewood.

The units based around both Baltimore and Washington, DC, operated the sites until 1965, when Baltimore's 4/1st acquired sole control of the remaining Regular Army sites. The AADCP for the combined Baltimore-Washington Defense Area was located at Fort George G. Meade.

Site Location	Radars	Magazines, Missiles, Launchers	Convert to Herc	Units (years)
Towson				HQ 691st Gp (3/593/63)
				HHB/684th (10/56-6/59)
				HHB/1/70th (6/5910/62)
	LOC:	1035 N. York Rd		
	CUR:	MDArNG Towson Armory		
BA-03	HIPAR	1A/1B/1C	12/60-	A/602d (11/55-8/56)
Phoenix/Sweet Air		18H/30A	7/61	A/54th (8/56-9/58)
		12L-UA		A/4/1st (9/58-12/62)
		(8L-H)		D/1/70th (12/62-4/74)
	LOC:	C - Sunnybrook Rd, N of Merrymans Mill		
		L - 3101 Paper Mill Rd		
	CUR:	C - (O) private owner		
		L - (P) Paper Mill Recreation Center; Jacksonville Senior Center; Baltimore County Fire Department training site		
BA-09		2A/1B		D/54th (11/55-9/58)
Fork		30A		D/4/1st (9/58-9/59)
		12L-A		D/1/70th (9/59-12/62)
	LOC:	C - end of Hutchensreuter Rd, S of MD 147		
		L - Stockdale Rd, S of MD 147		
	CUR:	C - (O) private owner		
		L - (I) private owner		

83

Site Location	Radars	Magazines, Missiles, Launchers	Convert to Herc	Units (years)
BA-14 **Army Chemical Center/Edgewood Arsenal** **Aberdeen Proving Ground**				HQ 17th Gp (/55-12/61) HHB/54th (12/54-9/58) HHB/4/1st (9/58-8/74)
	LOC: *CUR:*	*Aberdeen Proving Ground* *Aberdeen Proving Ground: Army Ordnance Center & School; HQ Army Test & Evaluation Command; HQ Soldier & Biological Chemical Command; Army Research Laboratory-Aberdeen; Medical Research: US Army Ordnance Museum*		
BA-18 **Edgewood Arsenal** DOUBLE SITE	ABAR/75 SMFU	3A/2B/1C 18H/30A 24L-UA (12L-H)	5/58- 1/59	C/54th (?/54-9/58) C/4/1st (9/58-4/74)
	LOC: *CUR:*	*Aberdeen Proving Grounds/Edgewood Arsenal* *C&L - (P) MDARng Edgewood Armory*		
BA-30/31 **Tolchester Beach/** **Chestertown** DOUBLE SITE	HIPAR	2A/2B/2C 18H/30A 23L-UA (12L-U)	5/58- 3/59	D/36th (/54-9/58) D/1/562d (9/58-12/62) D/4/1st (12/62-4/74)
	LOC: *CUR:*	*C - E of Tolchester Beach, MD 21* *L - SE Tolchester Beach, MD 445* *C - (P) Kent County Agricultural Center* *L - (P) Kent County*		
Fort Smallwood				HHB/683d (1/55-6/59) HHB/1/70th (6/59-4/74)
	LOC: *CUR:*	*Rocky Point, Fort Smallwood Rd* *(P) City of Baltimore Parks Department*		
BA-43 **Jacobsville**		2A/1B 30A 12L-A		C/36th (/54-9/58) C/1/562d (9/58-3/60) A/1/70th (3/60-12/62)
	LOC: *CUR:*	*C - 9034 Fort Smallwood Rd* *L - Old Nike Site Rd, S of Fort Smallwood Rd* *C - (P) Anne Arundel County Schools Maintenance & Operations* *L - (P) storage/work site*		
BA-79 **Granite** DOUBLE SITE	ABAR/75 FPA-16	2A/2B/2C 24H/30A 24L-UA (16L-H)	3/58- 2/59	A/54th (12/54-8/56) A/602d (8/56-9/58) A/4/5th (9/58-8/60) B/4/1st (8/60-12/62) A/2/70th (12/62-3/63) HHB/1/70th (10/62-8/74) B/1/70th (12/62-4/74)

84

Site Location	Radars	Magazines, Missiles, Launchers	Convert to Herc	Units (years)
	LOC:	C - Hernwood Rd, .5 N of Woodstock Rd		
		L - Hernwood Rd, 1.2 N of Woodstock Rd		
	CUR:	C - (I) Abandoned; former MDArng 70th Gen Spt Bn		
		L - (P) Maryland Police & Correctional Training Commissions		
Owings Mills				HHB/2/70th (6/59-3/63)
BA-92		2A/1B		B/54th (12/54-9/58)
Cronhardt		30A		B/4/1st (9/58-9/59)
		12L-A		D/2/70th (9/59-9/63)
	LOC:	C - 12100 Greenspring Rd, N of Broadway Rd		
		L - 2515 Baublitz Rd		
	CUR:	C – (O) SSG Isadore R. Jachman USAR Center		
		L - (O) Worthington Valley Swim Club		

BARKSDALE DEFENSE AREA

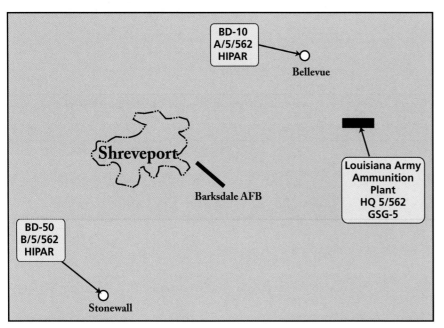

The Barksdale AFB defense was built as part of the second group of Nike-Hercules construction. Stationed at Barksdale at the time of the Nike deployment were HQ Second Air Force, the 4238th Strategic Wing, and 2d Bombardment Wing (Heavy). The AADCP was located at the Doyline Army Ammunition Plant, 24 miles east of Shreveport. Long-range acquisition and tracking data was provided by Air Force radar sites at England AFB, Alexandria, LA, and Texarkana AFS, AR. The city of Sheveport was a major transportation and agricultural center on the Upper Red River. Barksdale AFB is now the HQ of the Eighth Air Force and one of the last two Air Force bases operating the B-52H strategic bomber.

Site Location	Radars	Magazines, Missiles, Launchers	Convert to Herc	Units (years)
BD-10 **Bellevue**	HIPAR	3AG 12H 12L-H		A/5/562d (11/60-3/66)
	LOC:	C - S Bellevue Bodcau Dam Rd off of Hwy 157		
		L - 1 E Bellevue Bodcau Dam Rd		
	CUR:	C - (I) Bossier Parish Community College Criminal Justice Institute		
		L - (I) Bossier Parish Community College Criminal Justice Institute		
Louisiana Army Ammunition Plant	AN/GSG-5 BIRDIE	AADCP		HHB/5/562d (3/60-3/66)
	LOC:	2 N Doyline		
BD-50 **Stonewall**	HIPAR	3AG 12H 12L-H		B/5/562d (11/60-3/66)
	LOC:	4 NE Stonewall, intersection Missile Base Rd and Powell Rd		
	CUR:	C - (P) LSU School of Medicine		
		L - (P) private?		

BERGSTROM DEFENSE AREA

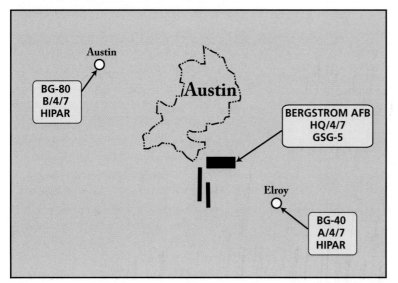

The 4th Missile Battalion, 7th Artillery defended the Austin/Bergstrom AFB region for almost six years. By the 1950s Austin was one of the fastest growing cities in the state both in terms of size and economic importance. Bergstrom was established in 1942 and hosted the 12th and 27th Fighter wings from 1950 to 1958. The Strategic Air Command resumed operational control of the base in late 1958 with the activation of the 910th Air Refueling Squadron and a squadron of B-52Ds followed in January 1959. Bomber and tanker operations continued there through October 1966 under the 4130th Strategic Wing and the 340th Bombardment Wing (Heavy). The Air Force closed the installation as an active base on 30 September 1993, turning over portions to the Air Force Reserve and the city of Austin.

Site Location	Radars	Magazines, Missiles, LaunchersConvert to Herc	Units (years)
Bergstrom AFB	AN/GSG-5	AADCP	HHB/4/7th (4/60-6/66)
		BIRDIE	
	LOC:	*SE Austin, US 183*	
	CUR:	*Commercial airport*	
BG-40	HIPAR	3AG	A/4/7th (11/60-6/66)
Elroy		12H	
		12L-H	
	LOC:	*C - 3.5 SE Austin, N of FR 2430*	
		L - 4 SSE Austin, S of FR 2430, Ensign- Bickford Rd	
	CUR:	*C - (I) private owner*	
		L - (P) private owner	
BG-80	HIPAR	3AG	B/4/7th (11/60-6/66)
Austin		12H	
		12L-H	
	LOC:	*C - 6 WNW Austin, St Stephens School Rd off of Bee Cave Rd*	
		L - 7 WNW Austin, Crystal Creek Dr off of Bee Cave Rd	
	CUR:	*C - (I) TXArNG 111th Support Group*	
		L - (I) Bee Cave Research Center	

BOSTON DEFENSE AREA

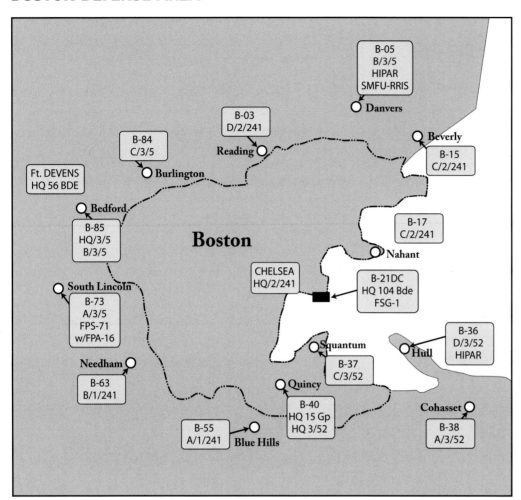

The Boston defense started in the mid-1950s as a major, multibattalion organization with AA brigade and multi-battalion group assigned. The city was a major American governmental, industrial, commercial, and transportation center in the New England area and that mandated the deployment of Nike in the area. Important military sites included the Boston Naval Shipyard, Hanscom AFB, the Boston Army Base, and Fort Devens.

In 1961 Boston's remaining sites were merged with those in Providence, Hartford, and Bridgeport to form the New England Defense Area. With the consolidation, Boston's Missile Master at Fort Banks was inactivated and the area command and control operations were assumed by the Missile Mentor facility at Site PR-69DC, Coventry, RI.

Boston was included in later site surveys for the proposed deployment of the Sentinel ABM system. The area was dropped after the Sentinel program was superceded by the Safeguard program in 1969.

Site Location	Radars	Magazines, Missiles, LaunchersConvert to Herc	Units (years)
B-03		2A/1B	B/24th (6/55-11/56)
Reading		30A	D/605th (11/56-9/58)
		2L-A	D/1/57th (9/58-8/59)
			D/2/241st (8/59-3/63)
	LOC:	*C Bear Hill*	
		L - 1.3 NE, Range Rd off of Haverhill St (Bear Hill)	
	CUR:	*C - (O) condominiums*	
		L - (O) skating rink, ex-firing range	

Site Location	Radars	Magazines, Missiles, Launchers	Convert to Herc	Units (years)
B-05 **Danvers**	HIPAR SMFU RRIS	1A/1B/1C 18H/30A 12L-UA (7L-U)	7/60- 1/61	B/605th (11/56-9/58) B/1/57th (9/58-6/60) B/3/5th (6/60-9/72) D/1/5th (9/72-4/74)
	LOC:	*C - 1.6 NW, North St* *L - 2.5 NNW, US 1 (Nike Village)*		
	CUR:	*C - (I) 1LT J.C. Ferra USAR Center; abandoned* *L - (I) Salem and Beverly Water Districts* *A - housing for the homeless*		
B-15 **Beverly**		2A/1B 30A 12L-A		A/605th (2/57-9/58) A/1/57th (9/58-8/59) C/2/241st (8/59-3/63)
	LOC:	*C - Brimball Hill Dr* *L - Beverly Airport LP Henderson Rd*		
	CUR:	*C - (O) abandoned* *L - (I) municipal airport, slated for demolition*		
B-17 **Nahant**		2A/1B 30A 12L-A		A/24th (6/55-11/56) C/605th (11/56-9/58) C/2/241st (8/59-3/63)
	LOC:	*C - Bailey's Hill, Nahant* *L - Nahant Rd at East Point (Ft. Ruckman)*		
	CUR:	*C - (O) park* *L - (P) Northeastern University - Edwards Marine Science Center*		
Chelsea				HHB/772d (11/57-5/59) HHB/2/241st (5/59-3/63)
B-21DC/R **Fort Heath/** **Fort Banks**	Missile Master AN/FSG-1 4 x AN/FPS-6 FAA ARSR-1	AADCP		HQ 56th Bde (11/51- /61) HQ 104th Bde (/59-3/63) HHB/24th (6/55-11/56) HHB/605th (/57-9/58) HHB/1/57th (9/58-6/60) Radar Section, 56th Bde
	LOC:	*1 NW Winthrop*		
B-35R **Long Island**				Radar Section, 56th Bde
	LOC:	*Long Island, Boston Harbor*		

Site Location	Radars	Magazines, Missiles, Launchers	Convert to Herc	Units (years)
B-36 **Ft. Duvall/Hull**	HIPAR	2B 12H/20A 8L-U	5/58- 11/58	D/514th (1/56-9/58) D/3/52d (9/58-12/61) B/3/5th (12/61-8/64) B/1/241st (8/64-4/74)
	LOC:	C - 1 E Hull; Hog Island L - 3 NW Hingham, River St		
	CUR:	C - (O) condominiums L - (O) park		
B-37 **Squantum/Quincy**		2B 20A 12L-A		C/514th (1/56-9/58) C/3/52d (9/58-12/61)
	LOC:	C - N Squantum, Dorchester St L - Long Island		
	CUR:	C - (P) American Legion post/day care center L - (I) former library storage		
B-38 **Cohasset/Hingham**		2A/1B 30A 12L-A		A/605th (11/56- /57) A/514th (/57-9/58) A/3/52d (9/58-12/61)
	LOC:	C - 1.5 SE Hingham, Leavitt St (Turkey Hill Rd) L - 2 W Cohasset, Cushing Hwy (Crocker Ln, Scituate Hill)		
	CUR:	C - (O) park L – (P) highway maintenance facility		
B-40 **Quincy**				HQ 15th Gp (-12/61) HHB/514th (1/56-9/58) HHB/3/52d (9/58-12/61)
	CUR:	Koch Family Park & Rec Area, Merrimount Park		
B-55 **Blue Hills**		2A/1B 30A 12L-A		C/24th (6/55- /56) B/514th (/56-9/58) B/3/52d (9/58-8/59) A/1/241st (8/59-3/63)
	LOC:	C - S Milton, Chickatawbut Hill L - N Randolph, on Middle St in Blue Hills Reservation off of High St		
	CUR:	C - (I) MDC Auburn Education Center L - (P) Metropolitan District Commission; dump		

Site Location	Radars	Magazines, Missiles, Launchers	Convert to Herc	Units (years)
B-63 **Needham**	2A/1B 30A 12L-A			D/24th (6/55-9/58) D/3/5th (9/58-8/59) B/1/241st (8/59-3/63)
	LOC:	C - 1.2 NW, Dwight Rd off of Central Ave L - 2.2 WSW, Pine St intersection with Charles River St		
	CUR:	C - (O) Charles River Association for Retarded Persons L - (P) Town of Needham		
B-71 **Natick**				HHB/605th (11/56- /57) HHB/704th (/57-5/59) HHB/1/241st (5/59-11/74)
B-73 **South Lincoln**	ABAR/71 FPA-16	2B 12H/20A 8L-U	5/58- 12/58	A/514th (1/56- /57) A/24th (/57-9/58) A/3/5th (9/58-8/64) A/1/241st (8/64-4/74)
	LOC:	C - Lincoln, S. Great Rd (Route 117) L - Oxbow Rd		
	CUR:	C - (O) Massachusetts Audubon Society; Drumlin Farm L - (I) Drumlin Farm Education and Wildlife Center		
B-75R Fort Strong				Radar Section, 15th Gp
	LOC:	Noodle's Island, Boston Harbor		
	CUR:	City Hospital		
B-82 Fort Devens				HQ 56th Bde (/61-9/66)
	LOC:	SW Ayre, US 202		
	CUR:	Devens Reserve Forces Training Area		
B-84 **Burlington**		2B 20A 8L-A		B/514th (1/56- /56) C/24th (/56-9/58) C/3/5th (9/58-8/63)
	LOC:	C - End of Edgemere Ave L - Northeastern University		
	CUR:	C - (I) Town of Burlington DPW L - (O) Northeastern University; Bedford St parking lot A - barracks is university library		

Site Location	Radars	Magazines, Missiles, Launchers	Convert to Herc	Units (years)
B-85		2A/1B		HHB/24th (11/56-9/58)
Bedford		30A		B/24th (11/56-9/58)
		12L-A		HHB/3/5th (9/58-8/63)
				B/3/5th (9/58-12/61)
	LOC:	*C - 1.4 W Bedford, Battle Flagg Rd & Notre Dame Rd off of Davis Rd*		
		L - 1.7 NW, Old Causeway Rd off of Carlisle Rd		
	CUR:	*C - (O) homes*		
		L - (P) Harvard University; zoological study facility		

BRIDGEPORT DEFENSE AREA

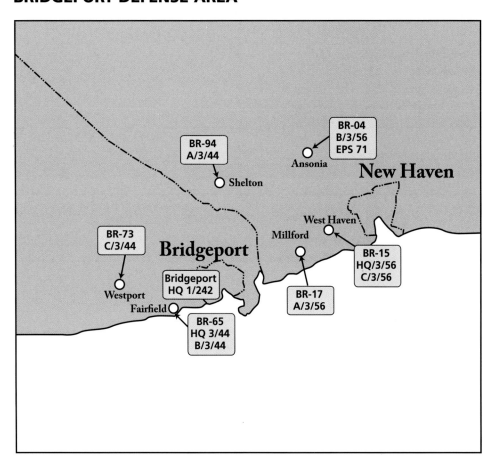

Established in 1956 with the arrival of the 967th AAAMBn, Bridgeport held six sites, with shared operations at one of the Hartford installations. This was the old industrial center of Connecticut along with substantial transportation facilities and the Sikorsky Aircraft Corporation plant at Stratford.

Only one of the six was modified for Hercules, and with the inactivation of both Regular Army battalions in 1961, Bridgeport was merged into the greater New England Defense Area.

BR-04	ABAR/71	3B	8/58-	B/967th (/56-9/58)
Ansonia		18H/30A	2/59	B/3/56th (9/58-9/61)
		12L-U		B/2/55th (9/61-8/64)
				D/1/192d (8/64-6/71)
	LOC:	C - N of Ford St west of Ford Rd		
		L - off of Ford Rd past Mulberry		
	CUR:	C - (I) US Forest Service Insect & Disease Laboratory		
		L - (P) Copper Ridge Farm; private owner		

BR-15		2A/1B	HHB/967th (/56-9/58)
Westhaven		30A	C/967th (/56-9/58)
		2L-A	HHB/3/56th (9/58-9/61)
			C/3/56th (9/58-9/61)
	LOC:	C&A – off of US 1, March Hill	
		L – Hilton Dr off of Bull Hill Ln	
	CUR:	C - (P) Orange ANG Communication Station; CTANG 103d ACS	
		L - (O) Town of West Haven Parks & Recreation Department; Nike Site Park	

BR-17		2A/1B	A/967th (/56-9/58)
Milford		30A	A/3/56th (9/58-1/61)
		12L-A	A/1/242d (1/61-3/63)
	LOC:	C - Eels Hill Rd, N of Rt 162 (New Haven Rd)	
		L - Rock Rd near Quirk	
	CUR:	C - (P) Town of Milford Board of Education	
		L - (O) industrial park	

BR-65		2A/1B	B/967th (/56- /57)
Fairfield		30A	HHB/741st (/57-9/58)
		12L-A	B/741st (/57-9/58)
			HHB/3/44th (9/58-3/61)
			B/741st (9/58-3/61)
	LOC:	C - One Rod Hwy, off Reef	
		L - Old Dam Rd, off Pine Creek	
	CUR:	C – (P) Town of Fairfield; fire training and canine center	
		L – (O) South Pine Creek Park	

BR-73		2A/1B	C/967th (/56- /57)
Westport		30A	C/741st (/57-9/58)
		12L-A	C/3/44th (9/58-1/61)
			B/1/242d (1/61-3/63)
	LOC:	C - Bayberry Ln at Merritt Pkwy	
		L - 85 North Ave	
	CUR:	C - (I) Town of Westport; Westport/Weston Health Dist; Bayberry Spec. Ed. Cnt.,	
		Westport Astronomy Society	

Site Location	Radars	Magazines, Missiles, Launchers	Convert to Herc	Units (years)
		L - (O) Staples High School grounds		
Bridgeport				HHB/1/242d (5/59-3/63)
BR-94		2A/1B		A/741st (/57-9/58)
Shelton		30A		A/3/44th (9/58-3/61)
		12L-A		
	LOC:	C - Eagle Dr extension		
		L - 49 Mohegan Rd		
	CUR:	C – (O?) US Government; storage and maintenance support site for Fort Devens		
		L – (O) Town of Shelton; park		

BUFFALO DEFENSE AREA

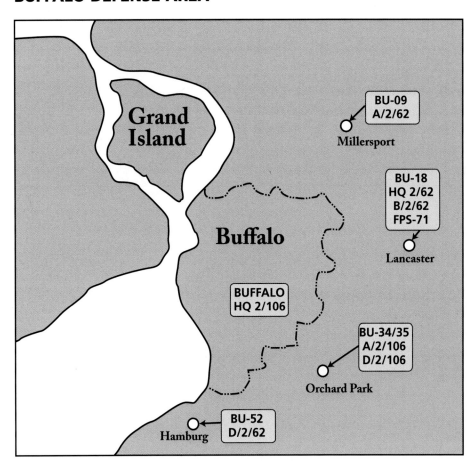

Buffalo and Niagara Falls initially commenced operations as separate defense areas, sharing a common AADCP at Lockport AFS. Buffalo was then the second largest city in the state of New York and the state's primary Great Lakes port. Local industries included rail, chemical, electronics manufacturing, agricultural processing, automotive parts and a large complex of iron and steel mills. With the inactivation of the 2/62nd in late 1961, the defense area was merged with Niagara Falls leaving a total of five firing batteries.

Site Location	Radars	Magazines, Missiles, Launchers	Convert to Herc	Units (years)
BU-09 **Ransom Creek/** **Millersport**		2A/1B 30A 2L-A		A/465th (6/56-9/58) A/2/62d (9/58-12/61)
	LOC:	C - Smith Rd, E of New Rd L - NY 263, N of Smith Rd, Town Rd 4845		
	CUR:	C - (I) Town of Amherst record department L - (I) Town of Amherst police department		
BU-18 **Lancaster/Milgrove**	ABAR/71	3B 18H/30A 12L-H	6/58- 4/59	HHB/465th (/56-9/58) B/465th (6/56-9/58) HHB/2/62d (9/58-12/61) B/2/62d (9/58-12/61) A/1/4th (12/61-4/63) HQ 209thGp (3/63-3/70) HHB/2/209th(3/63-3/70) B/2/209th (4/63-3/70)
	LOC:	C - Pavement Rd, N of Walden Ave L – Peppermint Rd, W of Ransom Rd		
	CUR:	C - (I) Lancaster Town Center L - (I) First Squared Element Company		
BU-34/35 **Orchard Park** DOUBLE SITE		4A/2B 60A 24L-AA		C/465th (6/56-9/58) D/2/62d (9/58-8/60) A/2/106th (8/60-3/63) D/2/106th (8/60-3/63)
	LOC:	C - Transit Rd (Hwy 187) , N of Mile Strip Rd L - end of N. Davis Rd at Willardshire Rd, E of Transit Rd		
	CUR:	C&L - (O) HGM Land Corporation		
BU-52 **Hamburg** DOUBLE SITE		4A/2B 60A 24L-AA		D/465th (6/56-9/58) D/2/62d (9/58-12/61)
	LOC:	C - New Lake View Rd, 2 E Heltz Rd L - New Lake View Rd, 1 E Heltz Rd		
	CUR:	C - (O) Hamburg town park L - (P) Town offices		
Buffalo				HHB/2/106th(5/59-3/63)

CHICAGO DEFENSE AREA

The Chicago-Gary area was one of the major defense areas in the Nike program—the "Windy City" constituted the single largest grouping of government, financial, business, industrial, and military activities in the upper Midwest. To guard this complex, ARADCOM constructed twenty-two firing sites in upstate Illinois and Indiana, under the operational control of one brigade, three groups, and several battalions.

The AADCP was located at Arlington Heights; the facility also provided command and control for other Nike batteries in Milwaukee to the north. Long-range detection and tracking data was provided by a co-located Air Force radar squadron and a ring of ARADCOM air defense radars (see next entry). The SAGE command post was located at Truax Field, Madison, WI, and the Air Force also maintained interceptors at O'Hare International Airport from February 1952 through January 1959.

Notable among the firing units was the 485th AAAMBn, which performed ARADCOM's fourth operational Nike-Hercules firing at Fort Bliss, TX, on 2 May 1958; and manned the first operational Hercules site, C-03 Montrose, on 30 June 1958.

The Milwaukee defense area was merged with Chicago in 1968 and Detroit's surviving sites were combined in 1971. The Chicago-Detroit Defense Area remained operational right up until the demise of ARADCOM in 1974.

Site Location	Radars	Magazines, Missiles, Launchers	Convert to Herc	Units (years)
C-03 **Montrose/Belmont** DOUBLE SITE	ABAR/75	2A/3B 18H/50A 20L-UA (12L-H)	3/58- 5/59	HHB/485th (10/55-9/58) A/485th (10/55-9/58) D/485th (/56-9/58) HHB/2/57th (9/58-8/63) A/2/57th (9/58-8/63) D/2/57th (9/58-5/59) HHB/6/3d (8/63-6/65) A/6/3d (8/63-6/65)
	LOC:	*C - Montrose Wilson Beach, end of Montrose Ave* *L - Montrose Wilson Beach, end of Belmont St*		
	CUR:	*C - (O) Lincoln Park; Montrose Wilson Beach* *L - (O) Lincoln Park; yacht club*		
		NOTE: First operational Hercules site in ARADCOM		
C-32 **Porter/Chesterton**	HIPAR SMFU	3B 18H/20A 12L-U	5/58- 10/58	B/79th (/57-9/58) B/1/60th (9/58-4/74)
	LOC:	*C - 3 WSW Tremont, N. Mineral SpringsRd, N of E. Oak Hill Rd* *L - 2 WSW Tremont, off East Oak Hill Rd on Wagner Rd*		
	CUR:	*C - (P) National Park Service; Indiana Dunes National Lakeshore* *L - (I) private owner*		
Museum of Science **and Industry**				HQ 56thBde (7/52-11/53) (7/55- /57)
	LOC:	*57th St & Lakeshore Dr*		
	CUR:	*Museum of Science and Industry*		
C-40 **Burnham Park**		2A/1B 30A 12L-A		B/485th (3/55-9/58) B/2/57th (9/58-8/63)
	LOC:	*C - Lake Shore Dr & 31st St* *L - Lake Shore Dr & 26th St*		
	CUR:	*C – (O) Burnham Park* *L – (O) Burnham Park*		
C-41 **Jackson Park**	ABAR/71	1B/2C 18H/30A 12L-U	6/58- 4/59	C/485th (3/55-9/58) C/2/57th (9/58-8/63) B/6/3d (8/63-6/65) D/1/60th (6/65-6/71)
	LOC:	*C - Lake Shore Dr & 55th St* *L - Lake Shoe Dr off end of 61st St*		
	CUR:	*C – (O) Jackson Park* *L – (O) Jackson Park*		

Site Location	Radars	Magazines, Missiles, Launchers	Convert to Herc	Units (years)
C-44 **Hegewisch/Wolf Lake** DOUBLE SITE		4A/2B 60A 24L-AA		D/485th (3/55-11-56) HHB/49th (11/56-9/58) B/49th (11/56-9/58) D/49th (11/56-9/58) HHB/4/52d (9/58-12/60) B/4/52d (9/58-12/59) D/4/52d (9/58-12/59) A/2/202d (12/59-3/63) D/2/202d (12/59-3/63)
	LOC:	*C - N of 136th St, Hegewisch, NNE of Ave K and 136th St* *L - off of "O" Blvd, north section of Wm W. Powers Conservation Area, Wolf Lake*		
	CUR:	*C- (P) State land, part of William Powers State Cons. Area, towers only* *L- (P) County Land, part of W.W. Powers State Cons. Area, foundations*		
C-45 **Gary Municipal Airport**		2B 20A 8L-A		HHB/79th (/57-9/58) C/79th (/57-9/58) HHB/1/60th(9/58-11/68) C/1/60th (9/58-6/60)
	LOC:	*C - NNW corner Gary Municipal Airport, off US 12* *L - W end Gary Municipal Airport*		
	CUR:	*C- (O) Gary Municipal Airport* *L- (P) Gary Municipal Airport, police firing range*		
C-46 **Munster**	ABAR/75	1B/1C 12H/20A 8L-U (8L-H)	10/60- 6/61	C/49th (11/56-9/58) C/4/52d (9/58-6/60) C/1/60th (6/60-11/68) HHB/1/60th(11/68-9/74)
	LOC:	*C - 1 S Munster, W side Columbia Ave (Sheffield Ave)* *L - 2 S Munster, W side Columbia Ave*		
	CUR:	*C - (O) industrial park* *L - (I) Salyer Plumbing Company*		
C-47 **Hobart/Wheeler**	HIPAR	2?B/1C 12H/20A 8L-U (8L-H)	10/60- 6/61	A/49th (11/56- /57) D/49th (11/56- /57) A/79th (/57-9/58) A/1/60th (9/58-4/74)
	LOC:	*C - 1 N Wheeler, County Rd 600* *L - 2 NNE Wheeler, Porter County Rd 700*		
	CUR:	*C - (I) private* *L - (I) Portage Township School Corporation,* *Listed on the National Register of Historic Places on 01/21/2000*		

Site Location	Radars	Magazines, Missiles, Launchers	Convert to Herc	Units (years)
C-48 **South Gary**		2B 20A 8L-A		D/79th (/57-9/58) D/1/60th (9/58-6/60)
	LOC:	C - on Grant St, near West 35th Ave L - W of Grant St, off of West 35th Ave (Glen Park)		
	CUR:	C - (O) city property L - (P) city property		
C-49 **Homewood**	HIPAR	1B/2C 18H/30A 11L-U	6/58- 7/59	A/49th (/57-9/58) A/4/52d (9/58-6/60) A/6/3d (6/60-8/63) A/1/202d (8/63-4/74)
	LOC:	C - W of IL 1, off of 187th St L - IL 1(S. Halstead St), S of 187th St		
	CUR:	C - (P) ILArnG recruiting L - (P) Mercy Health Care/USAR Center		
C-50R **Homewood**	LOC: CUR:	W of IL 1, N of 187th St (P) ILArnG recruiting		
C-51 **Worth/Palos Heights/** **La Grange**		2A/1B 30A 12L-A		C/13th (/56-9/58) C/2/60th (9/58-12/59) C/2/202d (12/59-3/63)
	LOC:	C - S of I 294, W Plattner Dr (P?) L - 1 W, S of I 294, Ridgeland Ave (P)		
C-54 **Orland Park**		2A/1B 30A 12L-A		HQ 22d Gp (-12/61) HHB/13th (/56-9/58) B/13th (/56-9/58) HHB/2/60th (9/58-12/61) B/2/60th (9/58-12/61)
	LOC:	C - SW Orland Park, S of 153d St L - SE Orland Park, N of 159th St		
	CUR:	C- (O) private L- (P) Village of Orland Park, Illinois Natl. Guard		

Site Location	Radars	Magazines, Missiles, Launchers	Convert to Herc	Units (years)
C-61 **Lemont**	ABAR/71	2B 12H/20A 8L-U (8L-H)	6/58- 6/59	C/86th (/55- /56) D/13th (/56-9/58) D/2/60th (9/58-12/61) C/6/3d (12/61-4/64) C/1/202d (4/64-11/68)
	LOC:	*C - 91st St, E of Cass Rd*		
		L - SW corner, I 55/Cass Rd interchange (South Frontage Rd)		
	CUR:	*(O) Argonne National Laboratories, Waterfall Glen Forest Preserve*		
C-70 **Naperville**		2A/1B 30A 12L-A		A/13th (/56-9/58) A/2/60th (9/58-12/59) B/2/202d (12/59-3/63)
	LOC:	*C - 2 SE Warrenville, Warrenville Rd, 1.5 M West of Naperville Rd*		
		L - E. Diehl Rd 1.5 M West of Naperville Rd		
	CUR:	*C – (O) AMOCO research center*		
		L – (O) Napier Park District		
C-72 Addison	HIPAR	1B/2C 18H/30A 10L-U	6/58- 6/59	B/86th (/57-9/58) B/6/3d (9/58-8/63) B/1/202d (8/63-4/74)
	LOC:	*L - E of Lombard & East Jeffery Dr S of Fullerton*		
		C – E of Rohlwing Rd (St. Rt. 53) N of Fullerton		
	CUR:	*C - (P) City of Addison park*		
		L - (O) Addison Department of Public Works		
C-80 **Arlington Heights** *shared launch site with C-81*		2A/1B 30A 12L-A		HHB/86th (/56-9/58) A/86th (/55-9/58) D/86th (/55-9/58) HHB/6/3d (9/58-6/65) A/6/3d (9/58-6/60) D/6/3d (9/58-12/60) HHB/1/202d (/59-8/74)
	LOC:	*C - N side Algonquin & Golf Rd*		
		L - S of W Central Rd, W of State Rd		
	CUR:	*C - (O) park/mini-mall*		
		L - (P) ILArNG; Special Forces Group		

Site Location	Radars	Magazines, Missiles, Launchers Convert to Herc	Units (years)
C-80DC **Arlington Heights**	AN/FSG-1 Missile Master AN/TSQ-51 Missile Mentor 2 x AN/FPS-6 (AN/FPS-6B) (AN/FPS-90) AN/FPS-20A (AN/FPS-67)	AADCP	HQ 45th Bde (/50-5/71) HQ 202d Gp (/59-3/63) USAF 755th RADS (SAGE)) (4/60-9/69
	LOC:	*Central Rd, E of Arlington Heights Rd*	
	CUR:	*(I) USAR 85th Division (Training Support)*	
C-81 **Arlington Heights** *shared launch site with C-80*		2A/1B 30A 12L-A	D/86th (/55-9/58) D/6/3d (9/58-12/60)
	LOC:	*C - W of State Rd, S of White Oak Rd* *L - S of W. Central Rd, W of State Rd*	
	CUR:	*C - (O) park/Juliet Lowe School* *L - (P) ILArNG*	
C-84 **Palatine**		2A/1B 30A 12L-A	C/86th (/56-9/58) C/6/3d (9/58-9/60) B/1/202d (9/60-3/63)
	LOC:	*C - N of W. Lake Cook Rd W of IL 53/Rand Rd* *L - W. Field Pkwy, E of Quentin Rd*	
	CUR:	*C - (O) field* *L - (O) Lake County administrative storage site*	
C-92 **Mundelein**		2A/1B 30A 12L-A	C/49th (11-56- /57) HHB/78th (/57-9/58) A/78th (/57-9/58) HHB/1/517th(9/58-12/60) A/1/517th (9/58-8/60) A/1/202d (8/60-3/63)
	LOC:	*between Half Day Rd & Milwaukee Ave*	
	CUR:	*(O) recreational complex*	
	NOTE:	*colocated with C-94 on former Naval Outlying Field Libertyville*	

Site Location	Radars	Magazines, Missiles, Launchers	Convert to Herc	Units (years)
C-93 **Northfield/Skokie**	HIPAR	2B 12H/20A 8L-U (8L-H)	4/58- 11/58	B/86th (/55- /57) D/78th (/57-9/58) D/1/517th (9/58-12/60) D/6/3d (12/60-4/64) D/1/202d (4/64-4/74)
	LOC:	*C - Hohfeler Rd, N of Tower Rd*		
		L - N of Tower Rd, W of Forest Way		
	CUR:	*C - (O) William N. "Bill" Erickson Forest Preserve*		
		L - (O) William N. "Bill" Erickson Forest Preserve		
C-94 **Libertyville**		2A/1B 30A 12L-A		B/78th (10/55-9/58) B/1/517th (9/58-8/60) C/1/202d (8/60-3/63)
	LOC:	*between Half Day Rd & Milwaukee Ave*		
	CUR:	*(O) Recreational complex*		
	NOTE:	*colocated with C-92 on former Naval Outlying Field Libertyville*		
C-98 **Fort Sheridan**		2A/1B 30A 12L-A		HQ 5ARADCOM (7/54-4/66) HQ 45th Bde (11/53-7/55) HQ 16th Gp (-12/61) HQ 28th Gp (5/71-9/74) HHB/78th (10/55- /57) HHB/86th (/55- /56) C/78th (10/55-9/58) C/1/517th (9/58-8/60) D/1/202d (8/60-3/63)
	LOC:	*C - NW Ft Sheridan, adjacent to National Cemetery*		
		L - NE Ft Sheridan, 12th Rd		
	CUR:	*(O) Town of Fort Sheridan;*		
		NOTE: Fort Sheridan inactivated as a military post on 28 May 1993 following 103 years of service to the Army and the nation. The Army retained a portion of the cantonment for reserve training purposes.		
Chicago				HHB/2/202d (3/59-3/63)

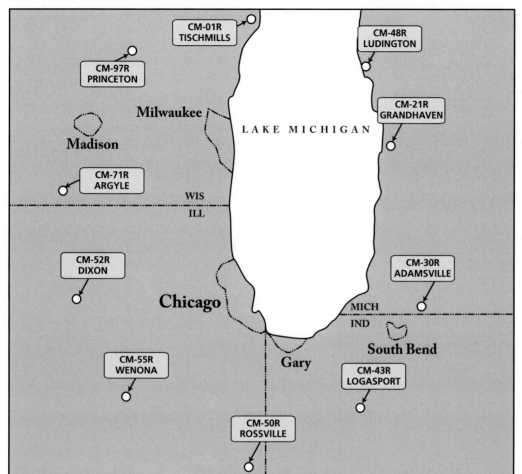

CHICAGO–MILWAUKEE RADAR RING

The Chicago–Milwaukee region featured a ring of ten radar sites separate from the Nike AADCP and battery radars in the two defense areas. Operated by detachments of the 16th, 22d, and 61st Artillery Groups, control of the sites eventually passed to the 45th Brigade. The employment of a separate radar defense ring was not repeated in ARADCOM. The type radars utilized at these sites has not been determined.

CM-01R	Tisch Mills, WI	61st Arty Gp det	Two Creeks AFS,then Two Creeks GFA
CM-21R	Grandhaven, MI	22d Arty Gp det	
CM-30R	Adamsville, MI	22d Arty Gp det	
CM-43R	Logansport, MI	22d Arty Gp det	
CM-48R	Ludington, MI	22d Arty Gp det	
CM-50R	Rossville, IL	16th Arty Gp det	
CM-55R	Wenona, IL	16th Arty Gp det	
CM-62R	Dixon, IL		16th Arty Gp det
CM-71R	Argyle, WI		16th Arty Gp det
CM-97R	Princeton, WI	61st Arty Gp det	

CINCINNATI-DAYTON DEFENSE AREA

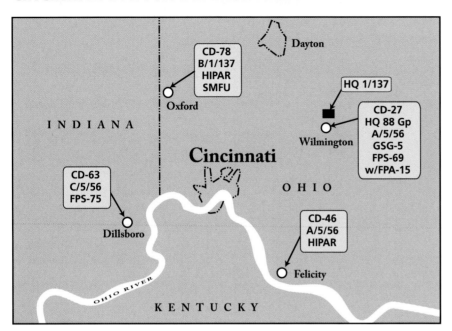

Built during the second series of Nike construction, the Cincinnati–Dayton defense protected the industrial areas of the upper Ohio River Valley; Air Force Systems Command's Wright Air Development Center/Aeronautical Systems Division; Strategic Air Command's 4043d STRATW/17th BW(H) at Wright-Patterson AFB; and the Air National Guard/Air Force units at Clinton County AFB.

The 1/137th, OHArNG, was originally activated for service in the Cleveland Defense Area. Following the conversion to Hercules, the battalion manned sites in both defenses.

One of the magazines at CD-46L, Dillsboro, was converted into a house following the shutdown of Nike operations.

Site Location	Radars	Magazines, Missiles, LaunchersConvert to Herc	Units (years)
CD-27DC **Wilmington**	AN/GSG-5 BIRDIE AN/FPA-16	AADCP	HQ 88th Gp (3/66- /70) HHB/5/56th (/60-3/70) HHB/1/137th(/64-3/71)
	LOC:	*4 SE, SR 730 and Osborne*	
	CUR:	*(I) Nike Center Town & Country School/Orion Industries*	
CD-27 **Wilmington**	ABAR/69	3D 18H 12L-U	A/5/56th (4/60-3/70)
	LOC:	*C - 4 SE, SR 730 and Osborne*	
		L - 4 SE, Osborne Rd	
	CUR:	*C - (I) Nike Center Town & Country School/Orion Industries*	
		L - (I) private owner	
CD-46 **Felicity**	HIPAR	3D 18H 12L-U	B/5/56th (4/60-5/65) A/1/137th (4/65-3/70)
	LOC:	*C - 3 W Felicity, S of OH 756, Fruit Ridge Rd*	
		L - 3.5 W Felicity, S of OH 756, Neville Penn Schoolhouse Rd	
	CUR:	*C – (I) OHArNG; Company C, 216th Engineer Bn*	
		L – (I) Industrial park	

Site Location	Radars	Magazines, Missiles, LaunchersConvert to Herc	Units (years)
CD-63 **Dillsboro**	ABAR/75	3D 18H 12L-U	C/5/56th (4/60-3/70)
	LOC:	C - 4 SE Dillsboro, S of US 50 on Texas Gas Rd L - 3 SE Dillsboro, S of US 50 on St Rt 262	
	CUR:	C- (I) L - (I) private home	
CD-78 **Oxford**	HIPAR SMFU	3D 18H 12L-U	D/5/56th (4/60-4/65) B/1/137th (4/65-3/70)
	LOC:	C - 3 NW Oxford, Todd Rd N of US 27 L - 4 NW Oxford, Taylor Rd N of US 27	
	CUR:	C - (I) USAR Center L - (I) Miami University storage	

CLEVELAND DEFENSE AREA

The city of Cleveland was one of the major industrial centers of the old "Rust Belt," built on steel and Great Lakes transportation. The opening of the Saint Lawrence Seaway in the late 1950s boosted the city's importance as a seaport, manufacturing center, and international transportation center.

Early in ARAACOM's history, the city hosted the 53rd Artillery Brigade, the initial controlling command for the AA units Pittsburgh, Buffalo, Niagara Falls, and Ohio. Following the establishment of a two-battalion Nike defense area, several artillery groups were stationed here. The AADCP and group HQ was located at Site CL-43C, Warrensville. The Cleveland Defense Area was merged with Detroit in November 1968.

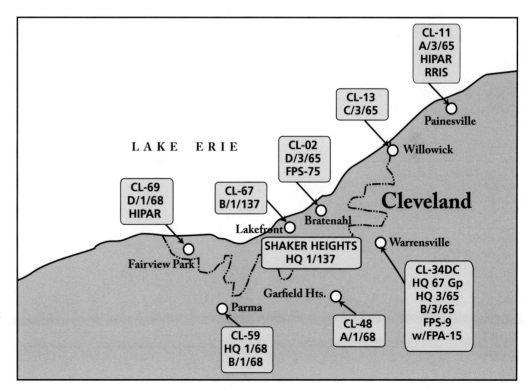

Site Location	Radars	Magazines, Missiles, Launchers	Convert to Herc	Units (years)
CL-02 **Bratenahl**	ABAR/75	3B 18H/30A 12L-U (12L-H)	5/58- 11/58	HHB/508th (/57-9/58) D/508th (2/57-9/58) HHB/3/65th (9/58- /59) D/3/65th (9/58-6/71)
	LOC:	C - N. Marginal Rd off of E. 55th St		
		L - Access Road off of Lakeshore Dr off of end of Martin Luther King I 90 exit		
	CUR:	C - (O) state waterfront park		
		L - (P) US Navy Finance Center parking lot		
CL-11 **Painesville**	HIPAR RRIS	3B(D?) 18H/30A 12L-U (12L-H)	6/58- 9/59	A/508th (2/57-9/58) A/3/65th (9/58-6/71)
	LOC:	C - Freedom Rd off of Newell St		
		L- Blackbrook Rd off of St Hwy 44		
	CUR:	C – (P) Lubizoil Corporation; storage yard		
		L – (I) County Engineer's office		
CL-13 **Willowick**		3B 30A 12L-A		C/508th (2/57-9/58) C/3/65th (9/58-6/61) A/1/137th (6/61- /63)
	LOC:	C - 30100 Arnold Rd		
		L - 33525 Curtis Rd, W of 337 St		
	CUR:	C - (O) Robert Maury Park W of W. 305th St		
		L - (I) Willoughby-Eastlake School District; school bus terminal and storage area, John F. Kennedy Senior Center		
Shaker Heights Armory				HQ 191st Gp(/59- /63) HHB/1/137th(/59- /64)
	LOC:	2500 E 130th		
CL-34DC **Warrensville/** **Highland Hills**	AN/GSG-5 BIRDIE AN/FPS-69 AN/FPA-15	AADCP		HQ 40th Gp (/56-3/58) HQ 67th Gp (3/58-8/61) HQ 90th Gp (3/66-5/69) HHB/3/65th (/59-6/71)
	LOC:	S of OH 87		
	CUR:	(O) field		
CL-34 **Warrensville /** **Highland Hills**		3B 30A 12L-A		B/351st (7/56-2/57) B/508th (2/57-9/58) B/3/65th (9/58-1/61)

Site Location	Radars	Magazines, Missiles, Launchers	Convert to Herc	Units (years)
				C/1/137th (1/61- /63)
	LOC:	C - S of OH 87		
		L - 3978 Richmond Rd & Harvard Rd		
	CUR:	C - (P) USAR Center; 319th Quartermaster Battalion, 444th Quartermaster Company		
		L - (O) abandoned		
CL-48		2A/1B		A/351st (7/56-9/58)
Garfield Heights		30A		A/1/68th (9/58-8/61)
		12L-A		
	LOC:	C - 5640 Briarcliff		
		L – End of Tulip Trail off of Stone Rd		
	CUR:	C - (O) Garfield Heights Board of Education School District administration		
		L - (I) parking lot, private?		
Cleveland				HQ 53d Bde (/55- /56)
CL-59		2A/1B		HHB/351st (7/56-9/58)
Parma/Midpark Station		30A		B/351st (7/56-9/58)
		12L-A		HHB/1/68th (9/58-8/61)
				B/1/68th (9/58-8/61)
	LOC:	C - 7300 York Rd		
		L – Bicentennial Dr off of Pleasant Valley Rd		
	CUR:	C - (O) Nathan Hale Park		
		L - (O) Cuyahoga Community College, Western Campus parking lot		
CL-67		3B		C/351st (7/56-9/58)
Lakefront Airport		30A		C/1/68th (9/58-1/61)
		12L-A		B/1/137th (1/61- /63)
	LOC:	C - 4200 S Marginal		
		L - N of I-90, E of airport, off of Martin Luther King Blvd		
	CUR:	C - (O) City of Cleveland; Joseph L. Stamps District Service Center		
		L - (P) Airport property, launchers paved over under runway 6L		
CL-69	HIPAR	3B	5/58-	HHB/508th (7/56- /57)
Lordstown Military		18H/30A	11/58	D/351st (7/56-9/58)
Reservation/		12L-U		D/1/68th (8/61-2/63)
Fairview Park				C/3/65th (8/61-2/63)
				C/1/137th (2/63-6/71)
	LOC:	C – North of Westwood Ave		
		L - 21700 Westwood Ave		
	CUR:	C - (O) park and housing		
		L - (O) Tri-City Park		

COLUMBUS DEFENSE AREA

During the late 1950s ARADCOM performed site surveys for a possible Nike-Hercules missile defense in the vicinity of Columbus AFB, Mississippi. No battalion was selected and the sites were never constructed. The two-letter designation for the proposed sites has not been identified. The air field at Columbus dated from its establishment in August 1941 as the Air Corps Advanced Flying School. Units assigned at Columbus AFB—which reactivated on 20 December 1950—including the 3301st Pilot Training Group (Contract-Primary) through January 1955 and the SAC's 4228th Strategic Wing, which activated at the base on 1 July 1958 with B-52Fs and KC-135As.

Site Location	Radars	Magazines, Missiles, Launchers	Convert to Herc	Units (years)
Cx-15 **Columbus**	*Site Survey Only			
Cx-60 **Columbus**	*Site Survey Only			

DALLAS–FORT WORTH DEFENSE AREA

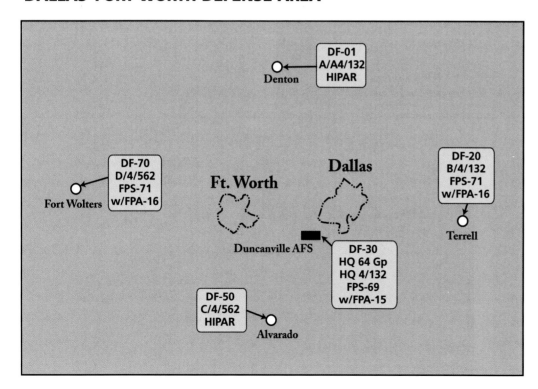

During the late 1950s ARADCOM performed site surveys for a possible Nike-Hercules missile defense in the vicinity of Columbus AFB, Mississippi. No battalion was selected and the sites were never constructed. The two-letter designation for the proposed sites has not been identified. The air field at Columbus dated from its establishment in August 1941 as the Air Corps Advanced Flying School. Units assigned at Columbus AFB—which reactivated on 20 December 1950—including the 3301st Pilot Training Group (Contract-Primary) through January 1955 and the SAC's 4228th Strategic Wing, which activated at the base on 1 July 1958 with B-52Fs and KC-135As.

Site Location	Radars	Magazines, Missiles, LaunchersConvert to Herc	Units (years)
DF-01 **Denton**	HIPAR	3D 18H 12L-U	A/4/562d (9/60-2/64) A/4/132d (2/64-10/68)
	LOC:	C - 3.5 N Denton, E side FR 2164 L - 4.5 N Denton, FR 2164 S of FR 3163	
	CUR:	C - (I) privately owned L - (I) University of North Texas; UNT Astronomics Research Lab	
DF-20 **Terrell**	ABAR/71 AN/FPA-16	3D 18H 12L-U	B/4/562d (9/60-2/64) B/4/132d (2/64-10/68)
	LOC:	C – CR 233 Colquitt Rd L - E side Griffith Rd	
	CUR:	C - (I) abandoned L - (I) private	
Dallas			HHB/4/562d (6/59- /59)
DF-30DC **Duncanville AFS**	AN/GSG-5 BIRDIE	AADCP ABAR/69 AN/FPA-15 AN/FPA-6 2x AN/FPA-10	HQ 64th Gp (3/66- /69) HHB/4/562d (/59-2/69) HHB/4/132d(3/63-10/68) USAF 745th AC&WS (2/53-9/69)
	LOC:	NE Duncanville-Wheatland Hwy & Duncanville Rd	
	CUR:	(O) City of Duncanville; Armstrong Park, municipal offices	
DF-50 **Alvarado**	HIPAR	3D 18H 12L-U	C/4/562d (9/60-10/68)
	LOC:	C - 3 SE Alvarado, N side FR 1807 (Nike Access Rd) L - 3.5 SE Alvarado, S side FR 1807	
	CUR:	C - (I) New Life Ministries L - (I) Private owner	
DF-70 **Fort Wolters**	ABAR/71 AN/FPA-16	3D 18H 12L-U	D/4/562d (9/60-10/68)
	LOC:	C - N Fort Wolters L - NW Fort Wolters	
	CUR:	C - (I) TXArNG; Unit Training Equipment Site No. 2 L - (I) Small arms storage; firing and maneuver range	

DETROIT DEFENSE AREA

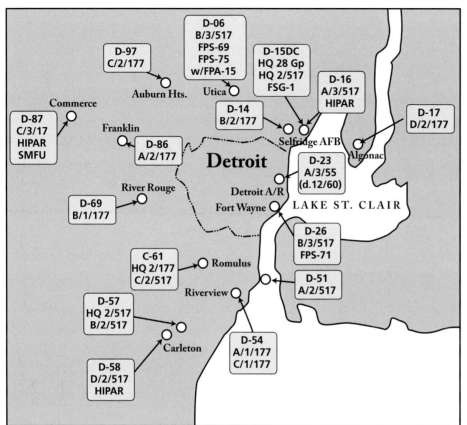

One of the major defense areas, Detroit remained operational until the end of ARAD-COM. Among the protected industries in the area were those of the automobile manufactures in Detroit, Dearborn, Flint, and Pontiac, and a substantial collection of steel mills.

Gun defense operations commenced in spring 1951, with the Illinois Guard's 698th AAABn (90 mm). The 698th was relieved by four Regular Army battalions, three of which were converted to Nike-Ajax (with a fourth new unit added later) that manned the 15 missile sites. Additional defense assets included the 1st Fighter Wing (Air Defense) at Selfridge AFB.

The AADCP was co-located with an Air Force radar site at the north end of Selfridge AFB. The NORAD SAGE command post was located 150 miles west of Detroit at Custer AFS. For two years, from 1969 until 1971, Detroit hosted the Second ARADCOM Region; as part of the June 1971 cut backs, the region was inactivated and the 28th Artillery Group moved to Chicago. The remaining three sites were closed in April 1974.

Site Location	Radars	Magazines, Missiles, Launchers	Convert to Herc	Units (years)
D-06	ABAR/69	2B	10/60-	B/516th (/55-9/58)
Utica	ABAR/75	12H/20A	4/61	B/3/517th (9/58-2/63)
	AN/FPA-15	8L-U		A/1/177th (2/63-4/74)
	LOC:	*L&C – River Bends Dr*		
	CUR:	*C - (P) admin site park HQ River Bends Park*		
		L - (P) River Bends Park		
D-14		2B		C/516th (/55-9/58)
Selfridge AFB		20A		C/3/517th (9/58-7/59)
Shared IFC with D-16		8L-A		B/2/177th (7/59-2/63)
	LOC:	*C - South Perimeter Rd, 1 W south gate*		
		L - South Perimeter Rd, 3 W south gate		
	CUR:	*C - (P) equipment storage*		
		L - (P) MIArNG vehicle storage		

Site Location	Radars	Magazines, Missiles, Launchers	Convert to Herc	Units (years)
D-15DC **Selfridge AFB**	AN/FSG-1 Missile Master AN/TSQ-51 Missile Mentor AN/CPS-5 AN/CPS-6 AN/FPS-6 (AN/FPS-26A) AN/FPS-6A AN/FPS-20 (AN/FPS-20A) (AN/FPS-35)	AADCP		HQ 2ARADCOM(12/69-6/71) HQ 28th Gp (9/58-6/71) HHB/516th (5/54-9/58) HHB/3/517th(9/58-9/72) HHB/2/3d (9/72-9/74) USAF 661st RADS (SAGE) (12/49-7/74)
	LOC:	Selfridge AFB, North Perimeter Rd		
	CUR:	(I) Selfridge ANGB; US Coast Guard Air Station Detroit; MIArNG Aviation Support Facility Selfridge; Selfridge Military Air Museum		
D-16 **Selfridge AFB** *Shared IFC with D-14*	HIPAR	2B 12H/20A 8L-U	5/58- 9/58	A/516th (/55-9/58) A/3/517th (9/58-6/71)
	LOC:	C - South Perimeter Rd, 1 W south gate L - South Perimeter Rd, .5 W south gate		
	CUR:	C - (P) equipment storage L - (P) boat/RV storage		
Detroit Artillery Armory				HHB/1/177th(6/59-8/74) HHB/2/177th(3/59- /59)
	LOC:	1500 W 8 Mile Rd		
D-17 **Algonac/Marine City**		2A/1B 30A 12L-A		D/18th (6/57- /58) D/516th (/58-9/58) D/3/517th (9/58-11/59) D/2/177th (11/59-2/63)
	LOC:	C - N side Shortcut Rd, E of Starville Rd, 6680 Short Cut Rd L - S side Shortcut Rd, E of Starville Rd, 6405 Short Cut Rd		
	CUR:	C - (O) private L - (P) private		
D-23 **Detroit City Airport/ Kercheval** * *Shared double launch with D-26;* *separate IFCs*		2B 20A 8L-A		A/85th (4/55-9/58) A/3/55th (9/58-12/60)
	LOC:	C - end of Lenox St L – Lakeside Dr East end of Belle Isle; South of Blue Heron Lagoon		
	CUR:	C - (O) Ford Brush Park L - (O) Field–part of Belle Isle Park		

111

Site Location	Radars	Magazines, Missiles, Launchers	Convert to Herc	Units (years)
D-26	ABAR/71	2B	5/58-	B/85th (4/55-9/58)
Detroit City Airport/		12H/20A	7/58	B/3/55th (9/58-12/60)
East Detroit		8L-UA		HHB/3/55th(/59-12/60)
* Shared double launch with D-23; separate IFCs				
	LOC:	C - end of Conner St		
		L - East end of Belle Isle; South of Blue Heron Lagoon		
	CUR:	C - (O) Maheras Memorial Park		
		L - (O) Field–part of Belle Isle Park		
Fort Wayne				HHB 85th (4/55-9/58)
				HHB 3/55th (9/58- /59)
	LOC:	6325 W. Jefferson Ave		
	CUR:	Historic Fort Wayne; city/county historical park, currently closed		
D-51		2A/1B		C/85th (4/55- /57)
NAS Grosse Isle		30A		A/504th (/55-9/58)
		12L-A		A/2/517th (9/58-2/63)
	LOC:	C - 8690 Groh Rd, W of E. River Rd, Grosse Isle		
		L - SE corner municipal airport off of E. River Rd		
	CUR:	C - (O) private		
		L - (O) EPA, nature area		
D-54		2A/4B		B/504th (1/55- /57)
Riverview/Wyandotte		60A		C/85th (/57-9/58)
DOUBLE SITE		24L-AA		C/3/55th (9/58-10/60)
				C/1/177th (11/59-2/63)
				A/1/177th (10/60-2/63)
	LOC:	C&L - N of Sibley Rd, E of Fort St		
		C S. Pennsylvania Rd?		
	CUR:	(O) park/school		
D-57		3B		HHB/504th (1/55-9/58)
Carleton		30A		B/504th (/57-9/58)
*Shared double launch with D-58;		12L-A		HHB/2/517th(9/58-2/63)
separate IFCs				B/2/517th (9/58-2/63)
	LOC:	C - S of Newport Rd, W of Telegraph Rd		
		L – S of Newport Rd		
	CUR:	C - (P) MiANG		
		L - (P) abandoned		

Site Location	Radars	Magazines, Missiles, Launchers	Convert to Herc	Units (years)
D-58 **Carleton/Newport**	HIPAR	3B 18H/30A 12L-UA	6/58- 6/59	D/504th (6/57-9/58) D/2/517th (9/58-2/63) C/1/177th (2/63-4/74)
Shared double launch with D-57; separate IFCs				
	LOC:	C - S of Newport Rd, W of Telegraph Rd L – S of Newport Rd		
	CUR:	C - (P) MiANG L - (P) abandoned		
D-61 **Romulus/Dearborn**	ABAR/75	1A/1B/1C 18H/30A 12L-UA (8L-H)	10/60- 6/61	C/504th (6/57-9/58) C/2/517th (9/58-2/63) HHB/2/177th(/59-2/63) C/1/177th (2/63-6/71)
	LOC:	Detroit Metropolitan Airport		
	CUR:	(O) Detroit Metropolitan Airport		
D-69 **River Rouge Park/Detroit**		2B 20A 8L-A		C/504th (1/55-6/57) A/18th (6/57-9/58) A/4/3d (9/58-11/59) B/1/177th (11/59-2/63)
	LOC:	C - Spinoza Dr L - W of Warren Ave, W. Outer Dr		
	CUR:	C - (P) Detroit Police training area L - (O) park		
D-86 **Franklin/Bingham**		2A/1B 30A 12L-A		C/85th (4/55-6/57) HHB 18th (6/57-9/58) B/18th (6/57-9/58) HHB/4/3d (9/58-12/60) B/4/3d (9/58-10/60) C/3/517th (12/60-9/72) C/2/3rd (9/72-4/74)
	LOC:	C – Center Rd, N side 11 Mile Rd, E of Inkster Rd L – Mel Bauman Dr, N side 11 Mile Rd, E of Inkster Rd		
	CUR:	C - (O) TV transmitter site L - (P) Army Reserve		

Site Location	Radars	Magazines, Missiles, Launchers	Convert to Herc	Units (years)
D-87 **Commerce/** **Union Lake**	HIPAR SMFU	1B/2C 18H/30A 12L-U (10L-H)	6/58- 8/59	D/504th (1/55-6/57) C/18th (6/57-9/58) C/4/3d (9/58-12/60) C/3/517th (12/60-9/72) C/2/3d (9/72-4/74)
	LOC:	C - S side Wise Rd, E of Carroll Lake L - S side Wise Rd, W of Union Lake Rd		
	CUR:	C - (P) Camp Oakland day camp L - (O) Proud Lake State Recreation Area		
D-97 **Auburn Heights**		2A/1B 30A 12L-A		D/516th (/55- /58) D/18th (/58-9/58) D/4/3d (9/58-11/59) C/2/177th (11/59-2/63)
	LOC:	C - N of MI 59, W of Squirrel Rd at Featherstone L - N of MI 59, E of I 75 interchange Mott Rd S of Featherstone		
	CUR:	C - (O) parking lot Oakland University L - (P) Oakland University, Auburn Hills Campus, next to baseball park, storage		

DYESS DEFENSE AREA

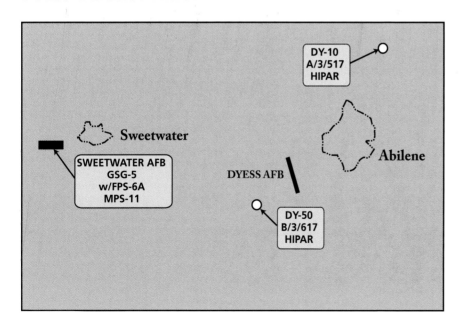

Units stationed at Dyess AFB while the 5/517th was operational included SAC's 819th Strategic Aerospace Division, the 96th BW(H), and the 578th Strategic Missile Squadron. Several of the 578th's Atlas F silos are located near the Nike sites. The Army Air Defense Command Post was located thirty-seven miles west at Sweetwater AFS. Both of the sites were located near former Army posts. Camp Barkeley served as a World War II infantry division training center, while Fort Phantom Hill was a frontier outpost and stop on the Butterfield stage route.

Site Location	Radars	Magazines, Missiles, Launchers	Convert to Herc	Units (years)
DY-10 **Fort Phantom Hill/** **Abilene**	HIPAR	3AG 12H 12L-H		A/5/517th (10/60-6/66)
	LOC:	C - 8 N Abilene, FR 600		
		L - 9 N Abilene, CR 341 at CR 317		
	CUR:	C - (I) Abilene Independent School District; Instructional Resources Center		
		L - (I) private owner		
Dyess AFB				HHB/5/517th(3/60-6/66)
	LOC:	3 SW Abilene		
	CUR:	Dyess AFB; 7th Wing (B-1B/C-130 operations)		
DY-50 **Camp Barkeley/** **Abilene**		3AG 12H 12L-H		B/5/517th (10/60-6/66)
	LOC:	C - 12 SW Abilene, W of US 277		
		L - 13 SW Abilene, W of US 277		
	CUR:	C - (I) private owner		
		L - (I) private owner		
Sweetwater AFS	AN/GSG-5 BIRDIE AN/MPS-11 AN/TPS-10D AN/FPS-6A AN/FPS-6B AN/FPS-90	AADCP		USAF 683d AC&WS (4/56-9/69)
	LOC:	NW Sweetwater, I 20		
	CUR:	(P) Avenger Field		

ELLSWORTH DEFENSE AREA

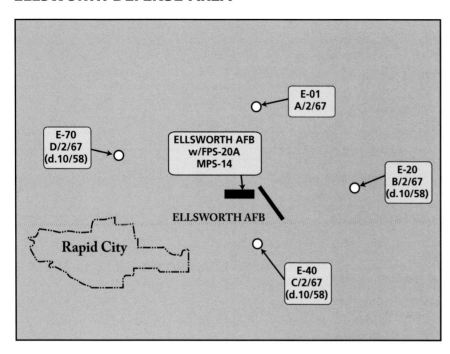

Defender of the 821st Strategic Aerospace Division (STRAD), 28th BW, and 850th Strategic Missile Squadron (Titan I), the Ellsworth, SD, defense was unique: three of the four sites were of standard below-ground configuration, and only one battery was modified for Hercules. This site was eventually disassembled and sent to HA-48 in the Hartford defense. Following the departure of the Nike defense, the Air Force activated the 44th Strategic Missile Wing which was equipped with the LGM-30F Minuteman II ICBMs. The three Titan I missile sites that followed were inactivated in late 1964.

Following the departure of the ARADCOM defense, the Air Force activated the 44th Strategic Missile Wing, equipped with the LGM-30B Minuteman I and HGM-25A Titan I ICBMs. The first-generation Titans inactivated in late 1964, leaving 150 Minuteman missiles scattered around the Black Hills region.

Site Location	Radars	Magazines, Missiles, Launchers	Convert to Herc	Units (years)
E-01	HIPAR	3B	6/58-	A/531st (6/57-9/58)
Ellsworth AFB		18H/30A	10/58	A/2/67th(9/58-1/61)
Hercules equipment to HA-48		12L-U		
	LOC:	C - 7 ENE, Elk Creek Rd		
		L - 6 ENE, Horseshoe Rd		
	CUR:	C - (P) private owner		
		L -(P) Douglas School District- East Nike School		
E-20		3A		B/531st (6/57-9/58)
Ellsworth AFB		30A		B/2/67th (9/58-10/58)
		12L-A		
	LOC:	C -6 N, Mead County 224th Pl (E. Nike)		
		L -5 N, Mead County off of 224th PL E of launch area		
	CUR:	C -(P) private owner		
		L -(P) private owner		

Site Location	Radars	Magazines, Missiles, Launchers	Convert to Herc	Units (years)
Ellsworth AFB	AN/GSG-5	AADCP		HHB/531st (6/57-9/58)
	BIRDIE			HHB/2/67th (9/58-8/61)
	AN/MPS-7			USAF 740th AC&WS
	AN/MPS-14		(2/53-8/62)	
	AN/FPS-20A			
	LOC:	*5 NE Rapid City, I 90*		
	CUR:	*Ellsworth AFB; South Dakota Air and Space Museum*		
E-40		3A		C/531st (6/57-9/58)
Ellsworth AFB		30A		C/2/67th (9/58-10/58)
		12L-A		
	LOC:	*C -2 WSW, Radar Hill Rd/Pennington County C212*		
		L -1 WSW, Bus Barn Rd		
	CUR:	*C -(P) Communications facility*		
		L -(P) (UASF Elsworth Academic Annex), Douglas County School System		
E-70		2B		D/531st 96/57-9/58)
Ellsworth AFB		20A		D/2/67th (9/58-10/58)
		8L-A		
	LOC:	*C -4 WNW, Meade County T252 Pioneer Trail*		
Note: unusual set of four		*L -5 WNW, Mead County T252 Pioneer Trail*		
launch pads located away		*C -(P) private owner*		
from the magazines proper		*L -(P) private owner*		

ENT AFB, CO

Ent AFB, named for Major General Uzal G. Ent, World War II commander of Second Air Force, was activated in January 1951 as the primary command and control site for North American air defense activities.

The base hosted NORAD, Air Defense Command, CONAD, Naval Forces-CONAD, Fourteenth Aerospace Force, and ARAACOM/ARAD-COM. The Army organization at the base included Headquarters and Headquarters Battery ARADCOM (there were no Nike sites at Ent); US Army Element Headquarters CONAD; and Headquarters, Special Troops, ARADCOM.

Ent was located at Boulder Street and Union Boulevard in downtown Colorado Springs. The base now serves as a US Olympic Training Complex; appropriate use for a group of office buildings with no runways.

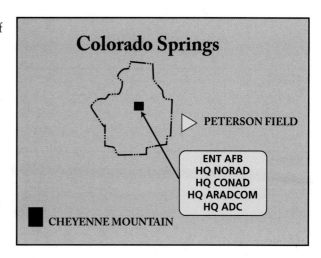

FAIRBANKS DEFENSE AREA

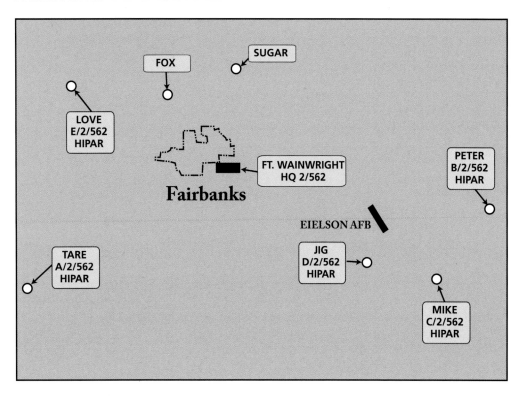

The northern half of the Alaskan defenses, the Fairbanks area consisted of five sites around Fort Wainwright and Eielson AFB, and hosted US Army Alaska Air Defense Group. Fairbanks was particularly notable for being the first defense to live fire from one of its own sites; on 16 December 59, B/2/562d launched a Hercules from Site Peter.

Ladd AFB served as an Alaskan Air Command fighter interceptor installation through 1 January 1961, when it was turned over to the Army. USARAL activated the site as Fort Wainwright. Eielson AFB served as a cold weather test facility and hosted rotational bombers and tankers under the 4157th STRATW. The Fairbanks sites closed down as part of the 1971 Defense cut backs, leaving Anchorage as the sole remaining Nike defense in Alaska.

Site Location	Radars	Magazines, Missiles, Launchers	Convert to Herc	Units (years)
FOX				
Land acquired and surveyed; not developed				
	LOC:	5 N Fairbanks, Chena Ridge Rd E. Tanna River.		
	CUR:	Never constructed		
SUGAR				
Land acquired and surveyed; not developed				
	LOC:	12 ENE Fairbanks, Lakloey Hill and Richardson Park subdivision		
	CUR:	Never constructed		
PETER	HIPAR	2AK / 16H / 8L-H		B/2/562d (3/59-4/71)
	LOC:	15 E Eielson AFB		
	CUR:	(P) US Army Yukon Training Area, abandoned		

Site Location	Radars	Magazines, Missiles, LaunchersConvert to Herc	Units (years)
MIKE	HIPAR	2AK 16H 8L-H	C/2/562d (3/59-4/70)
	LOC:	10 SE Eielson AFB	
	CUR:	(O) US Army Yukon Training Area, abandoned	
JIG	HIPAR	2AK 16H 8L-H	D/2/562d (3/59-4/70)
	LOC:	32 SE Fairbanks, near Richardson Hwy, on Site Rd near intersection Johnson Rd	
	CUR:	C - (O) L - Explosives storage	
Fort Wainwright (Ladd AFB)		AADCP	HQ USARALADG (4/64-) HQ 87th Arty Gp (- /79)
Eielson AFB			HHB/2/562d (9/58-6/71)
	LOC:	NE Fairbanks	
	CUR:	Fort Wainwright: HQ US Army Alaska	

Note: A former Alaskan Air Command fighter interceptor base, Ladd AFB transferred to the U.S. Army in January 1961.

Site Location	Radars	Magazines, Missiles, LaunchersConvert to Herc	Units (years)
TARE	HIPAR	2AK 16H 8L-H	A/2/562d (3/59-4/71)
	LOC:	18 SE Fairbanks, N. Richardson Hwy, Moose Creek Bluff	
	CUR:	C - (O) Chena River Recreation Area L - (O) Chena River Recreation Area	
Murphy Dome AFS			USAF 744th AC&WS
	LOC:	18 WNW Fairbanks, Murphy Dome Rd	
	CUR:	FAA Joint Surveillance System site A-02; Eleventh Air Force North Alaska Regional Control Center	
LOVE	HIPAR	2AK 16H 8L-H	E/2/562d (3/59-4/71)
	LOC:	10 NW Fairbanks, Murphy Dome Rd, 9E Elliot Hwy	
	CUR:	C/L - (O)	

FAIRCHILD DEFENSE AREA

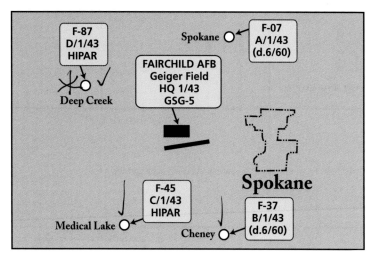

Activated in 1957, the Fairchild AFB defense was of standard design and operated both Ajax and Hercules. Air Force units at the base during the period of Nike operations included the 18th STRAD, 92d Strategic Aerospace Wing, and 576th SMS (Atlas E). Air Force fighter interceptor squadrons at Geiger Field, southwest of Spokane, and Larson AFB, near Moses Lake, provided additional defense for Washington's Inland Empire.

The NORAD SAGE command post was located at Larson; it was operational under the Spokane Air Defense Sector from 8 September 1958 through 1 September 1963. After its closure the Fairchild Defense Area drew tracking data from the SAGE command post at McChord AFB, Tacoma, WA.

Site Location	Radars	Magazines, Missiles, Launchers	Convert to Herc	Units (years)
F-07		2A/1B		A/10th (12/56-9/58)
Spokane		30A		A/1/43d (9/58-6/60)
		12L-A		
	LOC:	C - 6 NE, Newkirk Rd & Lyons Rd		
		L - 4.5 NE, Craig Rd N of Deno Rd		
	CUR:	C & L - (P) Fairchild Communications Facility Annex, USAF		
		Later - White Bluff Communications Site, Spokane Satellite Tracking Site No. 1		
F-37		2A/1B		B/10th (12/56-9/58)
Cheney		30A		B/1/43d (9/58-6/60)
		12L-A		
	LOC:	C - 1.8 E Four Lakes, Needham Hill access from launch area		
		L - 3.6 ESE Four Lakes, Andrus Rd, Needham Hill		
	CUR:	C - (I) private owner		
		L - (I) private owner		

NOTE: Former WAANG Four Lakes Air NG Station, 105th Air Control Station

Site Location	Radars	Magazines, Missiles, Launchers	Convert to Herc	Units (years)
F-45	LOPAR	2B/1C	6/60-	C/10th (12/56-9/58)
Medical Lake		18H/30A	1/61	C/1/43D (9/58-3/66)
		12L-UA		
	LOC:	C - Booth Hill, End of S. Washington Rd		
		L - S. Graham Rd, N of Espanola Rd		
	CUR:	C - (P) communications site		
		L - (P) communications company		

Site Location	Radars	Magazines, Missiles, Launchers	Convert to Herc	Units (years)
Geiger Field	AN/GSG-5	AADCP		HHB/10th (12/56-9/58)
	BIRDIE			HHB/1/43d (9/58-3/66)
	LOC:	*12 W Spokane, US 2*		*USAF 823rd AC&WS*
	CUR:	*Fairchild AFB*		
F-87	LOPAR	2B/1C	7/58-	D/1/43d (9/58-3/66)
Deep Creek		18H	3/59	
Hercules Only ✓		11L-U		
	LOC:	*C – W. Bowie Rd, W of Wood Rd*		
		L – W. Sprague Rd, E of Wood Rd		
	CUR:	*C – (P) Valley Electrical Service*		
		L – (P) William F. Spelker & Sons		

FORT BLISS, TX

Located on the northeast side of El Paso, under the Franklin Mountains and anchoring the southern end of the White Sands Missile Range, Fort Bliss has served for over fifty years as the "Home of Air Defense Artillery." During the development, deployment and operational use of Nike-Ajax and Nike-Hercules, the fort served as ARADCOM's training and evaluation center. Along with Nike, all major Army air defense systems and weapons have been tested at Fort Bliss.

Initial activities on the site at what is now El Paso commenced in 1848 at the Post in Franklin at Smith's Ranch. A more permanent post was established in December 1853 and renamed Fort Bliss on 8 March 1854. Lt. Col. William W. S. Bliss was a veteran of the Florida Indian and Mexican Wars who died in 1853. The fort site was relocated several times between 1854 and 1890, finally settling in its current location with the arrival of the 18th Infantry.

The US Army Coast Artillery Antiaircraft School relocated from Camp Davis, NC, to Bliss in 1944. The 1st Antiaircraft Guided Missile Battalion was established in 1945; the Antiaircraft Artillery and Guided Missile Center activated on the post in July 1946 and was redesignated the US Army Air Defense Center on 1 July 1957. Since that date the fort, Center and Air Defense Artillery School have provided all weapon systems, operations and basic training for air defense personnel.

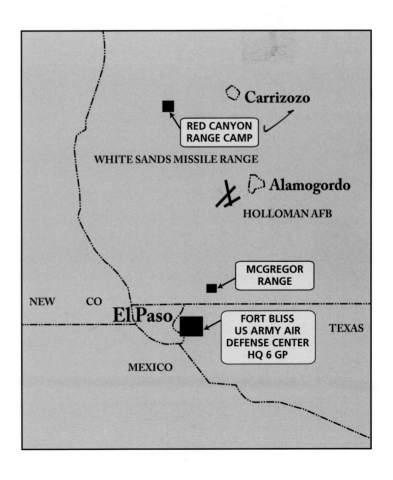

121

Nike training and launch facilities were built at two locations: Red Canyon Range Camp, 140 miles north of Fort Bliss and 16 miles west of Carrizozo; and McGregor Range, located immediately north of the Texas/New Mexico border near the Hueco Mountains. Each site was equipped with underground magazines, launch, and control facilities.

All CONUS Nike battalions returned to the range on a yearly basis for live-fire exercises and training. Red Canyon served as the annual service practice (ASP) training site for Nike-Ajax units from 1953 to 1957. Nike-Ajax and Hercules live firing, including post-1961 short-notice annual practice (SNAP) shots, were held at McGregor from 1957 to 1974.

Units assigned to Fort Bliss as of 1 January 2001:

US Army Air Defense Artillery Center & School
6th ADA Brigade

    1/6th ADA (THAAD)
    2/6th ADA (SHORAD)
    3/6th ADA (Patriot)
    4/6th ADA (Student Battalion)

1/56th ADA (Advanced Individual Training)
32nd Army Air & Missile Defense Command
11th ADA Brigade

    3/43rd ADA (Patriot)
    5/52nd ADA (Patriot)

31st ADA Brigade

    1/1st ADA (Patriot)
    3/2nd ADA (Patriot)

35th ADA Brigade

    2/1st ADA (Patriot)

108th ADA Brigade

    1/7th ADA (Patriot)
    2/43rd ADA (Patriot)
    1st ADA Battalion, 362nd Regiment (USAR)
    US Army Sergeants Major Academy
    US Army NCO Academy
    German Air Force Air Defense School (Raketenschule der Luftwaffe USA)
    62nd Army Band
    76th MP Battalion
    204th MI Battalion (Aerial Reconnaissance)
    US Army Combined Arms Support Battalion

5035th Garrison Support Unit
Allied Liaison Officers Group

    Joint Task Force Six
    William Beaumont Army Medical Center
    Biggs AAF
    507th Medical Company (Air Ambulance)

Fort Bliss is also the site of the Army Air Defense Artillery Museum.

FRANCIS E. WARREN AFB, WY (Safeguard)

Francis E. Warren AFB, located near Cheyenne, WY, possesses a lengthy history dating to its service as a cavalry post. The installation was first established in the mid-1860s as the Post at Crow Creek, and was renamed Fort D.A. Russell on 8 September 1867. Initially manned to protect Union Pacific Railroad crews, the post was granted permanent status due to its strategic location.

On 1 January 1930, it was renamed Fort Francis E. Warren for the Civil War veteran, first governor, and first senator from the state of Wyoming. On 1 April 1948, the property was transferred to the Air Force as Francis E. Warren AFB. Ten years later Warren became a SAC ICBM installation; it continues to serve in that role under the 90th Missile Wing, with three squadrons of LGM-30G Minuteman IIIs and one of the LGM-118 Peacekeeper.

Warren was never scheduled to receive either Nike or BOMARC. Plans were made during the mid-1960s to emplace a Sentinel installation. Following the change to the Safeguard program, Francis E. Warren was formally selected as the fourth ABM missile complex.

The Warren installation would have been unique in that it would not have had a Perimeter Acquisition Radar, but would have had four remote Sprint sites. The MSR installation was to be located east of Chugwater. The four RSLs were to be emplaced east of Wheatland; southeast of Chugwater; west of Springs; and west of Meridian.

Following the passage of the SALT I treaty and ABM protocol, site surveys for the Francis E. Warren complex were suspended. Safeguard deployment at Warren was formally cancelled on 2 October 1975.

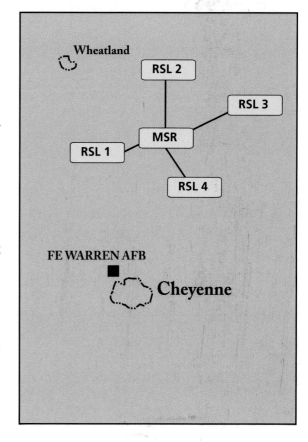

GRAND FORKS AFB, ND (Safeguard)

The Grand Forks area was initially selected for Nike-Zeus, then for Sentinel, and finally for Safeguard. The latter weapon system made it to operational status as ARADCOM's only completed assigned Safeguard complex.

Grand Forks AFB was built in the late 1950s as an Air Defense Command interceptor field and SAGE site; for a brief period, the base hosted the Grand Forks Air Defense Sector. B-52s and KC-135 tankers were introduced to the base in 1960; the base was transferred to SAC in 1963. The units the ABM site was intended to protect were the three Minuteman II/III squadrons of the 321st Strategic Missile Wing. The 319th BW(H) was also stationed at the base.

US Army SAFEGUARD Command, ARADCOM, assumed control of the Stanley R. Mickelson SAFEGUARD Complex on 1 March 1974.

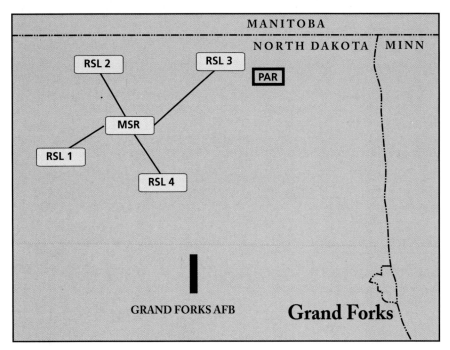

ARADCOM's responsibility for the site and all ballistic missile defense in CONUS was transferred to the Ballistic Missile Defense Program Manager (BMDPM) on 3 September 1974. Initial operational capability (IOC), with twenty-eight Sprint and eight Spartan missiles, was achieved on 1 April 1975. Full Operational Capability (FOC) was declared on 1 October 1975, with seventy Sprints and thirty Spartans. Congress decided to inactivate the site the very next day. The MSR facility was shut down in February, 1976; the PAR site was retained and loaned to the Air Force.

All components of the SAFEGUARD complex are still in place. The MSR is located east of Nekoma, ND; the PAR west of Cavalier; and the three Remote Sprint Launchers east of Hampden; northwest of Langdon; and northwest of Concrete.

HANFORD DEFENSE AREA

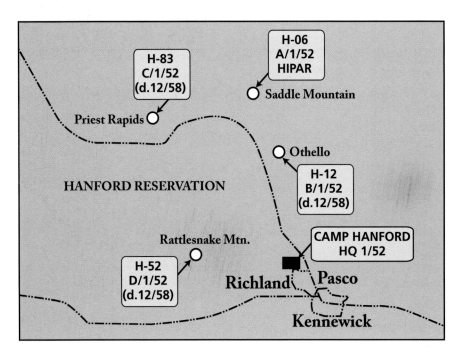

The Hanford defense was activated quickly for the purpose of protecting the massive nuclear research and weapons complex located in southeastern Washington. Camp Hanford was established in March 1950 to house the air defense units; four Regular Army 120mm gun battalions and two National Guard Special Security Force (SSF) units were assigned in short order. As with the Fairchild defense, only one of the Ajax sites was converted to Hercules. The site was later dismantled and the equipment relocated to the Norfolk Defense Area.

Site Location	Radars	Magazines, Missiles, Launchers	Convert to Herc	Units (years)
H-06		2B	5/58-	A/83d (/55-9/58)
Saddle Mountain		12H/20A	12/58	A/1/52d (9/58-12/60)
equipment to N-52, Norfolk		8L-U		
	LOC:	C - 2 S Corfu, Saddle Mountain		
		L - 5 S Corfu, N of WA 24		
	CUR:	(P) abandoned		
H-12		2B		B/83d (/55-9/58)
Othello		20A		B/1/52d (9/58-12/58)
		8L-A		
	LOC:	C - 14 SW Othello		
		L - 15 SW Othello, Grant/Franklin County Line		
	CUR:	(P) abandoned		
Camp Hanford	Manual AADCP			HQ 5th Gp (3/50-8/60)
				HHB/83d (12/54-9/58)
				HHB/1/52d (9/58-12/60)
	LOC:	10 NW Richland		
	CUR:	Hanford Works; Flour-Hanford contract operations for the Dept. of Energy. Battelle Pacific Northwest National Laboratory, Bechtel-Hanford Inc.		
H-52		2B		D/83d (/55-9/58)
Rattlesnake Mountain		20A		D/1/52d (9/58-12/58)
		8L-A		
	LOC:	C - 11 WNW Benton City, Rattlesnake Mountain		
		L - 10 NW Benton City, off of St Hwy 240		
	CUR:	C - (P) Battelle Northwest Observatory		
		L - (P) arid land reserve		
H-83		2B		C/83d (/55-9/58)
Priest Rapids		20A		C/1/52d (9/58-12/58)
		8L-A		
	LOC:	C - 8 E Desert Aire, N of WA 24		
		L - 8 E Desert Aire, N of WA 24		
	CUR:	(P) abandoned, Saddle Mountain National Wildlife Refuge		

HARTFORD DEFENSE AREA

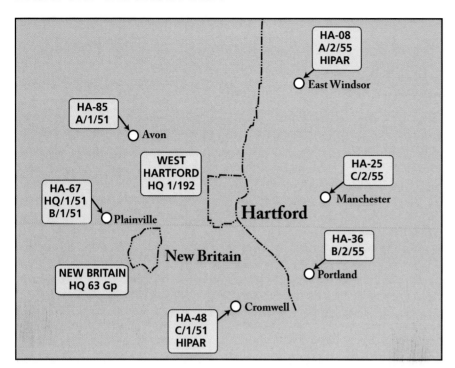

One of the four New England defenses, Hartford hosted one artillery group and two battalions, each operating three batteries. Operations at HA-67 Plainville were shared with one of the Bridgeport battalions.

The location of the capital of Connecticut on the Connecticut River helped contribute to its early development as a manufacturing and business center. Often called the "Insurance City" due to the presence of over forty major insurance companies, Harford also had several major heavy industries during the 1950s. The defense area covered Hartford and several other nearby cities including Manchester, Middletown, and New Britain. Boston's Missile Master facility at Fort Banks served as the first AADCP for the Hartford defense until its replacement by the Coventry, RI, installation. Hartford became part of the New England Defense Area in 1961.

Site Location	Radars	Magazines, Missiles, Launchers	Convert to Herc	Units (years)
HA-08	HIPAR	1B/2C	5/58-	A/11th (/56-9/58)
East Windsor/		18H/30A	1/59	A/2/55th (9/58-12/64)
Warehouse Point		10L-U		A/3/5th (12/64-11/68)
				B/1/192d (11/68-6/71)
	LOC:	C - Scantic Rd		
		L - Phelps Rd (SH 191)		
	CUR:	C – (P) Victory Outreach Ministries Church		
		L – (O) USAR Center		
HA-25		2A/1B		HHB/11th (/56-9/58)
Manchester		30A		C/11th(/56-9/58)
		12L-A		HHB/2/55th (9/58-1/61)
				C/2/55th (9/58-1/61)
	LOC:	C - 110 Garden Grove Rd		
		L – S of Line St		
	CUR:	C – (P) Town of Manchester, Recreation Center		
		L – (P) Hartford Electric Light Company		

Site Location	Radars	Magazines, Missiles, Launchers	Convert to Herc	Units (years)
HA-36		2A/1B		B/11th (/56-9/58)
Portland		30A		B/2/55th (9/58-1/61)
		12L-A		A/1/192d (1/61- /63)
	LOC:	C - off of Clark Hill Rd		
		L – N. Mulford Rd		
	CUR:	C – (O) Meskomasic State Forest		
		L – (O) Meskomasic State Forest		
HA-48	HIPAR	1A/1B/1C	7/60-	C/34th (10/56-9/58)
Cromwell		18H/30A	1/61	C/1/51st (9/58-3/61)
		12L-U		D/2/55th (3/61-8/64)
Hercules equipment from E-01		(7L-H)		B/1/192d (8/64-11/68)
	LOC:	C – End of County Squire Rd		
		L - Middletown, Mile Ln		
	CUR:	C – (O) Roncelli Christ Church; housing for the elderly		
		L – (P) USAR center		
New Britain				HQ 63d Gp (-9/61)
				HHB/2/55th(1/61-12/64)
	LOC:	Rocky Hill Rd		
HA-67		2A/1B		HHB/34th (10/56-9/58)
Plainville		30A		B/34th (10/56-9/58)
		12L-A		D/741st (/57-9/58)
				HHB/1/51st (9/58-3/61)
				B/1/51st (9/58-3/61)
				D/3/44th (9/58-3/61)
	LOC:	C - N Mountain, off Loon Lake, Metacomet Rd		
		L - Hyde Rd off Scott Swamp (US 6)		
	CUR:	C - (O) abandoned		
		L – (P) Stanley Works, Magic Door Division parking lot		
West Hartford				HHB/1/192d (5/59-6/71)
HA-85		2A/1B		A/34th (10/56-9/58)
Avon/Simsbury		30A		A/1/51st (9/58-1/61)
		12L-A		B/1/192d (1/61- /63)
	LOC:	C - 824 Montivideo Dr to Gibraltar Ln		
		L - Hilltop Dr		
	CUR:	C – (P) Talcott Mountain Service Center		
		L – (O) RWR Associates/Tower View Condominiums		

HOMESTEAD–MIAMI DEFENSE AREA

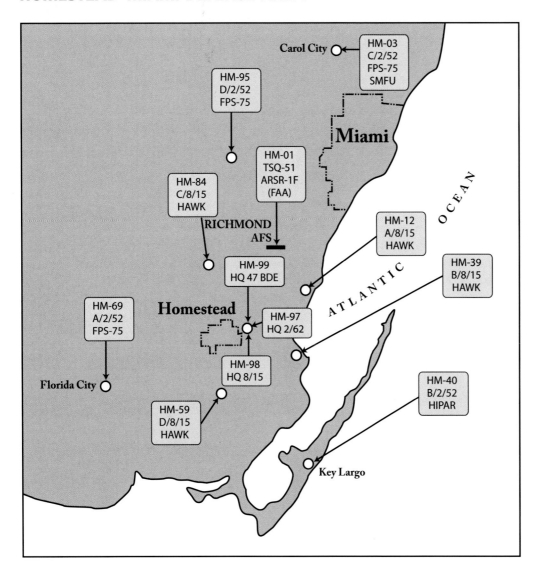

The Homestead–Miami defense was established as a result of the Cuban Missile Crisis (as was the Key West defense). Homestead-Miami featured both Nike-Hercules and HAWK battalions: the 2/52d (Nike-Hercules) relocated from Fort Bliss while the 8/15th activated on site.

Operations at Homestead AFB dated to World War II, when it served as an Air Transport Command terminal. Units assigned during the period of Nike/HAWK defenses included the 19th BW(H); 31st Tactical Fighter Wing; 4531st TFW; and 79th Airborne Early Warning and Control Squadron, which operated EC-121s. ADC's 319th Fighter Interceptor Squadron provided air defense with F-104As from 1963 to 1969. The defenses at Homestead–Miami and Key West remained operational well past the demise of ARADCOM. The transfer of the 2/52d back to Fort Bliss as a training unit in 1979 ended Nike-Hercules air defense activities in North America.

Site Location	Radars	Magazines, Missiles, Launchers	Convert to Herc	Units (years)

HM-01
Opa Locka

*Site redesignated to HM-03

Site Location	Radars	Magazines, Missiles, LaunchersConvert to Herc	Units (years)
HM-01DC **Richmond AFS**	AN/GSG-5 BIRDIE AN/TSQ-51 MISSILE MENTOR ARSR-1F 2 x AN/FPS-6	AADCP	31st Bde Det (6/71-6/79) 47th Bde Det (11/68-6/71) 13th Gp Det (10/62-11/68) USAF 644th RADS (4/60-4/78)
	LOC:	*Coral Reef Dr*	
	CUR:	*FAA JSS facility J-06 MIAMIFA was abandoned in 1992 due to Hurricane Andrew. A new radar facility was built several miles away in Tamiami, FL.*	
HM-03 **Opa Locka/** **Carol City**	ABAR/75 SMFU	3AG	C/2/52d (10/62-6/79)
	LOC:	*C- 2 WNW Carol City Red Ave at Miami Gardens Dr* *L - NW 202 Rd (NW 55th Ave), off of Red Rd (Honey Hill Dr)*	
	CUR:	*C – (O) private* *L – (I) USN; Naval Facilities Engineering Command, now private*	
HM-05 Goulds	*Site redesignated HM-12*		
HM-12 **Miami**	HAWK		A/8/15th (10/62-9/71) A/3/68th (9/71-6/79)
	LOC:	*SW 87th Ave at Hailin Mill Dr*	
	CUR:	*(I) ownership?*	
HM-39 Miami	HAWK		B/8/15th (3/65-9/71) B/3/68th (9/71-6/79)
	LOC:	*8 E Homestead AFB, SW 334th St*	
	CUR:	*(I) ownership?*	
HM-40 **Key Largo**	HIPAR	3AG	B/2/52d (6/65-6/79)
	LOC:	*FL 905 & Old Card Sound Rd*	
	CUR:	*C – (P) USN, NAVFACENGCOM* *L – (P) USN, NAVFACENGCOM*	
HM-59 Miami	HAWK		D/8/15th (6/65-9/71) D/3/68th (9/71-6/79)
	LOC:	*6 S Florida City SW 424th St*	
	CUR:	*(I) ownership?*	

Site Location	Radars	Magazines, Missiles, LaunchersConvert to Herc	Units (years)
HM-60 Miami	HAWK		D/8/15th (10/62-6/65)
	battery relocated to HM-59		
	LOC:	4 SW Florida City	
HM-65 Florida City	*site redesignated HM-66*		
HM-66 **Florida City**	HIPAR	3AG	B/2/52d (10/62-6/65)
	battery relocated to HM-40		
	LOC:	8 SW Florida City	
HM-69 **Florida City**	Mobile HIPAR	3AG	A/2/52d (6/65-6/79)
		ABAR/75	
	LOC:	12 WSW Florida City on State Rd 9336 (Launch S of Research Rd, IFC on Research Rd	
	CUR:	C&L – (I) National Park Service; Everglades National Park; nominated to Natl. Register	
HM-80 **Miami**	*site redesignated HM-84*		
HM-82 **Naranja**			HHB/8/15th (10/62-6/65)
HM-84 **Miami**	HAWK		C/8/15th (6/65-9/71) C/3/68th (9/71-6/79)
	LOC:	7 NNW Homestead Hainlin Mill Dr W. of SW 207th Ave	
	CUR:	(P) private?	
HM-85 **South Miami Heights**			HQ 13th Gp (10/62-) HHB/2/52d (10/62-)
	LOC:	Intersection SW 200th St (Caribbean Blvd) & SW 116th Ave	
HM-95 **Southwest Miami**	ABAR/75	3AG	D/2/52d (10/62-6/79)
	LOC:	C - 12 W Miami	
		L – SW 12th St, off of State Rd 997 (Krome Ave) and State Rd 41 (Tamiami Trail)	
	CUR:	C&L – (O) DOD communications facility, federal detention center	

Site Location	Radars	Magazines, Missiles, LaunchersConvert to Herc	Units (years)
HM-97 **West Homestead**			HHB/2/52d (10/62-6/79)
	LOC:	*Homestead AFB*	
	CUR:	*Homestead ARB; AFRES 482d Fighter Wing, FLANG det 1, 125th Fighter Group (alert detachment); Naval Security Group Activity Homestead*	
HM-98 **Homestead AFB**			
HM-99 **West Homestead**			HQ 31st Bde (6/71-6/79) HQ 47th Bde (11/68-6/71) HQ 13th Gp (-11/68)
	LOC:	*Homestead AFB*	
	CUR:	*Homestead ARB; as above*	

NOTE: Homestead AFB was closed following its destruction by Hurricane Andrew in 1992. The base was rebuilt for a reserve mission.

KANSAS CITY DEFENSE AREA

As part of the second round of Nike construction, the Kansas City sites covered the business, financial, industrial and rail facilities of the area as well as Richards-Gebauer AFB. The field, south of Grandview, MO, served as an ADC fighter interceptor base during the Nike period. Units assigned included HQ 29th Air Division and the 328th Fighter Wing (Air Defense). SAGE command post operations were held by HQ Kansas City Air Defense Sector. After the inactivation of KCADS in 1962, SAGE tracking data was provided by the Sioux City ADS, Sioux City, IA.

The AADCP was located at Naval Air Station Olathe, a Naval Air Reserve training base. The Air Force's 738th Radar Squadron (SAGE) was assigned to the co-located Olathe AFS.

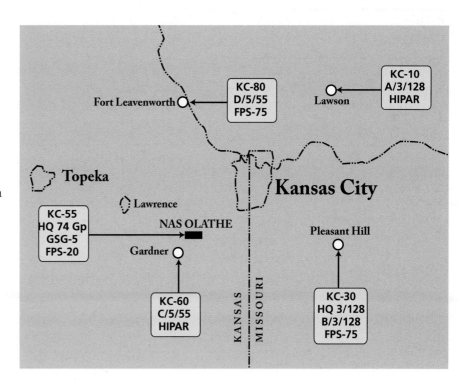

Site Location	Radars	Magazines, Missiles, LaunchersConvert to Herc	Units (years)
KC-10 **Lawson**	HIPAR	3D 18H 12L-U	A/5/55th (11/59-2/64) A/3/128th (2/64-2/69)
	LOC:	C - 1.5 E Lawson, S of W. 180th St L - 1.5 E Lawson, N. of W. 180th St	
	CUR:	C - (P) abandoned, for sale L - (P) SteamAction manufacturing plant	
KC-30 **Pleasant Hill**	ABAR/75	3D 18H 12L-U	B/5/55th (11/59-2/64) HHB/3/128th(1/64-2/69) B/3/128th (2/64-2/69)
	LOC:	C - 3 S Lone Jack, County Rd KK L - 4 SSE Lone Jack E. 163rd St at end of CR KK	
	CUR:	C - (I) abandoned L - (I) W.R. Gibson Farms; Flight Systems International rocket manufacturing	
Kansas City			HQ 74th Gp (/59- /59) HHB/5/55th (6/59- /59)
KC-60 **Gardner**	HIPAR	3D 18H 12L-U	D/5/55th (11/59-2/69)
	LOC:	C - 2 S Gardner, S. Gardner Rd, N W. 199th L - 3 S Gardner, S. Garner Rd S. W 199th	
	CUR:	C - (I) Gardner Unified School District; Nike Middle School L - (I) Gardner Unified School District	
KC-65DC **NAS Olathe**	AN/GSG 5 BIRDIE AN/FPS-20 AN/FPS-3 AN/FPS-4 2x AN/FPS-6A AN/FPS-20A	AACDP	HQ 74th Gp (/59- /69) HHB/5/55th (/59-2/69) USAF 738th RADS (2/53-9/68)
	LOC:	1.5 NNE Gardner, adjacent to former NAS Olathe	
	CUR:	(I) NARCEN Olathe; HQ Readiness Command Region 18	

Site Location	Radars	Magazines, Missiles, LaunchersConvert to Herc	Units (years)
KC-80	ABAR/75	3D	D/5/55th (11/59-2/69)
Fort Leavenworth		18H	
		12L-U	
	LOC:	C - SW Fort Leavenworth, Government Hill	
		L - NW Fort Leavenworth, Sheridan Dr	
		A - Fort Leavenworth, 5th Artillery Rd	
	CUR:	C - (P) abandoned	
		L - (P) KSArNG/Fort Leavenworth Rod & Gun Club parking lot	
		A - (I) US Army Space Institute; Medical Material Branch, Fort Leavenworth	

KEY WEST DEFENSE AREA

As with Homestead-Miami, Key West's defense was a result of the Cuban Missile Crisis; along with it's neighbor to the north, Key West remained operational after the inactivation of ARADCOM. Key West was the sole HAWK-only defense in ARADCOM. Key West had served as a Naval installation since 1822; its location only 90 miles from Cuba made it a primary staging point for American military forces (as well as a primary target) for the Cuban Missile Crisis in 1962. Naval Station Key West remained in service through 1975 as a destroyer and submarine homeport and ASW training center. Naval Air Station Key West hosted fleet aviation activities, including Reconnaissance Attack Wing One (RA-5Cs; 1974–1979).

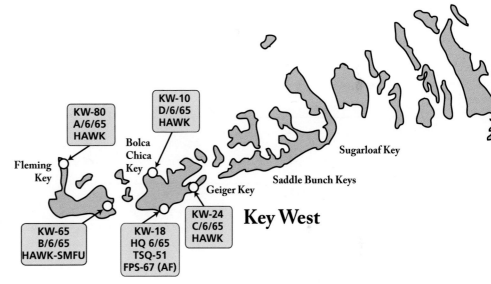

Site Location	Radars	Magazines, Missiles, LaunchersConvert to Herc	Units (years)
KW-10	HAWK		D/6/65th (10/62-9/72)
Boca Chica Key			D/l/65th (9/72-6/79)
	LOC:	I NNW NAS Key West, NAS exit off of US 1 (P) North access road	
KW-15	HAWK		C/6/65th (10/62-6/65)
Sugarloaf Key			
	LOC:	2 W Perky	
	CUR:	Southern Division, NAVFACENGCOM	

Site Location	Radars	Magazines, Missiles, LaunchersConvert to Herc	Units (years)
KW-18DC **NAS Key West**	AN/TSQ-38 Missile Monitor AN/TSQ-51 Missile Mentor AN/FPS-67 2 x AN/FPS-6	AADCP	HHB/6/65th (-9/72) HHB/1/65th (9/72-6/79) USAF 671st RADS (6/62-6/80)
	LOC:	Boca Chica Key, 5 E Key West	
	CUR:	NAS Key West: Caribbean Regional Operations Center, Joint Southern Surveillance Reconnaissance Operations Center, HQ Joint Interagency Task Force East, CGAS Key West, US Army Special Forces Underwater Training School, FAA Joint Surveillance System radar site J-07	

NOTE: The AN/TSQ-38 Battalion Operations Center was the only component of the AN/MSG-4 Missile Monitor fire distribution system employed by ARADCOM

KW-24	HAWK		C/6/65th (6/65-9/72)
Geiger Key			C/1/65th (9/72-6/79)
	LOC:	2 E NAS Key West, off of FL 941	
	CUR:	(P) Southern Division, NAVFACENGCOM, abandoned	
KW-65 **Key West**	HAWK		B/6/65th (10/62-9/72) B/1/65th (9/72-6/79)
	LOC:	N side Key West International Airport end of Government Rd	
	CUR:	(I) Southern Division, NAVFACENGCOM	
KW-80 **Fleming Key**	HAWK		A/6/65th (10/62-9/72) A/1/65th (9/72-6/79)
	LOC:	3 N Key West, N end Fleming Key end of Mustin St	
	CUR:	(P) US Army Special Forces installation	
KW-95 **Key West**			HHB/6/65th (10/62-)
	LOC:	SW Key West	
	CUR:	Southern Division, NAVFACENGCOM	

LINCOLN DEFENSE AREA

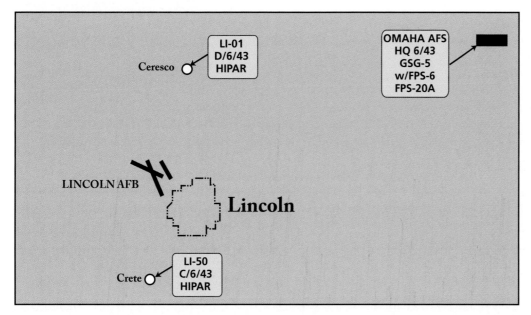

One battalion operated the Nike-Hercules sites at Nebraska's two Strategic Air Command bases, Lincoln and Offutt, due to their proximity. The battalion headquarters and AADCP were located at the Air Force long-range radar site, Omaha AFS. Lincoln AFB dated to 1954. During the Nike period the base hosted the 818th STRAD, the 551st SMS (Atlas F), and two wings of B-47s; the 98th Strategic Aerospace Wing and 307th Bombardment Wing (Medium). The base was inactivated in June 1966 following the retirement of the B-47 and was turned over to the city.

Site Location	Radars	Magazines, Missiles, Launchers	Convert to Herc	Units (years)
LI-01	HIPAR?	3AG		D/6/43d (6/60-6/66)
Ceresco/Davey		12H		
		12L-H		
	LOC:	C - Agnew Rd, 5 W US 77		
		L - end N 12th St		
	CUR:	C - (P) Raymond High School		
		L - (I) abandoned		
LI-50	ABAR/75	3AG		C/6/43d (6/60-6/66)
Crete		12L		
		12L-H		
	LOC:	C - 7800 N Roca Rd/NE 33rd		
		L - SW 72d St		
	CUR:	C - (I) Christ Town Apartments		
		L - (I) private owner		

LITTLE ROCK DEFENSE AREA

One of several Strategic Air Command bases considered for a Nike-Hercules defense, Little Rock AFB followed the pattern of other installations like Mountain Home and Malmstrom, undergoing a site survey but never receiving missiles.

The base activated on 1 February 1955 and housed two wings of B-47s; the 70th Strategic Reconnaissance Wing and 384th Bombardment Wing (Medium) fell under the operational control of the 825th Air Division. SAC also introduced a wing of Titan II

ICBMs under the 308th Strategic Missile Wing in late 1961 and—following the departure of the last B-47s—made Little Rock one of two B-58 Hustler bases.

Since 1970 Little Rock has served as the Air Force's center for C-130 training and operations with the 314th Airlift Wing conducting all C-130 crew and personnel training for the Department of Defense and several allied nations. The base also hosts the Arkansas Air National Guard's 189th Airlift Wing.

Site Location	Radars	Magazines, Missiles, Launchers	Convert to Herc	Units (years)
LR-10				
Cabot	*Site Survey Only*			
LR-80				
Conway	*Site Survey Only*			

LORING DEFENSE AREA

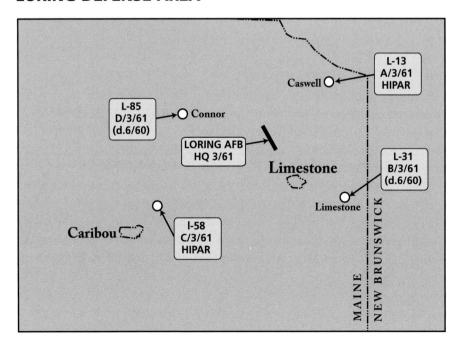

Covering the approaches to the northeastern United States, the Loring defense featured four standard Nike sites, two of which were converted to Hercules. As with the other SAC base defenses, operations were suspended in 1966. The units operational at Loring during the 1957–1966 period included the 45th Air Division, 42d Bombardment Wing (Heavy), and 27th Fighter Interceptor Squadron. Caribou Air Force Station, adjacent to the base, served as a nuclear weapon storage site. Early warning services were provided by Caswell AFS, seven miles to the northwest. The SAGE command post for the defense was located at Topsham AFS, near Brunswick, ME, under the direction of the Bangor Air Defense Sector.

Site Location	Radars	Magazines, Missiles, Launchers	Convert to Herc	Units (years)
L-13 **Caswell**	LOPAR	1B/2C 18H/30A 10L-U	6/58- 2/59	A/548th (3/57 - 9/58) A/3/61st (9/58-6/66)
	LOC:	*W. of Route 1A*		
	CUR:	*L - (I) private owner* *C - (I) private owner*		
L-31 **Limestone**		2A/1B 30A 12L-A		B/548th (3/57-9/58) 6/3/61st (9/58-6/60)
	LOC:	*C&L - N.&S. of Route 229*		
	CUR:	*C - (P) private owner* *L - (I) private owner*		
Loring AFB		Manual AADCP		HHB/548th (3/57-9/58) HHB/3/61st (9/58-6/66)
	LOC:	*3 NNW Limestone, US 1A*		
	CUR:	*Loring Commerce Center; commercial/industrial park* *NOTE: Loring AFB was inactivated 30 September 1994*		
L-58 **Caribou**	LOPAR	1B/2C 18H/30A 12L-U	6/60- 11/60	C/548th (3/57-9/58) C/3/61st (9/58-6/66)
	LOC:	*C - Albair Rd* *L - US Rt. 1*		
	CUR:	*C - (P) FAA ARSR-4 radar installation* *L - (P) VFW post*		
L-85 **Conner**		2A/1B 30A 12L-A		D/548th (3/57-9/58) D/3/61st (9/58-6/60)
	LOC:	*C&L - East of Rt. 1*		
	CUR:	*C - (?) Louis Blotner Radar Bomb Scoring Site, L. B. Communications Facility Site No. 1,* *L.B. Satellite Tracking Site 1* *L - (I) private owners*		

LOS ANGELES DEFENSE AREA

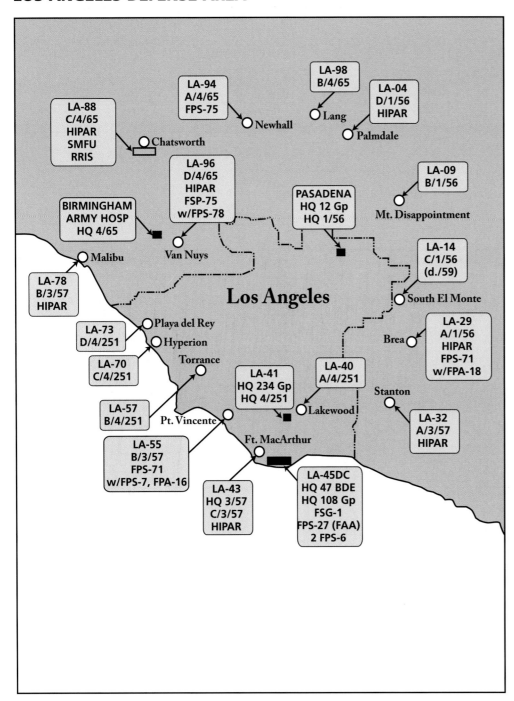

Los Angeles was one of the largest defenses, covering a large amount of territory and featuring sites that were located on ocean shore bluffs up to 8,000 foot plus mountain ridges. The defended facilities included a major portion of the nation's aerospace industry, several other large industries, shipyards, communications, transportation, and several military installations. LA had several unique features; the mountain sites had buildings with peaked roofs, due to the substantial annual snowfall. One of these sites, LA-04 Mt Gleason, was called "the world's highest Nike base," and was also considered the most remote Nike site in the continental United States. Several of the sites in the Los Angeles Defense also were threatened by forest fires.

Los Angeles was also the defense selected for initial Army National Guard Nike operations. In 1958 the California Guard's 720th Antiaircraft Missile Battalion (Nike-Ajax) acquired four sites, setting the standard for other defense areas.

The primary long-range radar for the LA defense was initially located at San Clemente Island Air Force Station; the site was later relocated to San Pedro Hill AFS, overlooking Terminal Island and Long Beach. The SAGE command post for the Los Angeles region was located at Norton AFB, near San Bernardino. Reduced from brigade to group status in November 1968, the Los Angeles defense continued operations until summer 1974.

Site Location	Radars	Magazines, Missiles, Launchers	Convert to Herc	Units (years)
LA-04 **Mount Gleason/** **Palmdale**	HIPAR	1B/2C 18H/30A 11L-U (10L-H)	6/58- 6/59	C/933d (12/55- /58) D/933d (/58-9/58) D/1/56th (9/58-12/68) A/4/65th (12/68-9/72) A/2/65th (9/72-3/74)
	LOC:	C - Mount Gleason, 9.8 W Mill Creek Forest Station		
		L - Mount Gleason, 6.8 W Mill Creek Forest Station		
	CUR:	C - (P) abandoned		
		L - (P) Los Angeles County prison camp		
		A - (P) Los Angeles County prison camp		
LA-09 **Mount Disappointment/** **Barley Flats**		2A/1B 30A 12L-A		B/933d (12/56-9/58) B/1/56th (9/58- /61)
	LOC:	C - Mount Disappointment		
		L - Barley Flats, 4 N Angeles Crest Hwy		
	CUR:	C - (P) radio relay site		
		L - (P) LA-County Sheriff Air Station		
		A- (I) youth camp/work camp		
Pasadena Army **Support Center**				HQ 12th Gp (/62) HHB/933d (12/55-9/58) HHB/1/56th (9/58-6/64)
	LOC:	126 S Grand		
	CUR:	Federal court annex, US Court of Appeals		
LA-14 **South El Monte**		2B 20A 8L-A		A/933d (12/55- /58) C/933d (/58-9/58) C/1/56th (9/58- /61)
	LOC:	C - 3600 Workman Mill Rd		
		L - 1201 N. Potrero Rd		
	CUR:	C - (O) radio relay site		
		L - (P) Los Angeles County parks workyard		
		A - (P) USAR Center		

Site Location	Radars	Magazines, Missiles, Launchers	Convert to Herc	Units (years)
LA-29 **Brea/** **Puente Hills**	HIPAR ABAR/71 AN/FPA-16	1A/1B/1C 18H/30A 12L-UA (7L-H)	12/60- 4/61	A/933d (/58-9/58) A/1/56th (9/58-4/64) C/4/251st (4/64-6/71)
	LOC:	C - Site Dr, off Central Ave, N of Brea Blvd		
		L - Site Dr, off Central Ave, N of Brea Blvd		
	CUR:	C/L - (O) Shell Oil Company; oil field; housing developments		
LA-32 **Garden Grove**	HIPAR	1B/1C 12H/20A 8L-U	6/58- 12/58	A/554th (/56-9/58) A/3/57th (9/58-6/63) A/4/251st (6/63-3/74)
	LOC:	C - SE corner Knott & Peterson		
		L - 11751 Western Ave		
	CUR:	C - (O) industrial park		
		L - (P) CAArNG; 458th MASH		
Fountain Valley * Temporary Site				8/933d (12/55- /57) C/933d (12/55- /57) D/933d (12/55- /57)
	LOC:	Fairview Rd & Fair Dr		
	CUR:	Orange County Fairgrounds		
NOTE: Former Santa Ana AFB; 1 NW John Wayne/Orange County IAP				
LA-40 **Long Beach Airport/** **Lakewood**		2A/1B 30A 12L-A		C/865th (6/55-9/58) C/4/62d (1-13 Sept 58) A/720th (9/58-5/59) A/4/251st (5/59- /63)
	LOC:	C - SW Spring & Clark		
		L - SW Spring & Lakewood		
	CUR:	C - (O) Hotel and commercial development		
		L - (O) commercial development, Kilroy Airport Center		
		A - (I) CAArNG center		
LA-41 **Signal Hill/** **Long Beach**				HQ 234th Gp (/59- /63) HHB/720th (6/57-5/59) HHB/4/251st (5/59-7/74)
	LOC:	2200 Redondo Blvd		
	CUR:	CAArNG Armory		

Site Location	Radars	Magazines, Missiles, Launchers	Convert to Herc	Units (years)
LA-43 **Fort MacArthur** **(Upper Res/White Point)**	HIPAR	1B/1C 12H/20A 8L-UA	12/60- 4/61	HHB/554th (11/54-9/58) C/554th (/56-9/58) HHB/3/57th (9/58-4/64) C/3/57th (9/58-6/63) D/4/251st (6/63-3/74)
	LOC:	C - Battery Leary-Merriam, Upper Reservation L - White Point, below Battery No. 127		
	CUR:	C - (I) City of Los Angeles; Angels Gate Park, Angels Gate Cultural Center L - (I) City of Los Angeles; White Point Park		

NOTE: Listed as a State of California Cultural and Historic Site on 08/11/2000

Site Location	Radars	Magazines, Missiles, Launchers	Convert to Herc	Units (years)
LA-45 **Fort MacArthur** **(Lower Res)**	AN/FSG-1 Missile Master AN/TSQ-51 Missile Mentor	AADCP		HQ 47th Bde (11/52-11/68) HQ 19th Gp (11/68-8/74) HQ 108th Gp (/56-9/59) HHB/55lst (8/54- /56) HHB/554th (11/54-9/68) HHB/865th (6/55-9/58) HHB/3/57th (9/58-4/64) HHB/4/62d (1-13 Sept 58)
	LOC:	Pacific Ave, between 22d and 36th Sts		
	CUR:	Los Angeles AFB Annex; housing/support activities		

Site Location	Radars	Magazines, Missiles, Launchers	Convert to Herc	Units (years)
RP-39 (Z-39) **San Pedro Hill AFS**	FAA ARSR-1 AN/FPS-27		USAF 670th RADS (4/61-4/76) 2 x AN/FPS-6 2 x AN/FPS-6A/6B	
	(AN/FPS-26A) (AN/FPS-90)			
	LOC:	Ranchos Palos Verdes, off Crest Rd		
	CUR:	FAA JSS Facility J-31 San Pedro		

Site Location	Radars	Magazines, Missiles, Launchers	Convert to Herc	Units (years)
LA-55 **Point Vicente**	ABAR/71 AN/FPS-7 AN/FPA-16	2B 12H/20A 8L-U	6/58- 12/58	D/554th (11/54-9/58) B/3/57th (9/58-4/64) B/4/251st (4/64-3/74)
	LOC:	C - SW Crenshaw & Seacrest L - between Hawthorne & Palos Verdes Dr		
	CUR:	C - (O) City of Rancho Palos Verdes; Del Cerro Park L - (I) City of Rancho Palos Verdes; city hall/admin		

Site Location	Radars	Magazines, Missiles, Launchers	Convert to Herc	Units (years)
LA-57 **Redondo Beach/** **Torrance**		2A/1B 30A 12L-A		D/865th (6/55-9/58) D/4/62d (1-13 Sept 58) B/720th (9/58-5/59) B/4/251st (9/59- /63)
	LOC:	C - 1102 Camino Real L - 30940 Crenshaw Blvd		
	CUR:	C - (O) City of Redondo Beach; Hopkins Wilderness Park L - (P) City of Torrance; Torrance Airport/Civil Air Patrol		
LA-70 **Hyperion/** **Playa del Rey**		2A/1B 30A 12L-A		A/865th (6/55-9/58) A/4/62d (1-13 Sept 58) C/720th (9/58-5/59) C/4/251st (5/59- /63)
Shared launch/admin facility with LA-73				
	LOC:	C - W of Pershing, off LAX L - 9014 Pershing Dr		
	CUR:	C - (O) private owner L - (O) Los Angeles Airport Authority A - (P) Jet Pets		
LA-73 **Playa del Rey/** **Los Angeles Airport**		2A/1B 30A 12L-A		B/865th (6/55-9/58) B/4/62d (1-13 Sept 58) D/720th (9/58-5/59) D/4/251st (5/59- /63)
Shared launch/admin facility with LA-70				
	LOC:	C - Manchester Ave & Redlands L - 9014 Pershing Dr		
	CUR:	C - (O) commercial/residential L - (O) Los Angeles Airport Authority		
LA-78 **Malibu**	HIPAR	1B/2C 18H/30A 12L-U	6/58- 6/59	B/554th (/56-9/58) B/3/57th (9/58-4/64) B/4/65th (4/64-9/72) B/2/65th (9/72-3/74)
	LOC:	C - 24666 W. Saddle Peak Rd L - 1900 Rambla Pacifica		

	CUR:	C - (O) National Park Service, Santa Monica Mountains NRA; microwave
		    communications facility
		L - (I) National Park Service, Santa Monica Mountains NRA; LA County
		    Fire Camp No. 8		

Site Location	Radars	Magazines, Missiles, Launchers	Convert to Herc	Units (years)
LA-88	HIPAR	1B/2C	5/58-	C/551st (/57-9/58)
Chatsworth/	SMFU	18H/30A	6/59	C/4/65th (9/58-9/72)
Oat Mountain	RRIS	11L-U		C/2/65th (9/72-3/74)
	LOC:	C - Oat Mountain		
		L - end of Browns Canyon Rd		
	CUR:	C - (I) abandoned, radio/communications relay site nearby		
		L - (I) State of California; abandoned		
LA-94	ABAR/75	1A/1B/1C	12/60-	A/551st (/55-9/58)
Los Pinetos/		12H/30A	6/61	A/4/65th (9/58-11/68)
Newhall		12L-UA		
		(8L-H)		
	LOC:	C - Los Angeles National Forest, Contract Point		
		L- Los Angeles National Forest W of Pacoima Res		
	CUR:	C - (P) ITT Gilfillon; radar test site		
		L - (P) ITT Gilfillon; radar test site		
		A - (P) LA County Fire Department		
Birmingham Army				HHB/551st (/56-9/58)
Hospital				HHB/4/65th (9/58-11/68)
	LOC:	6631 Balboa Ave, Van Nuys		
	CUR:	Birmingham High School, Birmingham Junior High School,		
		West Valley Special Education Center		
LA-96	HIPAR	1A/1B/1C	12/60-	D/933d (12/55- /58)
Van Nuys/	ABAR/75	18H/30	7/61	D/551st (/58-9/58)
Sepulveda	AN/FPS-78	12L-U		D/4/65th (9/58-6/71)
		(8L-H)		HHB/4/65th (/64-9/72)
				HHB/2/65th (9/72-9/74)
	LOC:	C - San Vicente Mountain, off Mulholland		
		L - 15990 Victory Blvd		
	CUR:	C - (P) San Vicente Mountain Park		
		L - (I) Sepulveda ANG Station, CAANG		
LA-98		2A/1B		B/551st (12/55-9/58)
Magic Mountain/		30A		B/4/65th (9/58- /63)
Lang/Saugus		12L-A		HHB/1/56th(6/64-12/68)
	LOC:	C - Los Angeles National Forest, Magic Mountain		
		L - Lang Station, CA 14		
	CUR:	C - (O) microwave relay site		
		L - (P) private owner; construction company		

MALMSTROM AFB, MT (Safeguard)

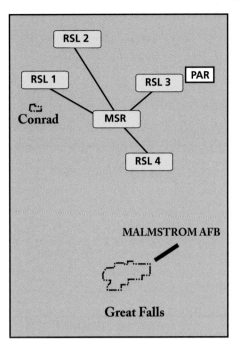

In 1958 the Air Force announced plans to deploy a squadron of BOMARCs to defend Malmstrom AFB near Great Falls, MT. One year later, Army Air Defense Command initiated site surveys for a two-battery Nike-Hercules defense at the same installation; the planned combination of both point and area missile defense systems was rare. Units at Malmstrom during this period included Strategic Air Command's 4061st Air Refueling Wing, Air defense Command's Headquarters Great Falls Air Defense Sector, and the 29th Fighter Interceptor Squadron. On 23 March 1960, BOMARC deployment was reduced to eight sites in the northeastern United States. On 18 May, the Joint Chiefs of Staff also cancelled construction of two Nike batteries.

Eight years later, Malmstrom/Great Falls was selected as the second site for the Safeguard ABM system. The Great Falls PAR installation was to be located approximately fifty miles north of that city and about fifteen miles east of Ledger, MT. The primary missile base and MSR were to be placed seven miles southeast of Conrad. The four remote Sprint batteries would be located north of Conrad; south of Shelby; east of Ledger; and east of Collins. Construction started in Montana in summer 1970; following several revisions, the planned completion date became February 1974. Following the passage of the ABM treaty in 1972 and subsequent protocol, construction of the Great Falls complex was suspended. The unfinished shell of the Perimeter Acquisition Radar remains in place east of Ledger, standing silent watch over the wheat fields.

MILWAUKEE DEFENSE AREA

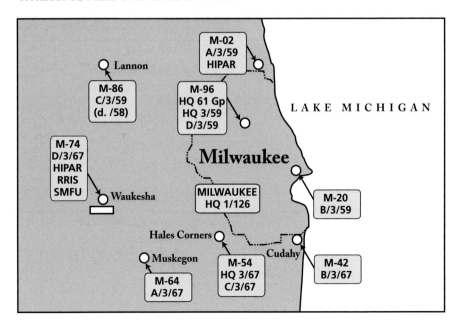

The Milwaukee defense was established with two battalions under the operational control of a single group. They protected the industrial, transportation, and governmental assets of southeastern Wisconsin (as well as the breweries). The AADCP for the Milwaukee batteries was C-80DC, Arlington Heights, in the Chicago defense. The SAGE command post for the area was located at Truax Field, Madison, WI, under the Chicago Air Defense Sector, and later, the 20th Air Division. Milwaukee was merged into the Chicago-Gary Defense Area in November 1968; the remaining Regular Army and Guard batteries continued operations until June 1971.

Site Location	Radars	Magazines, Missiles, Launchers	Convert to Herc	Units (years)
M-02 **Milwaukee**	HIPAR	1B/2C 18H/30A 12L-U	6/58- 6/59	A/852d (3/56-9/58) A/3/59th (9/58-6/71)
	LOC:	2040 W Brown Deer (River Hills)		
	CUR:	C - (O) upscale subdivision L - (O) upscale subdivision		
M-20 **Milwaukee**	LOPAR	3B 18H/30A 12L-U	6/58- 10/58	B/852d (3/56-9/58) B/3/59th (9/58-6/71)
	LOC:	1200 N. Harbor Dr		
	CUR:	C - (O) destroyed L - (O) Summerfest Park on lake front		
M-42 **Cudahy**		2A/1B 30A 12L-A		B/401st (5/56-9/58) B/3/67th (9/58-8/61)
	LOC:	6100 S Lake		
	CUR:	L- (O) golf course C- (P) ownership?		
M-54 **Hales Corners/** **Paynesville**		2A/1B 30A 12L-A		HHB/401st (5/56-9/58) C/401st (5/56-9/58) HHB/3/67th (9/58-8/61) C/3/67th (9/58-8/61)
	LOC:	2400 W Ryan		
	CUR:	(O) private		
M-64 **Muskego/** **Prospect**		2A/1B 30A 12L-A		A/852d (3/56- /57) A/401st (/57-9/58) A/3/67th (9/58-2/61) A/1/126th (2/61-3/63)
	LOC:	C - Martin Dr L - End of Adrian Dr off of Williams Dr		
	CUR:	C - (P) private owner L - (P) private owner		

Site Location	Radars	Magazines, Missiles, Launchers	Convert to Herc	Units (years)
M-74 **Waukesha**	HIPAR RRIS	1B/2C 18H/30A 12L-U	6/58- 8/59	B/852d (3/56- /57) D/401st (/57-9/58) D/3/67th (9/58-8/61) C/3/59th (8/61-6/64) B/2/126th (6/64-6/71)
	LOC:	C – S. of Davidson Rd		
			L – W. Cleveland Ave	
	CUR:	C - (P) Hillcrest Park L - (O) Missile Park		
M-86 **Lannon**		2A/1B 30A 12L-A		C/852d (3/56-9/58) C/3/59th (9/58-8/61)
	LOC:	C - Lannon Rd (Menomonee Falls) L - Menomonee Rd & Lannon Rd		
	CUR:	C - (P) Menomenee Park Headquarters L - (I) private owner		
M-96 **Milwaukee**		2A/1B 30A 12L-A		HQ 61st Gp (/55-8/61) HHB/852d (3/56-9/58) D/852d (3/56-9/58) HHB/3/59th (9/58-6/71) D/3/59th (9/58-3/61) B/1/126th (3/61-3/63) HHB/2/126th(3/63-6/71)
	LOC:	C - 4228 Silver Spring L - 5010 Silver Spring (N. Hopkins at W. Douglas Ave)		
	CUR:	L - (O) flood pond retention, parking lot?		
Milwaukee				HHB/1/126th (/59-3/63)

MINNEAPOLIS-ST PAUL DEFENSE AREA

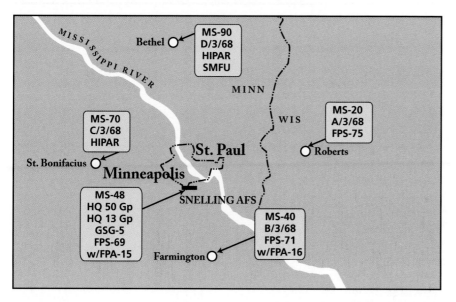

The Twin Cities defense was built for Hercules operations and served for twelve years. The missiles effectively replaced an Air Defense Command squadron of F-89s, based at Minneapolis-St Paul International Airport. The AADCP was located at Fort Snelling/Snelling Air Force station.

The fort dated to 24 August 1819 and saw use as a frontier outpost, supply base, and recruit training center. The Air Force acquire a portion of the post for use as headquarters of the 31st Air Division and as an aircraft control and warning squadron activation and training site. Long-range detection services were provided to the defense by Osceola AFS, WI, approximately forty miles to the north-northeast on the St Croix River. The SAGE command post for the region was located at Duluth Airport.

Site Location	Radars	Magazines, Missiles, Launchers	Convert to Herc	Units (years)
MS-20	ABAR/75	3D		A/3/68th (10/59-6/71)
Roberts		18H		
		12L-U		
	LOC:	C - 2.5 N Roberts, E of N 120th St		
		L - 3.5 N Roberts, W. of N 120th St		
	CUR:	C - (I) Nike Storage Center		
		L - (I) private owner		
MS-40	ABAR/71	3D		B/3/68th (10/59-6/71)
Farmington		18H		
		12L-U		
	LOC:	C – W. of Alvanero St		
		L – S. of 260st St W		
	CUR:	C - (I) private owner		
		L - (I) Govt. property		
MS-48DC	AN/GSG-5			HQ 50th Gp (/59-11/68)
Snelling AFS	BIRDIE			HQ 13th Gp (11/68-6/71)
	AN/FPA-69			HHB/3/68th (10/59-6/71)
	LOC:	S Minneapolis, I 494		
	CUR:	(O) National Cemetery		

NOTE: located in former Air-Defense Control Center building. BIRDIE blockhouse destroyed

Site Location	Radars	Magazines, Missiles, LaunchersConvert to Herc	Units (years)
MS-70 **St Bonifacius**	HIPAR	3D 18H 12L-U	C/3/68th (10/59-6/71)
	LOC:	C – Nike Rd L – W. CR 127	
	CUR:	C – (I) private owner L – (I) private?	
MS-90 **Bethel/Ishanti**	HIPAR	3D 18H 12L-U	D/3/68th (10/59-6/71)
	LOC:	C – end of Dahlia St NW, S. of 261st Ave NW L – 261st Ave NW at Lily StNW	
	CUR:	C - Ishanti County Sheriffs Department L – (P) private owner	

MOUNTAIN HOME DEFENSE AREA

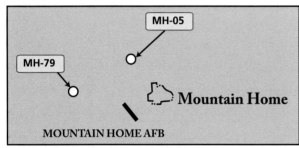

As with Malmstrom AFB, SAC's Mountain Home AFB was surveyed for a Nike-Hercules installation. Prior to cancellation, the 6th Missile Battalion of the 51st Artillery was selected to operate the two sites. The battalion was never activated.

Units assigned to Mountain Home included the 813th Air Division, 9th Strategic Aerospace Wing, and the 569th Strategic Missile Squadron; the latter's three Titan I complexes are identified for information purpos-

Site Location	Radars	Magazines, Missiles, LaunchersConvert to Herc	Units (years)
MH-05 Mountain Home *Site survey only*			
	LOC:	C - 8 NNE Mountain Home AFB, S of I 80 L - 8 N Mountain Home AFB, S of I 80	
	CUR:	range	
MH-79 Mountain Home *Site survey only*			
	LOC:	C - 10 WNW Mountain Home AFB, Dorsey Butte L - 11 WNW Mountain Home AFB	
	CUR:	range	

NEW YORK DEFENSE AREA

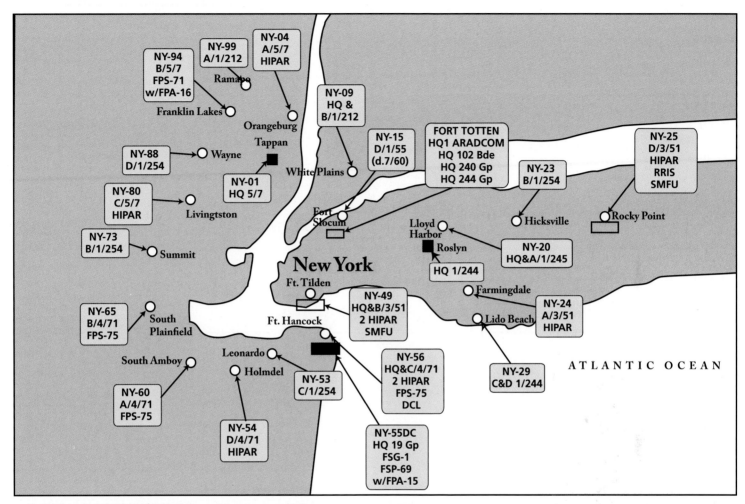

New York was the linchpin of the northeastern defenses; the initial Nike-Ajax laydown consisted of nineteen firing batteries (including three double-Ajax sites), two brigades, three groups, and five Regular Army battalions. Following the transfer of several batteries to the Guard, the number of battalions increased to ten. New York also hosted the First ARADCOM region for several years.

The original AADCP for New York was a manual installation at Fort Wadsworth, one of four fortifications in the defense area. The Missile Master installation was at Highlands Air Force Station (later Army Air Defense Base) on the north Jersey Shore.

The SAGE command post for the region was at Stewart AFB, near Newburgh on the Hudson River.

In the long run, New York was just as susceptible to personnel and battery reductions as the other defense areas; perhaps more so, considering its extent. The defense was merged with Philadelphia in September 1966, when the Missile Master at PH-64, Pedricktown, NJ, was inactivated. However, the last Regular Army Nike-Hercules battalion to man New York batteries was Philadelphia's 3/43d.

Site Location	Radars	Magazines, Missiles, Launchers	Convert to Herc	Units (years)
NY-01 **Tappan**				HHB/737th (3/56-9/58) HHB/5/7th (9/58-11/68)
	LOC:	Western Hwy		
	CUR:	USAR Center		
NY-03/04 **Orangeburg/** **Mount Nebo** DOUBLE SITE	HIPAR	3A/2B/1C 18H/60A 24L-UA (12L-H)	5/58- 12/58	A/66th (/55-1/57) A/737th (1/57-9/58) A/5/7th (9/58-6/64) C/1/244th (6/64-4/74)
	LOC:	C - Mt Nebo, W of US 9W Nike Ln off of Tweed Blvd (2 separate IFC sites) L - Palisades Pkwy & NY 303		
	CUR:	C - (P) City of Orangeburg; park L - (I) USAR Center; 812th Military Police Company		
NY-04R **Orangeburg Section No. 2**				52d Arty Bde Radar
	LOC:	Mt Nebo, W of US 9W		
	CUR:	(P) City of Orangeburg; park		
NY-09 **Kensico/** **White Plains** **Harrison**		2A/1B 30A 12L-A		B/66th (/55-9/58) B/1/55th (9/58-6/60) HHB/773d (/58-3/59) HHB/1/212th(3/59-3/63) B/1/212th (6/60-3/63)
	LOC:	C – Quarry Hieghts, off Route 22 L - Park Ln between Indian Hill Rd & Burns Rd		
	CUR:	C – (P) Town of Harrison L – (O) NYANG		
Fort Totten **(9/50-6/64)**				HQ First ARADCOM Region HQ 102d Bde (/59- /63) HQ 7th Gp (10/65-12/65) HQ 240th Gp (/59- /63) HQ 244th Gp (/59- /63) HHB/66th (8/54-9/58) HHB/1/55th (9/58-7/60)
	LOC:	N Queens, off Cross Island Pkwy		
	CUR:	City of New York		

Site Location	Radars	Magazines, Missiles, Launchers	Convert to Herc	Units (years)
		NOTE: Headquarters, Eastern Defense Command during WWII		
NY-15		2B		D/66th (/55-9/58)
Fort Slocum		20A		D/1/55th (9/58-7/60)
		8L-A		
	LOC:	*C - Davids Island*		
		L - Hart Island		
	CUR:	*C - (P) City of New Rochelle; private development planned*		
		L - (P) City of New York Dept. of Corrections		
NY-20		2A/1B		A/66th 1/57-9/58)
Lloyd Harbor/		30A		A/1/55th (9/58-6/60)
Huntington		12L-A		HHB/1/245th(3/59-4/63)
				A/1/245th (3/59-4/63)
	CUR:	*C - (O) private owner*		
		L - (O) private owner		
Roslyn ANGS				HHB/259th (2/58-3/59)
				HHB/1/244th(3/59-9/74)
	LOC:	*Roslyn Heights, N of NY 495*		
	CUR:	*Roslyn ANGS; scheduled for closure*		
NY-23		2A/1B		C/66th (/55-9/58)
Hicksville/Oyster Bay		30A		C/1/55th (9/58-6/60)
		12L-A		B/1/245th (6/60-4/63)
	LOC:	*C - W of NY 107/Cedar Swamp Rd (McClean Dr?)*		
		L - W of Brookville Rd, N of NY 106		
	CUR:	*C - (O) housing development*		
		L - (P) Nassau Board of Cooperative Education; Brookville Nature Park and		
		Outdoor Education Center		
NY-24	HIPAR	3B	5/58-	A/505th (/57-9/58)
North Amityville/		18H/30A	6/59	A/3/51st (9/58-6/64)
Farmingdale		12L-U		A/1/244th (6/64-7/74)
	LOC:	*L - Baiting Place Rd, S. of Allen Blvd, Farmingdale*		
		C - off Albany Rd, S. of New Hwy		
	CUR:	*C - (P) NYANG Training Center*		
		L - (I) USAR motor pool		

Site Location	Radars	Magazines, Missiles, Launchers	Convert to Herc	Units (years)
NY-25 **Rocky Point/** **Brookhaven**	HIPAR SMFU RRIS LOC: CUR:	1B/2C 18H/30A 10L-U C - between Wading River Manor Rd & NY 46, S of NY 25A L – Major Braxton Mem. Ave, and Cpl Tony Casamento Hwy C - (P) abandoned L - (I) Rocky Point USAR Center H - (I) City of Brookhaven; Harry Chapin Inn homeless shelter	5/58- 6/59	D/505th (/57-9/58) D/3/51st (9/58-6/64) B/1/244th (6/64-6/71)
NY-29/30 **Lido Beach** DOUBLE SITE	 LOC: CUR:	4A/2B 60A 24L-AA C - end of Blackheath Rd, Lido Beach L - N. of Lido Blvd C - (O) nature park L - (I) Long Beach School District		C/505th (/55-9/58) C/3/51st (9/58-12/60) C/1/244th (12/60- /63) D/1/244th (12/60- /63)
NY-49 **Fort Tilden** DOUBLE SITE (HERC)	2x HIPAR SMFU LOC: CUR:	4B 18H/40A 16L-U C&L - Rockaway Point Rd C - (O) National Park Service; Gateway National Recreation Area L - (P) National Park Service; Gateway National Recreation Area	3/58- 9/58	HHB/505th (6/54-9/58) B/505th (/55-9/58) HHB/3/51st (9/58-6/64) B/3/51st (9/58-9/72) B/1/51st (9/72-6/73) D/3/43d (6/73-4/74)
NY-53 **Leonardo/** **Belford**	 LOC: CUR:	2A/1B 30A 12L-A C - N of Highlands Rd, 0.5 E of Sleepy Hollow L - 0.5 S Highlands Rd, E of US Govt Railroad (Kings Hwy E.?) C - (O) Naval Weapons Station, Earle L - (O) housing		B/526th (/57-9/58) B/4/71st (9/58-6/60) C/1/254th (6/60-4/63)

Site Location	Radars	Magazines, Missiles, Launchers	Convert to Herc	Units (years)
NY-54	HIPAR	1A/2B	5/58-	D/526th (/57-9/58)
Homdel/Hazlet		30A	3/59	D/4/71st (9/58-6/64)
		12L-A		D/3/51st (6/64-11/68)
	LOC:	C - off Telegraph Hill Rd		
		L - N of NJ 34 off Homdel Rd		
	CUR:	C - (O) Phillips Park; communications facility, Admin area intact		
		L - (O) Holmdel County Park		
NOTE:		rare "hardened" site with heavily constructed blast-resistant structures at both the IFC and launch areas. Specially built protection for the control vans		
NY-55DC	AN/FSG-1	AADCP		HQ 52d Bde (11/68-6/71)
Highlands	Missile			HQ 19th Gp (12/61-11/68)
AFS/AADB	Master			HQ 16th Gp (6/71-9/74)
	AN/TSQ-51			HHB/3/51st (11/68-9/72)
	AN/TSQ-51			HHB/3/51st (11/68-9/72)
	Missile			HHB/1/51st (9/72-6/73)
	Mentor			USAF 646th RADS (SAGE)
	AN/FPS-69			(3/51-7/66)
	AN/FPA-15			
	AN/CPS-6/6B			
	AN/FPS-8			
	AN/GPS-3/3B			
	2 x AN/FPS-6/6B			
	(AN/FPS-26A)			
	(AN/FPS-90)			
	AN/FPS-7			
	LOC:	Portland Rd, 1S Navesink Twin Lights		
	CUR:	(O) Rocky Point Section, Hartshorne Woods County Park		
NY-56	2x HIPAR	4B	5/58-	HQ 52d Bde(/60-11/68)
Fort Hancock	ABAR/75	24H/40A	4/59	HQ 254th Gp(/59- /63)
DOUBLE SITE (HERC)	DCL	16L-UU		HHB/526th (2/54-9/58)
				C/526th (/55-9/58)
				HHB/4/71st (9/58-6/64)
				C/4/71st (9/58-6/64)
				HHB/3/51st(6/64-11/68)
				C/3/51st (6/64-6/71)
	LOC:	C - 3S Fort Hancock, Sandy Hook		
		L - 4S Fort Hancock, Sandy Hook		
	CUR:	C - (I) National Park Service; Gateway National Recreation Area		
		L - (I) National Park Service maintenance yard		

Site Location	Radars	Magazines, Missiles, Launchers	Convert to Herc	Units (years)
Fort Wadsworth		Manual AADCP		HQ 52d Bde (6/52- /60)
				HQ 80th Gp (-6/64)
	LOC:	*Bay & Seaside, Staten Island*		
	CUR:	*National Park Service, Gateway National Recreation Area*		
		NOTE: Former Naval Station New York, recently closed		
NY-58/60	ABAR/75	2B	1/61-	A/526th (/55-9/58)
South Amboy		12H/20A	5/61	A/4/71st (9/58-6/64)
		8L-U		A/3/51st (6/64-11/68)
	LOC:	*C - Jake Brown Rd, 1W of US 9*		
		L - Jake Brown Rd, 0.1 W of US 9		
	CUR:	*C - (O) open field*		
		L - (O) Old Bridge Township Board of Education		
NY-60R				52d Arty Bde Radar
South Amboy Section No. 1				
	CUR:	*(O) obliterated*		
Camp Kilmer				HHB/483d (3/55-9/58)
				HHB/2/65th (9/58-7/60)
	LOC:	*2 E New Brunswick*		
	CUR:	*state/commercial use*		
NY-65	ABAR/75	2B	1/61-	B/483d (/55-9/58)
South Plainfield		12H/20A	5/61	B/2/65th (9/58-7/60)
		8L-U		B/4/71st (7/60-4/63)
				C/7/112th (4/63-6/71)
	LOC:	*C - N of I 287, E of Durham*		
		L - Hadley Rd & Durham Rd		
	CUR:	*C - (O) Hadley Plaza office park*		
		L - (O) field		
NY-73		2A/1B		A/483d (3/55-9/58)
Summit/		30A		A/2/65th (9/58-7/60)
Watchung		12L-A		HHB/1/254th(5/59-4/63)
				B/1/254th (9/59-4/63)
	LOC:	*C - N of NJ 78*		
		L - Summit Ln		
	CUR:	*C - (O) Governor Livingston High School*		
		L - (O) Watchung Stables, Union County Park Commission		

Site Location	Radars	Magazines, Missiles, Launchers	Convert to Herc	Units (years)
NY-80R **Morristown**				Radar Section, 2/65th
NY-80 **Livingston/** **Essex Fells** **East Hannover** DOUBLE SITE	HIPAR	3A/2B/1C 18H/60A 23L-UA (12L-H)	5/58- 6/59	C/483d (3/55-9/58) C/2/65th (9/58-7/60) C/5/7th (7/60-4/63) HHB/7/112th(3/63-6/71) B/7/112th (4/63-6/71) HHB/1/254th(6/71-9/74) B/1/254th (6/71-4/74)
	LOC:	C – off of Beaufort Ave, off Eisenhower L – Nike Dr off of River Rd & NJ 10, East Hannover		
	CUR:	C - (P) Riker Hill Park, studios L - (O) housing development		
NY-88 **Mountain View/** **Wayne/Packanack Lakes**	12L-A	2A/1B 30A	D/1/254th (9/59-4/63)	D/483d (3/55-9/58) D/2/65th (9/58-9/59)
	LOC:	C - Ratzer Rd & Alps Rd L – off of NJ 23, N of I 80		
	CUR:	C - (I) development planned L - (P) Passaic County		
NY-93/94 **Ramsey/** **Darlington/** **Mahwah** DOUBLE SITE	ABAR/71 AN/FPA-16	2A/4B 18H/60A 24L-UA (12L-H)	5/58- 5/59	A/483d (3/55- /58) B/737th (/58/-9/58) B/5/7th (9/58-11/68) D/7/112th (11/68-6/71)
	LOC:	C - Campgaw Mountain; end of Shadow Ridge Rd L - 1S Darlington, W side Campgaw Rd		
	CUR:	C - (P) stables, Bergen County Parks; Saddle Ridge Horseback Riding Area L - (O) abandoned, A - (I) to be developed		
NY-99 **Spring Valley/** **Ramapo**		3B 30A 12L-A		C/737th (3/56-9/58) C/5/7th (9/58-6/60) A/1/112th (6/60- /63)
	LOC:	C - Grandview Ave L – Applegate Ln off of New Hempstead Rd		
	CUR:	C - (P) East Ramapo School District; warehouses L - (P) East Ramapo School District; school bus maintenance		

NIAGARA FALLS DEFENSE AREA

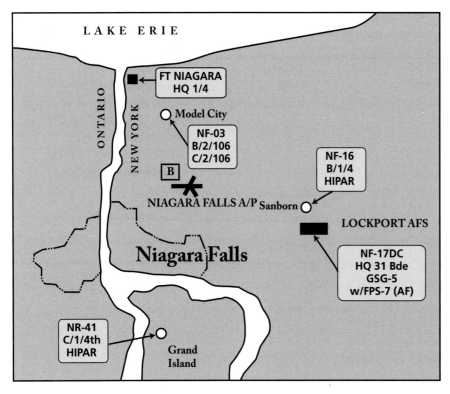

Niagara Falls, the northern half of the ARADCOM laydown in western New York, was merged with Buffalo on 15 December 1961, forming the Niagara Falls–Buffalo Defense Area. Until the merger, the headquarters for the defense area was Fort Niagara. The first fortification on the site dated to 1679; it served with the Army from 1796 until 1945, when it was turned over to the New York State Parks. The Army leased Fort Niagara in 1953, specifically as the manual command post for the coming Nike batteries. The post was returned to the state on 30 June 1962.

The primary AADCP for the Niagara Falls–Buffalo defense was located at Lockport AFS. SAGE-generated early warning and tracking data was provided by the NORAD command post at Hancock Field, Syracuse, NY. Niagara Falls International Airport hosted both ADC interceptor operations, from November 1952 to July 1960; and BOMARC B operations under the 35th Air Defense Missile Squadron, from June 1960 to December 1969.

Site Location	Radars	Magazines, Missiles, Launchers	Convert to Herc	Units (years)
Fort Niagara	Manual AADCP		HQ 2d Gp (3/58-12/61)	
				HHB/44th (3/53-9/58)
				HHB/465th (9/56- /56)
				HHB/1/4th (9/58-6/62)
	LOC:	3 NW Youngstown; on Lake Erie		
	CUR:	State park		
NF-03		4A/2B		A/44th (3/55-9/58)
Model City		60A		A/1/4th (9/58-7/60)
DOUBLE SITE		24L-AA		B/2/106th (7/60-3/63)
				C/2/106th (7/60-3/63)
	LOC:	C - Porter Center Rd & Langdon Rd		
		L - Balmer Rd & Porter Center Rd		
	CUR:	C - (P) private? abandoned		
		L - (P) USAF Youngstown Test Site, abandoned		

Site Location	Radars	Magazines, Missiles, Launchers	Convert to Herc	Units (years)
NF-16 **Sanborn/** **Cambria** DOUBLE SITE	HIPAR	3A/2B/1C 18H/60A 24L-UA (11L-H)	5/58- 5/59	B/44th (3/55-9/58) B/1/4th (9/58-3/70)
	LOC:	C - Shawnee Rd, S of Upper Mountain Rd		
		L - Upper Mountain Rd & Cambria Rd		
	CUR:	C - (I) Franklin Transportation Company		
		L - (I) Cambria Town Hall; vehicle maintenance yard; senior citizen's housing		
NF-16R Cambria				Radar Section, 2d Arty Gp
	LOC:	Shawnee Rd, S of Upper Mountain Rd		
	CUR:	(I) BOCES		
NF-17DC **Lockport AFS**	AN/GSG-5 BIRDIE AN/FSG-1 MISSILE MASTER AN/FPS-1 AN/CPS-6B 2x AN/FPS-6/6A AN/FPS-7 AN/FPS-26	AADCP		HQ 31st Bde (12/61-9/66) HQ 18th Gp (11/68-3/70) HQ 101st Gp (9/66-3/70) HHB/1/4th (6/62-3/70) USAF 763d RADS (1/51-6/79)
	LOC:	Shawnee Rd/NY 425, S of Sanders Settlement Rd		
	CUR:	(I) private owners; portions abandoned		
NF-41 **Grand Island**	HIPAR	2B/1C 18H 11L-U	5/58- 4/59	C/1/4th (4/59-4/63) A/2/209th (4/63-3/70)
	LOC:	C - S of White Haven Rd E of West River Pkwy		
		L - Staley Rd E of West River Pkwy		
	CUR:	C - (I) Town of Grand Island Nike Base Park/Senior Citizen Center		
		L - (I) Eco Island Ecology Reserve		

NOTE: Former dual NF-74/75, redesignated to NF-41 following conversion to Hercules

Site Location	Radars	Magazines, Missiles, Launchers	Convert to Herc	Units (years)
NF-74 Grand Island *dual site; shared launch facility with NF-75* *redesignated NF-41*		1A/2B 30A 12L-A		C/44th (3/55-9/58) C/1/4th (9/58-4/59)
NF-75 Grand Island *dual site; shared launch facility with NF-75* *redesignated NF-41*		2A/1B 30A 12L-A		D/44th (3/55-9/58) D/1/4th (9/58-4/59)

NORFOLK DEFENSE AREA

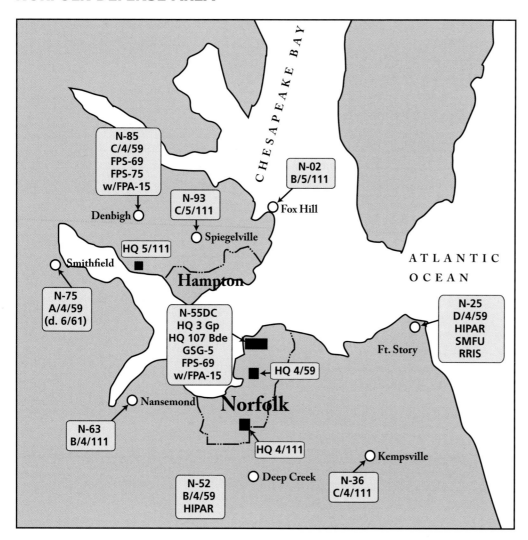

The Norfolk defense was initially constituted with two Nike-Ajax battalions covering the Hampton Roads/James River area of Virginia known as Tidewater. Two Army National Guard battalions acquired several Ajax sites in fall 1959; Battery B, 4th Missile Battalion, 111th Artillery, had the honor of retiring the Ajax from ARADCOM at site N-63 Nansemond.

Like the Niagara Falls defense, Norfolk hosted the two competing SAM systems; the 22d ADMS operated BOMARC from a site in Newport News from September 1958 through October 1972. Early warning for the Tidewater air defense missile installations was provided by Cape Charles AFS on the Delmarva Peninsula; the SAGE command post was located at Fort Lee AFS, near Petersburg. Concurrent with the inactivation of the Hampton Roads AADCP in June 1971, Norfolk was merged with Washington-Baltimore.

Site Location	Radars	Magazines, Missiles, Launchers	Convert to Herc	Units (years)
N-02		2A/1B		A/56th (3/55-9/58)
Fox Hill		30A		A/4/51st (9/58-3/60)
		12L-A		B/5/111th (3/60-3/63)
	LOC:	C - NE Hampton, Windmill Point Ln off of Beach Rd		
		L - end of Grundland Dr off of Beach Rd		
	CUR:	C - (P) Hampton City School District maintenance		
		L - (I) private owner		

Site Location	Radars	Magazines, Missiles, Launchers	Convert to Herc	Units (years)
N-08 **Fort Monroe**				HHB/56th (3/55-9/58) HHB/4/51st (9/58-7/60)
	LOC:	*Old Point Comfort, Hampton*		
	CUR:	*Fort Monroe; HQ Training & Doctrine Command, US Army ROTC Cadet Command,* *Virginia Operational Support Airlift Command*		

NOTE: Battery DeRussy serves as a Coast Artillery Corps memorial

Site Location	Radars	Magazines, Missiles, Launchers	Convert to Herc	Units (years)
N-20 **Ocean View**		3AG 12A 12L-A		D/38th (1/55- /57)

Temporary site; battery ops to Fort Story

	LOC:	*Ocean View Ave*		
	CUR:	*residential/commercial*		

Site Location	Radars	Magazines, Missiles, Launchers	Convert to Herc	Units (years)
N-25 **Fort Story** **(N-29)**	HIPAR SMFU RRIS	2B/1C 18H/6030A 12L-UA (8L-H)	5/58- 5/59	D/38th (/57-9/58) D/5/59th (9/58-6/71) HHB/4/59th (/64-6/71) B/4/1st (6/71-4/74)
	LOC:	*C - Atlantic & Vung Tau* *L – Desert Rd off of Al JubaylRd.*		
	CUR:	*C - (I) USMC/Amphibious Reconnaissance Training Board* *L - (I) USAR 159th Transportation Group (Det)(not DS? 2nd set of launchers destroyed?)*		

Site Location	Radars	Magazines, Missiles, Launchers	Convert to Herc	Units (years)
N-36 **Kempsville** **(N-49)**		2A/1B 30A 12L-A		C/38th (1/55-9/58) C/4/59th (9/58-9/59) C/4/111th (9/59-11/64)
	LOC:	*C – N of Lynnhaven Pkwy, 2.3 W of Salem* *L – S of Lynnhaven Pkwy, .8 W of Salem*		
	CUR:	*C - (P) City of Virginia Beach Parks & Recreation Department; admin* *L - (P) City of Virginia Beach Parks & Recreation Department; vehicle maintenance*		

Site Location	Radars	Magazines, Missiles, Launchers	Convert to Herc	Units (years)
Ballentine School				HHB/38th (1/55-9/58) HHB/4/59th (9/58- /59)
	LOC:	*Ballentine Blvd & Dana St*		
	CUR:	*Ballentine Elementary School*		

Site Location	Radars	Magazines, Missiles, Launchers	Convert to Herc	Units (years)
Reidsville/ **South Norfolk**				HHB/615th (2/58-6/59) HHB/4/111th (6/59-11/64)
	LOC:	*probably Bainbridge Blvd & Falcon Ave*		

Site Location	Radars	Magazines, Missiles, Launchers	Convert to Herc	Units (years)
Craddock Branch/ **Portsmouth**				HHB/4/59th (/59-12/61)
N-52 **Deep Creek/** **Portsmouth**	HIPAR	2B 18H/30A 8L-UA	6/60- 9/60	B/38th (1/55-9/58) B/4/59th (9/58-12/64) HHB/4/111th(11/64-8/74) B/4/111th (12/64-4/74)

Hercules equipment transferred from H-06

	LOC:	C - Minuteman Dr, N of Number 10 L - end of Sentry Rd S of Number 10		
	CUR:	C - (P) Chesapeake Alternative School L - (P) Public Safety Training Center		

N-55DC **Hampton Roads** **Army Terminal**	AN/GSG-5 BIRDIE AN/FPS-69 AN/FPA-15			HQ 107th Bde (/59- /63) HQ 3d Gp (3/58-12/61) HQ 100th Gp (/64-11/68) HQ 17th Gp (11/68-6/71)
	LOC:	7739 Hampton Blvd		
	CUR:	(O) Norfolk International Terminals		

N-63 **Nansemond/** **Suffolk** **(N-69)**		1A/2B 30A 12L-A		A/38th (1/55-9/58) A/4/59th (9/58-9/59) B/4/111th (9/59-11/64)
	LOC:	C - Bennetts Creek Park Rd, S of Bridge L - end of Bennets Creek Park Rd, 1 W of N-63C		
	CUR:	C - (O) USAR Center L - (O) Bennett's Creek Park		

NOTE: Last CONUS Ajax site; missiles released 18 November 1964

N-75 **Smithfield/** **Carrollton**		2A/1B 30A 12L-A		D/56th (3/55-9/58) D/4/51st (9/58-7/60) A/4/59th (7/60-6/61)
	LOC:	C - Boundary Rd & Wood Duck Rd L - Nike Park Rd & Titus Creek		
	CUR:	C - (P) Isle of Wight County; Jones Creek Dump Site L - (P) Carrolton Nike Park; Isle of Wight County Public Recreation Authority		

N-85 **Denbigh/**	ABAR/69 ABAR/75	1A/2B 18H/30A	3/60- 8/60	C/56th (3/55-9/58) C/4/51st (9/58-7/60)

Site Location	Radars	Magazines, Missiles, Launchers	Convert to Herc	Units (years)
Patrick Henry/ Camp Patrick (N-97)	AN/FPA-15	12L-UA (8L-H)		C/4/59th (7/60-12/64) C/4/111th (12/64-4/74)
	LOC:	*C - Newport News-Williamsburg International Airport; end of Cherokee Dr*		
		L - Denbigh Blvd & MacManus Blvd		
	CUR:	*C - (P) Peninsula Airport Commission; abandoned*		
		L - (O) Mary Immaculate Hospital/Warwick Forest Retirement Home		
N-93 Hampton/ Spiegelville (N-99)		2A/1B 30A 12L-A		B/56th (4/55-9/58) B/4/51st (9/58-3/60) C/5/111th (3/60-3/63)
	LOC:	C - N of Marcella Rd, E of VA 172		
		L - S of Hampton Roads Pkwy, E of Airborne Dr		
	CUR:	C - (P) USAR 359th Transportation Company (site scheduled for demolition)		
		L - (P) USAR 302d Transportation Company		
Newport News				HHB/5/111th (6/59-3/63)
	LOC:	*probably near Warwick & 25th*		

OAHU DEFENSE AREA

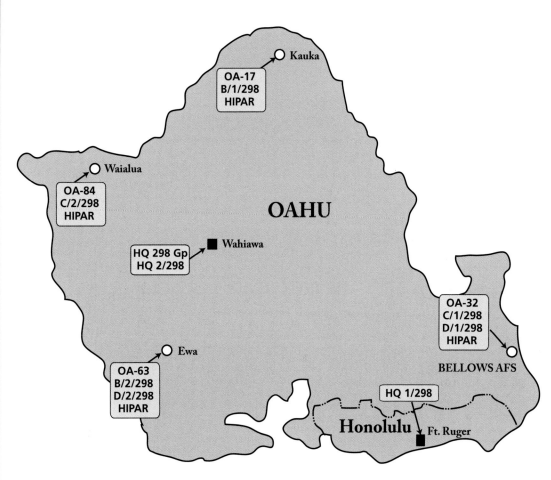

This Nike-Hercules defense was notable for being manned solely by Army National Guard personnel. Early plans called for six individual batteries; this was later modified to six batteries at four locations, ringing the island. Overall command of the defense came under US Army, Pacific (USARPAC). Units and installations defended by Guard included the massive Pearl Harbor Naval Base, Naval Submarine Base and Naval Shipyard; Marine Corps Air Station Kaneohe Bay; NAS Barbers Point; Wheeler AFB; and Hickam AFB.

No information has been found to indicate the type command and control equipment operated by the Oahu defense. The AADCP was located at Wahiawa; the early warning radar site was Mt Kaala AFS, operated jointly by Pacific Air Forces (PACAF), the FAA, and Hawaiian Air National Guard. Nike operations in Hawaii were suspended as part of the 1970 defense cutbacks.

Site Location	Radars	Magazines, Missiles, Launchers	Convert to Herc	Units (years)
OA-17		2AG		B/1/298th (1/61-3/70)
Kauka/Kahuku		12H		
			8L-H	
	LOC:	*C - 2.6 WNW Kahuku, Kawela Camp Rd*		
		L - 2.5 NNW Kahuku		
	CUR:	*C - US Army; range control facility*		
		L - US Army; Kahuku Army Training Area		

Site Location	Radars	Magazines, Missiles, LaunchersConvert to Herc	Units (years)
OA-32 **BellowsAFS/** **Waimanalo** *double site		4AG 24H 16L-H	C/1/298th (3/61-3/70) D/1/298th (3/61-3/70)
	LOC:	C - Kamehameha Ridge L - SE corner Bellows AFS off Tinker Rd	
	CUR:	C - US Army; abandoned L - (P) Bellows AFS; PACAF communications facility, DOD recreation facility	
Fort Ruger			HHB/158th (1/59-5/59) HHB/1/298th (5/59-3/70)
	LOC:	SE Diamond Head, Honolulu	
	CUR:	Fort Ruger; Hawaii State Dept of Defense, DOD recreation facility	
OA-63 **Ewa/Makakilo** *double site		4AG 24H 16L-H	B/2/298th (1/61-3/70) D/2/298th (1/61-3/70)
	LOC:	C - 2.3 NNW Ewa, off of Palehua Rd L - 2.3 NW Ewa off of Pale	
	CUR:	C - (I) USAF Palehua Solar Observatory Research Site L - (I) USAF Palehua Solar Observatory Research Site	
OA-84 **Waialua/Dillingham**		2AG 12H 8L-H	C/2/298th (1/61-3/70)
	LOC:	C - 5 SW Waialua, Peacock Flat Access Rd L - 3 WSW Waialua, Dillingham Field	
	CUR:	C - USAF training site L - Dillingham Airport; site abandoned NOTE: Former Dillingham AFB; HIANG interceptor alert site	
Wahiawa	AADCP		HQ 298th Gp (/57-3/70) HHB/297th (1/59-5/59) HHB/2/298th (5/59-3/70)
	LOC:	Kamehameha Hwy	
	CUR:	HIArNG Armory	

OFFUTT DEFENSE AREA

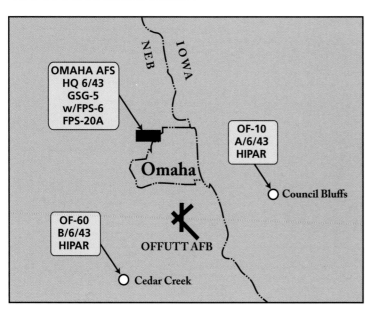

The Offutt defense was manned by the headquarters and head-quarters battery and two firing batteries of the 6th Missile Battalion, 43d Artillery; the other two batteries constituted the Lincoln AFB defense. The installation that became Offutt AFB was first activated in the late 1870s as Fort Crook, named for General George Crook. The flying field was named for First Lieutenant James Offutt in 1924, Omaha's first aviation casualty of World War I. Post World War II, the base became the headquarters of Strategic Air Command. As such, it was a primary target for the Soviets. The AADCP for the defense was located at Omaha AFS; SAGE tracking data came from the command post at Sioux City, IA. Units assigned to Offutt during the Nike period included HQSAC, the 385th Strategic Aerospace Wing, 4231st Strategic Wing, and the 549th Strategic Missile Squadron, equipped with nine Atlas Ds.

Site Location	Radars		Magazines, Missiles, LaunchersConvert to Herc	Units (years)
Omaha AFS	AN/GSG-5			HHB/6/43d (6/60-6/66)
	BIRDIE			USAF 789th RADS (SAGE)
	AN/CPS-4			(5/51-9/68)
	AN/FPS-3			
	AN/FPS-4			
	AN/FPS-6			
	AN/FPS-20			
	AN/FPS-20A			
	LOC:	N Omaha, 72d St & NE 36th		
	CUR:	multiple private and commercial use		
OF-10	HIPAR	3AG		A/6/43d (6/60-6/66)
Council Bluffs		12H		
		12L-H		
	LOC:	C - 5.8WCouncil Bluffs, S of IA 92		
		L - 6.3W Council Bluffs, S of IA 92, Treynor		
	CUR:	C - (I) Area Education Agency, 13/Loess Hills Halvorsen Center		
		L - (I) private owner		
OF-60		3AG		B/6/43d (6/60-6/66)

Site Location	Radars	Magazines, Missiles, LaunchersConvert to Herc	Units (years)
Cedar Creek		12H	
		12L-H	
	LOC:	C – 4SSE Cedar Creek, 10312 Agnew Rd, E of 108th St	
		L - 4S Cedar Creek, S side of Agnew Rd, W of 108th St	
	CUR:	C - (I) Camp of the Risen Son, religious retreat center	
		L - (I) Private residence and equipment storage	

PHILADELPHIA DEFENSE AREA

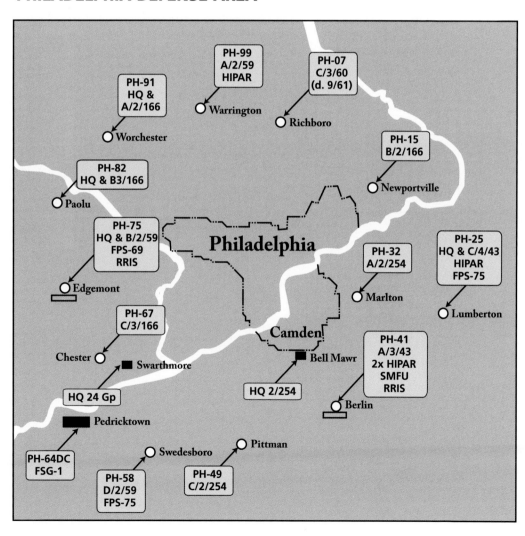

A major defense protecting multiple military installations as well as a substantial metropolitan, government, industrial region, Philadelphia was within the operations area of the 52d Brigade in New York City. The AADCP was located at Pedricktown AADB, an old Army depot site on the Delaware River that was updated to house a Missile Master blockhouse. After the merger in 1966, command post operations shifted to Highlands AADB, NJ, in the New York defense.

Nearby Air Force radar sites included Gibbsboro and Moorestown AFSs; SAGE tracking information was transmitted to Pedricktown from a command post at McGuire AFB, NJ. McGuire also hosted a BOMARC site under the 46th ADMS, from June 1961 through July 1972.

The transfer of the 24th Group out of the Philadelphia Defense Area in September 1966 resulted in the merger of the New York and Philadelphia defenses. Philadelphia's 3d Battalion, 43d Air Defense Artillery was the last Regular Army Nike battalion in the combined defense.

Site Location	Radars	Magazines, Missiles, Launchers	Convert to Herc	Units (years)
PH-07 **Richboro**		2B 20A 8L-A		C/506th (/56-9/58) C/3/60th (9/58-9/61)
	LOC:	*C - 2 N Richboro, N off Twining-Ford Rd* *L - 1 E Richboro, N off Newtown-Richboro Rd,*		
	CUR:	*C - (P) Council Rock School District; offices* *L - (P) Northampton Tennis & Fitness Center*		
PH-15 **Newportville/** **Corydon**		2A/1B 30A 12L-A		D/506th (/55-9/58) D/3/60th (9/58-4/60) B/2/166th (4/60-3/63)
	LOC:	*C - .5 W PA 413, S of I 276 behind shopping center off of Durham Rd* *L - .5 W PA 413, S off Ford Rd*		
	CUR:	*C - (P) private owner* *L - (P) USAR Center*		
Fort Dix *Temporary site				HQ 24th Gp (7/52- /58) B/738th (/55- /56) D/738th (/55- /56)
	LOC:	*SE Wrightstown*		
	CUR:	*Fort Dix; USAR/ArNG Training Installation*		
PH-23/25 **Lumberton** DOUBLE SITE	HIPAR ABAR/75	2A/2B/2C 24H/60A 22L-UA (14L-H)	3/58- 6/59	HHB/738th (7/54-9/58) C/738th (/56-9/58) HHB/3/43d (9/58-10/63) C/3/43d (9/58-10/63) A/7/112th (10/63-6/71) A/1/254th (6/71-4/74)
	LOC:	*C -2 S Mount Holly, N. off Municipal Dr at Eayrestown Rd* *L -2 S Mount Holly, S off Municipal Dr*		
	CUR:	*C - (I) Midway School* *L - (P) Lumberton Township Municipal Complex*		
PH-32 **Marlton**		2B 30A 8L-A		D/738th (/56-9/58) D/3/43d (9/58-10/60) A/2/254th (10/60-3/63)
	LOC:	*C - .5 N Tomlinson Mill, vicinity Tomlinson Mill Rd & S Elmwood Rd* *L - .8 NE Tomlinson Mill, E of Tomlinson Mill Rd behind subdivision off Washington Dr*		
	CUR:	*L - (P) Evesham Board of Education* *C - (O) subdivision?*		

Site Location	Radars	Magazines, Missiles, Launchers	Convert to Herc	Units (years)
Bell Mawr				HHB/116th (2/58-3/59)
				HHB/2/254th (3/59-3/63)
PH-41/43	2x HIPAR	1A/2B/3C	6/58-	A/738th (/55-9/58)
Berlin/	SMFU	18H/60A	7/61	A/3/43d (9/58-4/74)
Clementon	RRIS	23L-UA		
	DCL	(17L-U)		

DOUBLE SITE, converted from 6/58-6/59 and 1/61-7/61; Ajax operations through 1/61

	LOC:	C – W. off Williamstown Erial Rd		
		L – W. off Berlin-Cross Keys Rd, N of Atlantic City Expy		
	CUR:	C - (P) private owner		
		L - (P) US Government, abandoned		
PH-49		**2**A/1B		B/738th (/56-9/58)
Pittman		30A		B/3/43d (9/58-10/60)
		12L-A		C/2/254th (10/60-3/63)
	LOC:	C - 1 WNW Pittman, S off Golf Club Rd		
		L - Pittman-S. off Jefferson Rd		
	CUR:	C - (P) Gloucester County Christian School		
		L - (I) Kraemer Construction Company		
Fort Mott				A/738th (/55- /56)
*temporary site				C/738th (/55- /56)
	LOC:	7 WNW Salem		
	CUR:	Fort Mott State Park; wildlife refuge		
PH-58	ABAR/75	1A/1B/1C	1/61-	D/176th (/57-9/58)
Swedesboro		18H/30A	6/61	D/2/59th (9/58-10/64)
		12L-UA		B/3/43d (10/64-4/74)
		(7L-H)		
	LOC:	C - 1 NNE, E off Paulsboro Swedesboro Rd N of US 322		
		L - 1.4 NNE, E off Paulsboro Swedesboro Rd at Viereck Rd		
	CUR:	C - (I) private owner		
		L - (P) US Government?		

NOTE: "A damn good asparagus farm shot to hell." (quote from the owner)

Site Location	Radars	Magazines, Missiles, Launchers	Convert to Herc	Units (years)
PH-64DC **Pedricktown** **AADB**	AN/FSG-1 Missile Master			HQ 24th Gp (10/63-9/66) HHB/3/43d (10/63-9/66)
		AN/FPS-20 AN/FPS-6		
	LOC:	US 130, 2 NE Penns Grove		
	CUR:	USAR Center; 550th MI Battalion, Salem Community College		
		NOTE: Pedricktown USAR Center scheduled for closure		
RP-63/Z-63 **Gibbsboro, NJ**		AN/FPS-66 (AN/FPS-27) 2 x AN/FPS-6 2 x AN/FPS-6/6A (ANFPS-26A)		USAF 772nd Radar Sqdn (SAGE)
Swarthmore **PH-67** **Chester/** **Village Green/Media**		2A/1B 30A 12L-A		HQ 24th Gp (/58-10/63) C/176th (2/55-9/58) C/2/59th (9/58-4/60) C/3/166th (4/60-3/63)
	LOC:	C - PA 452, N of US 322 Pennell Rd & Weir Rd		
		L - E of Cherry Tree Rd, N of Conchester Rd (322)		
	CUR:	C - (P) Penn Del County School District; Stuart H. Smith Environmental Center		
		L - (P) Conchester School Board/Hilltop Elementary School parking lot		
PH-75 **Edgemont/** **Delaware City** DOUBLE SITE	ABAR/69 RRIS	3A/2B/1C 18H/60A 23L-UA (11L-H)	6/58- 9/59	HHB/176th (2/55-9/58) B/176th (/56-9/58) HHB/2/59th(9/58-10/64) B/2/59th (9/58-10/64) HHB/3/43d (9/66-4/74) C/3/43d (10/64-11/68)
	LOC:	C - 1.2 W Castle Rock, N of PA 3, on Delchester Rd		
		L - 1.2 W Castle Rock, S of PA 3, E off Delchester Rd		
	CUR:	C - (P) county road maintenance facility		
		L - (P) USAR Center		

Site Location	Radars	Magazines, Missiles, Launchers	Convert to Herc	Units (years)
PH-82 **Paoli/** **Valley Forge**		2A/1B 30A 12L-A		A/176th (2/55-9/58) A/2/59th (9/58-4/60) HHB/3/166th(6/59-3/63) B/3/166th (4/60-3/63)
	LOC:	*C - 1 SW Valley Forge NHP, Horseshoe Pt off Horseshoe Trail* *L - NE intersection Swedesford & Le Boutillier Rds*		
	CUR:	*C - (O) private, housing development* *L - (O) private, housing development*		
PH-91 **Worchester/** **Center Square**		2A/1B 30A 12L-A		A/506th (/55-9/58) A/3/60th (9/58-4/60) HHB/2/166th(3/59-10/64) A/2/166th (4/60-3/63)
	LOC:	*C - S Worchester, N. Trooper Rd* *L – N off Berks Rd*		
	CUR:	*C - (O) Worchester Nike Park* *L - (P) USAR Center; 330th Combat Engineer Battalion*		
PH-97R **Eureka**				Radar Section, 24th Gp
	LOC:	*2 NNW NAS Willow Grove, N side Folly Rd*		
	CUR:	*(P) Warrington Township; Igoe-Porter-Wellings Memorial Park, Twin Oaks Summer* Camp		
PH-99 **Warrington/** **Eureka** DOUBLE SITE (HERC)	2x HIPAR	4B/2C 36H/60A 22L-UU (22L-H)	4/58- 6/59	HHB/506th (12/54-9/58) B/506th (/55-9/58) HHB/3/60th (9/58-9/61) B/3/60th (9/58-9/61) A/2/59th (9/61-10/64) HHB/2/166th(10/64-9/69) A/2/166th (10/64-9/69) B/2/166th (10/64-8/68)
	LOC:	*C - 2 NNW NAS Willow Grove, N off Bradley Rd W of Folly Rd* *L - 2 NNW NAS Willow Grove, E side Folly Rd at Bradley Rd*		
	CUR:	*C - (P) Warrington Township; Igoe-Porter-Wellings Memorial Park, Twin Oaks Summer Camp* *L - (P) Warrington Township Lower Nike Site; partially destroyed*		

PITTSBURGH DEFENSE AREA

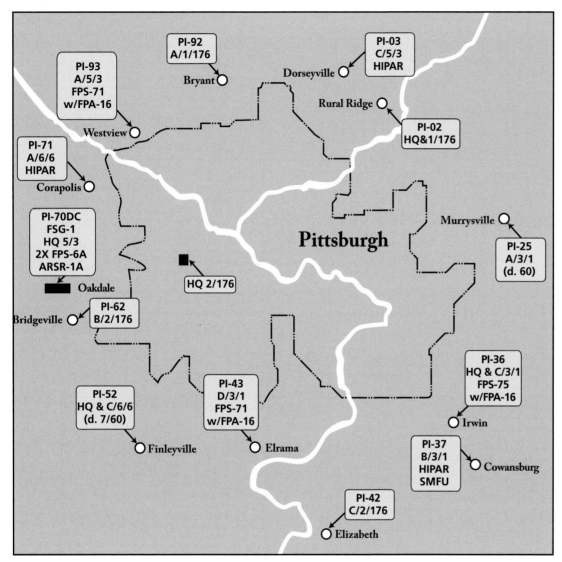

The Pittsburgh defense was fairly standard, with three Regular Army battalions initially assigned for the protection of the steel mills and other industry. The primary headquarters installation was the 18th Artillery Group, which went through three periods of operations, interspersed with the 31st Artillery Brigade. The AADCP was colocated with an Air Force radar site at Oakdale Army Air Defense Base.

During the course of Nike operations, SAGE date was inputted from command posts at Hancock Field, NY; Stewart AFB, NY; Custer AFS, MI; Fort Lee AFS, VA; and Duluth Airport, MN. Pittsburgh remained operational with one active Army and one National Guard battalion through 1974.

Site Location	Radars	Magazines, Missiles, Launchers	Convert to Herc	Units (years)
PI-02		2A/1B		D/1st (4/55-10/56)
Rural Ridge		30A		D/74th (10/56-9/58)
		12L-A		D/5/3d (9/58-4/60)
				HHB/1/176th(6/59-4/63)
				D/1/176th (4/60-4/63)

Site Location	Radars	Magazines, Missiles, Launchers	Convert to Herc	Units (years)
	LOC:	C - S Rural Ridge, End of Challenge Ln off of Lefever Hill Rd		
		L - N Rural Ridge, N off Crawford Run Rd		
	CUR:	C - (P) Teen Challenge; drug & alcohol rehab		
		L - (P) Pennsylvania Department of Transportation; road equipment yard, heavy equipment operator training		
PI-03	HIPAR	3B	5/58-	C/74th (9/56-9/58)
Dorseyville/		18H/30A	11/58	C/5/3d (9/58-10/63)
Indianola		12L-U		C/2/176th (10/63-3/74)
	LOC:	C - End of Charles St off of Saxonburg Rd		
		L - 1.3 N Dorseyville, W off Gibsonia Rd (PA 910)		
	CUR:	C - (I) American Indian Center Singing Winds Site		
		L - (I) Northwest Deer Township Senior Citizens Center		
Blawnox				HHB/708th (3/58-6/59)
				HHB/1/176th (6/59- /59)
PI-25		2A/1B		A/1st (4/55-9/58)
Murrysville/		30A		A/3/1st (9/58- /60)
Monroe		12L-A		
	LOC:	C - 713 New Texas Rd		
		L - 428 Presque Isle Rd (off of Golden Mile Hwy (PA 286) in subdivision)		
	CUR:	C - (P) Univ. Pittsburgh Primate Research Lab		
		L - (O) A.E. O'Block Elementary School, A.E. Stevenson High School		
PI-36	ABAR/75	1B/2C	6/58-	HHB/1st (4/55-9/58)
Irwin	AN/FPA-16	18H/30A	5/59	C/1st (4/55-9/58)
		10L-U		HHB/3/1st (9/58-8/74)
				C/3/1st (9/58-12/68)
	LOC:	C - 1 NNE North Irwin, 1600 block Morris Rd		
		L - 2 NW Manor, W of South Sandy Hill Rd, end of Nike Rd		
	CUR:	C - (P) Norwin Soccer Club, Norwin YMCA, Oak Hollow Seniors Center		
		L - (P) US Government ?		
PI-37	HIPAR	3B	6/58-	B/1st (/56-9/58)
Cowansburg/	SMFU	18H/30A	5/59	B/3/1st (9/58-3/74)
Herminie		12L-U		
	LOC:	C - 2 NNW Herminie, NW off Morris Ave		
		L - 2.5 NW Herminie, Nike Rd of off Sandy Hill Rd		
	CUR:	C - (P) private?		
		L - (P) Private owner, machine shop		

Site Location	Radars	Magazines, Missiles, Launchers	Convert to Herc	Units (years)
PI-42 **Elizabeth**		2A/1B 30A 12L-A		D/1st (/56-9/58) D/3/1st (9/58-4/60) C/2/176th (4/60-4/63)
	LOC:	C - 1 E Hillsdale, NW of Scenery Dr (PA 48) L - 1 W Mustard, NE off of Pineview Rd		
	CUR:	C - (P) Elizabeth Forward School District, A - private housing L - (I) Twin Pines Council of Governments Police Firing Range		
PI-43 **Elrama**	ABAR/71 AN/FPA-16	3B 18H/30A 12L-U	5/58- 11/58	D/509th (5/55-9/58) D/6/6th (9/58-7/60) D/3/1st (7/60-3/74)
	LOC:	C - 1.3 W Elrama end of Maple St off of Finley-Elrama Rd L - 2.2 W Elrama, E of Finley-Elrama Rd		
	CUR:	C - (P) PAArNG; D/876th Engineer Battalion L - (I) US government?, abandoned		

NOTE: *First operational Pittsburgh Nike site, 21 May 1955*

Site Location	Radars	Magazines, Missiles, Launchers	Convert to Herc	Units (years)
PI-52 **Finleyville**		2A/1B 30A 12L-A		HHB/509th (/58-9/58) C/509th (/55-9/58) HHB/6/6th (9/58-7/60) C/6/6th (9/58-7/60)
	LOC:	C - 1.2 N Finleyville, end of Hidden Hollow Rd N off of Orange Belt (PA 88) L - 2 N Finleyville, end of Walter Long Rd S off of Orange Belt (PA 88)		
	CUR:	C - (P) South Hills Christian School L - (P) Walter Long Manufacturing Company		
PI-62 **Bridgeville/** **Hickman**		2A/1B 30A 12L-A		B/509th (/56-9/58) B/6/6th (9/58-8/59) B/2/176th (8/59-4/63)
	LOC:	C - 1 ESE Oakdale, S off of Hilltop Rd L - 2 SE Oakdale, end of Will Way E off of Old Oakdale Rd		
	CUR:	C – (P) USAR L – (P) US Army? A – (I) Headquarters, Army Readiness Group, Pittsburgh		
Carnegie/Logan Armory				HHB/2/176th (/59-4/63)
PI-70 DC **Oakdale AADB**	AN/FSG-1 Missile Master AN/TSQ-51	AADCP		HQ 31st Bde (9/66-6/71) HQ 18th Gp (10/52-12/61, 12/63-9/66, 11/68-8/74) HHB/5/3d (12/61-10/63)

Site Location	Radars	Magazines, Missiles, Launchers	Convert to Herc	Units (years)
	Missile Mentor FAA ARSR-1A (AN/FPS-24) AN/FPS-20 2 x AN/FPS-6 2 x AN/FPS-6B (AN/FPS-26A) (AN/FPS-90)			USAF 662d RADS (SAGE) (7/60-12/69)
	LOC: 2 E Oakdale, Messerschmidt Rd off of Nike Site Rd off of Thomas Run and Oakdale Rd			
	CUR:(I) HQ USAR 99th Regional Support Command			
Moon Run				*HHB/724th (3/58-6/59)* *HHB/2/176th (6/59- /59)*
PI-71 **Coraopolis/** **Beacon**	HIPAR	1B/2C 18H/30A 10L-U	6/58- 3/59	A/509th (/55-9/58) A/6/6th (9/58-10/63) B/2/176th (10/63-3/74)
	LOC:	*C - Silver Ln, S off of Ewings Mill Rd, NNW of Forest Grove*		
		L - Nike Rd off of Ewings Mill Rd		
	CUR:	*C - (I) Robinson Department of Public Works*		
		L - (P) private owner		
PI-92 **Bryant/** **North Park**		2A/1B 30A 12L-A		B/74th (9/56-9/58) B/5/3d (9/58-8/59) A/1/176th (8/59-4/63)
	LOC:	*C - 2 NE Highland, N of Peebles Rd*		
		L - 3 NE Highland, W Ridge Rd E off of Kummer Rd		
	CUR:	*C - (P) USAR North Hills Army Reserve Center*		
		L - (P) Allegany County Police & Fire Academy		
PI-93 **West View**	ABAR/71 AN/FPA-16	1B/2C 18H/30A 10L-H	6/58- 6/59	HHB/74th (9/56-9/58) A/74th (9/56-9/58) HHB/5/3d (9/58-12/61) A/5/3d (9/58-12/63) HHB/2/176th (4/63-4/74) A/2/176th (10/63-6/71)
	LOC:	*C - .8 NW West View, Valley Hi Dr or Logan Dr off of Gass Rd*		
		L - 1.3 NNE Emsworth, Ben Avon Heights Rd		
	CUR:	*C - (P) PAArNG, 28th Signal Battalion*		
		L - (P) Avonworth High School, Private residence		

PITTSBURGH DEFENSE AREA

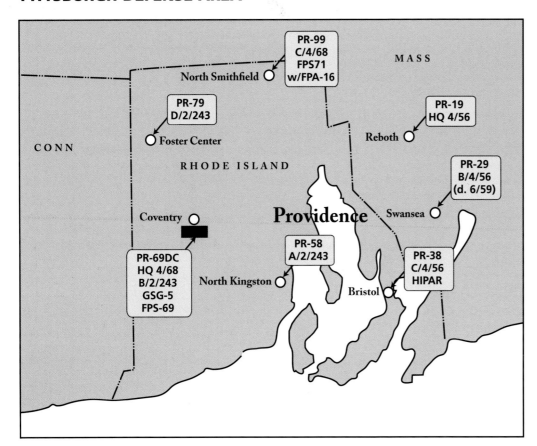

The Providence sites were manned by two Regular Army battalions that protected the governmental, industrial, and military center of Narragansett Bay. Included in the latter category were Naval Construction Battalion Center Davisville; Naval Air Station Quonset Point; Naval Station Newport; and the Naval War College.

Boston's 3d Missile Battalion, 5th Artillery, assumed responsibility for Providence's remaining Regular Army Nike-Hercules site in August 1963. The AADCP, at PR-69 Coventry, was upgraded to Missile Mentor standards and assumed command responsibility for the New England Defense Area in September 1966.

Site Location	Radars	Magazines, Missiles, Launchers	Convert to Herc	Units (years)
PR-19		2A/1B		HQ 11th Gp (5/58-8/60)
Rehoboth		30A		HHB/739th (/56- /58)
		12L-A		A/739th (6/56-9/58)
				A/4/56th (9/58-8/60)
				HHB/4/56th (8/60-8/63)
				HHB/3/5th (8/63-6/71)
	LOC:	*C - Meadow Hill, N off of Fairview Ave*		
		L - end of Nike Ct S off of Peck St		
	CUR:	*C – (P) MAArNG/USAR Center*		
		L – (P) Town of Rehoboth		

Site Location	Radars	Magazines, Missiles, Launchers	Convert to Herc	Units (years)
PR-29 **Swansea**		2A/1B 30A 12L-A		B/739th (1/56-9/58) B/4/56th (9/58-8/60)
	LOC:	*C – Nike Site Rd, W of Sharps Lot Rd, N of Marvel* *L – Data Vault Rd, E of Sharps Lot Rd, between Baker & Marvel*		
	CUR:	*C - (P) ball fields* *L – (P) Anderson Motor Company*		
PR-38 **Bristol**	HIPAR	1B/2C 18H/30A 10L-U	5/58- 6/59	HHB/739th (/58-9/58) C/739th (1/56-9/58) HHB/4/56th (9/58-8/60) C/4/56th (9/58-8/63) C/3/5th (8/63-9/72) C/1/5th (9/72-4/74)
	LOC:	*C - Mount Hope, end of Tower St* *L - Bristol Point, E of Metacom Ave (RI 136)*		
	CUR:	*C - (P) Brown University, museum* *L - (P) Roger Williams University/Bristol County Development Center*		
PR-58 **North Kingston/** **Davisville**		2A/1B 30A 12L-A		A/751st (5/56-9/58) A/4/68th (9/58-12/60) A/2/243d (12/60- /63)
	LOC:	*C - end of Signal Rock Dr N off of Fletcher Rd* *L - W of Perimeter Rd N of Davisville Rd, former NCBC Davisville*		
	CUR:	*C - (P) USAF North Kingston ANG Station, North Kingston Parks & Recreation Dept;* * Signal Rock Park* *L - (P) EECO*		
PR-69DC **Coventry**	AN/GSG-5 BIRDIE AN/TSQ-51 MISSILE MENTOR AN/FPS-69			HQ 24th Gp (9/66-10/74) HHB/751st (/56-9/58) HHB/4/68th (9/58-12/61) HHB/3/5th (6/71-9/72) HHB/1/5th (9/72-10/74)
	LOC:	*Nike Site Rd, E of Read School House Rd, N of Rt 117*		
	CUR:	*(I) RIANG*		

Site Location	Radars	Magazines, Missiles, Launchers	Convert to Herc	Units (years)
PR-69 **Coventry**		2A/1B 30A 12L-A		B/751st (5/56-9/58) B/4/68th (9/58-12/61) B/2/243d (12/60-6/63)
	LOC:	*C – Nike Site Rd, E of Read School House, N of Rt 117* *L - E of Phillips Hill, end of Provident Pl off of Phillips Hill Rd, S of Rt 117*		
	CUR:	*C - (I) Coventry ANF Station, RIANG; 281st Combat Communications Group, 282d CCS* *L - (P) Central Coventry Park*		
PR-79 **Foster Center/** **Woonsocket**		2A/1B 30A 12L-A		D/751st (5/56-9/58) D/4/68th (9/58-12/60) D/2/243d (12/60-6/63)
	LOC:	*C - Oak Hill, end of Theodore Foster Dr S of Hartford Pike (Rt 101)* *L - S off of Winsor Rd*		
	CUR:	*C – (P) Foster/Gloucester Regional School District Offices* *L – (I) State of Rhode Island; State Police Training Academy*		
PR-99 **North** **Smithfield/** **Foster**	ABAR/71 AN/FPA-16	1B/2C 18H/30A 11L-U (10L-H)	5/58- 6/59	C/751st (5/56-9/58) C/4/68th (9/58-12/61) D/4/56th (12/61-8/63) B/2/243d (8/63-6/71)
	LOC:	*C - Black Plain Hill, W off Old Oxford Rd* *L - N off of Pond Hill Rd, W of Black Plain Rd*		
	CUR:	*C - (P) North Smithfield ANG Station, RIANG/Air Force Reserve Center* *L - (I) RIANG motor pool*		

ROBINS DEFENSE AREA

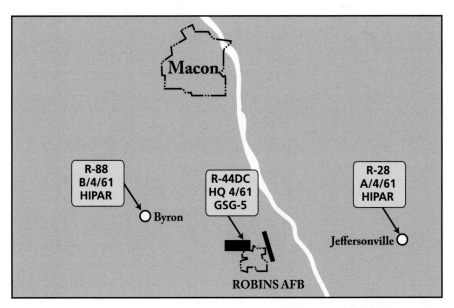

The Robins AFB Nike defense was a standard SAC-type installation. Units assigned to the base were the 4137th Strategic Wing, 456th Bombardment Wing (Heavy), HQ Warner Robins Air Materiel Area, HQ Continental Air Command, and HQ Fourteenth Air Force (CONAC). The 4/61st activated in the San Francisco defense and transferred to Robins following turnover of its Nike-Ajax sites to the California Army National Guard.

The AADCP was located on Robins AFB; SAGE data was furnished from the command post at Montgomery AFB, AL. The type radars assigned to the two firing batteries have not been determined.

Site Location	Radars	Magazines, Missiles, Launchers	Convert to Herc	Units (years)
R-28		3AG		A/4/61st (11/60-3/66)
Jeffersonville		12H		
		12L-H		
	LOC:	C – Missile Base Rd near interchange of I-16 & GA Hwy 96		
		L – W off Hamlin-Floyd Rd		
	CUR:	C - (I)		
		L - (P) Twiggs County Board of Education, high school		
R-44DC	AN/GSG-5			HHB/4/61st (7/59-3/66)
Robins AFB	BIRDIE			
	LOC:	15 SSE Macon, US 129		
	CUR:	Robins AFB: HQ Warner Robins Air Logistics Center, HQ Air Force Reserve		
		Command; GAANG; Robins AFB Museum of Aviation		
R-88		3AG		B/4/61st (11/60-3/66)
Byron		12H		
		12L-H		
	LOC:	C - Boy Scout Rd at Juniper Creek Rd		
		L – S of Juniper Creek Rd at Oleo Acres		
	CUR:	C - (P)		
		L (P) Pyrotechnics, Inc.		

ST LOUIS DEFENSE AREA

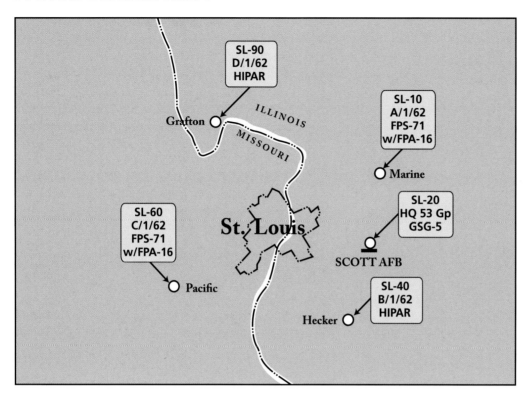

St Louis was furnished with four Nike-Hercules batteries during the second round of ARADCOM construction. The sites were placed to defend the city's substantial rail and industrial assets as well as Military Air Transport Service (MATS) activities at Scott AFB. Air Defense Command's 85th Fighter Interceptor Squadron operated out of Scott during this period.

The AADCP was co-located with an ADC radar squadron at Belleville Air Force Station. SAGE input was from the command post at Truax Field, WI, under the Chicago Air Defense Sector.

Site Location	Radars	Magazines, Missiles, Launchers Convert to Herc	Units (years)
SL-10	ABAR/71	3D	A/1/62d (5/60-12/68)
Marine	AN/FPA-16	18H	
		12L-U	
	LOC:	C - 3 NW Marine, IL 4	
		L - 5 NNW Marine, Fruit Rd	
	CUR:	C - (O) private	
		L - (I) Madison County DPW storage facility; Sheriff's Department firing range	
SL-20			HQ 53d Gp (3/66-12/69)
Scott AFB			HHB/1/62d (/59-1/69)
	LOC:	6 ENE Bellville, I 64	
	CUR:	Scott AFB: HQ US Transportation Command; HQ Air Mobility Command,	
		HQ Air Weather Service; HQ Air Force Communications Agency; AFRES	

Site Location	Radars	Magazines, Missiles, Launchers	Convert to Herc	Units (years)
SL-40 **Hecker**	HIPAR	3D 18H 12L-U		B/1/62d (5/60-12/68)
	LOC:	C - 3.5 SE Hecker, 6137 Beck Rd L - 4.5 SE Hecker, M road W of Beck		
	CUR:	C - (I) Beck Vocational Technology School; day care center L - (I) Hecker/Red Bud School District, vocational training		
SL-47DC **Belleville AFS**	AN/GSG-5 BIRDIE AN/FPS-3 AN/CPS-4 2x AN/FPS-6 AN/FPS-90	AADCP		USAF 789th RADS(SAGE) (5/51-6/68)
	LOC:	8 E Belleville, IL 158		
SL-60 **Pacific**	ABAR/71 AN/FPA-16	3D 18H 12L-U		C/1/62d (5/60-12/68)
	LOC:	C- 5S off of County Rd NN L - 6S 2 SW Catawissa, S of County Rd AP (Nike Base Rd)		
	CUR:	C - (P) private, MPL Industries L - (I) Nike School, school district support services, 1 building destroyed		
SL-90 **Alton/** **Pere Marquette**	HIPAR	3D 18H 12L-U		D/1/62d (5/60-12/68)
	LOC:	C - 5 WNW Grafton, Marquette State Park; off of Scenic Dr L - 6 WNW Grafton, Pere Marquette State Park; end of Scenic Dr		
	CUR:	C - (P) Pere Marquette State Park; equipment storage (foundations) L - (P) Pere Marquette State Park; abandoned, buried		

SAN FRANCISCO DEFENSE AREA

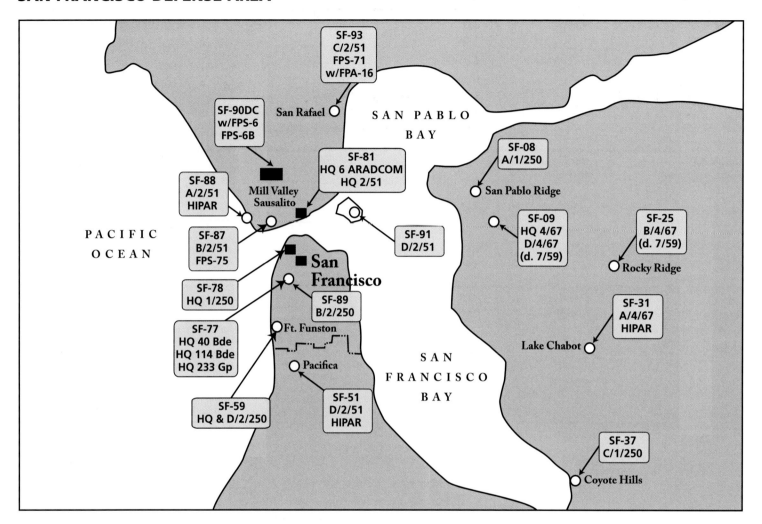

The San Francisco–Oakland Bay Area was filled with major military installations, shipyards, industrial sites, communications systems, and financial and governmental concerns; as a leading Pacific Rim city, it was an obvious candidate for a major Nike defense.

The SF defense hosted the Sixth ARADCOM Region and stood up with one brigade, one group, and three battalions. The AADCP was located at Mill Valley AFS, on the summit of Mt. Tamalpais in Marin County. The SAGE command posts providing early warning and initial target tracking information were

located at Beale AFB, CA (San Francisco ADS, 2/59-8/63); Adair AFS, OR (Portland ADS/26th Air Division, 8/63-9/69); Norton AFB, CA (27th AD, 9/69-11/69), and Luke AFB, AZ (26th AD, 11/69-8/74).

In June 1971, HHB/1/61st transferred to Fort Baker from Elmira in the Travis AFB defense and assumed operational control of the remaining Regular Army firing battery in the Bay Area. Notably, many of the former ARADCOM sites in the San Francisco area are now owned by the National Park Service's Golden Gate National Recreation Area.

Site Location	Radars	Magazines, Missiles, Launchers	Convert to Herc	Units (years)
Berkeley				HHB/728th (/58-5/59)
				HHB/2/250th (5/59-7/59)
SF-08		2A/1B		C/441st (/56-9/58)
San Pablo Ridge		30A		C/4/67th (9/58-7/59)
shared IFC & launch with SF-09		12L-A		A/1/250th (7/59-3/63)
	LOC:	C - San Pablo Ridge		
		L - Nike Site Rd		
	CUR:	(P) Wildcat Canyon Regional Park		
SF-09		2A/1B		HHB/441st (8/55-9/58)
San Pablo Ridge/		30A		HHB/4/67th (9/58-3/63)
Berkeley		12L-A		D/441st (/56-9/58)
shared IFC & launch with SF-08				D/4/67th (9/58-7/59)
	LOC:	C - San Pablo Ridge		
		L - Nike Site Rd		
	CUR:	(P) Wildcat Canyon Regional Park		
Benecia				B/740th (7/54- /55)
Temporary site				C/740th (7/54- /55)
				C/441st (/55- /57)
SF-25		2A/1B		B/441st (/56-9/58)
Rocky Ridge		30A		B/4/67th (9/58-7/59)
		12L-A		
	LOC:	C - 4 N Crow Canyon Rd, end of Bollinger Canyon Rd		
		L - 5 N Crow Canyon Rd, Bollinger Canyon Rd		
	CUR:	C - (unknown) Mount Martell ANG Radio Relay Annex; Las Trampas Regional Park/ microwave communications site		
		L - (P) Tracor Aerospace/California Dept. of Forestry/Las Trampas Regional Park offices		
T-25				D/441st (8/55- /56)
Parks AFB				
temporary site				
	LOC:	2 N Livermore, I 580		
	CUR:	Camp Parks; USAR, CAArNG activities, INS detention center		

Site Location	Radars	Magazines, Missiles, Launchers	Convert to Herc	Units (years)
SF-31 **Lake Chabot/** **Castro Valley**	HIPAR	2B 12H/20A 8L-U	5/58- 6/59	A/441st (8/55-9/58) A/4/67th (9/58-6/63) B/1/250th (3/63-3/74)
	LOC:	C - 0.5 W intersection of Fairmont Dr & Lake Chabot Rd		
		L - 17930 Lake Chabot Rd		
	CUR:	C - (I) communications facility		
		L - (P) East Bay Regional Park District; Lake Chabot Park; Department of Public Safety service yard		
SF-37 **Coyote Hills/** **Newark**		2A/1B 30A 12L-A		D/740th (/55-9/58) D/4/61st (9/58-7/60) C/1/250th (7/59-3/63)
	LOC:	C - S Red Hill Coyote Hills		
		L - N Red Hill Coyote Hills		
	CUR:	C - (P) East Bay Regional Park District; Coyote Hills Regional Park/Alameda County Sheriffs Department, radio transmitter		
		L - (O) Coyote Hills Regional Park		
		A - (I) Coyote Hills Regional Park visitors center		
SF-51 **Milagra/** **Pacifica**	HIPAR	2B 12H/20A 8L-U	5/58- 4/59	C/740th (/56-9/58) C/4/61st (9/58-7/59) D/2/51st (7/59-6/63) A/1/250th (6/63-4/74)
	LOC:	C - Sweeney Ridge (no vehicle access)		
		L - Milagra Ridge, off Sharp Park Rd		
	CUR:	C - (P) Golden Gate NRA; Sweeney Ridge Skyline Preserve		
		L - (P) Golden Gate NRA; Milagra Ridge tops of magazines remain		
SF-59 **Fort Funston/** **Mt. San Bruno**		2A/1B 30A 12L-A		A/740th (/56-9/58) A/4/61st (9/58-7/59) HHB/2/250th (7/59-3/63) D/2/250th (7/59-3/63)
	LOC:	C - Mount San Bruno, Radio Rd		
		L - 500 Skyline Blvd, Fort Funston		
	CUR:	C - (P) communications site		
		L - (P) Golden Gate NRA parking lot		
		A - (I) Golden Gate NRA; Ocean District Headquarters. Environmental Science Center/ Air Quality Monitoring Center		

Site Location	Radars	Magazines, Missiles, Launchers	Convert to Herc	Units (years)
SF-77 **Presidio of** **San Francisco**				HQ 40th Bde (-6/71) HQ 114th Bde (/59- /63) HQ 13th Gp (6/71-8/74) HQ 233d Gp (/59- /63)
	LOC:	*Ralston Ave, Bldg 1201*		
	CUR:	*(I) Golden Gate NRA; unoccupied*		
SF-78 **Presidio of** **San Francisco**				HHB/1/250th (5/59-7/74)
	LOC:	*Bldg 1648, Battery Bowman*		
	CUR:	*(I) Golden Gate NRA; unoccupied*		
SF-81 **Fort Baker**				HQ 6ARADCOM (/51-8/74) HQ 47th Bde (3/52-11/52) HHB/9th (10/54-9/58) HHB/2/51st (9/58-6/71) HHB/1/61st (6/71-8/74)
	LOC:	*Marin County, N end Golden Gate Bridge*		
	CUR:	*(I) (I) GGNRA. Bldg. 601, Cavallo Lodge*		
SF-87 **Fort Cronkhite/** **Sausalito**	ABAR/75	2B 12H/20A 8L-U	5/58- 6/59	B/9th (/55-9/58) B/2/51st (9/58-6/71)
	LOC:	*C - Battery Hill 129* *L - Bunker Rd*		
	CUR:	*C - (P) Golden Gate NRA Hawk Hill observation site* *L - (P) Golden Gate NRA; California Marine Mammal Center*		
SF-88 **Fort Barry/** **Sausalito**	HIPAR	2B 12H/20A 8L-U	5/58- 11/58	A/9th (/55-9/58) A/2/51st (9/58-6/71) B/1/61st (6/71-3/74)
	LOC:	*C - Wolf Ridge, Fort Cronkhite (no vehicle access)* *L – Field Rd, Adjacent to Battery Alexander*		
	CUR:	*C - (I) Golden Gate NRA* *L - (I) Golden Gate NRA; RESTORED SITE—National Park Service*		

Site Location	Radars	Magazines, Missiles, LaunchersConvert to Herc		Units (years)
Fort Barry				HQ 30th Gp (3/58-8/61)
	LOC:	*N end, Golden Gate Bridge*		
	CUR:	*(I) Golden Gate NRA*		
SF-89		2A/1B		HHB/740th (7/54-9/58)
Presidio of		30A		C/740th (/55-9/58)
San Francisco/		12L-A		HHB/4/61st (9/58-7/59)
Mt Sutro				C/4/61st (9/58-7/59)
				B/2/250th (7/59-3/63)
	LOC:	*C – Top of Mount Sutro*		
		L - Presidio, Battery Caulfield Rd		
	CUR:	*C - (P) Television/communications facility*		
		L - (I) Golden Gate NRA; parking storage		
		NOTE: named "Battery Caulfield"		
T-89				
Presidio of				
San Francisco				
temporary site elsewhere on reservation				
	LOC: unknown			
	CUR: National Park Service; Golden Gate NRA			
SF-90DC	AN/TSQ-51			40th Arty Gp Det
Mill Valley AFS	Missile			13th Arty Gp Det
	Mentor			USAF 666th RADS
	2x AN/CPS-6B		(11/50-3/81)	
	AN/FPS-8			
	AN/FPS-4			
	AN/GPS-3			
	2x AN/FPS-6			
	AN/FPS-6B			
	AN/FPS-26A			
	AN/FPS-7C			
	AN/FSS-7 SLBM			
	LOC:	*Mount Tamalpais, E. Ridgecrest Blvd*		
	CUR:	*FAA JSS Facility J-33 Mill Valley; National Park Service, Golden Gate NRA*		

NOTE: Sea-Launched Ballistic Missile (SLBM) detection site under Det 3, Fourteenth Air Force (7/67-7/72) and Det 3, 14th Missile Warning Squadron (7/72-4/80). The National Park Service cleared all of the former Air Force properties during the early 1990s, leaving only the Federal Aviation Administration radar facility.

Site Location	Radars	Magazines, Missiles, Launchers	Convert to Herc	Units (years)
SF-91 **Angel Island**		2A/1B 30A 12L-A		D/9th (/55-9/58) D/2/51st (9/58- /61)
	LOC:	C - Mount Caroline Livermore, Angel Island L - Fort McDowell, Angel Island		
	CUR:	C - (O) Angel Island State Park, pads only L - (I) closed/Angel Island State Park		
SF-93 **San Rafael**	ABAR/71 AN/FPA-16	3B 18H/30A	5/58- 2/59	C/9th (/56-9/58) C/2/51st (9/58-6/71)
	LOC:	C - top of Bayhills Dr L - N of Smith Ranch Rd		
	CUR:	C - (P) Harry A. Barbier Memorial Park, towers & pads only L - (P) Marin County waste treatment plant A - (I) Youth guidance center		

SAULT STE MARIE DEFENSE AREA

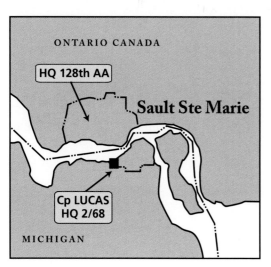

ARADCOM retained two gun-only defense areas after the completion of Nike-Ajax deployment. The defense at Sault Ste Marie, MI, was unique in that it fielded both ARADCOM and Royal Canadian Artillery Units.

The defense was first established at Camp Lucas during World War II to protect the Sault Ste. Marie Canal and Locks and St Marys River. The combined US Army/Canadian command was emplaced in 1951 as part of the general upgrading of continental air defense. Camp Lucas housed the AADCP; operations were strictly manual. The NORAD regional command post was located at K.I. Sawyer AFB, near Marquette, MI.

For whatever reason, neither Sault Ste Marie nor the other gun defense at Savannah River were ever considered for Nike-Ajax deployment. The Air Force did base a squadron of CIM-10B BOMARCs at Raco, MI, under the 37th ADMS, from March 1960 through October 1972. The two American and single Canadian battalions were inactivated on 15 June 1960, ending ARADCOM gun operations.

Site Location	Radars	Magazines, Missiles, Launchers	Convert to Herc	Units (years)
Camp Lucas	Manual AADCP			HHB/8th AAABn (/51-9/58) HHB/2/68th (9/58-6/60)
	LOC:	Sault Ste Marie		
	CUR:	(P) Lake Superior State University		

SAVANNAH RIVER DEFENSE AREA

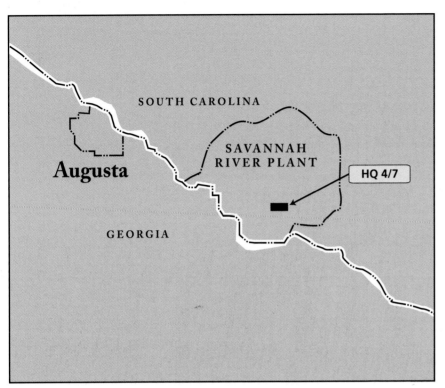

The Atomic Energy Commission's Savannah River Plant was located twelve miles south of Aiken, SC, and covered some 300 square miles in Aiken, Barnwell and Allendale Counties. ARAD-COM provided two battalions for the defense: the 33d Antiaircraft Artillery (90mm gun) and 425th Antiaircraft Artillery (Skysweeper) Battalions. The 33d converted to Skysweeper in early 1956. One battalion was replaced by a CARS unit on 1 September 1958; the unit inactivated on 20 January 1960. ARADCOM declined to provide a Nike-Ajax battalion for the Savannah River defense.

Site Location	Radars	Magazines, Missiles, Launchers	Convert to Herc	Units (years)
Savannah River Plant		Manual AADCP		HHB/33d AAABn (5/55-9/58)
				HHB/425th (5/55-9/58)
				HHB/2/68th (9/58-1/60)
	LOC:	*12 SE Aiken, SC*		

SCHILLING DEFENSE AREA

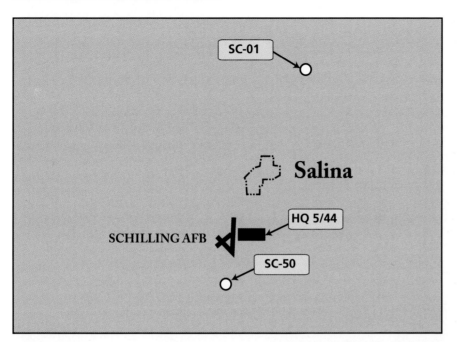

Schilling was one of two SAC defenses that were constructed and manned but never went on alert. The 5th Missile Battalion, 44th Artillery, was activated in April 1960 to control the two sites, but was inactivated slightly over two months later. SAC operations at Schilling AFB in 1960 included the 820th Air Division, 40th Bombardment Wing (Medium), and 310th Strategic Aerospace Wing. The 550th Strategic Missile Squadron, equipped with twelve Atlas Fs, was assigned to the latter wing. Schilling AFB was closed in April 1967. Topographic maps indicate the existence of SAC-style above-ground launchers at SC-01; no evidence of similar construction remains at SC-50.

Site Location	Radars	Magazines, Missiles, Launchers	Convert to Herc	Units (years)
SC-01 **Schilling AFB** *Not operational*		3AG		
	LOC:	C - 5 S Bennington, E off 160th Rd, S of Buffalo Rd		
		L - 3.5 SSE Bennington, E off 160th Rd, N of Coronado Rd		
	CUR:	C - (I) Bennington Fiberglass		
		L - (I) private owner		
Schilling AFB				HHB/5/44th (4/60-6/60)
	LOC:	SW Salina, W of I 135		
	CUR:	Salina Municipal Airport		
SC-50 **Schilling AFB** *Not operational*				
	LOC:	C - 6 SSW Smolan, E of S Burma Rd at W Hedburg Rd		
		L - S off W. Thorstenburg Rd, E of S. Muir Rd		
	CUR:	C - (P) private ownership; housing		
		L - (I) 80% completed, private		

SEATTLE DEFENSE AREA

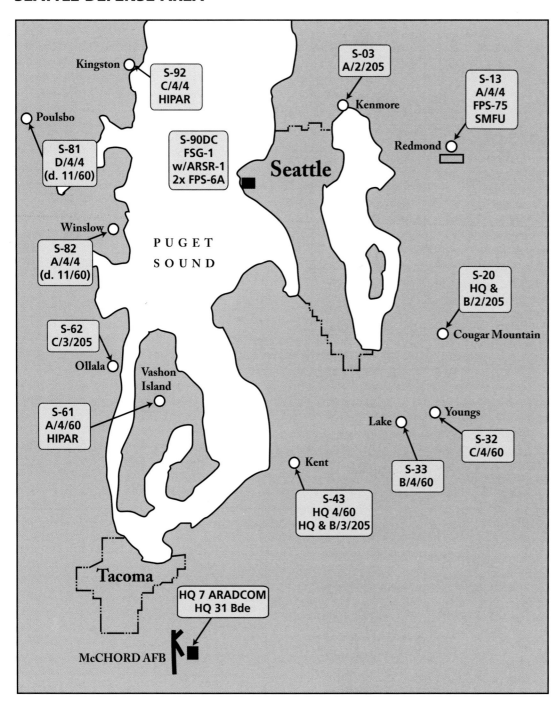

As a major industrial and financial center of the Pacific Northwest, Seattle rated a Nike defense. Eleven batteries were emplaced, under the operational direction of a brigade and three battalions. The Washington Army National Guard later contributed two battalions. The AADCP was located at Fort Lawton on the Puget Sound, a historic old military post that had seen varied use since 1900. Following the conversion to Nike-Hercules (and subsequent reduction to three Hercules batteries), the Missile Master was replaced by a BIRDIE.

Local Air Force defense operations included the SAGE command post at McChord AFB; interceptor squadrons at Paine and McChord AFBs; and long-range radars at Fort Lawton and Blaine AFS. At one time Paine AFB was scheduled to receive BOMARC.

Site Location	Radars	Magazines, Missiles, Launchers	Convert to Herc	Units (years)
S-03 **Kenmore**		2B 20A 8L-A		C/28th (/56-9/58) C/2/43d (9/58-6/59) A/2/205th (6/59-3/64)
	LOC:	C - 47th Ave NE, S of 201st L - 130 228th SW at Meridian Ave S		
	CUR:	C - (O) Horizon Heights Park L - (P) FEMA Region X Headquarters/USAR Center		
S-12 **Phantom Lake** *Gun site*				HHB/770th (6/58-4/59) HHB/2/205th (4/59-6/60)
S-13 **Redmond** DOUBLE SITE	ABAR/75 SMFU	3A/2B/1C 18H/60A 23L-UA (11L-H)	6/58- 4/59	A/28th (/56-9/58) D/28th (/57-9/58) A/2/43d (9/58-4/59) D/2/43d (9/58-11/60) A/4/4th (11/60-10/64) A/2/205th (10/64-3/74)
	LOC:	C - end of 95th NE, off 171st L – end of 95th NE, off 195th NE		
	CUR:	C - (P) US Army National Guard, private housing development L - (I) Nursery		
S-14 **Redmond**				HHB/28th (8/54-9/58) HHB/2/43d (9/58-11/60) HHB/2/205th (3/64-7/74)
	LOC:	L - end of 95th NE, off 171st		
	CUR:	L - (O) housing development		
Seattle Artillery Armory		HQ 115th Bde (4/59- /63)		
S-20 **Cougar Mountain/** **Issaquah**		2B 20A 8L-A		B/28th (/57-9/58) B/2/43d (9/58-6/59) B/2/205th (6/59-3/64) HHB/2/205th(6/60-3/64)
	LOC:	C - end of Cougar Mtn Rd L - S of SE 65th Pl		
	CUR:	C - (O) Cougar Mountain County Park L - (O) Cougar Mountain Regional Wildland Park		

Site Location	Radars	Magazines, Missiles, LaunchersConvert to Herc	Units (years)
S-32		2A/1B	C/433d (/56-9/58)
Lake Youngs		30A	C/4/60th (9/58-12/61)
shared launch facility with S-33		12L-A	
	LOC:	C – SE 184th St & SE Old Petrovitsky Dr	
		L - end of 174th SE off of E Lake Desire Dr	
	CUR:	C - (P) King County Sheriffs Department	
		L - (I) Maple Valley Christian School/South King County Activity Center	
S-33		2A/1B	B/433d (/56-9/58)
Lake Youngs/		30A	C/4/60th (9/58-12/61)
Renton		12L-A	
shared launch facility with S-32			
	LOC:	C - 14631 SE 192nd St & 148th Ave SE	
		L - end of 174th SE off of E Lake Desire Dr	
	CUR:	C – (P) USAR Center; 104th Division (Training) Drill Sergeant School	
		L – (I) Maple Valley Christian School/South King County Activity Center	
S-41			HHB/240th (4/58-4/59)
O'Brien			HHB/3/205th (4/59-6/59)
gun site			
S-43		2A/1B	D/433d (/55-9/58)
Kent/Midway		30A	D/4/60th (9/58-6/59)
		10L-A	B/3/205th (6/59-2/63)
	LOC:	C - Military Rd, N of WA 516 (229th Pl)	
		L - Military Rd & 38th Ave S	
	CUR:	C - (O) King County Parks/Kent School District	
		L - (P) WAArNG; 3/161st Infantry (Mech)	
S-45			HHB/433d (/56-9/58)
Kent			HHB/3/205th (6/59-2/63)
	LOC:	Military Rd & 38th Ave S	
	CUR:	(P) WAArNG; 3/161st Infantry (Mech)	
McChord AFB	SAGE Command Post	HQ 7ARADCOM (7/60-4/66)	
	2x AN/CPS-6B	HQ 31st Bde (-12/61)	
			USAF HQ 25th AD (10/51- /90)
			USAF HQ Seattle ADS (1/58-4/66)
			USAF 635th AC&WS

Site Location	Radars	Magazines, Missiles, Launchers	Convert to Herc	Units (years)
				(5/47-4/60)
	LOC:	*10 S Tacoma, I 5*		
	CUR:	*McChord AFB: HQ ANG Western Air Defense Sector; McChord AFB Museum*		
	Note:	*McChord was one of Air Defense Command's primary fighter interceptor bases*		
		from 1948 through 1989 and also hosted a SAGE direction center/combat center under		
		25th Air Division. The former headquarters site of the Seventh ARADCOM Region		
		and 31st Artillery Brigade, adjacent to the flight line, is now a parking lot.		
S-61 **Vashon Island**	HIPAR	1A/1B/1C 18H/30A 12L-UA (7L-H)	6/60- 3/61	A/433d (/56-9/58) A/4/60th (9/58-12/61) B/4/4th (12/61-10/64) B/2/205th (10/64-3/74)
	LOC:	*C - SW 210th St* *L – end of 119 Ave SW, N of SW 220th St*		
	CUR:	*C - (P) commercial use, ball park* *L - (P) Vashon Island Equestrian Park/Nike Events Center*		
S-62 **Ollala**		2A/1B 30A 12L-A		B/513th (/56-9/58) B/4/4th (9/58-6/59) C/3/205th (6/59-3/63)
	LOC:	*C - .5 N Ollala, 12700 Lala Cove Ln* *L - 1.5 SW Ollala, 7450 SE Nelson Rd, W of Klahanine Ln SE*		
	CUR:	*C - (P) Ollala Guest Lodge; substance abuse rehab center* *L - (P) private ownership*		
S-81 **Poulsbo**		2A/1B 30A 12L-A		D/433d (9/55- /56) HHB/513th (/55-9/58) D/513th (/56-9/58) HHB/4/4th (9/58-10/64) D/4/4th (9/58-11/60)
	LOC:	*C - 1.5 SE Poulsbo, 18360 Caldart Ave* *L - W Poulsbo, Finn Hill Rd*		
	CUR:	*C - (I) South Kitsap School District admin offices/Frank Raab Municipal Park* *L - (O) private development*		
S-82 **Winslow/** **Bainbridge Island**		1A/2B 30A 12L-A		A/513th (/56-9/58) A/4/4th (9/58-11/60)
	LOC:	*C - S Winslow, 4900 Rose Ave NE* *L – NE High School Rd*		
	CUR:	*C - (O) Bainbridge Parks District, Eagledale Park* *L - (P) Bainbridge Parks District, Strawberry Hill Park*		

Site Location	Radars	Magazines, Missiles, Launchers	Convert to Herc	Units (years)
S-90DC **Fort Lawton**	AN/FSG-1 Missile Master AN/GSG-5 BIRDIE FAA ARSR-1C 2 x AN/FPS-6A	AADCP	USAF 635th RADS (6/61-8/63) (AN/FPS-26)	HQ 26th Gp (12/61-3/66) HQ 49th Gp (3/66-8/74) HHB/433d (9/55- /56) HHB/4/4th (10/64-9/72) HHB/1/4th (9/72-7/74)
	LOC:	*W Seattle, W Government Way*		
	CUR:	*Seattle Discovery Park; USAR Fort Lawton; FAA radar site*		

Note: The majority of the former Fort Lawton is now Seattle Discovery Park with some historic structures remaining, including the Missile Master/BIRDIE blockhouse. The city demolished the remainder of the ARADCOM command/support buildings in 2001. The US Army Reserve's Fort Lawton is below the original post and incorporates two reserve centers.

Site Location	Radars	Magazines, Missiles, Launchers	Convert to Herc	Units (years)
S-90 **Fort Lawton** *temporary site*				D/513th (/55- /56)
	LOC: W Seattle, W Government Way			
	CUR: (P) City of Seattle Discovery Park; USAR Center			

Site Location	Radars	Magazines, Missiles, Launchers	Convert to Herc	Units (years)
S-92 **Kingston**	HIPAR	2B 12H/20A 8L-U	6/58- 1/59	C/513th (/56-9/58) C/4/4th (9/58-9/72) C/1/4th (9/72-3/74)
	LOC:	*C -*	*1 N Kingston, 27055 Ohio Ave*	
		L -	*W Kingston, 8998 NE West Kingston Rd*	
	CUR:	*C -*	*(O) Associated General Contractors of Oregon & Washington*	
		L -	*(O) North Kitsap County School District; Spectrum School, school bus maintenance facility*	

Site Location	Radars	Magazines, Missiles, Launchers	Convert to Herc	Units (years)
S-93R **Fort Worden** *radar located on Protection Island until 1957*				Radar Section, 31st Arty Bde
	LOC: Battery Benson			
	CUR: Fort Worden State Park			

SHEPPARD DEFENSE AREA

In the late 1950s Army Air Defense Command surveyed a multiple Strategic Air Command base for deployment of a Nike-Hercules battalions. One was the large technical training installation of Sheppard AFB, near Wichita Falls, TX, which in 1957 gained a wing of B-52s.

As with Malmstrom and Mountain Home AFBs, Nike deployment never got beyond the proposal and survey stages. Units assigned to Sheppard included the 4245th Strategic Wing and the 3740th Technical Training Wing.

Site Location	Radars	Magazines, Missiles, Launchers	Convert to Herc	Units (years)
SH-20 Petrolia	*Site survey only*			
SH-70 Burkburnett	*Site survey only*			

THULE DEFENSE AREA

Thule Air Base, Greenland, is named for the village of Ultima Thule (Danish for "The Utmost End"), and is located all of 900 miles from the North Pole. The Air Force established operations at the field in the 1950s as an air defense, tanker, and (later) missile warning base. Thule is still considered the ultimate remote tour.

The Army maintained a gun battalion at the base from 1955 through 1958, followed by a Nike-Hercules battalion. The sites were considered to be part of ARADCOM as they were dedicated to the defense of the CONUS. It appears that each battery had two magazines, with four batteries ringing the base. Sites were labeled 01, 13, 40, and 60 and constructed 1957-58. The sites were of a different design than others in ARADCOM, a direct result of the extreme weather conditions. Known as "Rising Star," each magazine had two elevators and no rail launchers. Additional information on ARADCOM operations at Thule is scarce.

Apparently, Nike operations were suspended about the same time that the Air Force removed the last interceptor squadron (322d FIS, flying F-102s), and the Tanker Task Force. Other units assigned during the Nike period included 4734th Air Defense Group, 4683d Air Defense Wing, and BMEWS Site I (Ballistic Missile Early Warning).

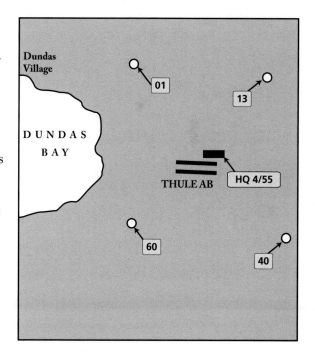

TRAVIS DEFENSE AREA

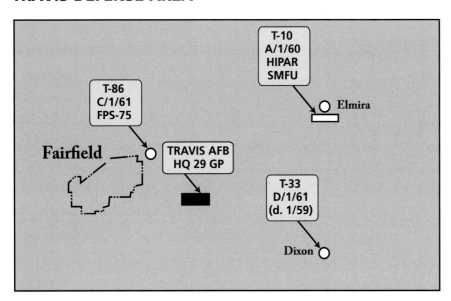

Long time trans-Pacific air terminal for the Air Force, Travis AFB also hosted a Strategic Air Command bombardment wing during the 1950s and 1960s. The base was selected for Nike-Hercules deployment during the first round of construction; in an interesting turn of events, the Travis battalion eventually assumed responsibility for the San Francisco Defense Area.

Air Force operations at the base during the Nike period included SAC's 14th Strategic Aerospace Division and 5th Bombardment Wing (Heavy); ADC's 82d Fighter Interceptor Squadron; MATS' 1501st Air Transport Wing; and MAC's 60th Military Airlift Wing. Fairfield AFS, adjacent to Travis, served as an Air Materiel command nuclear weapon storage and maintenance depot.

Site Location	Radars	Magazines, Missiles, Launchers	Convert to Herc	Units (years)
T-10	HIPAR	3B	6/58-	A/436th (1/57-9/58)
Elmira	SMFU	18H/30A	1/59	HHB/1/61st (9/58-6/71)
		12L-U		A/1/61st (9/58-3/74)
	LOC:	C - 3 SE Elmira, N of Hay Rd		
		L - 2 S Elmira, Hay Rd at Lewis Rd		
	CUR:	C - (P) low income housing, no radars		
		L - (I) private owner		
T-33		3AG		D/436th (1/57-9/58)
Dixon/Lambie		12A		D/1/61st (9/58-1/59)
		12L-A		
	LOC:	C - Lambie Rd E of Goose Haven Rd		
		L - Bithell Rd, N of Lambie Rd		
	CUR:	C - (P) California Department of Health Services/youth correctional facility		
		L - (O) agricultural		
T-53		2A/1B		B/436th (1/57-9/58)
Potrero Hills		30A		B/1/61st (9/58-1/59)
		12L-A		
	LOC:	C - 2.5 SSW Travis AFB, end of Branscombe Rd, Explosives Technology Rd		

Site Location	Radars	Magazines, Missiles, Launchers	Convert to Herc	Units (years)
	CUR:	L - 2.5 S Travis AFB, end of Branscombe Rd, Explosives Technology Rd		
		C - (P) Explosives Technology		
		L - (P) USAF Potrero Hill Storage Annex; Explosives Technology; one elevator operational		
Travis AFB	AN/GSG-5 BIRDIE	AADCP		HQ 29th Gp (/57- /62) HHB/436th (1/57-9/58) HHB/1/61st (9/58- /58)
	LOC:	4 E Fairfield		
	CUR:	Travis AFB; David Grant Medical Center; Travis AFB Museum		
T-86 Fairfield/ Cement Hills	ABAR/75	1A/1B/1C 18H/30A 12L-UA (8L-U)	12/60- 6/61	C/436th (1/57-9/58) C/1/61st (9/58-6/71)
	LOC:	C - N Fairfield, Cement Hill (no vehicle access)		
		L - N Fairfield, Clay Bank Rd N off of Air Base Pkwy		
	CUR:	C - (P) private ownership		
		L - (P) Solano County Detention Center/Solano County Animal Shelter/Suisun Unified School District vehicle maintenance		

TURNER DEFENSE AREA

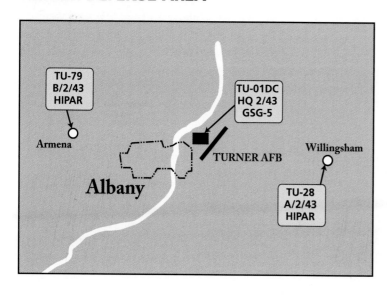

Turner AFB was transferred from Tactical Air Command to Strategic Air Command in 1959. The transfer resulted in the departure of a fighter wing and the arrival of B-52 and tanker operations, which led to the installation of a Nike-Hercules defense. The two batteries were of standard SAC design and protected the men and equipment of the 822d Air Division, 4138th Strategic Wing, 484th Bombardment Wing (Heavy), and MATS' 1370th Photo Mapping & Charting Wing. The AADCP was located on base; the Air Force installation providing long-range detection and tracking information was located at Eufala AFS, AL.

Turner AFB was transferred to the Navy as NAS Albany one year after the demise of the Nike-Hercules battalion. It continued in service with the Navy as the homeport of the RA-5C squadrons of Reconnaissance Attack Wing One through 1974.

Site Location	Radars	Magazines, Missiles, Launchers	Convert to Herc	Units (years)
TU-01 **Turner AFB**	AN/GSG-5 BIRDIE	AADCP		HHB/2/43d (7/59-3/66)
	LOC:	*NE Albany, US 82*		
	CUR:	*(P) Miller Brewing Company, Federal Job Corps Center*		
TU-28 **Willingsham/** **Sylvester**		3AG 12H 12L-H		A/2/43d (11/60-3/66)
	LOC:	*C - 4 W Sylvester, Pinckral Rd, N off of GA 520/US 82* *L - 3 W Sylvester, Pine Knoll Rd, N off of GA 520/US 82*		
	CUR:	*C - (I) private retirement home* *L - (I) Midway Auto Parts*		
TU-79 **Armena/Sasser**		3AG 12H 12L-H		B/2/43d (11/60-3/66)
	LOC:	*C - 9 NW Albany, S of US 82, Joiner Dr, W off Hampton Ln, W off N Doubletree Dr* *L - 10 NW Albany, S of US 82, E of Winnifred Rd, N of Martindale Dr*		
	CUR:	*C - (I) Anchorage; drug & alcohol rehab center* *L - (O) housing development*		

WALKER DEFENSE AREA

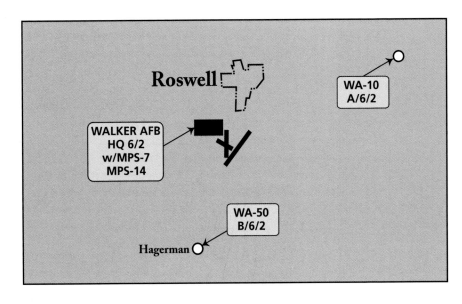

Walker was particularly unusual: the sites were selected and built, the battalion activated, batteries were assigned—and the whole setup was shut down. Many of the personnel, including the battalion commander, LCOL Fred Ruck, were later transferred to the Omaha Defense Area.

Air Force units at Walker AFB during this brief period were the 6th Bombardment Wing (recently converted from B-36s) and the 58th Fighter Interceptor Squadron.

Site Location	Radars	Magazines, Missiles, LaunchersConvert to Herc	Units (years)
WA-10 **Roswell** *not operational*		3AG	A/6/2d
	LOC:	C - 10.5 E Roswell, Alamo Rd at Hatchita Rd, 2 N US 380	
		L - 11.5 E Roswell, Hatchita Rd, 2 N US 380	
	CUR:	C - (I) NMArNG Military Academy	
		L - (I) NMARnG training site	
Walker AFB	AN/MPS-7 AN/MPS-14	AADCP	HHB/6/2d (4/60-6/60) USAF 686th AC&WS (10/53-8/63)
	LOC:	5 S Roswell	
	CUR:	Roswell Industrial Air Center	
WA-50 **Hagerman** *not operational*		3AG	B/6/2d
	LOC:	C - 13 S Roswell, 5 W US 285, W Chickasaw Rd	
		L - 14 S Roswell, 5 W US 285, Des Moines Rd	
	CUR:	C - (I) Roswell Correctional Center	
		L - (P) abandoned	

WASHINGTON DEFENSE AREA

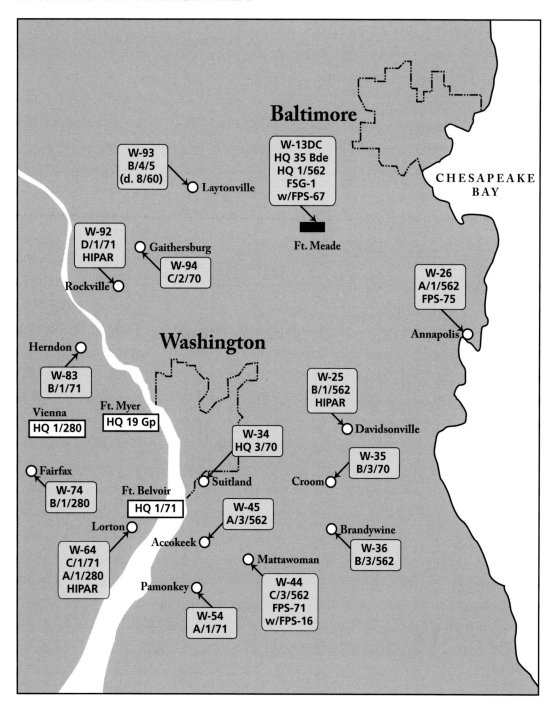

Baltimore

W-93
B/4/5
(d. 8/60)

○ Laytonville

W-13DC
HQ 35 Bde
HQ 1/562
FSG-1
w/FPS-67

CHESAPEAKE
BAY

Ft. Meade

W-92
D/1/71
HIPAR

○ Gaithersburg

W-94
C/2/70

Rockville ○

W-26
A/1/562
FPS-75

Annapolis ○

Washington

Herndon ○

W-83
B/1/71

W-25
B/1/562
HIPAR

Vienna   Ft. Myer
HQ 1/280   HQ 19 Gp

○ Davidsonville

W-34
HQ 3/70

W-35
B/3/70

○ Fairfax

W-74
B/1/280

Ft. Belvoir

HQ 1/71

○ Suitland   Croom ○

W-45
A/3/562

Lorton ○

Accokeek ○

○ Brandywine

W-36
B/3/562

W-64
C/1/71
A/1/280
HIPAR

○ Mattawoman

Pamonkey ○

W-44
C/3/562
FPS-71
w/FPS-16

W-54
A/1/71

Two-thirds of the combined Washington–Baltimore defense, the nation's capitol Nike organization possessed several notables: the first operational Nike-Ajax battalion, the 36th AAMBn; the first operational battery, a temporary site at Fort Meade; as well as a designated "National Site" for VIP tours.

The purpose of the defense was obvious: to protect the military and Federal center of the nation. The AADCP was located at Fort Meade, with a co-assigned Air Force radar squadron. SAGE input data was provided by the command post at Fort Lee AFS, Petersburg, VA.

Washington operated under the 35th Brigade until very late, with operations under a group level command for the final ten months of the defense. In 1971 Washington–Baltimore merged with the Hampton Roads defense; by shutdown in 1974, the three defense areas operated only nine batteries.

Site Location	Radars	Magazines, Missiles, Launchers	Convert to Herc	Units (years)
W-13 DC **Fort George G.** **Meade**	AN/FSG-1 Missile Master AN/TSQ-51 Missile Mentor AN/FPS-67 2 x AN/FPS-6 2 x AN/FPS-6B (AN/FPS-90)	AADCP		HQ 2ARADCOM (3/51-8/61) HQ 35th Bde (2/50-12/73) HHB/36th (1/54-9/58) HHB/1/562d (9/58-12/62) USAF 770th RADS (10/61-1/80)
	LOC:	*MD 175 & MD 198*		
	CUR:	*Fort George G. Meade: HQ First US Army (Forward); National Security Agency;* *HQ Army Intelligence & Security Command; Defense Information School.*		
	NOTE:	*The former AADCP is occupied by the fort's Director of Information Services*		
W-13 **Fort George G. Meade** *temporary site*				B/36th (5/54-6/55)
	LOC:	*unknown*		
	CUR:	*Fort George G. Meade* *NOTE: First operational Nike site, 30 May 1954*		
W-25 **Davidsonville**	HIPAR	2B 12H/20A 8L-U	3/58- 6/58	B/36th (6/55-9/58) B/1/562d (9/58-12/62) B/1/71st (12/62- /65) B/4/1st (/65-11/68) A/1/70th (11/68-4/74)
	LOC:	*C - Anne Bridge Rd & Wayson Rd* *L - Elmer F. Hagner Ln and Anne Bridge Rd, E of Wayson Rd*		
	CUR:	*C - (I) recreational area* *L - (I) Anne Arundel County Police Training Academy*		
NOTE: National Site, 1963-1974				
W-26 **Annapolis/** **Skidmore/** **Bay Bridge**	ABAR/75	1A/1B/1C 18H/30A 12L-U (8L-H)	12/60- 6/61	A/36th (/55-9/58) A/1/562d (9/58-12/62) A/1/70th (12/62-11/68)

Site Location	Radars	Magazines, Missiles, Launchers	Convert to Herc	Units (years)
	LOC:	C - N of US 50, Benson Ln off of Broadneck Rd		
		L - N of US 50, Bay Head Rd at Woods Landing Dr		
	CUR:	C - (P) USAR Center		
		L - (P) U.S. Government		
		NOTE: First ArNG Nike-Hercules operations		
W-34 Suitland				HHB/686th (/59-5/59) HHB/3/70th (5/59-3/63) HHB/1/71st (3/63- /65)
W-35 **Croom/Marlboro**		2B 20A 8L-A		HHB/75th (11/54-9/58) B/75th (/55-9/58) HHB/3/562d (9/58-6/60) B/3/562d (9/58-6/60) B/3/70th (6/60-3/63)
	LOC:	C – N of Mt. Calvert Rd, .9 E of MD 382		
		L -, E of Duvall Rd		
	CUR:	C - (P) Croom Vocational High School		
		L - (I) Croom Vocational High School		
W-36 **Brandywine/** **Naylor**		2A/1B 30A 12L-A		D/75th (/57-9/58) D/3/562d (9/58-12/61)
	LOC:	C - end of Edgemeade Rd, W of Molly Berry Rd, 2 W of MD 382		
		L - S off Candy Hill Rd, 1 W of MD 382		
	CUR:	C - private?		
		L - (P) private owner;		
W-44 **Mattawoman/** **Waldorf/** **La Plata**	ABAR/71 AN/FPA-16	2B 12H/20A 8L-UA	6/58- 12/58	C/75th (/55-9/58) C/3/562d (9/58-12/61) A/1/71st (12/61-3/63) C/1/70th (3/63-6/71)
	LOC:	C - 5 N Waldorf, Country Ln		
		L - 6 NE Waldorf, Country Ln, S of Cedarville Rd		
	CUR:	C - (P) park?		
		L - (P) American Indian Cultural Center/Maryland Indian Heritage Society of Waldorf		

Site Location	Radars	Magazines, Missiles, Launchers	Convert to Herc	Units (years)
W-45 **Accokeek**		2B 20A 8L-A		HHB/686th (2/59- /59) A/75th (/55-9/58) A/3/562d (9/58-6/60) B/3/70th (6/60-12/61)
	LOC:	C - 4 W Waldorf, S side Bensville Rd (MD 228) L - 4 W Waldorf, N side Bensville Rd (MD 228)		
	CUR:	C - (I) Naval Research Laboratory Field Site Lower Waldorf L - (P) Naval Research Laboratory Waldorf Annex		
W-54 **Pamonkey**		2B 20A 8L-A		A/71st (/55-9/58) A/1/71st (9/58-12/61)
	LOC:	C – end of Gwynn Rd L - W off Bumpy Oak Rd		
	CUR:	C - (P) Charles County Alternative School L - (P) Pamonkey Naval Research Laboratory		
W-64 **Lorton** DOUBLE SITE	HIPAR	2A/2B/2C 24H/60A 24L-UA (16L-H)	6/58- 3/59	C/71st (/54-9/58) C/1/71st (9/58-8/63) A/1/280th (9/59-3/63) A/4/111th (8/63-4/74)
	LOC:	C - S of Silver Brook and W of VA 600 L - Hooes Rd (VA 636), N off Furnace Rd (VA 611)		
	CUR:	C - (P) former District of Columbia maximum security prison L - (P) former District of Columbia maximum security prison		

NOTE: Lorton was the first fixed battery site built and served as the National Site from 1957 to 1963. In 2001, The National Cold War Museum had acquired the property and will restore the former ARADCOM installation as a museum site.

Alexandria				HHB/125th (2/58-6/59) HHB/1/280th (6/59- /59)
Fort Belvoir				HHB/71st (7/54-9/58) HHB/1/71st (9/58-3/63)
	LOC:	5 S Alexandria, US 1		
	CUR:	Fort Belvoir: Defense Logistics Agency; Defense Contract Audit Agency; HQ Criminal Investigation Command; Night Vision & Electronics Sensors Directorate; Information Systems Software Center; National Imagery & Mapping College; Defense Systems Management College; Army Management Staff College; USAR ArNG		

Site Location	Radars	Magazines, Missiles, Launchers	Convert to Herc	Units (years)
W-74 **Fairfax/Pohick**		2B 20A 8L-A		D/71st (/54-9/58) D/1/71st (9/58-9/59) B/2/280th (9/59-3/63)
	LOC:	C - Ladue Ln, S of Popes Head Rd L - 1 W, Quiet Brook Rd, S of Popes Head Rd		
	CUR:	C - (P) Fairfax County maintenance yard L - (O) Fairfax County park		
Fort Myer				HQ 19th Gp (/59- /63)
	LOC:	Arlington		
	CUR:	Fort Myer: HQ 3rd US Infantry Regiment (The Old Guard; ceremonial unit); The US Army Band		
Vienna				HHB/1/280th (/59-3/63)
W-83 **Herndon/** **Dranesville**		2A/1B 30A 12L-A		B/71st (/55-9/58) B/1/71st (9/58-11/62)
	LOC:	C - Springvale Rd, S of VA 193/Georgetown Pike L - Utterback Store Rd, N of Leesburg Pike (VA 3)		
	CUR:	C - (O) USAR? L - (O) Great Falls Nike Park		
W-92 **Rockville**	HIPAR	1B/2C 18H/30A 12L-U	6/58- 6/59	A/71st (/54-9/55) D/602d (9/55-9/58) D/4/5th (9/58-8/60) D/1/71st (8/60- /65) A/4/1st (/65-4/74)
	LOC:	C - 10901 Darnestown Rd L - 770 Muddy Branch Rd at School Dr		
	CUR:	C - (P) US Consumer Products Safety Commission Engineering Laboratory L - (P) National Institute for Standards and Technology/USACE		
W-93 **Laytonville/** **Derwood**		2A/1B 30A 12L-A		B/602d (9/55-9/58) B/4/5th (9/58-8/60)
	LOC:	C - 21515 Zion Rd L - 5321 Riggs Rd A - 5115 Riggs Rd		
	CUR:	C - (O) American Foundation for Autistic Children L - (P) MDArNG; unit unknown A - (I) MDArNG B/1/115th Infantry		

Site Location	Radars	Magazines, Missiles, Launchers	Convert to Herc	Units (years)
W-94		2A/1B		C/602d (9/55-9/58)
Gaithersburg		30A		C/4/5th (9/58-6/60)
		12L-A		C/2/70th (6/60-3/63)
	LOC:	C - Calypso Ln, access S off of Snouffers School Rd		
		L - 8791 Snouffers School Rd		
	CUR:	C - (O) residential area		
		L - (P) MGEN Benjamin L. Hunton Memorial USAR Center; launchers abandoned		

WHITEMAN AFB (Safeguard)

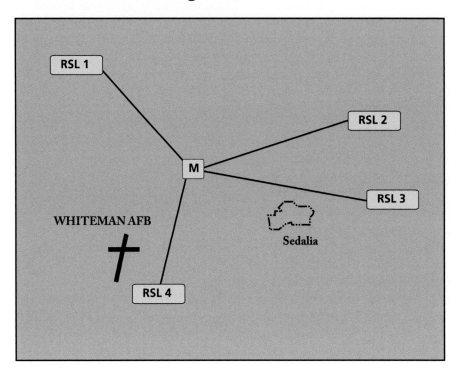

The fourth of four planned Safeguard installations, Whiteman AFB, MO, was scheduled to become operational in early 1976. The purpose of the defense was the protection of the 150 Minuteman II silos of the 351st Strategic Missile Wing. The Whiteman installation was similar to Francis E. Warren's in that the Perimeter Acquisition Radar was deleted and a fourth remote Sprint site was added. The main complex was to be placed immediately southwest of Hughesville, approximately ten miles northwest of Sedalia. The remote Sprint launchers would be located northeast of Concordia; southwest of Longwood; northwest of Otterville; and southeast of Whiteman AFB. The layout of the RSLs was dictated by bomber flyout corridors and approach and landing patterns. As with the Francis E. Warren complex in Wyoming, the site surveys for the Whiteman facility were suspended and the complex was cancelled on 2 October 1975.

US Army AAA Gun Site Program 1951-59

This is a compilation of information concerning the Army's AAA Gun Site program which ran from 1951 to 1959 and involved the placing of 90mm and 120mm gun batteries and supporting units in self-contained, permanent positions located in arcs around major cities and critical areas. In July 1950, there were seventeen 90mm AAA battalions in the Regular Army (two were in training) and five 120mm gun battalions. The Army National Guard had an additional eleven gun units.

Initially, the AAA gun program consisted of Active Army (Regular Army and mobilized Army National Guard (ArNG) units stationed at major Army installations such as Fort Bliss, TX, and Camp Stewart, GA, with missions to move to major cites on order. Subsequently, these units were moved to Army installations closer to their intended defense sites. Eventually the units manned the sites in a rotation, being billeting at the Army post.

In late 1952, the on-site positions became permanent stations for the batteries assigned to them and eventually barracks and administrative structures were built. During the winter of 1952-53, many AAA units lived in tents on site until permanent, usually prefabricated metal buildings were erected on concrete and wooden foundations. A typical AAA site consisted of eleven such buildings, eight for barracks, one each for maintenance, battery CP, and the dayroom. Additional tents or wooden buildings were erected for mess hall and latrine facilities.

Between 1952 and 1953 mobilized ArNG units were released from active duty, and in most cases new Regular Army units replaced then in place. Starting in early 1954 the Nike-Ajax surface-to-air guided missile system replaced AAA guns in Active Army AAA battalions (initially with 120mm units). Concurrent with this changeover, non-federalized ArNG units took over gun sites. These units had about ten full-time soldiers, but were primarily drilling guardsmen and usually had a home armory in addition to the gun site.

Starting in 1957, the Active Army began replacing Nike-Ajax with the next generation, Nike-Hercules, and the ArNG on-site program began receiving Nike-Ajax systems and moving units to Nike sites. The Active Army AAA gun program officially ended in October 1957 and the few remaining gun units were inactivated shortly thereafter. The ArNG gun program lasted at least until 1959.

Not included in this listing are numerous divisional and non-divisional AAA Automatic Weapons (AW) battalions, which were not involved in the static gun site program. Most of these were later converted to 75mm Skysweeper units. While technically an AAA gun, the Skysweeper was used tactically the same way the AW units were used and are not included here (except for the two deployed to the Savannah River Project). Only 90mm, 120mm, and headquarters units associated with the gun sites program are included on this listing.

Baltimore Defense Area

35th AAA Bn (90mm)
89th AAA Bn (90mm)
115th AAA Bn (90mm) (mob MS ArNG)
208th AAA Gp (mob CT ArNG)
602d AAA Bn (90mm)
683d AAA BN (90mm) (MD ArNG)
684th AAA BN (90mm) (MD ArNG)
736th AAA Bn (90mm) (mob DE ArNG)

Baltimore [Northern Point and Eastern Ave]
    D-602 (90mm) (53-54);
    ?-683 (90mm) (MD ArNG) (55-59)
Catonsville [BA-66] [St. Timothy's School for Girls] [Rolling Road & US Rte 40]
    D-35 (90mm);
    A-89 (90mm) (52-56);
    A-684 (90mm)(MD ArNG) (56-59)
Curtis Bay [Baltimore- Fort Armistead]
    A-35 (90mm) (?-57)
Dundalk, MD [BA-31] [Sollars Point]
    A-602 (90mm);
    D-35 (90mm); (?-55);
    ?-683 (90mm) (MD ArNG) (55-59)
Edgewood, MD [BA-16H] [Army Chem Ctr]
    602 (90mm) (53-55);
    B-602 (90mm) (53-55)
Essex [8 mi e of Baltimore; Golden Ring and Northern Ave.]
    B-602 (90mm);
    C-602 (90mm) (53-55);
    ?-683 (90mm) (MD ArNG) (55-59)
Fort Meade [BA-62H] [MD 175/198][current DOIM]
    35 (90mm)(52-54);
    89 (90mm);
    208th Gp (mob CT ArNG) (51-52)
Linthicum [BA-51][Friendship IAP]
    B-35 (90mm)(?-57)
Glen Burnie [BA-50]

C-35 (90mm) (?-57);
HHB-35 (54-57)
Gwynn Oaks [Gwynn Oaks Park]
    B-89 (90mm) (?-56);
    ?-684 (90mm)(MD ArNG) (56-59)
Parksville [Moore Ave/ Oakleigh Rd]
    (C-602 (90mm); (?-55);
    ?-683 (90mm) (MD ArNG) (55-59)
Pikesville [Smith Ave/ Old Pimlico Rd]
    (C-89 (90mm) (?-56);;
    ?-684 (90mm) (MD ArNG) (56-59)
Towson [York Road near Beltaway [Ruhl Armory?]
    D-89 (90mm) (52-55);
    D-683 (90mm) (MD ArNG) (56-59)

Boston Defense Area

56th AAA Bde
15th AAA Gp
16th AAA Bn (90mm)
514th AAA Bn (90mm)
605th AAA Bn (90mm)
685th AAA Bn (90mm) (mob MA ArNG)
704th AAA BN (90mm) (mob MA ArNG) (and on-site program)
772d AAA Bn (90mm) (MA ArNG)

Belmont [Concord Ave]
    A-16 (90mm) (52-57)
Brighton [Nonantum Street]
    B-16 (90mm) (52-55);
    A-704 (90mm) (MA ArNG) (55);
    D-772 (90mm) (MA ArNG) (56-58).
Fort Banks [B-21][Winthrop]
    HHB-704 (90mm) (52);
    HHB-685 (90mm)(52-53);
    HHB-514 (90mm) (53-55);
    HHB-16 (90mm) (52-57);
    D-704 (90mm) (MA ArNG) (55-58).
Fort Dawes [B-22] [Deer Island]

HHB/ C-704 (90mm) (52-53);
HHB/ C-605 (90mm) (53-56);
B-16 (90mm) (56-57).
Fort Duvall [B-31]
D-685 (90mm) (52-53);
D-514 (90mm) (53-55)
Hyde Park [B-51] [Farrar Ave]
A-685 (90mm) (52-53);
A-514 (90mm) (53-55);
B-704 (90mm) (MA ArNG) (55-58).
Lynn [B-10] [Rte 1A near Saugus line]
D-704 (90mm) (52-53);
D-605 (90mm) (53-56);
D-16 (90mm) (56-57))
Medford [B-90] [Medford Fells Park]
D-16 (90mm) (52-56);
A-772 (90mm) (MA ArNG) (56-58)
Milton [Randolph Ave]
B-685 (90mm) (52-53);
B-514 (90mm) (53-55);
A-704 (90mm) (MA ArNG) (55-58)
Nahant [East Point] [B-17]
A-704 (90mm) (52-53);
A-605 (90mm) (53-56)
Newton [Nahanton Street]
C-16 (90mm) (52-57)
Quincy [Merrymount Park]
C-685 (90mm) (52-53);
C-514 (90mm) (53-55);
B-16 (90mm) (55-56);
C-704 (90mm) (MA ArNG) (55-58)
Saugus [Main St]
B, 704 (90mm) (52-53);
B-605 (90mm) (53-56);
C-772 (90mm) (56-58)

Bridgeport Defense Area
211th AAA Bn (90mm) (CT ArNG)
283d AAA Bn (90mm) (CT ArNG)

Camp Hanford, WA Defense Area
5th AAA Gp
83d AAA Bn (120mm)
501st AAA BN (120mm)
518th AAA Bn (120mm)
519th AAA Bn (120mm)
SSF for Hanford: 2 ArNG 120mm BNs: 420th (WA ArNG) and unspecified)

HA-01 [North Slope]
D-519 (120mm)
HA-03 [Riverland]
5th AAA Gp
HA-04 [North Slope]
C-519 (120mm)
HA-10 [North Slope]
HHB/ B-519 (120mm)
HA-12 [North Slope]
A-519 (120mm)
HA-21 [North Slope]
B-518 (120mm)
HA-40 [200 East Hill] [Central Area]
(D-518 (120mm)
HA-42 [Army Loop Road] [Central Area]
(A-518 (120mm))
HA-50 [Army Loop Road] [Central Area]
C-518 (120mm)
HA-51 [Army Loop Road] [Central Area]
B-501 (120mm)
HA-61H [Central Area]
HHB/ A-501 (120mm)
HA-70 [Base Camp 130] [Riverland below Columbia River, abandoned in 54]
D-501 (120mm)
HA-71 [Riverland below Columbia River, abandoned in 54]
D-83 (120mm)
HA-72 [Riverland]
C-83 (120mm)
HA-80 [Central Area
C-501 (120mm)

HA-80 [North Slope]

    B-83 (120mm)

HA-90 [North Slope]

    HHB/ A-83 (120mm)

Chicago Defense Area

13th AAA Bn (90mm)

22d AAA Gp

23d AAA Gp

45th AAA Bde

49th AAA Bn (90mm)

51st AAA Bde (mob PA ArNG)

79th AAA Bn (120mm)

86th AAA Bn (120mm)

101st AAA Bn (90mm) (mob GA ArNG) ?

496th AAA Bn (90mm)

713th AAA BN (90mm) (mob SC ArNG) ????

734th AAA Bn (90mm)

768th AAA Bn (90mm) (mob IL ArNG)

Argo [C-62]

    A-13 (90mm)

Argonne National Labs [C-86]

    D-13 (90mm)

Chicago [1660 East Hyde Park Blvd]

    13th (90mm)

Chicago [1660 East Hyde Park Blvd]

    13th (90mm)

Chicago [Navy Pier]

    A-79 (120mm);

    C-13 [A-49?] (90mm) (52-54)

Fort Sheridan/ Skokie

    49 (90mm);

    D-49 (90mm);

    C-13 [A-49?] (90mm) (54-55)

LaGrange [C-66]

    C-49 (90mm)

LaGrange [C-71] [Westchester]

    (13th (90mm))

Maywood [C-76]

    B-13 (90mm)

Oaklawn [130th St & Cicero]

    734 (90mm) 53-57)

Palatine (C-61)

    D-13 (90mm)

Skokie [C-91] [Lalse & Lowell Aves.]

    HHB-49 (52-56)

Dallas-Fort Worth Defense Area

DFW-60 [Grounds of AF Plant No. 4 (Convair now Lockheed] (75mm) (>1958)

    546th AAA Bn (75mm)

Detroit Defense Area

18th AAA BN (90mm)

28th AAA Gp

99th AAA Bn (90mm)

228th AAA Gp (mob SC ArNG)

504th AAA Bn (90mm)

516th AAA Bn

698th AAA Bn (90mm) (mob IL ArNG)

Algonac [D-17]

    D-18 (90mm);

    D-518 90mm) (56-58)

Algonquin [Dearborn] [D-26]

    C-504 (55)

Dearborn [D-62] [Greenfield & Dearborn Sts.]

    HHB-504 (53-55)

Detroit [D-50] [6301 W. Jefferson]

    516 (53-55)

Detroit [Mark Twain & Belton [D-72]]

    18 (90mm);

    B-18 (90mm);

    C-504 (90mm) (54-55)

Ferndale [D-90]

    D-504 (90mm) (54-56)

Fort Wayne

A-504 (90mm) (55)
Grosse Island NAS [D-51] [Ryan & 10 Mile Road?]
Hazel Park, MI [D-91]
A-99 (90mm); D-516 (90mm) (56)
Newport [D-58T]
C-504 (90mm) (55)
Park Grove [Crusade & Novaro Rd, Detroit]
99 (90mm)

Los Angeles Defense Area

47th AAA Bde
77th AAA Bn (90mm)
551st AAA Bn (90mm)
554th AAA Bn

Fort MacArthur
77 (90mm)
Long Beach [LA-40]
B-554 (56)
Manhattan Beach
77 (90mm);
C-77(90mm)
San Pedro [LA-43]
B-554 (56)
Starston [LA-32]
B-551 (90mm) (55)
Van Nuys [LA-96][Birmingham Hosp]
551 (90mm)

New York City Defense Area

11th AAA Gp
12th AAA Bn (90mm)
16th AAA Gp
34th AAA Bn (90mm)
41st AAA Bn (90mm)
52d AAA Bde
66th AAA Bn (120mm)
69th AAA Bn (90mm)
80th AAA Gp

98th AAA Bn (90mm)
102d AAA Bde (mob NY ArNG)
109th AAA Bn (90mm) (NJ ArNG)
209th AAA Gp (mob NY ArNG) ?
245th AAA BN (120mm) (NY ArNG)
259th AAA Bn (120mm) (mob NY ArNG)
505th AAA Bn (120mm)
526th AAA Bn (90mm)
554th AAA Bn ?
712th AAA Bn (90mm) (mob FL ArNG)
737th AAA Bn (90mm)
749th AAA Bn (90mm)

Belleville, NJ [NY-81] [Branch Brook Park]
HHB-98 (53-56);
B-109 (90mm)(NJ ArNG)(57?-58)
Bronx [NY-08] [Kingsbridge Rd & Jerome Ave]
C-749 (90mm) 56-57)
Brooklyn
245 (120mm)
Crawfords Corners [Ft. Hancock?]
B-749 (90mm) (54-58)
East Rutherford, NJ
HHB-749 (54-57)
Elizabeth, NJ [NY-67] [Richmond & Brunswick Ave]
HHB, 254th AAA Gp (NJ ArNG) (58);
A-109 (90mm) (58))
Englewood, NJ
749 (90mm) (53-54)
Fort Hamilton
66 (120mm) (52-54);
69 (90mm) (54-57);
B-66 (120mm) (52-54)
Fort Hancock, NJ
D-12 (90mm);
HHB-66 (54-55);
B-66 (120mm) (54-55);
A-34 [D-11?] (90mm)(56);
B-34 (90mm) (56);
A-737 (90mm) (54-56);

B-749 (90mm) (52-53);

C-505 (120mm)

Fort Lee [NY-03] [Hudson Terrace]

C-749 (90mm) 53-56);

D-109 (90mm) (NJ ArNG) (55-58)

Fort Slocum, NY [NY-16]

D-66 (120mm);

B-98 (90mm)(Jun 56-Jun 57);

A-749 (90mm) (55-57)

Fort Tilden [NY-43]

69 (90mm) (51-54);

505 (120mm);

737 (90mm);

A-69 (90mm)(51-52);

HHB- 737 (53-57);

HHB- 505 (52-54);

A-505 (120mm) (52-55);

C-505 (120mm) (52-55)

Fort Totten [NY-19]

41 (90mm);

34 (90mm) (52-56);

HHB-69 (50-51);

HHB-66 (55)

Fort Wadsworth, Staten Island

102d AAA Bde (50-52);

C-66 (120mm);

12 (90mm)

Miller Field, Staten Island

12 (90mm); HHB-66 (Jun 52-Nov 52);

A-737 (90mm) (52)

Moonachie, NJ

New York [NY-30]

D-69 (90mm)(52-56)

New York [NY-34]

B-69 (90mm) (52-56)

New York [NY-40]

D-69 (90mm)(56-57)

New York [NY-41]

B-69 (90mm)(56-57);

A-66(90mm)

New York [NY-45]

C-737 (90mm) (53-56)

Newark, NJ [NY-74] [South Munn & South Orange Aves, Vailsburg Park]

HHB-109 (90mm) (NJ ArNG)

C-109 (90mm) (58)

Nutley, NJ [Camp Avondale]

B-738 (90mm) (52-54)

Secaucus, NJ

98 (90mm)

Teaneck, NJ [NY-96]

B-98 (90mm);

A-749 (90mm) (53-55)

Teterboro Airport, NJ

Wallington, NJ [NY-91]

HHB-98 (May 56-Jun 57)

Niagara Falls Defense Area

2d AAA Gp

44th AAA Bn (90mm)

336th AAA Bn (90mm) (mob NY ArNG)

606th AAA Bn (90mm)

Grand Island [Staley Rd]

HHB/ D-606 (90mm) (53-57)

Grand Island [NF-30]

B-606 (90mm) (53-55)

Lewiston, NY [NF-10]

A-606 (90mm))

Lewiston, NY [NF-92]

B-606 (90mm) (55-57)

Youngstown, NY [Fort Niagara]

Norfolk Defense Area

3d AAA Gp

38th AAA Bn (90mm)

56th AAA Bn (90mm)

550th AAA Bn (90mm)

Churchland
    A/ B-38 (90mm)
Fort Monroe [N-03]
    56 (90mm);
    A-56 (90mm)
Fort Story
    38 (90mm);
    550 (90mm) (53-54)
Lafayette Station, Norfolk
    D-38 (90mm)
Newport News
    D-56 (90mm)
Norfolk (Capeview & Parkview Sta.)
    HHB-550 (54-57)
Ocean View 3, Norfolk
    A/ B/ C/ D-550 (90mm) (53-55)
Phoebus
    B-56 (90mm)
Pine Chapel Rd, Hampton
    D-56 (90mm)
Portsmouth
    C-38 (90mm)

Philadelphia Defense Area

19th AA Bn (90mm)
24th AAA Gp
51st AAA Bn (90mm)
53d AAA Bde
108th AAA Bde (mob GA ArNG)
116th AAA Bn (90mm) (NJ ArNG)
150th AAA Bn (90mm) (mob NC ArNG)
209th AAA Gp (mob NY ArNG) ???
226th AAA Gp (mob AL ArNG)
337th AAA Bn (90mm) (mob PA ArNG)
506th AAA Bn (90mm)
738th AAA Bn (90mm)
Camden [PH-30]
    B-19 (90mm)(52-56)
Germantown, PA [PH-02] [Ardleigh St, Logan Sta., Phila 41

[Logan Station] [Swarthmore]
HHB-506 (52-53);
    B-506th (90mm) (52-55)
Media, PA (Marple)
    51 (90mm)
Marple, PA [PH-73]
    A-51 (90mm)
Merchantville, NJ [PH-29] [Camden] [Cornell Ave & Rte 70]
    738 (90mm) (52-56);
HHB-116 (90mm) (NJ ArNG) (58);
    A-116 (90mm) (NJ ArNG) (58)
Mount Ephraim, NJ [Bellmawr, NJ]] [PH-39] [Browning Rd]
    19 (90mm) (53-57)
Pennsauken [PH-23] [Union Ave]
    B-116 (90mm) (NJ ArNG) (58)
Philadelphia IAP [PH-57]
    B-19 (90mm) (56-57)
Roxboro [PH-94]
    A-51 (90mm) (55-56)
Swarthmore [PH-03]
    C-506 (90mm) (52-55)
Swarthmore [PH-09]
    C-506 (90mm) (52-55)
Swarthmore
    HHB-19 (52-53)

Pittsburgh Defense Area

18th AAA Gp
74th AAA Bn (90mm) [repl 102 NY ArNG]
102d AAA Bn (90mm) (mob NY ArNG)
182d AAA Bn (90mm) (mob OH ArNG)
509th AAA Bn (90mm) [repl 708 PA ArNG]
701st AAA BN (90mm) [repl 182 OH ArNG]
708th AAA Bn (90mm) (mob PA ArNG) and on-site program
724th AAA Bn (90mm) (PA ArNG) on-site program

Blawnox [Blawnox Prison Farm Rd]
    D-74 (90mm) (52-55);
    (?-708 (PA ArNG) (56-59?)
Brentwood [Brentwood Rd]

D-701 (90mm) (52-55))

Bridgeville [Cook School Rd]

B-509 (90mm);

(?-724 (PA ArNG) (56-59?)

Etna [Middle Road]

C-74 (90mm) (52-55);

(?-708 (PA ArNG) (56-59?)

Heidelburg [Collier Rd]

C-509 (90mm);

(?-724 (PA ArNG) (56-59?)

Kenmawr [Phillips Rd]

D-509 (90mm));

(?-724 (PA ArNG) (56-59?)

Kennywood Park

(B-701 (90mm) (52-55))

Millvale [McKnight Road]

B-74 (90mm) (52-55);

(?-708 (PA ArNG) (56-59?)

Moon Run [Planet Way]

HHB/ A-509 (90mm) (52-55);

(?-724 (PA ArNG) (56-59?)

South Park, Broughton

74 (90mm);

509 (90mm);

HHB/ C-701 (90mm) (52-55)

West View Park

HHB/ A-74 (90mm) (52-55);

(?-708 (PA ArNG) (56-59?)

Wilkinsburg [Frick Park]

A-701 (90mm) (52-55)

Providence Defense Area

Providence

243d AAA Bn (90mm)

705th AA Bn (90mm)

San Diego Defense Area

730th AA Bn (90mm) (CA ArNG)

San Francisco Defense Area

9th AAA Bn (120mm)

30th AAA Gp

271st AA Bn (90mm)(CA ArNG)

718th AAA Bn (90mm) (mob CA ArNG)

728th AA Bn (90mm)(CA ArNG) (also mob)

740th AAA Bn (90mm)

752d AAA Bn (90mm)

Alameda

728 (90mm)

Fort Baker

740 (90mm)

Fort Barry [SF-9T]

B-752 (90mm);

D-9 (120mm) (53-54)

Fort Funston

D-752) (90mm)

Fort Winfield Scott

9 (120mm);

(A-9 (120mm)

Grizzly Peak, Berkeley

752 (90mm)

Presidio San Francisco

HHB-9th (51-54)

San Francisco

271st (90mm)

Savannah Defense Area

Savannah River Project, AEC Installations, Jackson, SC

33d AAA Bn (90mm)

425th AAA Bn (75mm)

478th AAA Bn (75mm)

Seattle Defense Area

20th AAA Bn (90mm)

26th AAA Gp

28th AAA Bn (120mm)

31st AAA Bde

420th AAA Bn (90mm) (mob WA ArNG)

513th AAA Bn (90mm)

Fort Lawton
  20 (90mm);
  28 (120mm);
  513 (90mm)
Winslow, Bainbridge Island
  B-20 (90mm)
S-71
S-60
S-41 O'Brien [S-41]
S-12 Phantom Lake [S-12][Bellevue;

Washington, DC

3d AAA Gp
14th AAA Bn (90mm)
19th AAA Gp
35th AAA Bde
36th AAA Bn (120mm)
70th AAA Bn (90mm)
71st AAA Bn (120mm)
75th AAA Bn (120mm)
125th AAA Bn (120mm) (VA ArNG)
260th AAA Bn (90mm) (mob DC ArNG)
340th AAA Bn (DC ArNG) (on-site program)
380th AAA Bn (DC ArNG) (on-site program)
601st AAA Bn (90mm)
736th AAA Bn (90mm) (mob DE ArNG) ?

Andrews AFB, MD [W-32]
  B-75 (120mm) (51-53);
  C-75 (120mm) (51-54);
  HHB-75 (120mm) (53-54);
  HHB-601 (90mm) (53-57);
  A-601 (90mm) (53)
Annandale, VA [W-63]
  ?-710 (90mm) (mob VA ArNG);
  C-14 (90mm) (52-57);
  B-70 (90mm) (57)

Bethesda, MD [W-82]
  A-70 (90mm) 51-57)
Brookland, DC [12 & Kearney NE]
  19 Gp (52-56)
Cabin John, MD
  B-34 (120mm) (51-53);
  C-70 (90mm) 54-57)?;
  A-240 (120mm) (DC ArNG) (54-57)
Carmody Hills, MD
  C-75 (120mm) (52-53);
  (A-380 (120mm);
  B-340 (120mm) (DC ArNG) (54-57)
Chillum [W-03]
  D-70 (90mm); (51-54);
  C-70 (90mm) (53-54);
  D-340 (90mm) (DC ArNG) (54-59)
College Park, MD [W-10]
  D-70 (90mm) (53, 54-57);
  HHB (-)-70 (90mm) (53-54) DC ArNG 57-58
Forestville, MD [W-24]
  B-260 (90mm) (mob DC ArNG) (52-53);
  B-601 (90mm) (53-57)
Fort Belvoir, VA [Mount Vernon, Gum Springs]
  A-71 (120mm) (51-53);
  HHB-71 (120mm) (51-54); ?-125 (120mm) (VA ArNG)
(55?-58?)
Fort Meade, MD [W-13]] [MD 175/198] [current DOIM]
  35th AAA Bde (51-57+);
  19th AAA Gp (51-53);
  HHB-75 (120mm) (51-52);
  HHB-601 (90mm) (53);
  HHB-260 (120mm) (mob DC ArNG) (51-53);
  HHB-36 (120mm) (51-54);
  HHB-70 (90mm) (51-54);
  HHB-736 (90mm) (mob DE ArNG) (51-52)
Fort Myer, VA [W-61] [Washington Forest] [Alexandria] (2)
  HHB-710 (90mm) (mob VA ArNG) (51-52);
  ?-710 (90mm) (mob VA ArNG) (51-52);

C-70 (90mm) (51-53);
HHB-14 (90mm) (52-57);
B/D-14 (90mm) (52-57);
19 Gp (56-58);
HHB-70 (90mm) (57)

Fort Reno, DC

Franconia, MD
B-71 (120mm) (51-54)

Friendly, MD
A-75 (120mm) (51-54 (57?);
A-380 (DC ArNG (55?-58?)

Hillandale, MD (2)
D-36 (120mm);
A-260 (120mm) (mob DC ArNG) (51-53);
B-75 (120mm) (54-56);
C-340 (120mm) (DC ArNG) (54-59)

Hybla Valley, VA [W-51]
C?-710 (90mm) (mob VA ArNG) (51-52);
B-14 (90mm) (52-53);
A-71 (120mm) (53-54);
D-125 (120mm) (VA ArNG) (54?-58?);
C-70 (90mm) (58)

Landover, MD
?-260 (90mm) (mob DC ArNG) (51-53);
B-75 (120mm) (53-54);
C-75 (120mm) (53-54);
A-601 (90mm) (53-57)

Langley, VA [W-72]
?-710 (90mm) (mob VA ArNG) (51-52)?;
A-14 (90mm) (52-57);
A-125 (120mm) (VA ArNG) (57-59?)

McLean (Hunting Ridge), VA
D-71 (120mm) (51-54);
HHB (-)-71 (120mm) (53-54);
A-70 (90mm) (57)

Oxon Hill, MD
D-260 (90mm) (mob DC ArNG) (51-53);
D-601 (90mm) (53-57)

Rosemary Hills, MD [W-91]
C-36 (120mm) (51-54);
HHB-36 (90mm) (53-54);
?-380 (120mm) (DC ArNG) (54-57)

Suitland Federal Center, MD

Temple Hills, MD
C-260 (90mm) (mob DC ArNG) (51-53);
C-601 990mm) (53-57) DC ArNG (380) (57-58?)

Vienna, VA
C-71 (120mm) (51-54);
B-125 (120mm) (VA ArNG) (54-57)

Woodmoor, MD
B-70 (90mm) (51-57);
HHB-70 (90mm) (54-57)

The ARAACOM/ARADCOM Battalions

The following lists and provides brief unit histories for the antiaircraft Regular Army, Organized Reserve/Army Reserve (USAR) and Army National Guard (ArNG) artillery battalions assigned to ARAA-COM/ARADCOM. Those that served at Fort Bliss, TX, during the ARADCOM era are also listed. Battalions activated for service elsewhere in the US Army are not listed.

A unit is constituted when its designation is placed on the official rolls of the US Army. It is organized through the assignment of personnel and equipment and activated on a specific date of establishment. Army National Guard units were organized and not activated but instead received Federal Recognition from the government when they were determined to have adequate personnel, equipment and organization. The Army consolidated units through the merger of two or more battalions. The resulting unit inherited the history, lineage and honors of its component units.

Concerning National Guard/Army National Guard units, they received Federal Recognition under Title 32 of the United States Code upon certification of adequate organization, manning and equipment. In effect, the recognition date served as the unit's "activation" date although they remained in state service. The Army's removal of a unit's federally recognized status was tantamount to inactivation of the unit and usually reflected a decline in personnel and operational readiness, but more often was part of unit reorganizations into other missions.

1st Antiaircraft Artillery Missile Battalion

1st AAAMBn A. 15 Apr 55, Irwin, PA

I. 1 Sept 58

A	PI-25 Murrysville	4/55-9/58	to A/3/1st
B	PI-37 Cowansburg	/56-9/58	to B/3/1st
C	PI-36 Irwin	4/55-9/58	to C/3/1st
D	PI-02 Rural Ridge	4/55-9/56	to D/74th
	PI-42 Elizabeth	9/56-/58	to D/3/1st

Irwin

First constituted 1 July 1924 as 1/1st Coast Artillery Harbor Defense; organized 1 June 1926 at Fort Randolph, CZ. Replaced in the Pittsburgh Defense Area by 3/1st Artillery; consolidated with the 1st Artillery 19 March 1959.

1st Guided Missile Battalion

1st AAAGMBn A. 11 Oct 45, Fort Bliss, TX; rd GMBn 4 Jun 47

I.

A/1st GMBn	Fort Bliss
B/1st GMBn	Fort Bliss
C/1st GMBn	Fort Bliss
D/1st GMBn	Fort Bliss

Fort Bliss

The 1st AAA Guided Missile Battalion formed on 11 October 1945 from conventional antiaircraft battalions and a detachment of personnel at Fort Miles, DE. It gave way to the 1st Guided Missile Regiment on

21 April 1948 and eventually served as the foundation for the 1st Guided Missile Group and Brigade at Fort Bliss.

The battalion regularly operated detachments at location s such as Camp Davis, NC; Fort Miles, DE; Naval Ordnance Test Station Inyokern, CA; and Point Mugu, CA. In 1953 it shifted to training Nike Ajax units for ARAACOM out of Red Canyon Range Camp. The battalion provided the first all-Army crew for a missile launch in the United States in 1947 and fired the first Ajax from Red Canyon in September 1953.

2nd Guided Missile Battalion

2nd GMBn A. 15 Oct 52, Fort Bliss, TX;

    I.

E/2nd GMBn	Fort Bliss
F/2nd GMBn	Fort Bliss
G/2nd GMBn	Fort Bliss

    Fort Bliss

Organized and activated on 15 October 1952 as a unit of the 1st Guided Missile Group, the 2nd Guided Missile Battalion stood up specifically to compile Nike Ajax lesson plans, training aids and schematics developed at the White Sands Proving Ground. It then assumed a primary role in Nike unit package training.

8th Antiaircraft Artillery Battalion

8th AAAAWBn A. 13 Jan 49, Fort Bliss, TX; rd AAABn 3 Jan 51

    I. 1 Sept 58

    Fort Bliss (/50) Camp Lucas

First constituted and organized 1 June 1918 as 2/68th Artillery Coast Artillery Corps at Fort Terry, NY. Replaced in the Sault Ste Marie Defense Area by 2/68th Artillery; consolidated with the 68th Artillery Regiment on 31 July 1959.

9th Antiaircraft Artillery Missile Battalion

9th AAABn (120mm Gun) A. 15 Sept 50, Fort Bliss, TX; rd AAABn (120mm Gun, Static) 20 Jul 53, rd AAAMBn 1 Oct 54

    I. 1 Sept 58

A	SF-88 Fort Barry	/55-9/58	to A/2/51st
B	SF-87 Fort Cronkhite	/55-9/58	to B/2/51st
C	SF-93 San Rafael	/57-9/58	to C/2/51st
D	SF-91 Angel Island	/55-9/58	to D/2/51st

    Fort Bliss ( ) San Francisco

First constituted 1 July 1924 as 1/9th Coast Artillery Harbor Defense; organized 10 February 1941 at Fort Warren, MA. Replaced in the San Francisco Defense Area by 2/51st Artillery.

10th Antiaircraft Artillery Missile Battalion (Nike)(Continental)

10th AAAAWBn (Mobile) A. 20 Dec 51, Camp Edwards, MA; rd AAABnAW (Semimobile) 18 Apr 52,
rd AAAMBn (Nike)(Continental) 5 Dec 56

I. 1 Sept 58

A	F-07 Spokane	/57-9/58	to A/1/43rd
B	F-37 Cheney	/57-9/58	to B/1/43rd
C	F-45 Medical Lake	/57-9/58	to C/1/43rd

Camp Edwards ( ) Fairchild AFB

First constituted 21 May 1942 as 2/509th Coast Artillery Antiaircraft; activated 10 November 1942 at Fort Bliss, TX. Replaced in the Fairchild Defense Area by 1/43rd Artillery.

11th Antiaircraft Artillery Missile Battalion (Nike)

11th AAAMBn (Nike) A. 2 Apr 56, Fort Hancock, NJ

I. 1 Sept 58

A	HA-08 East Windsor	/56-9/58	to A/2/55th
B	HA-36 Portland	/56-9/58	to B/2/55th
C	HA-25 Manchester	/56-9/58	to C/2/55th

Fort Hancock ( ) Manchester

First constituted and organized 1 March 1918 as 3/66th Regiment, Coast Artillery Corps, at Fort Adams, RI. Replaced in the Hartford Defense Area by 2/55th Artillery.

12th Antiaircraft Artillery Battalion

12th AAAGBn A. 8 Apr 52, Fort Hancock, NJ; rd AAABn 15 May 53;

I. 20 Dec 57

Fort Hancock ( ) New York

First constituted 1 July 1924 as 2nd Coast Artillery Harbor Defense; Headquarters & Headquarters Battery activated 1 August 1940, Fort Monroe, VA. Consolidated with the 2nd Artillery on 15 December 1961.

13th Antiaircraft Artillery Battalion

13th AAAGBn A. 2 Apr 52, Camp McCoy, WI; rd AAABn 24 Jul 53; rd AAAMBn 16 Jul 56

I. 1 Sept 58

A	C-70 Naperville	/56-9/58	to A/2/60th
B	C-54 Orland Park	/56-9/58	to B/2/60th
C	C-51 Worth	/56-9/58	to C/2/60th
D	C-71 La Grange	-7/56	gun site
	C-61 Lemont	7/56-9/58	to D/2/60th

Camp McCoy (6/52) Orland Park

First constituted 1 July 1924 as 2/13th Coast Artillery. Headquarters & Headquarters Battery activated at Fort Moultrie, SC, 1 August 1940. Replaced in the Chicago Defense Area by 2/60th Artillery.

14th Antiaircraft Artillery Battalion

14th AAAGBn A. 7 Apr 52, Fort Myer, VA; rd AAABn 22 Jul 53

    I. 15 Jun 57

    *Fort Myer

First constituted as 1/14th Coast Artillery Harbor Defense; partially organized 1 July 1924 at Fort Worden, WA.

16th Antiaircraft Artillery Battalion

16th AAGBn A. 10 Apr 52, Fort Banks, MA; rd AAABn 15 May 53

    I. 20 Dec 57

    *Fort Banks

First constituted and organized 1 July 1924 as 1/16th Coast Artillery Harbor Defense in Hawaii.

18th Antiaircraft Artillery Missile Battalion

18th AAAGBn A. 2 May 52, Fort Custer, MI; rd AAABn 24 Jul 53; rd AAAMBn 15 Jun 57

    I. 1 Sept 58

A	D-69 River Rouge	/57-9/58	to A/4/3rd
B	D-86 Franklin	/57-9/58	to B/4/3rd
C	D-87 Commerce	/57-9/58	to C/4/3rd
D	D-17 Algonac	/57- /58	to D/516th
	D-97 Auburn Heights	/58-9/58	to D/4/3rd

    Fort Custer (6/57) Franklin

First constituted 1 July 1924 as 2/3rd Coast Artillery Harbor Defense; Headquarters & Headquarters Battery organized 2 December 1940, Harbor Defenses of Los Angeles. Replaced in the Detroit Defense Area by 4/3rd Artillery; consolidated with the 3rd Artillery 15 December 1961.

19th Antiaircraft Artillery Battalion

19th AAAGBn A. 5 May 52, Sandia Base, Albuquerque, NM; rd AAABn 24 Jul 53

    I. 15 Jun 57

    *Sandia Base ( ) Philadelphia

First constituted in the Organized Reserves as 1/625th Coast Artillery Harbor Defense; organized July 1924 in San Diego, CA.

20th Antiaircraft Artillery Battalion

20th AAAGBn A. 8 May 52, Fort Lewis, WA; rd AAABn 1 May 53;

    I. 20 Dec 57

    Fort Lewis ( ) Phantom Lake

First constituted 1 July 1924 as 2/4th Coast Artillery Harbor Defense; Headquarters, 2nd Battalion activated 18 August 1924 at Fort Amador, CZ. Consolidated with the 4th Artillery on 1 September 1958.

24th Antiaircraft Artillery Missile Battalion

24th AAAMBn A. 1 Jun 55, Fort Banks, MA

I. 1 Sept 58

A	B-17 Nahant	6/55-11/56	to C/605th
	B-73 South Lincoln	11/56-9/58	to A/3/5th
B	B-03 Reading	6/55-11/56	to D/605th
	B-85 Bedford	11/56-9/58	to B/3/5th
C	B-55 Blue Hills	6/55- /56	to B/514th
	B-84 Burlington	/56-9/58	to C/3/5th
D	B-63 Needham	6/55-9/58	to D/3/5th

Fort Banks (11/56) Bedford

First constituted and activated 5 May 1942 as 1/504th Coast Artillery Antiaircraft at Camp Hulen, TX. Replaced in the Boston Defense Area by 3/5th Artillery; consolidated with the 5th Artillery 26 August 1960.

28th Antiaircraft Artillery Missile Battalion

AAAGBn A. 15 Sept 50, Fort Bliss, TX; rd AAABn 20 Jul 53, rd AAAMBn 16 Aug 54;

I. 1 Sept 58

A	S-13 Redmond	/55-9/58	to A/2/43rd
B	S-20 Cougar Mountain	/56-9/58	to B/2/43rd
C	S-03 Kenmore	/55-9/58	to C/2/43rd
D	S-13 Redmond	/56-9/58	to D/2/43rd

Fort Bliss (8/54) Redmond

First constituted and activated 6 February 1942 as the 28th Coast Artillery Battalion (155mm Gun). Battery A activated at Camp Pendleton, VA. Replaced in the Seattle Defense Area by 2/43rd Artillery.

33rd Antiaircraft Artillery Battalion

33rd AAAGBn A. 17 Sept 52, Fort Bliss, TX; rd AAABn 8 May 53

I. 20 Dec 57

Fort Bliss ( ) Savannah River Project

First constituted on 1 July 1924 as 2/15th Coast Artillery Harbor Defense; organized 1 August 1942 in the Harbor Defenses of Pearl Harbor.

34th Antiaircraft Artillery Missile Battalion

34th AAAAWBn A. 31 Jul 49, Fort Bliss, TX; rd AAABn 3 Aug 53, Fort. Totten, NY (/56)-Plainville, rd AAAMBn 26 Oct 56

I. 1 Sept 58

A	HA-85 Avon	/56-9/58	to A/1/51st
B	HA-67 Plainville	/56-9/58	to B/1/51st
C	HA-48 Cromwell	/56-9/58	to C/1/51st

Fort Bliss ( ) Plainville

First constituted 3 November 1942 as the 484th Coast Artillery Battalion (Antiaircraft)(Automatic Weapons)(Colored); activated 10 December 1942 at Camp Stewart, GA. Replaced in the Hartford Defense Area by 1/51st Artillery.

35th Antiaircraft Artillery Battalion

35th AAAGBn A. 1 Apr 51, Camp Stewart, GA; rd AAABn (Gun) 22 Jul 53
    I. 20 Dec 57

    Camp Stewart ( ) Glen Burnie

First constituted July 1923 in the Organized Reserves as 1/514th Coast Artillery Antiaircraft; organized October 1923 in upstate New York.

36th Antiaircraft Artillery Missile Battalion

36th AAAGBn A. 15 Nov 49, Fort Bliss, TX; rd AAABn (120mm)(Static) 15 Jul 53; rd AAAMBn 25 Jan 54;
    I. 1 Sept 58

A	New Carrollton	-12/54	
	BA-79 Granite	12/54-8/56	to A/602nd
B	Jct 495/270	-12/53	
	W-13T Fort Meade	12/53-6/55	temp site
	W-25 Davidsonville	6/55-9/58	to B/1/562nd
C	Walter Reed Annex/Forest Glen		
	BA-43 Jacobsville	/54-9/58	to C/1/562nd
D	NSWC White Oak		
	BA-30 Tolchester Beach	/54-9/58	to D/1/562nd

    Fort Bliss (4/51) Fort George G. Meade (9/52) Fort Reno ( ) Fort George G. Meade

First constituted 13 January 1941 as 1/94th Coast Artillery (Antiaircraft)(Semimobile); activated 17 April 1941 at Camp Davis, NC.

When the 36th AAA Battalion arrived in Washington DC it assumed responsibility for the northwesterly gun sites under assignment to the 3rd AAA Group. In September 1952 the headquarters moved to Fort Reno to work the Anti-Aircraft Operations Center (AAOC) with the 70th AAABn. The 36th became the first operational Nike Ajax battalion by occupying Site W-13T in December 1953 and going operational on 10 May 1954. It made the second operational ARADCOM Nike Hercules firing on 29 April 1958 at Fort Bliss, TX. The 1/562nd Artillery replaced the 36th AAAMBn in the Baltimore Defense Area.

38th Antiaircraft Artillery Missile Battalion

38th AAAGBn A. 1 Dec 51, Camp Edwards, MA; rd AAABn 8 May 53, rd AAAMBn 23 Jan 55;
    I. 1 Sept 58

A	N-63 Nansemond	/55-9/58	to A/5/59th
B	N-52 Deep Creek	/55-9/58	to B/5/59th
C	N-36 Kempsville	/55-9/58	to C/5/59th
D	N-20T Ocean View	/55- /57	temp site

| | N-25 Fort Story | /57-9/58 | to D/5/59th |

Camp Edwards ( ) Norfolk

First constituted 29 July 1921 in the Organized Reserves on as 2/505th Coast Artillery Antiaircraft; organized in December 1921 in Ohio. Replaced in the Norfolk Defense Area by 4/59th Artillery.

41st Antiaircraft Artillery Battalion

41st AAAGBn A. 8 Jun 49, Fort Bliss, TX; rd AAABn 3 Aug 53

    I. 20 Dec 57

    Fort Bliss ( ) Fort Totten

First constituted 24 February 1943 as the 119th Coast Artillery Battalion (Antiaircraft)(Gun); activated 2 April 1943 at Camp Haan, CA.

44th Antiaircraft Artillery Missile Battalion

44th AAAGBn A. 1 Apr 51, Camp Stewart, GA; rd AAABn 3 Aug 53, rd AAAMBn 22 Mar 55

    I. 1 Sept 58

A	NF-03 Model City	/55-9/58	to A/1/4th
B	NF-16 Sanborn	/55-9/58	to B/1/4th
C	NF-74 Grand Island	/55-9/58	to C/1/4th
D	NF-75 Grand Island	/55-9/58	to D/1/4th

    Camp Stewart (3/55) Fort Niagara

First constituted 30 June 1924 as 3/4th Coast Artillery Harbor Defense; headquarters activated 14 March 1940 at Fort Kobbe, CZ. Replaced in the Niagara Falls Defense Area by 1/4th Artillery; battalion consolidated 1 September 1958 with the 4th Artillery.

49th Antiaircraft Artillery Missile Battalion

49th AAAGBn A. 13 May 52, Fort Sheridan, IL; rd AAABn 24 Jul 53, rd AAAMBn 10 Nov 56

    I. 1 Sept 58

A	C-47 Hobart	/56- /57	to A/79th
	C-49 Homewood	/57-9/58	to A/4/52nd
B	C-44 Hegewisch	/56-9/58	to B/4/52nd
C	C-92 Mundelein	/56- /57	to A/78th
	C-46 Munster	/57-9/58	to C/4/52nd
D	C-47 Hobart	/56- /57	to A/79th
	C-44 Hegewisch	/57-9/58	to D/4/52nd

    Fort Sheridan (/56) Hegewisch

First constituted and partially organized 1 July 1924 as 3/14th Coast Artillery Harbor Defense, at Fort Worden, WA. Replaced in the Chicago Defense Area by 4/52nd Artillery.

51st Antiaircraft Artillery Battalion

51st AAAGBn A. 13 May 52, Fort Dix, NJ; rd AAABn 20 Jun 53

    I. 31 May 56

Fort Dix ( ) Swarthmore

First constituted 30 June 1924 in the Organized Reserves as 3/625th Coast Artillery (Harbor Defense); organized July 1924 at San Diego, CA.

52nd Antiaircraft Artillery Battalion

52nd AAAAWBn, Mobile A. 26 Nov 52, Camp Roberts, CA; rd AAABn 31 Mar 53

I. 15 Jun 57

Camp Roberts ( ) Castle AFB

First constituted 9 October 1942 as 3/61st Coast Artillery; activated 8 January 1943 at Reykjavik, Iceland. Consolidated on 25 August 1961 with the 61st Artillery.

54th Antiaircraft Artillery Missile Battalion

54th AAAMBn A. 15 Dec 54, Edgewood Arsenal, MD

I. 1 Sept 58

A	BA-79 Granite	12/54-8/56	to A/602nd
	BA-03 Phoenix	8/56-9/58	to A/4/1st
B	BA-92 Cronhardt	12/54-9/58	to B/4/1st
C	BA-18 Edgewood	/55-9/58	to C/4/1st
D	BA-09 Fork	11/55-9/58	to D/4/1st

Edgewood Arsenal

First constituted 1 June 1821 as elements of the 1st Regiment of Artillery. Reconstituted 1 July 1924 as 2/1st Coast Artillery Harbor Defense; activated 15 April 1932 at Fort Sherman, CZ. Replaced in the Baltimore Defense Area by 4/1st Artillery; consolidated with the 1st Artillery on 19 March 1959

56th Antiaircraft Artillery Missile Battalion

56th AAAGBn A. 10 Jan 52, Camp Stewart, GA; rd AAABn 22 Jul 53, rd AAAMBn 22 Mar 55

I. 1 Sept 58

A	N-02 Fox Hill	/55-9/58	to A/4/51st
B	N-93 Hampton	/55-9/58	to B/4/51st
C	N-85 Denbigh	/55-9/58	to C/4/51st
D	N-75 Smithfield	/55-9/58	to D/4/51st

Camp Stewart ( ) Norfolk

First constituted as the 993rd Antiaircraft Artillery Searchlight Battalion; activated 28 June 1946 in Hawaii. Replaced in the Norfolk Defense Area by 4/51st Artillery.

66th Antiaircraft Artillery Missile Battalion

66th AAAGBn A. 13 Jun 52, Miller Field, Staten Island, NY; rd AAABn 3 Aug 53, rd AAAMBn 6 Aug 54

I. 1 Sept 58

A	NY-03 Orangeburg	/55-1/57	to A/737th
	NY-20 Lloyd Harbor	1/57-9/58	to A/1/55th
B	NY-09 Kensico	/55-9/58	to B/1/55th

C	NY-23 Hicksville	/55-9/58	to C/1/55th
D	NY-15 Fort Slocum	/55-9/58	to D/1/55th

Staten Island ( ) Fort Totten

First constituted as 1/66th Artillery Coast Artillery Corps; Battery A organized 1 March 1918 at Fort Stark, NH. Replaced in the New York Defense Area by 1/55th Artillery

69th Antiaircraft Artillery Battalion

69th AAAGBn A. 8 Jun 49, Fort Bliss, TX; rd AAABn (Gun) 3 Aug 53

    I. 20 Dec 57

Fort Bliss ( ) Fort Hamilton

First constituted and organized 17 May 1918 as 1/69th Artillery Coast Artillery Corps, at Fort Worden, WA.

70th Antiaircraft Artillery Battalion

70th AAAGBn A. 15 Jan 49, Fort Bliss, TX; rd AAABn 15 May 53

    I. 20 Dec 57

Fort Bliss ( ) Bailey's Crossroads

First constituted on 5 September 1928 in the Organized Reserves as 1/562nd Coast Artillery Antiaircraft; redesignated 30 November 1928 as 1/917th Coast Artillery Antiaircraft and organized in Virginia the following year. Battalion consolidated 31 July 1959 with the 562nd Artillery.

71st Antiaircraft Artillery Missile Battalion

71st AAAGBn A. 30 Sept 49, Fort Bliss, TX; rd AAABn 22 Jul 53, rd AAAMBn 6 Jul 54;

    I. 1 Sept 58

A	W-92 Rockville	/54- /55	to D/602nd
	W-54 Pamonkey	/55-9/58	to A/1/71st
B	W-83 Herndon	/54-9/58	to B/1/71st
C	W-64 Lorton	/54-9/58	to C/1/71st
D	2-74 Fairfax	/54-9/58	to D/1/71st

Fort Bliss (/53) Fort Belvoir

First constituted 2 May 1918 as Headquarters & Headquarters Battery Company, 71st Artillery Coast Artillery Corps; organized 12 May 1918 at Fort Strong, MA. Replaced in the Washington, DC. Defense Area by 1/71st Artillery; consolidated 31 July 1959 with the 71st Artillery.

74th Antiaircraft Artillery Missile Battalion

74th AAAGBn Mobile A. 13 Jun 52, Fort Indiantown Gap, PA; rd AAABn 20 Jul 53; rd AAAMBn 1 Sept 56

    I. 1 Sept 58

A	PI-93 Westview	9/56-9/58	to A/5/3rd
B	PI-92 Bryant	9/56-9/58	to B/5/3rd
C	PI-03 Dorseyville	9/56-9/58	to C/5/3rd
D	PI-02 Rural Ridge	9/56-9/58	to D/5/3rd

Indiantown Gap Military Reservation ( ) Pittsburgh

First constituted 29 July 1921 in the Organized Reserves as 1/503rd Artillery Antiaircraft; organized in March 1922 at Tyrone, PA. Replaced in the Pittsburgh Defense Area by 5/3rd Artillery.

75th Antiaircraft Artillery Missile Battalion

75th AAAGBn A. 15 Jan 49, Fort Bliss, TX; rd AAABn (Gun) 22 Jul 53, rd AAAMBn 5 Nov 54

I. 1 Sept 58

A	W-45 Accokeek	/55-9/58	to A/3/562nd
B	W-35 Croom	/55-9/58	to B/3/562nd
C	W-44 Mattawoman	/55-9/58	to C/3/562nd
D	W-36 Brandywine	/57-9/58	to D/3/562nd

Fort Bliss ( ) Croom

First constituted 29 July 1921 in the Organized Reserves as 1st Battalion, 509th Artillery Antiaircraft, Coast Artillery Corps; organized at Seattle, WA, in November 1922. Replaced in the Washington, DC Defense Area by 3/562nd Artillery.

77th Antiaircraft Artillery Battalion

77th AAAGBn A. 10 Jan 52, Camp Stewart, GA; rd AAABn 20 Jul 53

I. 20 Dec 57

Camp Stewart ( ) Los Angeles

First constituted in the Organized Reserves in December 1921 as 1/505th Artillery Antiaircraft, Coast Artillery Corps; organized December 1921 in Cincinnati, OH.

78th Antiaircraft Artillery Missile Battalion (Nike)

78th AAAMBn A. 10 Nov 55, Fort Sheridan, IL

I. 1 Sept 58

A	C-92 Mundelein	11/55-9/58	to A/1/517th
B	C-94 Libertyville	11/55-9/58	to B/1/517th
C	Fort Sheridan	11/55-/56	
	C-98 Fort Sheridan	/56-9/58	to C/1/517th
D	Fort. Sheridan	11/55-3/56	
	C-80 Arlington Heights	3/56-/57	
	C-93 Northfield	/57-9/58	to D/1/517th

Fort Sheridan (/57) Mundelein

First constituted July 1923 in the Organized Reserves as 1/517th Artillery Antiaircraft, Coast Artillery Corps; organized in July 1925 at San Francisco, CA. Replaced in the Chicago Defense Area by 1/517th Artillery; battalion consolidated 31 July 1959 with the 517th Artillery.

79th Antiaircraft Artillery Missile Battalion

79th AAAGBn A. 15 Jan 49, Fort Bliss, TX; rd AAABn 24 Jul 53, rd AAAMBn 13 Dec 54

I. 1 Sept 58

A	C-51 Worth	3/55-	
	C-47 Hobart	/57-9/58	to A/1/60th
B	C-30T Dunes State Park	1/55-9/55	
	C-50 Homewood	9/55-	
	C-32 Porter	/57-9/58	to B/1/60th
C	C-45 Gary Airport	2/55-9/58	to C/1/60th
D	C-48 South Gary	2/55-9/58	to D/1/60th

Fort Bliss (/50) Fort Custer (10/52) Gary (2/55) South Gary

First constituted 13 January 1941 as 1/79th Coast Artillery (Antiaircraft)(Mobile); activated 1 June 1941 at Fort Bliss, TX. The battalion vacated its gun sites for Ajax training under the 86th AAAMBn on 24 January 1955. Replaced in the Chicago Defense Area by 1/60th Artillery.

83rd Antiaircraft Artillery Missile Battalion

83rd AAAGBn A. 13 Jun 52, Camp Hanford, WA; rd AAABn 20 Jul 53; rd AAAMBn 1 Aug 54

I. 1 Sept 58

A	H-06 Saddle Mountain	/55-9/58	to A/1/52nd
B	H-12 Othello	/55-9/58	to B/1/52nd
C	H-83 Priest Rapids	/55-9/58	to C/1/52nd
D	H-52 Rattlesnake Mountain	/55-9/58	to D/1/52nd

Camp Hanford

First constituted 15 January 1918 as 2/64th Regiment, Coast Artillery Corps; organized 17 May 1918 at Pensacola, FL. Replaced in the Hanford Defense Area by 1/52nd Artillery.

85th Antiaircraft Artillery Missile Battalion

85th AAAMBn A. 1 Apr 55, Fort Wayne, MI

I. 1 Sept 58

A	D-23 Detroit City Airport	/55-9/58	to A/3/55th
B	D-26 Fort Wayne	/55-9/58	to B/3/55th
C	D-54 Riverview	/57-9/58	to C/3/55th
D	D-26 Fort Wayne	/55-9/58	to D/3/55th

Fort Wayne

First constituted 19 January 1942 as 1/85th Coast Artillery (Antiaircraft Artillery)(Semimobile); activated 26 January 1942 at Camp Davis, NC. Replaced in the Detroit Defense Area by 3/55th Artillery.

86th Antiaircraft Artillery Missile Battalion

86th AAAGBn A. 13 Jul 52, Fort Sheridan, IL; rd AAABn (Gun) 24 Jul 53, rd AAAMBn 25 Mar 54

I. 1 Sept 58

A	C-42 Promontory Point	8/52-5/53	
	C-90 Chicago	5/53-1/54	
	C-94T Libertyville	/54-3/55	
	C-80 Arlington Heights	3/55-9/58	to A/6/3rd

B	C-28 Burnham Park	8/52-5/53	
	C-95 Skokie	5/53-4/54	to A/496th
	C-30T Dunes State Park	/54-1/55	
	C-93 Northfield	1/55- /57	to D/78th
	C-72 Addison	/57-9/58	to B/6/3rd
C	C-60T Lemont	/54-3/55	to D/86th
	C-61 Lemont	3/55- /56	to D/13th
	C-84 Palatine	/56-9/58	to C/6/3rd
D	C-95T Libertyville	/54-4/55	
	C-60T Lemont	4/55-9/55	
	C-72 Addison	9/55-	
	C-80 Arlington Heights	/55-9/58	to D/6/3rd

Fort Sheridan (9/53) C-90 Chicago (3/55) Arlington Heights

First constituted and organized 17 May 1918 as 2/69th Coast Artillery Coast Artillery Corps, at Fort Worden, WA. The 86th replaced the Pennsylvania Army National Guard 709th AAAGBn in the Chicago defense; it was in turn replaced by 6/3rd Artillery. It was the first antiaircraft battalion in the defense to stand down from gun operations for conversion to Nike Ajax, officially on 16 January 1954. On 28 August 1954 the 45th Antiaircraft Artillery Brigade declared the 86th operational in Nike.

89th Antiaircraft Artillery Battalion
89th AAAGBn A. 28 Jul 52, Fort George Meade, MD; rd AAABn 22 Jul 53

I. 31 Mar 56

Fort George G. Meade

First constituted 5 August 1942 as 1/89th Coast Artillery (Antiaircraft)(Semimobile); activated 10 August 1942 at Washington, DC

90th Antiaircraft Artillery Battalion
90th AAAGBn A. 14 Jul 52, Fort Bliss, TX; rd AAABn 8 May 53

I. 16 Dec 57

Fort Bliss

First constituted 29 July 1921 in the Organized Reserves as 2/509th Regiment, Coast Artillery Corps Antiaircraft; organized November 1922 at Seattle, WA.

93rd Antiaircraft Artillery Battalion
93rd AAAGBn A. 16 May 52, Oakland Army Base, CA; rd AAABn 1 Sept 53

I. 26 Dec 57

Oakland Army Base ( ) Ladd AFB

First constituted 4 November 1943 as the 93rd Antiaircraft Artillery Gun Battalion; activated 12 December 1943 at Aliea, TH.

96th Antiaircraft Artillery Battalion

96th AAAGBn A. 8 Jun 49, Fort Bliss, TX; rd AAABn 1 Sept 53

    I. 15 Sept 58

    Fort Bliss ( ) Fort Richardson

First constituted 13 January 1941 as 1/96th Coast Artillery Antiaircraft; activated 15 April 1941 at Camp Davis, NC. Replaced in the Anchorage Defense Area by 4/43rd Artillery

98th Antiaircraft Artillery Battalion

98th AAAGBn Semimobile A. 10 Aug 52, Fort Hancock, NJ; rd AAABn 3 Aug 53

    I. 15 Jun 57

    Fort Hancock

First constituted 13 January 1941 as 1/98th Coast Artillery (Antiaircraft)(Semimobile); activated 11 July 1941 at Schofield Barracks, TH.

99th Antiaircraft Artillery Battalion

99th AAAGBn A. 3 Aug 52, Fort Custer, MI; rd AABn (Gun)(90mm)(Static) 24 Jul 53

    I. 15 Jun 57

    Fort Custer Detroit

First constituted in the Organized Reserves July 1923 as 2/517th Coast Artillery (Antiaircraft); organized in August 1925 at San Francisco, CA. Battalion consolidated 31 July 1959 with the 517th Artillery.

101st Antiaircraft Artillery Battalion   GAArNG

101st AAAGBn FR. 17 Jun 47, Statesboro, GA; rd AAABn 1 Oct 53

    Cons. 1 Jul 59

    A   Statesboro
    B   Hinesville
    C   Swainsboro
    D   Waynesboro

    Statesboro

Originally constituted in the Georgia National Guard on 12 October 1940 as the 101st Separate Battalion, Coast Artillery (Antiaircraft), with the headquarters battery receiving its Federal recognition in Atlanta on 15 October 1940. Notably, Batteries A (the Georgia Hussars) and B (the Liberty Independent Troop) dated to 1785 and 1798 respectively and both served in the Confederate States Army during the Civil War.

    The battalion was called to Federal service on 14 August 1950 and apparently served in the Chicago Defense Area prior to its 13 April 1952 release. Consolidated into the 214th Artillery on 1 July 1959.

102nd Antiaircraft Artillery Battalion (Gun)   NYArNG

72nd AAAGBn (Mobile) FR 13 Nov 47, Buffalo, NY; rd 102nd AAAGBn 1 May 50, rd AAABn (Gun) 1 Oct 53

Rd. 106th AAABn 14 Feb 58

Buffalo (/51) Pittsburgh (7/52) Buffalo

Originally constituted in the New York National Guard on 23 July 1940 as the 1st Battalion, 209th Coast Artillery (Antiaircraft). The headquarters received its Federal recognition in Buffalo on 14 October 1940. The 74th AAABn replaced the 102nd in the Pittsburgh Defense Area.

106th Antiaircraft Artillery Missile Battalion   NYArNG

102nd AAAGBn rd 106th AAABn 14 Feb 58; rd AAAMBn 15 Feb 58

    Cons. 16 Mar 59

    Buffalo

    Not Operational with Nike

The battalion was first constituted on 23 July 1940 in the New York National Guard as 1/209th Coast Artillery (Antiaircraft); it organized and received its Federal recognition 14 October 1940 at Buffalo, NY. On 16 March 1959 the battalion consolidated into the 106th Artillery; the 1/106th replaced it in the Buffalo Defense Area prior to Nike Ajax operations.

109th Antiaircraft Artillery Missile Battalion   NJArNG

109th AAABn (120mm Gun) FR. 15 Jun 54, Newark, NJ; rd AAAMBn 1 Feb 58

    Cons. 1 Mar 59

A	Elizabeth
B	Belleville
C	Newark
D	Fort Lee

    Newark

    Not Operational with Nike

The battalion was constituted on 1 April 1954 as the 109th Antiaircraft Artillery Battalion (120mm Gun). Battalion consolidated with 254th Artillery, 1 March 1959; replaced in the New York Defense Area by 1/254th Artillery.

110th Antiaircraft Artillery Battalion (90mm Gun)   OHArNG

    Constituted on 1 November 1954 as the 110th Antiaircraft Artillery Battalion (90mm Gun) and allotted to the Ohio Army National Guard. However, on 15 March 1957 the US Army withdrew the battalion's allotment to the State of Ohio.

114th Antiaircraft Artillery Battalion   TNArNG

114th AAAGBn (Semimobile) FR. 23 Aug 51, Knoxville, TN; rd AAABn 1 Oct 53

    Cons.1 Mar 59

A	Maryville
B	Knoxville
C	Oak Ridge
D	Oak Ridge

*Knoxville

Originally constituted in the US Army on 19 December 1942 as the 114th Coast Artillery Battalion (Separate)(Antiaircraft) (Gun)(Semimobile) and activated on 10 February 1943 at Fort Bliss, TX. Consolidated into the 109th Armor on 1 March 1959.

115th Antiaircraft Artillery Battalion (90mm Gun)   MSArNG

115th AAGBn (Mobile) FR. 22 Jun 1949, Jackson, MS; rd AAABn (90mm Gun) 1 Oct 53

   B/U 1 May 59

   *Jackson

The battalion was first constituted on 8 February 1943 in the Army of the United States as the 115th Coast Artillery Battalion (Antiaircraft)(Gun)(Separate) and activated 20 March 1943 at Camp Davis, NC. It was called to active duty on 1 May 1951 and released from Federal service on 31 January 1953. On 1 May 1959 the battalion was broken up; the Headquarters & Headquarters Battery was consolidated with the 136th Transportation Group in Jackson as the 31st Administrative Company.

116th Antiaircraft Artillery Missile Battalion (Nike)   NJArNG

116th AAABn (90mm Gun) FR. 16 Apr 55, Camden, NJ; rd AAAMBn (Nike) 1 Nov 57

   Cons. 1 Mar 59
   A   Camden
   B   Pennsauken
   C   Bellwawr

   *Camden (11/57) Bellmawr

   Not operational with Nike

The battalion was constituted in the New Jersey National Guard on 8 April 1955 as the 116th Antiaircraft Artillery Battalion (90mm Gun). Battalion consolidated with the 254th Artillery, 1 March 1959; replaced in the Philadelphia Defense Area by 2/254th Artillery.

120th Antiaircraft Artillery Battalion (90mm Gun)   NMArNG

3630th Ordnance Maintenance Company, AA Rd. 120th AAAGBn 12 May 49, Roswell, NM; rd AAABn (90mm Gun) 1 Oct 53

   Cons. 1 Sept 59
   A   Belen
   B   Roswell
   C   Socorro
   D   Alamogordo

   *Roswell

Originally constituted in the New Mexico National Guard and organized at Roswell, NM during February 1910. Consolidated with the 200th Artillery on 1 September 1959.

125th Antiaircraft Artillery Missile Battalion (Nike)   VAArNG

125th AAAGBn (90mm) FR. 10 Nov 52, Alexandria, VA; rd AAABn (Gun, 90mm) 1 Oct 53; rd AAABn

(Gun, 120mm) 16 Apr 54

    rd AAAMBn 15 Feb 58

    Cons. 1 Jun 59

    HHB   Alexandria

    A   Camp Pendleton

    B   Langley

    C   Alexandria

    *Alexandria

Special Security Force, 1950s; not operational with Nike

The battalion was constituted in the Virginia National Guard on 3 January 1951 as the 125th Antiaircraft Artillery Gun Battalion (90mm). Battalion consolidated with the 280th Artillery, 1 June 1959; replaced in the Washington, DC Defense Area by 1/280th Artillery.

132nd Antiaircraft Artillery Battalion   WIArNG

132nd AAAAWBn FR. 15 Dec 49, Milwaukee, WI; rd AAABn (AW)(SP) 1 Oct 53

    Cons. 15 Feb 59

    A   West Bend

    B   Racine

    C   Two Rivers

    *Milwaukee

The battalion was constituted on 1 February 1949 in the Wisconsin National Guard as the 132nd Antiaircraft Artillery Automatic Weapons Battalion. The battalion consolidated with the 126th Artillery on 15 February 1959 with its personnel going to the 1/126th Artillery, Milwaukee Defense Area.

137th Antiaircraft Artillery Battalion (AW)(SP)   OHArNG

183rd AAAWBn FR 30 Oct 47, Columbus, OH; rd 137th AAAWBn 1 Feb 59, rd 137th AAABn (automatic weapons) (self-propelled) 20 May 53

    B/U 1 Sept 59

    *Columbus

The battalion was constituted in the Ohio National Guard on 3 July 1946 as the 183rd Antiaircraft Artillery Searchlight Battalion. It served in Federal service at Fort Hays, OH from 15 January 1952 to 15 June 1954. The battalion was broken upon 1 September 1959; the Headquarters & Headquarters Battery was redesignated the 37th Administrative Company.

150th Antiaircraft Artillery Gun Battalion   NCArNG

150th AAAGBn FR. 3 Nov 47, Wilmington, NC; rd AAAGBn (90mm)

    Cons.1 Apr 59

The battalion was constituted in the North Carolina National Guard as the 150th Antiaircraft Artillery Gun Battalion on 9 July 1946; notably, Battery A/150th at Wilmington dated to the 22 February 1853 organization of the Wilmington Light Artillery and saw service in the Confederate States Army as G/18th North Carolina Infantry. The battalion was ordered into Federal service on 1 May 1951 for duty in the

Philadelphia Defense Area and was released on 31 March 1953. It was consolidated with the 252nd Artillery on 1 April 1959.

156th Antiaircraft Artillery Battalion   DEArNG

156th AAABn FR. 9 Mar 49, Dagsboro, DE; rd AAAGBn 20 Jul 51, rd AAABn 1 Oct 53

Cons. 1 Apr 59

A	Wilmington
B	Wilmington
C	Newark
D	New Castle

Dagsboro (10/49) Wilmington

Originally constituted in the Delaware National Guard as the 156th Antiaircraft Artillery Automatic Weapons Battalion. The Headquarters & Headquarters Battery received its Federal recognition at Dagsboro on 9 March 1949 but was reorganized in Wilmington on 10 October 1949 through redesignation of D/736th AAAGBn. Consolidated on 1 April 1959 with the 198th Artillery under the Combat Arms Regimental System (CARS).

158th Antiaircraft Artillery Missile Battalion (Nike-Hercules)   THArNG

483rd FA FR. 7 Jul 47, Honolulu, Oahu, TH; rd AAABn (90mm) 1 Sept 55, rd AAAMBn (Nike-Hercules) 15 Jan 59

Cons. 1 May 59

Honolulu

Not operational with Nike

First constituted 19 May 1944 as 531st Field Artillery Battalion; activated 31 May 1944 at Schofield Barracks, TH. Battalion consolidated 1 May 1959 with the 298th Artillery, Territory of Hawaii Army National Guard; replaced in the Oahu Defense Area by 1/298th Artillery.

168th Antiaircraft Artillery Missile Battalion

168th AAABn (Light) A. 27 Oct 52, Fort Bliss, TX; rd AAAMBn 25 Jul 58

I. 1 Sept 58

Fort Bliss

First constituted 13 April 1942 as 1/607th Coast Artillery Antiaircraft; activated 1 June 1942 at Camp Hulen, TX.

176th Antiaircraft Artillery Missile Battalion

176th AAAMBn A. 15 Feb 55, Aberdeen Proving Ground, MD

I. 1 Sept 58

A	PH-82 Paoli	/55-9/58	to A/2/59th
B	PH-75 Edgemont	/56-9/58	to B/2/59th
C	PH-67 Chester	/55-9/58	to C/2/59th
D	PH-58 Swedesboro	/57-9/58	to D/2/59th

Aberdeen Proving Ground (/55) Edgemont

First constituted 19 May 1944 as the 176th Coast Artillery Battalion (155mm Gun); activated 31 May 1944 on Makin Atoll, Gilbert Islands. Replaced in the Philadelphia Defense Area by 2/59th Artillery.

177th Antiaircraft Artillery Battalion   OHArNG

177th AAAGBn FR. 1 Jun 51, Youngstown, OH; rd AAABn

Cons. 1 Sept 59
A	Youngstown
B	Alliance
C	Kent
D	Warren

Youngstown

Special Security Force, 1950s

Originally constituted in the US Army on 19 May 1944 as the 177th Coast Artillery Battalion (155mm Gun) and activated at Fort Ruger, TH on 31 May 1944. Served as part of the Special Security Force during the 1950s, consolidated with the 137th Artillery on 1 September 1959.

179th Antiaircraft Artillery Missile Battalion   OHArNG

179th AAAGBn FR. 2 May 51, Cleveland, OH; rd AAABn 1 Oct 53, rd AAAMBn (Nike) 1 Nov 58

Cons. 1 Sept 59
A	Akron
B	Cleveland
C	Kent

Cleveland (1/52) Lakewood

Special Security Force, 1950s; not operational with Nike

First constituted 19 May 1944 as the 179th Coast Artillery Battalion (155mm Gun); activated 31 May 1944 at Fort Ruger, TH. Battalion consolidated with the 137th Artillery, Ohio Army National Guard, on 1 September 1959; replaced in the Cleveland Defense Area by 1/137th Artillery

180th Antiaircraft Artillery Battalion (90mm Gun)   OHArNG

180th AAAGBn FR. 29 May 51, Dayton, OH

Rd. 174th Artillery 1 Sept 59
A	Middleton
B	Greenville
C	Lima
D	Piqua

Dayton

Originally constituted in the US Army on 19 May 1944 as the 180th Coast Artillery Battalion (155mm Gun) and activated at Fort Ruger, TH on 31 May 1944.   In a unique turn, the battalion was redesignated as the 174th Artillery under CARS on 1 September 1959 vice the usual consolidation method.

182nd Antiaircraft Artillery Gun Battalion   OHArNG
182nd AAAGBn FR 14 Jan 53, Canton, OH
>   Cons. 1 Sept 59

>   *Canton*

Originally constituted on 9 December 1952 in the Ohio Army National Guard as the 182nd Antiaircraft Artillery Gun Battalion; Federal service in the Pittsburgh Defense Area, May 1951 to December 1952. Battalion consolidated with the 137th Artillery on 1 September 1959.

201st Antiaircraft Artillery Gun Battalion   MOArNG
201st AAAGBn FR. 20 Apr 53, St Louis, MO
>   Db. 20 Apr 58
>   A   Jefferson Barracks
>   B   Jefferson Barracks
>   C   Jefferson Barracks
>   D   Jefferson Barracks

>   *St Louis*

First constituted in the US Army on 9 May 1942 as the 2nd Battalion, 606th Coast Artillery (Antiaircraft) and activated at Camp Edwards, MA on 20 January 1943. The unit was disbanded on 20 April 1958 when the government removed its Federal recognition.

202nd Antiaircraft Artillery Battalion (90mm Gun)   MOArNG
202nd AAAGBn FR. 16 Mar 53, St Charles, MO; rd AAABn (90mm Gun) 1 Oct 53
>   Rd. 204th Signal Bn 15 Apr 59
>   A   St Louis
>   B   St Louis
>   C   St Louis
>   D   St Louis

>   *St Charles*

Originally constituted in the Missouri Army National Guard on 1 December 1952 as the 202nd Antiaircraft Artillery Battalion.

203rd Antiaircraft Artillery Battalion (90mm Gun)   MOArNG
108th Mech Cavalry Reconnaissance Squadron rd 203rd AAAAWBn, Mobile 1 Nov 49, Joplin, MO; rd AAAGBn 1 Dec 52,
>   Rd. AAABn (90mm Gun) 1 Oct 53
>   Cons. 15 Apr 59

A   Anderson
B   Aurora
C   Monett
D   Pierce City

Joplin

Originally constituted in the Missouri National Guard on 27 June 1946 as the 108th Mechanized Cavalry Reconnaissance Squadron; the headquarters received its Federal recognition in Joplin on 21 October 1946. Consolidated into the 203rd Combat Arms Regiment on 15 April 1959. The unit probably receives the award for the best battalion motto: "Don't Kick Our Dog." It was known locally as "The Houn' Dawg Regiment."

210th Antiaircraft Artillery Battalion (90mm Gun)   NHArNG

210th AAAAWBn FR. 10 Oct 47, Berlin, NH; rd AAAGBn (90mm Gun) 16 Oct 50, rd AAABn (90mm Gun) 1 Oct 53

Cons. 1 Feb 59
A   Berlin
B   Franklin
C   Lancaster
D   Plymouth

Berlin

Originally constituted in the New Hampshire National Guard as the 2nd Battalion, 197th Artillery (Antiaircraft), Coast Artillery Corps the headquarters battalion received its Federal in Newport on 30 June 1922. Consolidated with the 197th Artillery under CARS on 1 February 1959.

211th Antiaircraft Artillery Missile Battalion   CTArNG

211th AAAAWBn FR. 6 Jan 47, Bridgeport, CT; rd AAAAGBn (90mm) 25 Jun 51, rd AAABn (90mm Gun) 1 Oct 53,

rd AAAMBn 1 Oct 58
Cons. 1 May 59
A   Bridgeport
B   Milford
C   West Hartford

Bridgeport

Not operational with Nike

First constituted in the Connecticut National Guard as the 1st Separate Squadron, Connecticut Cavalry; headquarters organized 3 May 1917 at Hartford. Battalion consolidated with the 242nd Artillery, 1 May 1959; replaced in the Bridgeport Defense Area by 1/242nd Artillery.

213th Antiaircraft Artillery Battalion (Gun)   PAArNG

73rd AAAGBn (Semimobile) FR. 30 Sept 46, Easton, PA; rd 213th 213th AAAGBn 1 Jun 50, rd 213th AAABn (Gun) 1 Oct 53

Cons.1 Jun 59

A   Reading

B   Allentown

C   Reading

D   Allentown

Easton (10/53) Bethlehem

First constituted in the Pennsylvania National Guard on 16 July 1919 as the 3rd Separate Battalion of Infantry. Notably, C/213th originally organized on 6 August 1849 at Allentown as the Lehigh Fencibles and served in the Union Army as I/1st Regiment, Pennsylvania Volunteer Infantry. The battalion was ordered into Federal service on 29 August 1950 and released on 28 May 1952; it consolidated with the 213th Artillery on 1 June 1959.

227th Antiaircraft Artillery Missile Battalion   MIArNG

227th AAABn (90mm Gun) Org. 1 Nov 54, Detroit, MI; rd AAAMBn 1 Mar 58

Cons. 15 Apr 59

Detroit

Not operational with Nike

First organized in the Michigan Army National Guard as the 227th Antiaircraft Artillery Battalion (90mm Gun) and federally recognized 1 November at Detroit. Battalion consolidated with the 177th Artillery, 15 April 1959; replaced in the Detroit Defense Area by 1/177th Artillery.

238th Antiaircraft Artillery Battalion   CTArNG

238th AAAGBn FR. 11 Feb 48, New London, CT; rd AAABn (90mm Gun) 1 Oct 53

Cons. 1 May 59

New London ( ) West Hartford

Not operational with Nike

First constituted in the Army of the United States on 1 April 1942 as 3/208th Coast Artillery Antiaircraft; activated 13 August 1942 at Townseville, Australia. The Army allotted the 238th Antiaircraft Artillery Searchlight to the Connecticut National Guard on 31 May 1946; it was ordered into Federal service on 14 August 1950 at New London and released on 13 June 1953. Battalion consolidated with the 192nd Artillery, 1 May 1959; replaced in the Hartford Defense Area by 1/192nd Artillery.

240th Antiaircraft Artillery Missile Battalion   WAArNG

240th AAAGBn Org. 15 Dec 48, Seattle, WA; rd AAABn (120mm) 1 Oct 53, rd AAABn (90mm) 1 May 54

rd AAAMBn (Nike) 2 Jan 58

Cons. 15 Apr 59

A   Kirkland

B   Poulsbo

C   Bellingham

Seattle (4/56) Houghton (4/58) Kent

Special Security Force, 1950s; not operational with Nike

First constituted in the Washington National Guard 27 May 1942 as 3/205th Coast Artillery Antiaircraft; organized 15 June 1942 at Camp Haan, CA. Battalion consolidated with the 205th Artillery, 15 April 1959; replaced in the Seattle Defense Area by 3/205th Artillery.

243rd Antiaircraft Artillery Missile Battalion   CTArNG
243rd AAAAWBn FR. 4 Dec 46, Providence, RI; rd AAAGBn (90mm) 1 Aug 51, rd AAABn (90mm) Gun 1 Oct 53

        rd AAAMBn 22 Dec 58;
        Cons. 1 Apr 59
        A   Bristol
        B   Newport
        C   Providence
        D   Woonsocket

    Providence

        Special Security Force, 1950s; not operational with Nike
First constituted in the Rhode Island National Guard as 1/243rd Artillery, Coast Artillery Corps. Headquarters organized 1 October 1923 in Providence. Battalion consolidated with the 243rd Artillery, 1 April 1959; replaced in the Providence Defense Area by 2/243rd Artillery

245th Antiaircraft Artillery Missile Battalion   NYArNG
245th AAASLBn Org. 29 Oct 47, Brooklyn, NY; rd AAAGBn 1 Dec 47, rd AAABn (120mm Gun) 1 Oct 53, rd AAAMBn 15 Feb 58
        Rd. 245th Artillery, 16 Mar 59

    Brooklyn

        Special Security Force, 1950s; not operational with Nike
First constituted as the 13th Regiment, New York State Militia; organized 5 July 1847 at Brooklyn. It was ordered into Federal service on 14 August 1950 at Brooklyn and released on 13 July 1952. Redesignated as the 245th Artillery on 16 March 1959 and replaced in the New York Defense Area by 1/245th Artillery.

248th Antiaircraft Artillery Missile Battalion (Nike)   ILArNG
210th FA FR. 18 Dec 46, Chicago, IL; rd AAABn (120mm Gun) 28 Feb 54; rd AAAMBn (Nike) 28 Feb 58
        rd 2/202nd Artillery 1 Mar 59

    Chicago

        Not operational with Nike
Constituted in the Illinois National Guard on 1 July 1897 as a Squadron of Cavalry and organized from existing troops.

250th Antiaircraft Artillery Battalion (Gun)   GAANrNG
250th AAASLBn FR. 28 May 47, Augusta, GA; rd AAAGBn 1 Dec 47, rd AAABn (Gun) 1 Oct 53
        Cons. 1 Jul 59
        A   Augusta

B	Augusta
C	Moultrie
D	Augusta

Augusta

Originally constituted on 27 may 1942 in the Georgia National Guard as the 3rd Battalion, 214th Coast Artillery (Antiaircraft) and activated at Benicia Arsenal, CA on 26 June 1942. Called to Federal active service 14 August 1950, released to state service 13 May 1952 and consolidated with the 214th Artillery on 1 July 1959.

257th Antiaircraft Artillery Battalion   MNArNG

257th AAAAWBn FR. 22 Oct 46, Cloquet, MN; rd AAAGBn (90mm), rd AAABn 1 Oct 53

Cons.22 Feb 59

A	Cloquet
B	Virginia
C	Pine City
D	White Bear

Cloquet

Originally constituted in the Minnesota National Guard on 21 June 1946 as the 257th Antiaircraft Artillery Automatic Weapons Battalion. Consolidated with the 125th Artillery under CARS on 22 February 1959.

259th Antiaircraft Artillery Missile Battalion (Nike)   NYArNG

259th AAAGBn rd 1 Mar 50, New York, NY; rd AAABn 1 Oct 53; rd AAAMBn (Nike) 14 Feb 58;

Cons. 244th Artillery 16 Mar 59

New York

Not operational with Nike

First constituted in the New York National Guard as 3/9th Coast Defense Area Command, Coast Artillery Corps; headquarters organized 10 December 1920 in New York, NY. AcDu NYC 1/51-2/52. Consolidated with 244th Artillery 16 March 1959; replaced in the New York Defense Area by 1/244th Artillery.

260th Antiaircraft Artillery Battalion (120mm Gun)   DCArNG

260th AAAGBn FR. 14 Nov 46, Washington, DC; rd 260th AAABn (120mm Gun) 1 Oct 53

Db. 19 Mar 54

First constituted in the District of Columbia National Guard as the 1st Battalion, 260th Coast Artillery (Harbor Defense) with headquarters organized and federally recognized on 3 September 1924. The battalion was ordered into Federal service in the Washington Defense Area on 1 May 1951, released on 31 March 1953 and was disbanded on 19 March 1954 following the removal of Federal recognition.

271st Antiaircraft Artillery Missile Battalion   CAArNG

271st AAAAWBn FR. 5 May 47, San Francisco, CA; rd AAAGBn (90mm)1 Jan 51, rd AAABn (90mm Gun) 1 Oct 53,

> rd AAABn (120mm Gun) 1 Sept 54, rd AAABn (90mm Gun) 1 Jan 56; rd AAAMBn 1 Mar 58
> Cons. 1 May 59

> *San Francisco*

Special Security Force, 1950s; not operational with Nike
First constituted in the California National Guard on 5 August 1946 as the 271st Antiaircraft Artillery Automatic Weapons Battalion. Consolidated with the 250th Artillery, 1 May 1959; replaced in the San Francisco Defense Area by 1/250th Artillery.

278th Antiaircraft Artillery Battalion   ALArNG

278th AAAAWBn FR. 23 Mar 53, Florence, AL; rd AAABn 1 Oct 53

> Cons. 2 May 59
> A   Florence
> B   Tuscumbia
> C   Florence
> D   Sheffield

> *Florence*

Originally constituted in the Alabama National Guard as the 278th Antiaircraft Artillery Automatic Weapons Battalion. On 15 June 1954 the Alabama Army National Guard consolidated the 104th Antiaircraft Artillery Battalion (Montgomery) into the 278th; the latter was consolidated with the 278th Artillery under CARS on 2 May 1959.

283rd Antiaircraft Artillery Battalion (90mm Gun)   CTArNG

283rd AAAAWBn FR. 23 Dec 46, Bridgeport, CT; rd AAAGBn 25 Jun 51, rd AAABn (90mm Gun) 1 Oct 53

> Cons. 1 May 59
> A   Bridgeport
> B   Bridgeport
> C   New Haven
> D   West Hartford

> *Bridgeport (9/56) Stratford*

Special Security Force, 1950s
First constituted in the Connecticut National Guard as the 242nd Coast Artillery Battalion (Harbor Defense); headquarters, 1/242nd Coast Artillery received its Federal recognition in Bridgeport on 13 December 1922. Consolidated with the 242nd Artillery on 1 May 1959.

286th Antiaircraft Artillery Battalion (90mm Gun)   WAArNG

286th AAABn (90mm Gun) FR. 29 Aug 55, Bellingham, WA

> Cons.15 Apr 59
> A   Seattle
> B   Puyallup

C   Anacortes
D   Bellingham

Bellingham

Originally constituted in the Washington Army National Guard on 15 May 1952 as the 286th Antiaircraft Artillery Gun Battalion. Headquarters—which dated its formation to the organization of Company F, 1st Infantry on 17 September 1890 at Whatcom—received its Federal recognition in Bellingham on 24 February 1948 as the 874th Coast Artillery Battery (90mm AMTB) and redesignated as HHB 286th AAABn on 29 August 1955.

297th Antiaircraft Artillery Missile Battalion (Nike-Hercules)   THArNG

297th AAABn (90mm) Org. 3 Dec 56, Wahiawa, Oahu, TH; rd AAAMBn (Nike-Hercules) 15 Jan 59

I. 1 May 59

A   Wahiawa
B   Wahiawa
C   Waialua
D   Pearl City

Wahiawa

Not operational with Nike

First constituted 10 October 1956 as the 297th Antiaircraft Artillery Battalion (90mm Gun) and allocated to the Hawaii Army National Guard. Organized 3 December 1956 from former elements of the 298th Infantry. Battalion consolidated 1 May 1959 with the 298th Artillery, Territory of Hawaii Army National Guard; replaced in the Oahu Defense Area by 2/298th Artillery

298th Antiaircraft Artillery Battalion   THArNG

298th AAABn (90mm) FR. 7 Jan 57, Honolulu, TH;

B/U 15 Jan 59

A	Honolulu	rd 1/299th CAR
B	Honolulu	rd 1/299th CAR
C	Kaneohe	rd B/158th AAAMBn
D	Honolulu	rd 1/299th CAR

Honolulu

Originally constituted in the Territory of Hawaii Army National Guard on 10 October 1956 as the 29th Antiaircraft Artillery Battalion (90mm). The battalion was broken up and its elements consolidated, redesignated or disbanded after 15 January 1959 with the Headquarters & Headquarters Battery and batteries A, B and D forming the 1st Battle Group, 299th Combat Arms Regiment.

300th Antiaircraft Artillery Battalion   MIArNG

593rd AAAAWBn rd 300th AAAGBn 1 Oct 50, Kingsford, MI; rd AAABn 5 Oct 53

Cons. 15 Mar 59

A   Manistee
B   Iron River

C   Baraga
D
*Kingsford

Originally constituted in the Michigan National Guard on 22 May 1946 at Kingsford as the 593rd Antiaircraft Artillery Automatic Weapons Battalion. Consolidated with the 182nd Artillery on 15 March 1959.

308th Antiaircraft Artillery Battalion (90mm Gun)   NJArNG

308th AAAGBn (90mm Gun) FR 1 Dec 47, Rio Grande, NJ

Rd. 286th 1 Feb 55
A   Rio Grande
B   Ocean City
C   Wildwood

*Rio Grande, NJ

First constituted in the New Jersey National Guard on 9 July 1946 as the 308th Antiaircraft Artillery Searchlight Battalion. Redesignated as the 286th Armored Field Artillery Battalion on 1 February 1955.

336th Antiaircraft Artillery Gun Battalion   NYArNG

336th AAAGBn FR. 30 Oct 47, Utica, NY

Rd. 3/101st Armored Cavalry 15 Mar 53

*Utica

First constituted in the New York National Guard and organized on 21 March 1898 as the 16th Battalion of Infantry. It was called to active Federal service on 15 May 1951 for duty in the Niagara Falls Defense Area, released on 14 March 1953 and redesignated as the 3rd Battalion, 101st Armored Cavalry on 15 March.

337th Antiaircraft Artillery Battalion (90mm Gun)   PAArNG

337th AAASLBn FR. I Dec 46, Reading, PA; rd AAABn (90mm Gun)

Cons 1 Jun 59

*Reading (5/51) Hamburg

First constituted in the Pennsylvania National Guard on 27 May 1942 as the 3/213th Coast Artillery (Antiaircraft). The battalion was ordered into Federal service on 1 May 1951 for duty in the Philadelphia Defense Area and was released on 31 December 1952. Battalion consolidated with the 213th Artillery, 1 June 1959.

340th Antiaircraft Artillery Missile Battalion (Nike)   DCArNG

340th AAASLBn Org. 4 Oct 46, Washington, DC; Rd. AAAGBn 1 Sept 50, Rd. AAABn (120mm Gun) 15 Nov 53,

Rd. AAAMBn (Nike) 10 Feb 58;
Db. 1 Mar 59

*Washington DC

Not operational with Nike

First constituted in the District of Columbia National Guard 15 June 1942 as 3/260th Coast Artillery (Antiaircraft); organized 15 June 1942 at Retsil, WA. Disbanded 1 March 1959; Headquarters & Headquarters Battery converted and redesignated as the 107th Engineer Company.

341st Antiaircraft Artillery Battalion   ALArNG

341st AAABn FR. 10 May 55, Jasper, AL

    B/U 2 May 59

A	Vernon	cons. C/877th Engineers
B	Double Springs	to B/1343rd Engineers
C	Carbon Hill	to B/1343rd Engineers
D	Dora	Rd. 402nd Ord Company

    Jasper

First constituted on 1 April 1955 in the Alabama Army National Guard as the 341st Antiaircraft Artillery Battalion; broken up and components redesignated on 2 May 1959.

351st Antiaircraft Artillery Missile Battalion

351st AAAMBn A. 15 Jul 56, Cleveland, OH

    I. 1 Sept 58

A	CL-48 Garfield Heights	/56-9/58	to A/1/68th
B	CL-34 Warrensville	/56- /57	to B/508th
	CL-59 Parma	/57-9/58	to B/1/68th
C	CL-67 Lakefront Airport	/56-9/58	to C/1/68th
D	CL-69 Lordstown	/56-9/58	to D/1/68th

    Cleveland

First constituted 1 January 1942 as the 351st Coast Artillery Searchlight Battalion; activated 12 January 1942 at Camp Haan, CA. Replaced in the Cleveland Defense Area by 1/68th Artillery.

369th Antiaircraft Artillery Battalion (90mm Gun)   NYArNG

369th AAAGBn (Colored) FR. 29 Oct 47, New York, NY; rd AAABn (90mm Gun) 1 Oct 53

    Rd. 1 Apr 55

    New York City

Originally constituted in the New York National Guard at New York on 2 June 1913 as the 1st Battalion, 15th Infantry (Colored). Redesignated as the 569th Field Artillery Battalion on 1 April 1955.

380th Antiaircraft Artillery Missile Battalion (Nike)   DCArNG

380th AAAAWBn Org. 10 Oct 46, Washington DC; rd AAABn (120mm Gun) 15 Nov 53, rd AAAMBn (Nike) 10 Feb 58

    Db. 1 Mar 59

    Washington DC

Not operational with Nike

First constituted in the District of Columbia National Guard 17 June 1924 as 2/260th Coast Artillery Harbor Defense. AcDu Wash DC, 11/52-4/53. AcDu Niagara Falls, 5/51-11/52; NYC 11/52-4/53. Disbanded 1 March 1959; Headquarters & Headquarters Battery redesignated 105th Military Police Detachment.

398th Antiaircraft Artillery Battalion (AW)(SP)   USAR

398th AAAAWBn (self-propelled) A. 21 Feb 47, Manchester, NH; rd AAABn (automatic weapons)(self-propelled) 13 Dec 54

    I. 30 Jun 59

    Manchester

Battalion first constituted in the Army of the United States as the 398th Coast Artillery Battalion (Antiaircraft) (Automatic Weapons) on 19 December 1942 and activated 20 February 1943 at Camp Edwards, MA. The 398th Antiaircraft Artillery Automatic Weapons Battalion (self-propelled) was allotted to the Organized Reserve and assigned to First US Army on 6 February 1947. It was called to active duty on Manchester on 11 September 1950 and released on 20 December 1954.

401st Antiaircraft Artillery Missile Battalion

401st AAAMBn A. 1 May 56, Milwaukee, WI

    I. 1 Sept 58

A	M-64 Muskegon	/57-9/58	to A/3/67th
B	M-42 Cuddahy	/56-9/58	to B/3/67th
C	M-54 Hales Corners	/56-9/58	to C/3/67th
D	M-74 Waukesha	/57-9/58	to D/3/67th

    Milwaukee ( ) Hales Corners

First constituted 31 January 1942 as the 401st Separate Coastal Artillery Battalion (Antiaircraft)(Gun); activated 1 April 1942 at Camp Haan, CA. Replaced in the Milwaukee Defense Area by 3/67th Artillery.

418th Antiaircraft Artillery Battalion (90mm Gun)   VAArNG

418th AAAGBn FR. 17 Oct 51, Danville, VA; rd AAABn (90mm Gun) 1 Oct 53

    Cons. 1 Jun 59

    A   Danville

    B   Attarisa

    C   Rocky Mount

    D   Chatham

    Danville (3/56) Chatham

Originally constituted in the Virginia National Guard on 2 July 1946 as the 418th Antiaircraft Artillery Automatic Weapons Battalion. Consolidated with the 246th Artillery on 1 June 1959.

420th Antiaircraft Artillery Battalion (90mm Gun)   WAArNG

420th AAAGBn FR. 14 Nov 47, Yakima, WA; rd AAABn (90mm Gun) 1 Oct 53

Cons. 15 Apr 59

Yakima

First constituted 5 July 1946 in the Washington National Guard as the 420th Antiaircraft Artillery Gun Battalion. It was ordered into active Federal service on 1 May 1951 for duty in the Seattle Defense Area and released on 31 December 1952. Battalion consolidated with the 205th Artillery on 15 April 1959.

425th Antiaircraft Artillery Battalion

425th AAABn A. 10 Mar 55, Camp Stewart, GA

I. 1 Sept 58

Camp Stewart ( ) Savannah River Project

First constituted 25 February 1943 as the 125th Coast Artillery Battalion (Separate)(Antiaircraft)(Gun)(Mobile); activated 24 May 1943 at Camp Haan, CA.

433rd Antiaircraft Artillery Missile Battalion (Nike)(Continental)

433rd AAAMBn A. 7 Sept 55, Fort Lawton, WA

I. 1 Sept 58

A	S-61 Vashon Island	/56-9/58	to A/4/60th
B	S-33 Lake Youngs	/56-9/58	to B/4/60th
C	S-32 Lake Youngs	/56-9/58	to C/4/60th
D	S-81 Poulsbo	/56- /58	to D/513th
	S-43 Kent	/58-9/58	to D/4/60th

Fort Lawton ( ) Midway

First constituted 31 January 1942 as the 433rd Separate Coast Artillery Battalion Antiaircraft Automatic Weapons; activated 1 March 1942 at Camp Stewart, GA. Replaced in the Seattle Defense Area by 4/60th Artillery.

436th Antiaircraft Artillery Missile Battalion

436th AAABn A. 6 Jan 55, Travis AFB, CA; rd AAAMBn 5 Jan 57

I. 1 Sept 58

A	T-10 Elmira	/57-9/58	to A/1/61st
B	T-53 Potrero Hills	/57-9/58	to B/1/61st
C	T-85 Fairfield	/57-9/58	to C/1/61st
D	T-33 Dixon	/57-9/58	to D/1/61st

Travis AFB

First constituted 10 April 1942 as the 436th Coast Artillery Battalion (Antiaircraft)(Automatic Weapons); activated 20 April 1942 at Camp Hulen, TX. Replaced in the Travis Defense Area by 1/61st Artillery

441st Antiaircraft Artillery Missile Battalion

441st AAAMBn A. 1 Aug 55, Fort Cronkhite, CA

I. 1 Sept 58

A	SF-31 Lake Chabot	/56-9/58	to A/4/67th
B	SF-25 Rocky Ridge	/56-9/58	to B/4/67th
C	Benicia	/55- /56	temp site

	SF-08 San Pablo Ridge	/56-9/58	to C/4/67th
D	Parks AFB	/55- /56	temp site
	SF-09 San Pablo Ridge	/56-9/58	to D/4/67th

Fort Cronkhite ( ) San Pablo Ridge

First constituted 21 May 1942 as the 441st Coast Artillery Battalion (Antiaircraft)(Automatic Weapons); activated 1 June 1942 at Camp Stewart, GA. Replaced in the San Francisco Defense Area by 4/67th Artillery.

450th Antiaircraft Artillery Battalion Automatic Weapons

450th AAAAWBn (Separate)(Mobile) A. 2 Jul 46, Fort Bliss, TX; rd AAABn (Automatic Weapons) 12 Oct 50;

I. 1 Nov 57

Fort Bliss ( ) Eielson AFB

First constituted 8 May 1942 as the 450th Coast Artillery Battalion (Antiaircraft)(Automatic Weapons)(Colored); activated 11 May 1942 at Camp Davis, NC.

451st Antiaircraft Artillery Battalion

451st AAABn A. 6 Jan 55, March AFB, CA

I. 15 Jun 57

March AFB

First constituted 9 May 1942 as the 451st Coast Artillery Battalion (Antiaircraft)(Automatic Weapons); activated 1 August 1942 at Camp Stewart, GA.

456th Antiaircraft Artillery Battalion   USAR

456th AAAAWBn (Mobile) A. 19 Nov 48, Providence, RI; rd AAABn 19 Jan 54

I. 18 Apr 55

Providence

The battalion was first constituted in the Army of the United States as the 456th Coast Artillery Battalion (Antiaircraft)(Automatic Weapons) and activated at Fort Sheridan, IL on 1 September 1942. The Army allotted the 456th Antiaircraft Artillery Automatic Weapons Battalion (Mobile) to the Organized Reserve Corps on 3 November 1948 and assigned it to the First US Army on 8 November 1948. It served on active duty in the Travis Defense Area from September 1950 to January 1955; the Regular Army 436th AAA Battalion replaced the 456th on 6 January.

464th Antiaircraft Artillery Battalion   ALArNG

464th AAAAWBn FR. 9 Jan 47, Talladega, AL; rd AAABn 1 Jan 53

Cons.2 May 59

Talladega (1/51) Camp Roberts (4/51) Castle AFB (12/52) Talladega

First constituted 30 August 1942 in the Army of the United States as the 464th Coast Artillery Battalion (Separate)(Antiaircraft) and activated 15 October 1942 at Camp Davis, NC. It was called to Federal service on 23 January 1951 for duty at Camp Roberts, CA and in the Castle Defense Area and released on 22 December 1952. Battalion consolidated with the 203rd Artillery on 2 May 1959.

465th Antiaircraft Artillery Missile Battalion

465th AAAMBn A. 1 Jun 56, Fort Niagara, NY

I. 1 Sept 58

A	BU-09 Ransom Creek	/56-9/58	to A/2/62nd
B	BU-18 Lancaster	/56-9/58	to B/2/62nd
C	BU-34 Orchard Park	/56-9/58	to C/2/62nd
D	BU-52 Hamburg	/56-9/58	to D/2/62nd

Fort Niagara ( ) Lancaster

First constituted 30 August 1942 as the 465th Coast Artillery Battalion (Antiaircraft)(Automatic Weapons); activated 15 October 1942 at Camp Davis, NC. Replaced in the Buffalo Defense Area by 2/62nd Artillery.

466th Antiaircraft Artillery Battalion   USAR

466th AAAAWBn (Semimobile)(Colored) A. 19 Nov 46, Richmond, VA; rd AAABn 13 Dec 50

I. 1 Jun 59

Richmond (3/55) Glassmere

The battalion was initially constituted in the Army of the United States on 30 August 1942 as the 466th Coast Artillery Battalion (Antiaircraft)(Automatic Weapons)(Colored) and activated 15 October 1942 at Camp Stewart, GA. It was allotted to the Organized Reserves on 8 November 1946, called to active duty on 11 September 1950 and released back to reserve status on 6 January 1955. On 21 March 1955 the Army Reserve reorganized the battalion at Glassmere, PA near Pittsburgh.

478th Antiaircraft Artillery Battalion

478th AAABn A. 25 Mar 55, Camp Stewart, GA

I. 15 Feb 58

Camp Stewart ( ) Savannah River Project

First constituted 3 November 1942 as the 478th Coast Artillery Battalion (Antiaircraft)(Automatic Weapons); activated 20 November 1942 at Camp Davis, NC.

483rd Antiaircraft Artillery Missile Battalion

483rd AAAMBn A. 11 Mar 55, Fort Hancock, NJ

I. 1 Sept 58

A	NY-93 Ramsey	/55- /58	to B/737th
	NY-73 Summit	/58-9/58	to A/2/65th
B	NY-65 South Plainfield	/55-9/58	to B/2/65th
C	NY-80 Livingston	/55-9/58	to C/2/65th
D	NY-88 Mountain View	/55-9/58	to D/2/65th

First constituted 19 December 1942 as the 483rd Coast Artillery Battalion (Antiaircraft)(Automatic

Weapons); activated 10 February 1943 at Fort Bliss, TX. Replaced in the New York Defense Area by 2/65th Artillery.

485th Antiaircraft Artillery Missile Battalion

485th AAAMBn A. 1 Mar 55, Fort Sheridan, IL

I. 1 Sept 58

A	C-03 Montrose	10/55-9/58	to A/2/57th
B	C-40 Burnham Park	/55-9/58	to B/2/57th
C	C-41 Jackson Park	/55-9/58	to C/2/57th
D	C-44 Hegewisch	/55- /56	to B/49th
	C-03 Montrose	/56-9/58	to D/2/57th

Fort Sheridan ( ) Montrose

First constituted 2 November 1942 as the 485th Coast Artillery Battalion (Antiaircraft)(Automatic Weapons); activated 10 February 1943 at Camp Hulen, TX. On 30 June 1958 Site C-03, A/485th became ARADCOM's first operational Nike Hercules battery.

Replaced in the Chicago Defense Area by 2/57th Artillery.

495th Antiaircraft Artillery Missile Battalion

495th AAABn (Light)(Mobile)(75mm) A. 27 Oct 52, Fort Bliss, TX; rd AAAMBn 10 Aug 53;

I. 28 Aug 58

A	10/52-	A>
B	10/52-	A>
C	9/54-	A>
D	9/54-	A>

Fort Bliss

First constituted 15 June 1942 as the 495th Coast Artillery Battalion (Antiaircraft)(Gun) and activated on 10 July 1942 in Iceland. Following reactivation as an AAA battalion (Light)(Mobile)(75mm) at Fort Bliss the 495th served as the Army's first training unit for the 75mm Skysweeper; the first two field batteries the battalion trained departed for Thule, Greenland in August 1953. The 495th subsequently redesignated as a missile unit and was the first Nike battalion to go through Annual Service Practice at Red Canyon Range Camp, between December 1954 and January 1955. Over January and February 1956 A/495th served as the first Nike unit to participate in an air transportability test, conducted at Biggs AFB. The 495th became the first semi-mobile Nike Ajax battalion in the Army on 20 December 1956 and on 3 May 1957 made the first Nike Ajax training launch from the new McGregor Range, where Batteries A and C/495th fired a total of six missiles. On 3 June 1957 D/495th moved to Camp Desert Rock, Nevada for Exercise Desert Rock, marking the first employment of an Ajax unit in a nuclear test.

496th Antiaircraft Artillery Battalion

496th AAAGBn A. 15 Sept 53, Camp Stewart, GA; rd AAABn 26 Aug 53

I. 20 Dec 57

A	C-96 Chicago	4/54-12/57
B	C-90 Chicago	4/54-12/57

245

| C | C-97 Chicago | 4/54-12/57 |
| D | C-98 Chicago | 4/54-12/57 |

Camp Stewart (4/54) C-90 Chicago

First constituted 19 December 1942 as the 496th Coast Artillery Battalion (Antiaircraft)(Gun); activated 10 January 1943 at Camp Stewart, GA.

501st Antiaircraft Artillery Battalion

501st AAAGBn A. 15 Jan 49, Fort Bliss, TX; rd AAABn (Gun) 20 Jul 53

I. 20 Dec 57

Fort Bliss ( ) Camp Hanford

First constituted 19 December 1942 as the 501st Coast Artillery Battalion (Antiaircraft)(Gun); activated 20 February 1943 at Camp Edwards, MA.

502nd Antiaircraft Artillery Battalion

502nd AAAGBn (Semimobile) A. 18 Nov 48, Fort Bliss, TX; rd AAABn 1 Sept 53

I. 15 Sept 58

Fort Bliss ( ) Ladd AFB ( ) Eielson AFB

First constituted 19 December 1942 as the 502nd Coast Artillery Battalion (Antiaircraft)(Gun); activated 20 February 1943 at Camp Edwards, MA.

504th Antiaircraft Artillery Missile Battalion

504th AAAGBn (Semimobile) A. 20 Nov 48, Fort Bliss, TX; rd AAABn 24 Jul 53, rd AAAMBn 10 Jan 55

I. 1 Sept 58

A	D-51 NAS Grosse Isle	/55-9/58	to A/2/517th
B	D-54 Riverview	/55- /57	to C/85th
	D-57 Carleton	/57-9/58	to B/2/517th
C	D-69 River Rouge	/56- /57	to A/18th
	D-61 Romulus	/57-9/58	to C/2/517th
D	D-58 Carleton	/56-9/58	to D/2/517th

Fort Bliss ( ) Carleton

First constituted 8 February 1943 as the 504th Coast Artillery Battalion (Antiaircraft)(Gun); activated 20 March 1943 at Camp Davis, NC. Replaced in the Detroit Defense Area by 2/517th Artillery.

505th Antiaircraft Artillery Missile Battalion

505th AAAGBn (Semimobile) A. 22 Nov 52, Fort Tilden, NY; rd AAABn (Gun) 3 Aug 53, rd AAAMBn 9 Jun 54

I. 1 Sept 58

A	NY-24 Amityville	/55-9/58	to A/3/51st
B	NY-49 Fort Tilden	/55-9/58	to B/3/51st
C	NY-29 Lido Beach	/55-9/58	to C/3/51st
D	NY-25 Rocky Point	/55-9/58	to D/3/51st

Fort Tilden

First constituted 25 February 1943 as the 505th Coast Artillery Battalion (Antiaircraft)(Gun); activated 10 April 1943 at Camp Stewart, GA. Replaced in the New York Defense Area by 3/51st Artillery.

506th Antiaircraft Artillery Missile Battalion

506th AAAGBn A. 1 Dec 52, Logan Station, Philadelphia, PA; rd AAABn (Gun) 24 Jul 53, rd AAAMBn 1 Dec 54

I. 1 Sept 58

A	PH-91 Worchester	/55-9/58	to A/3/60th
B	PH-99 Warrington	/55-9/58	to B/3/60th
C	PH-07 Richboro	/55-9/58	to C/3/60th
D	PH-15 Newportville	/55-9/58	to D/3/60th

Logan Station (/55) Warrington

First constituted 25 February 1943 as the 506th Coast Artillery Battalion (Antiaircraft)(Gun); activated 20 May 1943 at Camp Stewart, GA. Replaced in the Philadelphia Defense Area by 3/60th Artillery.

508th Antiaircraft Artillery Missile Battalion

508th AAAMBn A. 15 Feb 57, Lordstown Military Reservation, OH

I. 1 Sept 58

A	CL-11 Painesville	/58-9/58	to A/3/65th
B	CL-34 Warrensville	/57-9/58	to B/3/65th
C	CL-13 Willowick	/56-9/58	to C/3/65th
D	CL-02 Bratenahl	/57-9/58	to D/3/65th

Lordstown Military Reservation ( ) Cleveland

First constituted 25 February 1943 as the 508th Coast Artillery Battalion (Antiaircraft)(Gun); activated 20 May 1943 at Camp Stewart, GA. Replaced in the Cleveland Defense Area by 3/65th Artillery.

509th Antiaircraft Artillery Missile Battalion

509th AAGBn A. 1 Dec 52, Pittsburgh, PA; rd AAABn (Gun) 24 Jul 53, rd AAAMBn 1 Feb 55

I. 1 Sept 58

A	PI-71 Coraopolis	/55-9/58	to A/6/6th
B	PI-62 Bridgeville	/56-9/58	to B/6/6th
C	PI-52 Finleyville	/55-9/58	to C/6/6th
D	PI-43 Elrama	5/55-9/58	to D/6/6th

Pittsburgh ( ) Hickam

First constituted 25 February 1943 as the 509th Antiaircraft Artillery Gun Battalion Semimobile; activated 10 June 1943 at Camp Edwards, MA. Replaced in the Pittsburgh Defense Area by 6/6th Battalion.

513th Antiaircraft Artillery Missile Battalion

513th AAAGBn (Semimobile) A. 5 Dec 52, Fort Lawton, WA; rd AAABn (Gun) 20 Jul 53, rd AAAMBn 20

Dec 54

    I. 1 Sept 58

A	S-82 Winslow	/55-9/58	to A/4/4th
B	S-62 Ollala	/55-9/58	to B/4/4th
C	S-92 Kingston	/55-9/58	to C/4/4th
D	S-81 Poulsbo	/58-9/58	to D/4/4th

    *Fort Lawton ( ) Poulsbo

First constituted 25 February 1943 as the 513th Antiaircraft Artillery Gun Battalion Semimobile; activated 10 June 1943 at Camp Edwards, MA. Replaced in the Seattle Defense Area by 4/4th Artillery.

514th Antiaircraft Artillery Missile Battalion

514th AAAGBn (Semimobile) A. 26 Dec 52, Fort Banks, MA; rd AAABn 3 Aug 53, rd AAAMBn 5 Jan 55

    I. 1 Sept 58

A	B-73 South Lincoln	1/56-11 /56	to A/24th
	B-38 Cohasset	11/56-9/58	to A/3/52nd
B	B-84 Burlington	1/56- /56	to C/24th
	B-55 Blue Hills	/56-9/58	to B/3/52nd
C	B-37 Squantum	1/56-9/58	to C/3/52nd
D	B-36 Fort Duvall	1/56-9/58	to D/3/52nd

    *Fort Banks Squantum

First constituted 25 February 1943 as the 514th AAAGBn (Semimobile); activated 10 July 1943 at Camp Edwards, MA. Replaced in the Boston Defense Area by 3/52nd Artillery

516th Antiaircraft Artillery Missile Battalion

516th AAAGBn (Semimobile) A. 5 Jan 53, Detroit, MI; rd AAABn (Gun) 24 Jul 53, rd AAAMBn 20 May 54

    I. 1 Sept 58

A	D-16 Selfridge	/55-9/58	to A/3/517th
B	D-06 Utica	/55-9/58	to B/3/517th
C	D-14 Selfridge	/55-9/58	to C/3/517th
D	D-97 Auburn Heights	/55- /58	to D/18th
	D-17 Algonac	/58-9/58	to D/3/517th

    *Detroit ( ) Selfridge AFB

First constituted 25 February 1943 as the 516th Antiaircraft Artillery Gun Battalion (Semimobile); activated 1 October 1943 at Camp Haan, CA. Replaced in the Detroit Defense Area by 3/517th Artillery.

518th Antiaircraft Artillery Battalion Gun

518th AAAGBn A. 15 Jan 49, Fort Bliss, TX; rd AAABn (Gun) 20 Jul 53

    I. 20 Dec 57

    *Fort Bliss ( ) Camp Hanford

First constituted 25 February 1943 as the 518th Antiaircraft Artillery Gun Battalion (Semimobile); activated 12 November 1943 in New Caledonia.

519th Antiaircraft Artillery Battalion Gun

519th AAAGBn (Semimobile) A. 15 Jan 49, Fort Bliss, TX; rd AAABn (Gun) 20 Jul 53

    I. 20 Dec 57

    Fort Bliss ( ) Camp Hanford

First constituted 25 February 1943 as the 519th Antiaircraft Artillery Gun Battalion (Semimobile); activated 1 June 1943 at the Teaneck Armory, West Englewood, NJ.

526th Antiaircraft Artillery Missile Battalion

1/71st Coast Artillery (Antiaircraft)(Semimobile) A. 1 Jul 40, Fort Story, VA; rd 71st AAAGBn 1 Sept 43rd 526th AAA Composite Battalion 10 Jan 45, rd 526th AAAGBn 1 Sept 45, rd AAABn 3 Aug 53, rd AAAMBn 13 Feb 54,

    I. 1 Sept 58

A	NY-58 South Amboy	/55-9/58	to A/4/71st
B	NY-53 Leonardo	/55-9/58	to B/4/71st
C	NY-56 Fort Hancock	/55-9/58	to C/4/71st
D	NY-54 Holmdel	/55-9/58	to D/4/71st

    Fort Story Washington, DC Fort Hancock

First constituted 2 May 1918 as 1/71st Artillery Coast Artillery Corps; organized 12 May 1918 at Forts Strong and Andrews, MA. Replaced in the New York Defense Area by 4/71st Artillery; consolidated 31 July 1959 with the 71st Artillery.

527th Antiaircraft Artillery Battalion (90mm Gun)   LAArNG

527th AAAGBn FR. 23 May 49, New Orleans, LA; rd AAAAWBn 1 Oct 59, rd AAAGBn 1 Oct 52,

    rd AAABn (90mm Gun) 1 Oct 53

    Cons. 1 Jul 59

    New Orleans

Originally constituted in the Louisiana National Guard on 27 May 1946 as the 527th Antiaircraft Automatic Weapons Battalion. Consolidated with the 141st Artillery under CARS on 1 July 1959.

531st Antiaircraft Artillery Missile Battalion

531st AAABn (AW) A. 24 Jul 52, Fort Bliss, TX; rd AAAMBn 15 Jun 57

    I. 1 Sept 58

A	E-01 Ellsworth AFB	/57-9/58	to A/2/67th
B	E-20 Ellsworth AFB	/57-9/58	to B/2/67th
C	E-40 Ellsworth AFB	/57-9/58	to C/2/67th
D	E-70 Ellsworth AFB	/57-9/58	to D/2/67th

    Fort Bliss Ellsworth AFB

First constituted 6 July 1942 as the 531st Coast Artillery Battalion Antiaircraft Automatic Weapons; activated 15 July 1942 at Fort Bliss, TX. Replaced in the Ellsworth Defense Area by 2/67th Artillery.

546th Antiaircraft Artillery Battalion

546th AAABn A. 20 Nov 53, Fort Bliss, TX

    I. 15 Jun 57

    Fort Bliss ( ) Carswell AFB

First constituted 19 December 1942 as the 546th Coast Artillery Battalion Antiaircraft Automatic Weapons; activated 10 January 1943 at Camp Haan, CA.

548th Antiaircraft Artillery Missile Battalion

548th AAABn A. 15 Dec 53, Fort Bliss, TX; rd AAAMBn 1 Mar 57

    I. 1 Sept 58

A	L-13 Caswell	9/57-9/58	to A/3/61st
B	L-31 Limestone	9/57-9/58	to B/3/61st
C	L-58 Caribou	9/57-9/58	to C/3/61st
D	L-85 Conner	9/57-9/58	to D/3/61st

    Fort Bliss ( ) Loring AFB

First constituted 19 December 1942 as the 548th Coast Artillery Battalion Antiaircraft Automatic Weapons; activated 10 January 1943 at Camp Haan, CA. Replaced in the Loring Defense Area by 3/61st Artillery.

549th Antiaircraft Artillery Missile Battalion

549th AAAGBn A. 23 Jul 52, Camp Stewart, GA; rd AAABn 8 Jun 53, rd AAAMBn 14 Jul 58

    I. 1 Sept 58

    Camp Stewart (7/55) Thule AB

First constituted 19 December 1942 as the 549th Coast Artillery Battalion Antiaircraft Automatic Weapons; activated 20 January 1943 at Camp Edwards, MA. Replaced in the Thule Defense Area by 4/55th Artillery.

550th Antiaircraft Artillery Battalion Gun

550th AAAGBn A. 23 Jul 52, Camp Stewart, GA; AAABn (Gun) 8 May 53,

    I. 20 Dec 57

    Camp Stewart ( ) Norfolk

First constituted 19 December 1942 as the 550th Coast Artillery Battalion (Antiaircraft)(Automatic Weapons); activated 10 January 1943 at Camp Edwards, MA.

551st Antiaircraft Artillery Missile Battalion

551st AAAGBn A. 23 Jul 52, Camp Stewart, GA; rd AAABn (Gun) 8 May 53, rd AAAMBn 17 Aug 54;

    I. 1 Sept 58

A	LA-94 Los Pinetos	/55-9/58	to A/4/65th
B	LA-98 Magic Mountain	12/55-9/58	to B/4/65th
C	LA-88 Chatsworth	/57-9/58	to C/4/65th
D	LA-96 Van Nuys	/58-9/58	to D/4/65th

Camp Stewart (8/54) Fort MacArthur (/56) Birmingham Army Hospital

First constituted 19 December 1942 as the 551st Coast Artillery Battalion (Antiaircraft)(Automatic Weapons); activated 20 January 1943 at Camp Edwards, MA. Replaced in the Los Angeles Defense Area by 4/65th Artillery.

554th Antiaircraft Artillery Missile Battalion

554th AAABn A. 23 Jul 52, Camp Stewart, GA; rd AAAMBn 10 Nov 54

    I. 1 Sept 58

A	LA-32 Garden Grove	/56-9/58	to A/3/57th
B	LA-78 Malibu	/56-9/58	to B/3/57th
C	LA-43 Fort MacArthur	/56-9/58	to C/3/57th
D	LA-55 Point Vicente	/54-9/58	to D/3/57th

Camp Stewart (11/54) Fort MacArthur

First constituted 19 December 1942 as the 554th Coast Artillery Battalion (Antiaircraft)(Automatic Weapons); activated 20 February 1943 at Camp Hulen, TX. Replaced in the Los Angeles Defense Area by 3/57th Artillery.

598th Antiaircraft Artillery Battalion (90mm Gun)   MNArNG

598th AAABn (Semimobile) FR. 1 Oct 46, Duluth, MN; rd AAAAWBn (Mobile 1 Oct 49, rd AAAGBn (90mm) 16 Jul 51,

    Rd. AAABn (90mm Gun) 1 Oct 53

    B/U 22 Feb 59

A	Faribault	rd 114th Trans Co
B	St Peter	rd B/1/125th FA
C	New Ulm	rd 224th Trans Co
D	Olivia	rd 535th Trans Co

Duluth

Originally constituted in the Minnesota National Guard as the 1st Battalion, 215th Coast Artillery (Antiaircraft)(Semimobile; headquarters received its Federal recognition at St Cloud on 30 April 1921. Battalion broken up on 22 February 1959 with components converted or redesignated.

601st Antiaircraft Artillery Battalion

601st AAAGBn (Semimobile) A. 1 Jan 53, Fort George G. Meade, MD; rd AAABn 15 Jul 53

    I. 15 Jun 57

    Fort George G. Meade ( ) Andrews AFB

First constituted 19 January 1942 as 1/601st Coast Artillery Antiaircraft; activated 1 February 1942 at Fort

Bliss, TX.

602nd Antiaircraft Artillery Missile Battalion

602nd AAAGBn (Semimobile) A. 1 Jan 53, Essex, MD; rd AABn 22 Jul 53, rd AAAMBn 22 Sept 55

I. 1 Sept 58

A	BA-03 Phoenix	11/55-8/56	to A/54th
	BA-79 Granite	8/56-9/58	to A/4/5th
B	W-93 Laytonville	/55-9/58	to B/4/5th
C	W-94 Gaithersburg	/55-9/58	to C/4/5th
D	W-92 Rockville	9/58	to D/4/5th

Essex (11/55) Laytonville

First constituted 31 January 1942 as 1/602nd Coast Artillery Antiaircraft; activated 1 March 1942 at Fort Bliss, TX. Replaced in the Washington Defense Area by 4/5th Artillery.

605th Antiaircraft Artillery Missile Battalion

605th AAAGBn (Semimobile) A. 16 Feb 53, Fort Dawes, MA; rd AAABn 3 Aug 53, rd AAAMBn 19 Apr 56

I. 1 Sept 58

A	B-15 Beverly	2/57-9/58	to A/1/57th
B	B-05 Danvers	11/56-9/58	to B/1/57th
C	B-17 Nahant	11/56-9/58	to C/1/57th
D	B-03 Reading	11/56-9/58	to D/1/57th

Fort Dawes (/57) Fort Banks

First constituted 31 January 1942 as 1/605th Coast Artillery Antiaircraft; activated 1 March 1942 at Camp Stewart, GA. Replaced in the Boston Defense Area by 1/57th Artillery.

606th Antiaircraft Artillery Battalion

606th AAAGBn A. 14 Feb 53, Lewiston, NY; rd AAABn 3 Aug 53

I. 20 Dec 57

Lewiston ( ) Niagara Falls

First constituted 25 February 1943 as the 120th Coast Artillery Battalion (Antiaircraft)(Gun); activated 2 April 1943 at Camp Haan, CA.

615th Antiaircraft Artillery Missile Battalion (Nike)

615th AAABn90mm Gun FR. 13 Sept 54, South Norfolk, VA; rd AAAMBn (Nike) 15 Feb 58

Cons. 1 Jun 59

A   Craddock
B   Smithfield
C   Camp Pendleton
D   South Norfolk

South Norfolk

Special Security Force, 1950s; not operational with Nike

The 615th Antiaircraft Battalion was constituted on 26 June 1954 and organized on 13 September 1954 in South Norfolk. It was consolidated with the 111th Artillery on 1 June 1959 prior to operations with Nike Ajax; the 4/111th replaced it in the Norfolk Defense Area.

633rd Antiaircraft Artillery Battalion (90mm Gun)   NYArNG

102nd AAAAWBn rd 633rd 1 Mar 50, New York, NY; rd AAAGBn 1 May 50, rd AAAAWBn ca. 1952
    Db. 1 Oct 57

   New York

Originally constituted in the New York National Guard as the 1st Battalion, 96th Coast Defense Command, Coast Artillery Corps; the headquarters received its Federal recognition in New York on 19 July 1921. The battalion served on Federal active duty from 15 May 1951 through 14 April 1953 and was disbanded on 1 October 1957.

678th Antiaircraft Artillery Battalion (90mm Gun)   SCArNG

678th AAAAWBn (Mobile) FR. 15 Apr 47, Anderson, SC; rd AAAGBn (90mm) 1 Nov 52, rd AAABn (90mm Gun) 1 Oct 53
    Cons. 1 Apr 59
    A   Seneca
    B   Easley
    C   Greenville
    D   Williamston

   Anderson

Originally constituted 5 July 1946 in the South Carolina National Guard as the 678th Antiaircraft Artillery Automatic Weapons Battalion (Mobile); the Headquarters & Headquarters Battery dated its formation to the 21 July 1923 organization of the 2nd Battalion, 263rd Coast Artillery at Beaufort. Consolidated with the 263rd Artillery on 1 April 1959.

682nd Antiaircraft Artillery Battalion   CAArNG

682nd AAAAWBn FR. 2 Jun 47, Long Beach, CA; rd AAAGBn 1 Jan 51, rd AAABn 1 Oct 53
    Cons. 1 May 59
    A   San Pedro
    B   Compton
    C   Lynwood
    D   Norwalk

   Long Beach

Originally constituted in the California National Guard on 5 August 1946; the Headquarters & Headquarters Battery dated its formation to the 3 December 1924 organization of headquarters, 2nd Battalion, 251st Coast Artillery (Harbor Defense). Consolidated with the 251st Artillery on 1 May 1959.

683rd Antiaircraft Artillery Missile Battalion (Nike)   MDArNG

683rd AAABn (90mm Gun) FR. 21 Nov 55, Essex, MD; rd AAAMBn (Nike) 15 Jan 58

Cons. 1 Mar 59

Essex

Not operational with Nike

The battalion was first constituted on 10 July 1946 as the 683rd Antiaircraft Artillery Automatic Weapons Battalion and allotted to the Oregon National Guard; the allotment was withdrawn 1 November 1955 and given to the Maryland Army National Guard. The unit organized 21 November 1955 and consolidated with the 70th Artillery on 1 March 1959; the 1/70th replaced it in the Baltimore Defense Area before the battalion became operational with Nike Ajax.

684th Antiaircraft Artillery Missile Battalion   MDArNG

684th AAABn (90mm Gun) Org. 1 Oct 56, Towson, MD; rd AAAMBn (Nike) 15 Feb 58;

Cons. 1 Mar 59

A	Catonsville
B	Baltimore
C	Baltimore
D	Towson

Towson (1/57) Baltimore (2/58) Towson

Not operational with Nike

The battalion was constituted on 1 June 1956 and allocated to the Maryland Army National Guard. It organized and received its Federal recognition on 1 October 1956 and on 1 March 1959 consolidated into the 70th Artillery. The 2/70th replaced the 684th before it became operational with Nike Ajax.

685th Antiaircraft Artillery Battalion (90mm Gun)   MAArNG

685th AAAWBn FR. 27 Jan 48, Bourne, MA; rd AAAGBn 1 Jan 49, rd AAABn (90mm Gun) 1 Oct 53

Bourne

The battalion was first constituted in the Massachusetts National Guard on 8 July 1946 as the 685th Antiaircraft Artillery Automatic Weapons Battalion. It was ordered into active Federal service on 1 May 1951 for duty in the Boston Defense Area and released on 31 January 1953. Battalion consolidated with the 211th Artillery on 1 May 1959.

686th Antiaircraft Artillery Missile Battalion   MDArNG

686th AAAMBn constituted 12 Feb 59

Cons. 1 Mar 59

Original planned designation as the 103rd AAAMBn. The battalion was constituted 12 February 1959 in the Maryland Army National Guard, consolidated with the 70th Artillery on 1 March 1959 prior to organizing and was not operational with Nike Ajax.

688th Antiaircraft Artillery Battalion   PAArNG

688th AAAAWBn FR. 12 Dec 46, Allentown, PA; rd AAAGBn 1 Oct 51, rd AAABn 1 Oct 53

Db. 18 Oct 53

| A | Allentown |

B	Allentown
C	Tamaqua
D	Tamaqua

Allentown

Originally constituted in the Pennsylvania National Guard on 24 May 1946. The battalion was disbanded on 18 October 1953.

689th Antiaircraft Artillery Battalion (90mm Gun)   PAArNG

689th AAAAWBn FR 10 Dec 46, Pittsburgh, PA; rd AAAGBn (90mm Gun) 1 Jun 51
  Db. 30 Sept 53

Pittsburgh

Originally constituted in the Pennsylvania National Guard as the 1/176th Field Artillery (155mm Howitzer); the headquarters received its Federal recognition in Pittsburgh on 31 July 1920 as the 1/18th Infantry and was redesignated 1 April 1921. The Army disbanded the 689th on 30 September 1953 through withdrawal of its Federal recognition.

698th Antiaircraft Artillery Missile Battalion   ILArNG

689th AAAGBn Org. 14 Feb 47, Chicago, IL; rd AAABn (90mm Gun) 1 Oct 53, rd AAAMBn 27 Feb 58
  Rd. 202nd Regiment, 1 Mar 59

Chicago

Not operational with Nike

First constituted 27 May 1942 in the Illinois National Guard as 3/202nd Coast Artillery Antiaircraft; activated 15 June 1942 at Bremerton, WA. AcDu Detroit, May 1951 through February 1953.

  Redesignated 202nd Combat Arms Regiment 1 March 1959; replaced in the Chicago Defense Area by 1/202nd Artillery.

701st Antiaircraft Artillery Battalion Gun

701st AAAGBn (Semimobile) A. 1 Feb 53, Pittsburgh, PA; rd AAABn (Gun) 24 Jul 53
  I. 20 Dec 57

Pittsburgh

First constituted 20 September 1942 as 1/701st Coast Artillery (Antiaircraft); activated 1 October 1942 at Fort Totten, NY.

703rd Antiaircraft Artillery Battalion (90mm Gun)   MEArNG

703rd AAAGBn FR. 6 Feb 47, South Portland, ME; rd AAABn 1 Oct 53
  B/U 15 May 59

A	South Portland	rd D/103rd Armd Cav
B	Bath	rd Howitzer Bn, 3/103rd Armd Cav
C	Brunswick	rd Tank Co, 3/103rd Armd Cav
D	Rockland	Cons. B/1st AW Bn/240th Artillery

South Portland

Originally constituted in the Maine National Guard on 17 September 1923 as the 1st Battalion, 240th Artillery (Fixed Defense); headquarters, 1st Battalion received its Federal recognition in Bath on 9 January 1924. The battalion was broken up on 15 May 1959 with its components reorganized and redesignated or consolidated into other units.

704th Antiaircraft Artillery Missile Battalion MAArNG

704th AAAGBn FR. 3 Feb 48, Boston, MA; rd AAABn 1 Oct 53; rd AAAMBn 1 Feb 58

    Cons. 1 May 59

A	Boston
B	Boston
C	Boston
D	Hingham

    Boston

Special Security Force, 1950s; not operational with Nike

First constituted in the Massachusetts National Guard as 1/1st Coast Defense Command, Coast Artillery Corps and federally recognized on 14 March 1921. However, through consolidations the unit also drew its lineage from the South Regiment, organized 13 December 1636, making it one of the four oldest units the National Guard. The battalion served on active duty in Boston from 15 March 1951 through 15 March 1953.

It consolidated 1 May 1959 with the 241st Artillery and was replaced in the Boston Defense Area by 1/241st Artillery; the 704th was not operational with Nike

705th Antiaircraft Artillery Battalion (90mm Gun) RIArNG

705th AAAGBn (Semimobile) FR. 4 Dec 46, Providence, RI;

    Cons. 1 Apr 59

A	West Warwick
B	East Greenwich
C	Pawtucket
D	Westerly

    Providence

Originally constituted in the Rhode Island Militia and organized in January 1872 in Providence as the 2nd Battalion, 1st Light Infantry; the battalion served on Federal active duty from 14 August 1950 to 13 July 1952. Consolidated with the 243rd Artillery on 1 April 1959 under CARS.

707th Antiaircraft Artillery Missile Battalion (Nike) PAArNG

707th AAAGBn (90mm) FR. 2 Dec 46, Philadelphia, PA; rd AAABn (90mm Gun) 1 Oct 53, rd AAAMBn (Nike) 15 Feb 58

    Cons. 1 Jun 59

    Philadelphia ( ) Worchester

Special Security Force, 1950s; not operational with Nike

Battalion first constituted in the Pennsylvania National Guard on 24 May 1946 as the 707th Antiaircraft

Artillery Gun Battalion (90mm). Ordered into active Federal service on 14 August 1950 at Philadelphia, released 13 June 1952. Battalion consolidated with the 166th Artillery, 1 June 1959; replaced in the Philadelphia defense by 2/166th Artillery.

708th Antiaircraft Artillery Missile Battalion (Nike)   PAArNG
708th AAAGBn (Semimobile) FR. 12 Jan 48, Pittsburgh, PA; rd AAAMBN (Nike) 1 Feb 58

Cons. 1 Jun 59
A	Pittsburgh
B	Pittsburgh
C	Pittsburgh
D	Pittsburgh

Pittsburgh (3/58) Blawnox

Special Security Force, 1950s; not operational with Nike
Battalion first constituted in the Pennsylvania National Guard on 24 May 1946 as the 708th Antiaircraft Artillery Gun Battalion (Semimobile). Notably, A/708th first organized on 5 September 1831 in Pittsburgh as the Duquesne Greys, served in the Mexican War as K/1st Pennsylvania Volunteers and during the Civil War as B/12th Pennsylvania Volunteer Infantry. The battalion was called to Federal service for duty in the Pittsburgh Defense Area on 1 May 1951 and was released on 28 February 1953. Battalion consolidated 1 June 1959 with the 176th Artillery; replaced in the Pittsburgh Defense Area by 1/176th Artillery.

709th Antiaircraft Artillery Missile Battalion (Nike)   PAArNG
709th AAAGBn (120mm) FR. 30 Oct 47, Philadelphia, PA; rd AAAGBn (90mm) 14 Aug 52, rd AAABn (90mm) 1 Oct 53,
rd AAAMBn (Nike) 15 Feb 58
Cons. 1 Jun 59
C-42 Promontory Point	/50-5/52	to A/86th
C-28 Burnham Park	/50-8/52	to B/86th

Philadelphia (/50) Chicago (8/52) Philadelphia (4/58) Media ( ) Paoli

Special Security Force, 1950s; not operational with Nike
Battalion first constituted 24 May 1946 as the 709th AAAGBn (120mm) in the Pennsylvania National Guard. The battalion was ordered into Federal service in the Chicago Defense Area on 14 August 1950 and returned to state service on 13 August 1952. Battalion consolidated 1 June 1959 with the 166th Artillery; replaced in the Philadelphia Defense Area by 3/166th Artillery.

710th Antiaircraft Artillery Missile Battalion (Nike)   VAArNG
710th AAAGBn (Semimobile) FR. 15 Oct 46, Newport News, VA; rd AAABn (90mm Gun) 1 Oct 53, rd AAAMBn (Nike) 14 Feb 58;

Cons. 1 Jun 59
HHB	Newport News
A	Williamsburg
B	Hampton

C   Newport News

Newport News

Special Security Force, 1950s

The 710th was constituted on 2 July 1946 and allotted to the Virginia National Guard; it organized and received its federal recognition on 15 October 1946. It was called to Federal service in Newport News on 14 August 1950 and released on 13 April 1952. Battalion consolidated into the 111th Artillery on 1 June 1959 prior to operations with Nike Ajax; the 5/111th replaced it in the Norfolk Defense Area.

711th Antiaircraft Artillery Battalion (90mm Gun)   ALArNG

711th AAAGBn FR. 9 Jan 47, Mobile, AL; rd AAABn (90mm Gun) 1 Oct 53

Rd. 2 May 59

A   Mobile
B   Bay Minette
C   Luverne
D   Atmore

Mobile

Originally constituted in the Alabama National Guard on 24 July 1946 as the 711th Antiaircraft Artillery Gun Battalion; the Headquarters & Headquarters Battery drew its lineage from the 1836 organization of the Mobile Artillery Company. The battalion was reorganized and redesignated the 711th Signal Battalion on 2 May 1959.

712th Antiaircraft Artillery Battalion (90mm Gun)   FLArNG

712th AAAGBn (Semimobile) FR. 17 Dec 46, Miami, FL; rd AAABn (90mm Gun) 1 Oct 53

Cons. 15 Apr 59

Miami

Battalion first constituted in the Florida National Guard on 5 July 1946 as the 712th Antiaircraft Artillery Gun Battalion (Semimobile). Battalion called to Federal service 1 May 1951 for operations in the New York Defense Area, released 30 April 1953. Consolidated with the 265th Artillery on 15 April 1959.

713th Antiaircraft Artillery Battalion (90mm Gun)   SCArNG

713th AAAGBn (Semimobile) FR. 4 Apr 47, Lancaster, SC; rd AAAGBn (90mm) 1 Oct 53

Cons. 1 Apr 59

A   York
B   Camden
C   Cheraw
D   Florence

Lancaster (/50) Fort Sheridan (6/52) Lancaster

Constituted in the South Carolina National Guard on 5 July 1946. The battalion served on Federal active duty from 14 August 1950 to 13 June 1952 in the Chicago Defense Area; the 49th AAAGBn replaced it. The 713th was consolidated with the 263rd Artillery under CARS on 1 April 1959.

715th Antiaircraft Artillery Battalion (90mm Gun)   NYArNG

715th AAAGBn FR. 19 Jan 48, Brooklyn, NY; rd AAABn (90mm Gun) 1 Oct 53

    Rd. 1 Apr 55

    Brooklyn

Originally constituted in the US Army as the 192nd Coast Artillery Battalion (Harbor Defense) and organized at Fort Tilden, NY on 7 October 1945. The New York Army National Guard redesignated the battalion as the 715th Field Artillery on 1 April 1955.

716th Antiaircraft Artillery Battalion (90mm Gun)   NMArNG

716th AAAGBn FR. 27 Sept 47, Las Cruces, NM

    Cons.
HB	Deming
A	Las Cruces
B	Silver City
C	Lordsburg
C	Hot Springs/Truth or Consequences

    Las Cruces

Originally constituted in the New Mexico National Guard on 19 April 1921 as the 2nd Squadron, 1st Cavalry; however, it received its Federal recognition as the 2nd Squadron, 111th Cavalry at Santa Fe on 3 August 1923. The battalion was called to active Federal service on 14 August 1950 and returned to state control on 13 August 1952; it was consolidated with the 200th Artillery on 1 September 1959.

717th Antiaircraft Artillery Battalion (90mm Gun)   NMArNG

717th AAAGBn FR. 23 Jun 47, Albuquerque, NM; rd AAABn (90mm Gun) 1 Oct 53

    Cons.1 Sept 59
HB	Albuquerque
A	Farmington
B	Albuquerque
C	Socorro
D	Gallup

    Albuquerque

Battalion originally organized in the New Mexico National Guard as Headquarters, 120th Engineers and federally recognized 8 June 1924 in Las Cruces. The battalion was ordered to Federal service on 1 May 1951 for operations at Los Alamos and was released on 28 February 1953. Battalion consolidated with the 200th Artillery on 1 September 1959.

718th Antiaircraft Artillery Battalion   CAArNG

718th AAAGBn FR. 31 Jan 49, San Francisco, CA; rd AAABn 1 Oct 53

    Db. 30 Nov 54

    San Francisco (7/54) Alameda

Battalion originally constituted in the California National Guard as the 2nd Battalion, 250th Coast Artillery (Harbor Defense) with headquarters organized and federally recognized in San Francisco on 7 February 1925. The battalion was called to Federal service in the San Francisco Defense Area on 15 May 1951 and released on 14 May 1953. Battalion disbanded 30 November 1954.

719th Antiaircraft Artillery Battalion (90mm Gun)   CAArNG

719th AAAGBn FR. 22 Sept 47, Alameda, CA; rd AAABn (90mm Gun) 1 Oct 53

> Db. 28 Feb 58

> *Alameda*

Constituted in the California National Guard as the 719th Antiaircraft Artillery Gun Battalion on 5 August 1946. The battalion served on active duty from 21 August 1950 through 4 April 1952 in the Seattle Defense Area; notably, it was reorganized at Fort Lewis as a "colored" or segregated unit. The battalion was disbanded on 28 February 1958 through withdrawal of its Federal recognition.

720th Antiaircraft Artillery Missile Battalion (Nike)   CAArNG

720th AAAGBn FR. 10 Apr 47, Long Beach, CA; rd AAABn 1 Oct 53, rd AAAMBn (Nike) 1 Jun 57

> Cons. 1 May 59

A	Long Beach	4/47-9/58	
	LA-40 Long Beach	9/58-5/59	to A/4/251st
B	Long Beach	4/47-9/58	
	LA-57 Redondo Beach	9/58-5/59	to B/4/251st
C	Gardena	4/47-9/58	
	LA-70 Hyperion	9/58-5/59	to C/4/251st
D	Long Beach	4/47-9/58	
	LA-73 Playa del Rey	9/58-5/59	to D/4/251st

> *Long Beach*

The battalion was constituted in the California National Guard on 5 August 1946 as the 720th Antiaircraft Artillery Gun Battalion with Headquarters & Headquarters Battery federally recognized in Long Beach on 10 April 1947. This was the first operational Army National Guard Nike Ajax battalion, assuming responsibility for four batteries in the Los Angeles Defense Area in September 1958. Battalion consolidated 1 May 1959 with the 251st Artillery; replaced in the Los Angeles Defense Area by 4/251st Artillery.

724th Antiaircraft Artillery Missile Battalion (Nike)   PAArNG

724th AAASLBn Org. 16 Dec 47, Pittsburgh, PA; rd AAAGBn (Mobile) Dec 47; rd AAAAWBn (Mobile) 1 Oct 49

> rd AAAGBn (90mm) 1 Oct 51, rd AAABn (90mm) Gun 1 Oct 53; rd AAAMBn (Nike) 1 Feb 58

> Cons. 1 Jun 59

A	Everett
B	Pittsburgh
C	Pittsburgh
D	Pittsburgh

*Pittsburgh (3/58) Moon Run

Special Security Force, 1950s; not operational with Nike

First organized and federally recognized 16 November 1921 as Headquarters Battery and Combat Training, 2/176th Field Artillery, in Pittsburgh, PA. Consolidated 1 June 1959 with the 176th Artillery; battalion replaced in Pittsburgh Defense Area by 2/176th Artillery

726th Antiaircraft Artillery Battalion (90mm Gun)   NMArNG

726th AAASLBn FR. 23 Jun 47, Albuquerque, NM; rd AAAGBn 1 Dec 47, rd AAABn (90mm Gun) 1 Oct 53

Cons. 1 Sept 59

HB	Santa Fe
A	Taos
B	Las Vegas
C	Santa Fe
D	Española

*Albuquerque

Constituted in the New Mexico National Guard on 31 May 1946 as the 726th Antiaircraft Artillery Searchlight Battalion; Battery C dated its original organization to 1916 as Supply Company, 1st Infantry. The battalion served on Federal active duty from 14 August 1950 through 13 May 1952; it was consolidated into the 200th Artillery under CARS on 1 September 1959.

728th Antiaircraft Artillery Missile Battalion   CAArNG

728th AAASLBn Org. 3 Mar 47, San Francisco, CA; rd AAAGBn 1 Dec 47, rd AAABn 1 Oct 53; rd AAAMBn 1 Mar 58,

Cons. 1 May 59

A	San Francisco
B	San Francisco
C	San Francisco
D	San Francisco

*San Francisco (11/54) Alameda (6/58) Berkeley

Not operational with Nike

Battalion first constituted in the California National Guard on 5 August 1946 as the 728th Antiaircraft Artillery Searchlight Battalion with Headquarters & Headquarters Battery receiving its Federal recognition in San Francisco on 3 March 1947. The Department of Defense called the battalion to Federal service on 15 May 1951 for service at Fort Bliss, TX and in the San Francisco Defense Area; it was released on 14 May 1953. Battalion consolidated 1 May 1959 with the 250th Artillery; replaced in the San Francisco Defense Area by 2/250th Artillery.

730th Antiaircraft Artillery Battalion (90mm Gun)   CAArNG

730th AAASLBn FR. 25 Oct 47, San Diego, CA; rd AAAGBn (Mobile) 1 Dec 47, rd AAABn (90mm Gun) 1 Oct 53

Cons. 1 May 59
A   El Cajon
B   Coronado
C   San Diego
D   El Cajon

San Diego (9/49) National City

Special Security Force, 1950s
Originally constituted in the California National Guard as the 8th Company, Coast Artillery Corps with Federal recognition in San Diego on 11 May 1921. Consolidated with the 251st Artillery on 1 March 1959.

734th Antiaircraft Artillery Battalion
734th AAAGBn (Semimobile) A. 20 Mar 53, Chicago, IL; rd AAABn (Gun) 24 Jul 53;

I. 15 Jun 57

Chicago

First constituted 25 February 1943 as the 734th AAAGBn (Semimobile); activated 20 July 1943 at Camp Edwards, MA. The 734th replaced the ILArNG 768th AAAGBn in the Chicago Defense Area.

737th Antiaircraft Artillery Missile Battalion
737th AAAGBn (Semimobile) A. 15 Mar 53, New York, NY; rd AAABn (Gun) 3 Aug 53, rd AAAMBn 2 Mar 56

I. 1 Sept 58
A	NY-03 Orangeburg	1/57-9/58	to A/5/7th
B	NY-93 Ramsey	/58-9/58	to B/5/7th
C	NY-99 Spring Valley	3/56-9/58	to C/5/7th

New York ( ) Camp Shanks (3/56) Tappan

First constituted 21 May 1942 as 1/608th Coast Artillery Antiaircraft; activated 15 November 1942 at Fort Bliss, TX. Notably, the battalion only manned three batteries prior to its replacement by the 5/7th Artillery.

738th Antiaircraft Artillery Missile Battalion
738th AAAGBn (Semimobile) A. 1 Mar 53, Philadelphia, PA; rd AAABn (Gun) 20 Jul 53, rd AAAMBn 9 Jul 54

I. 1 Sept 58
A	Fort Mott	/55- /56	temp site
	PH-41 Berlin	/56-9/58	to A/3/43rd
B	Fort Dix	/55- /56	temp site
	PH-49 Pittman	/56-9/58	to B/3/43rd
C	Fort Mott	/55- /56	temp site
	PH-25 Lumberton	/56-9/58	to C/3/43rd
D	Fort Dix	/55- /56	temp site
	PH-32 Marlton	/56-9/58	to D/3/43rd

Philadelphia (/54) Fort Mott (/56) Lumberton

First constituted 21 May 1942 as 1/609th Coast Artillery Antiaircraft; activated 10 December 1942 at Camp Edwards, MA. The battalion recorded the first Nike Hercules firing by an operational ARADCOM unit at Fort Bliss's McGregor Range on 28 April 1948. The 3/43rd Artillery replaced the 738th in the Philadelphia Defense Area.

739th Antiaircraft Artillery Missile Battalion

739th AAAMBn A. 2 Jan 56, Fort Banks, MA

I. 1 Sept 58

A	PR-19 Rehoboth	/56-9/58	to A/4/56th
B	PR-29 Swansea	/56-9/58	to B/4/56th
C	PR-38 Bristol	/56-9/58	to C/4/56th

Fort Banks (/56) Rehoboth (/58) Bristol

First constituted 21 May 1942 as 1/610th Coast Artillery Antiaircraft; activated 10 December 1942 at Camp Davis, NC. Replaced in the Providence Defense Area by 4/56th Artillery.

740th Antiaircraft Artillery Missile Battalion

740th AAAGBn (Semimobile) A. 14 Apr 53, Presidio of San Francisco, CA; rd AAABn (Gun) 20 Jul 53, rd AAAMBn 9 Jul 54

I. 1 Sept 58

A	SF-59 Fort Funston	/54-9/58	to A/4/61st
B	SF-89 Fort Winfield Scott	/55-9/58	to B/4/61st
C	SF-51 Milagra	/56-9/58	to C/4/61st
D	SF-37 Coyote Hills	/54-9/58	to D/4/61st

Presidio of San Francisco ( ) Fort Winfield Scott

First constituted 21 May 1942 as 1/611th Coast Artillery Antiaircraft; activated 10 December 1942 at Fort Bliss, TX. Replaced in the San Francisco Defense Area by 4/61st Artillery.

741st Antiaircraft Artillery Missile Battalion

741st AAAMBn A. 1 Jan 57, Fort Hancock, NJ

I. 1 Sept 58

A	BR-94 Shelton	/57-9/58	to A/3/44th
B	BR-65 Fairfield	/57-9/58	to B/3/44th
C	BR-73 Westport	/57-9/58	to C/3/44th
D	HA-67 Plainville	/57-9/58	to D/3/44th

Fort Hancock ( ) Fairfield

First constituted 21 May 1942 as 1/612th Coast Artillery (Antiaircraft)(Colored); activated 1 September 1942 at Camp Stewart, GA. Replaced in the Bridgeport Defense Area by 3/44th Artillery.

744th Antiaircraft Artillery Battalion (90mm Gun)   NHArNG

744th AAAGBn (Mobile) FR. 4 Apr 47, Laconia, NH; rd AAABn (90mm Gun) 1 Oct 53

Cons. 1 Feb 59

A	Concord
B	Wolfboro
C	Laconia
D	Franklin

*Laconia

Originally constituted in the New Hampshire National Guard as 1st Battalion, 197th Artillery (Antiaircraft), Coast Artillery Corps; the headquarters received its Federal recognition at Laconia on 9 June 1922. The battalion was consolidated with the 197th Artillery on 1 February 1959.

745th Antiaircraft Artillery Battalion (90mm Gun)   CTArNG
745th AAAGBn FR. 16 Sept 47, Norwich, CT; rd 745th AAABn (90mm Gun)

>B/U 1 May 59

>*Norwich

Battalion first constituted in the Connecticut National Guard on 16 May 1940 as the 1st Battalion, 208th Coast Artillery (Antiaircraft) with headquarters receiving its Federal recognition on 13 November 1940 at Weathersfield. It was ordered into Federal service on 14 August 1950 for operations in the Hartford Defense Area and released on 13 April 1952. Battalion broken up on 1 May 1959; the Headquarters & Headquarters Battery was redesignated B/162nd Transportation Battalion.

746th Antiaircraft Artillery Battalion   CAArNG
746th AAAGBn FR 24 Feb 57, San Diego, CA; rd AAABn 1 Oct 53

>Cons.

>*San Diego

First constituted in the California National Guard as the 8th Company, 1st Coast Defense Command, Coast Artillery Corps with organization in San Diego on 16 May 1911. The battalion served on Federal active duty from 14 August 1950 to 13 June 1952; it was consolidated with the 251st Artillery under CARS on 1 May 1959.

747th Antiaircraft Artillery Battalion (90mm Gun)   MAArNG
747th AAAAWBn FR. 26 Jan 48, Fall River, MA; rd AAAGBn (90mm) 1 Jul 51, rd AAABn (90mm Gun) 1 Oct 53

>Cons. 1 May 59

>*Fall River

Originally constituted in the Massachusetts National Guard as the 4th Battalion, 241st Coast Artillery (Harbor Defense) and organized at Fall River. Consolidated with the 211th Artillery on 1 May 1959.

749th Antiaircraft Artillery Battalion Gun
749th AAAGBn A. 1 Apr 53, New York, NY; rd AAABn (Gun) 3 Aug 53

>I. 20 Dec 57

>*New York

First constituted 10 January 1942 as the 26th Separate Coast Artillery Battalion Harbor Defense; activated 28 January 1942 at Fort McKinley, ME.

751st Antiaircraft Artillery Missile Battalion

751st AAAMBn A. 1 May 56, Fort Banks, MA

I. 1 Sept 58

A	PR-58 North Kingston	/56-9/58	to A/4/68th
B	PR-69 Coventry	/56-9/58	to B/4/68th
C	PR-99 North Smithfield	/56-9/58	to C/4/68th
D	PR-79 Foster Center	/56-9/58	to D/4/68th

Fort Banks ( ) Coventry

First constituted 4 November 1943 as Headquarters & Headquarters Battery, 751st Antiaircraft Gun Battalion; activated 12 December at Fort Kamehameha, TH. Replaced in the Providence Defense Area by 4/68th Artillery.

752nd Antiaircraft Artillery Battalion

752nd AAAGBn A. 14 Apr 53, San Francisco, CA; rd AAABn 20 Jul 53;

I. 15 Jun 57

San Francisco ( ) Fort Winfield Scott

First constituted 13 January 1941 as 2/95th Coast Artillery Aircraft(Semimobile); activated 17 April 1941 at Camp Davis, NC.

768th Antiaircraft Artillery Battalion   ILArNG

768th AAAGBn FR. 13 Dec 48, Chicago, IL; rd AAABn (Gun) 1 Oct 53;

Cons. 27 Feb 58

Chicago (5/51) Camp McCoy (6/52) Chicago

First constituted 1 October 1920 as 1/6th Infantry and allotted to the Illinois National Guard; federally recognized 26 August 1924 as the 1/202nd Coast Artillery (Antiaircraft) at Chicago, IL. The battalion was called to Federal service on 15 May 1951 and released on 11 April 1953; the 734th AAAGBn (90mm) replaced it in the Chicago Defense Area. Battalion consolidated 27 February 1958 with the 698th Antiaircraft Artillery Missile Battalion, Illinois Army National Guard

770th Antiaircraft Artillery Missile Battalion   WAArNG

770th AAAGBn (Semimobile) FR. 12 May 47, Seattle, WA; rd AAABn (120mm) 1 Oct 53; rd AAAMBn 2 Jan 58

Cons. 15 Apr 59

Seattle ( ) Phantom Lake

Special Security Force, 1950s; not operational with Nike

First organized in the Washington National Guard as 1/205th Coast Artillery Antiaircraft; federally recognized 30 November 1939 at Seattle, WA. Consolidated 15 April 1959 with the 205th Artillery; replaced in the Seattle Defense Area by 2/205th Artillery.

771st Antiaircraft Artillery Gun Battalion (90mm) — NYArNG

176th MP Bn rd 771st AAAGBn (90mm) 1 Sept 50, Brooklyn, NY
>Db. 30 Nov 52

>*Brooklyn*

Constituted in the New York National Guard on 27 September 1946 as the 176th Military Police Company; the Headquarters and Headquarters Detachment at Brooklyn received its Federal recognition on 31 March 1948. The battalion was disbanded on 30 November 1952 through withdrawal of its Federal recognition.

772nd Antiaircraft Artillery Missile Battalion — MAArNG

772nd AAAGBn FR. 29 Jan 48, Chelsea, MA; rd AAAAWBn (Mobile) 1 Oct 49, rd AAAGBn (90mm) 1 Jul 51, rd AAABn (90mm Gun) 1 Oct 53; rd AAAMBn 1 Feb 58
>Cons. 1 May 59
>A Chelsea
>B Fort Banks
>C Winthrop

>*Chelsea (5/52) Boston (11/57) Chelsea*

Special Security Force, 1950s
First constituted in the Massachusetts National Guard as 2/1st Coast Defense Command, Coast Artillery Corps; federally recognized 22 November 1920 in Roslindale, MA. Through consolidations the unit also drew its lineage from the South Regiment, which formed on 13 December 1636, making it one of the four oldest units in the National Guard. Battalion consolidated 1 May 1959 with the 241st Artillery; replaced in the Boston Defense Area by 2/241st Artillery.

773rd Antiaircraft Artillery Missile Battalion (Nike) — NYArNG

773rd AAAGBn (Semimobile) FR. 6 Oct 47, New York, NY; rd AAABn (90mm Gun) 1 Oct 53; rd AAAMBn (Nike) 15 Feb 58
>Cons. 16 Mar 59

>*New York 7/58 Bronx 3/59 White Plains*

Not operational with Nike
The 773rd first organized in the National Guard, State of New York as companies of the 1st Battalion, 12th Regiment and activated in New York City. The oldest components were Companies A and B which formed on 16 November 1859; notably, both surrendered to Confederate Forces at Harpers Ferry, VA in 1862. The battalion was called to Federal active service in the New York Defense Area on 1 May 1951 and released on 30 April 1953. Battalion consolidated with the 212th Artillery on 16 March 1959; the 1/212th replaced it in the New York Defense Area.

852nd Antiaircraft Artillery Missile Battalion

852nd AAAMBn A. 2 Mar 56, Milwaukee, WI
>I. 1 Sept 58

A	M-64 Muskegon	/56- /57	to A/401st
	M-02 Milwaukee	/57-9/58	to A/3/59th
B	M-74 Waukesha	/56- /57	to D/401st
	M-20 Milwaukee	/57-9/58	to B/3/59th
C	M-86 Lannon	/56-9/58	to C/3/59th
D	M-96 Milwaukee	/56-9/58	to D/3/59th

Milwaukee

First constituted 2 November 1942 as the 487th Coast Artillery Battalion Antiaircraft; activated 10 December 1942 at Camp Haan, CA. Replaced in the Milwaukee Defense Area by 3/59th Artillery.

865th Antiaircraft Artillery Missile Battalion

865th AAAMBn A. 1 Jun 55, Los Angeles, CA
I. 1 Sept 58

A	LA-70 Hyperion	/55-9/58	to A/4/62nd
B	LA-73 Playa del Rey	/55-9/58	to B/4/62nd
C	LA-40 Long Beach	/55-9/58	to C/4/62nd
D	LA-57 Redondo Beach	/55-9/58	to D/4/62nd

Los Angeles ( ) Fort MacArthur

First constituted 27 May 1942 as 3/93rd Coast Artillery Antiaircraft Semimobile; activated 15 June 1942 in Hawaii. Replaced in the Los Angeles Defense Area by 4/62nd Artillery.

867th Antiaircraft Artillery Battalion

3/96th Coast Artillery (AA) rd AAAGBn (Semimobile) 12 Dec 43, Schofield Barracks, TA; rd AAAAWBn (Mobile) 14 Feb 49
    rd AAABn 1 Oct 50
    I. 1 Nov 57

Schofeld Barracks (2/44) Kwajalein (9/44) Schofeld Barracks ( ) Fort Richardson

First constituted 27 May 1942 as 3/96th Coast Artillery Antiaircraft(Semimobile); activated 15 June 1942 at Schofeld Barracks, TA.

870th Antiaircraft Artillery Battalion (90mm Gun)   NYArNG

870th AAAAWBn (Semimobile)(Colored) FR. 30 Oct 47, New York, NY; rd AAAGBn (90mm) 1 Sept 51,
    rd AAABn (90mm Gun) 1 Oct 53
    Rd. 1 Apr 55

New York

First constituted in the New York National Guard on 2 June 1913 as the 2nd Battalion, 15th Infantry (Colored). Redesignated as the 970th Field Artillery Battalion on 1 April 1955.

933rd Antiaircraft Artillery Missile Battalion

933rd AAAMBn A. 15 Dec 55, Fort MacArthur, CA

I. 1 Sept 58

A	LA-14 South El Monte	/56- /58	to C/933rd
	LA-29 Brea	/58-9/58	to A/1/56th
B	Fountain Valley	/56-12/56	temp site
	LA-09 Mt Disappointment	12/56-9/58	to B/1/56th
C	Fountain Valley	/56- /56	temp site
	LA-04 Mt Gleason	/56- /58	to D/933rd
	LA-14 South El Monte	/58-9/58	to C/1/56th
D	Fountain Valley	/56- /57	temp site
	LA-04 Mt Gleason	/57-9/58	to D/1/56th

Fort MacArthur ( ) Pasadena Army Support Center

First constituted in the Organized Reserves 29 July 1921 as 2/502nd Artillery Antiaircraft, Coast Artillery Corps; organized during November 1921 in New York, NY. Replaced in the Los Angeles Defense Area by 1/56th Artillery.

951st Antiaircraft Artillery Battalion   CAArNG

951st AAAWBn FR. 20 Mar 47, Richmond, CA; rd AAAGBn 1 Jan 51, rd AAABn 1 Oct 53

Cons. 1 May 59

A	Richmond
B	Richmond
C	Vallejo
D	Vallejo

Richmond

Constituted in the California National Guard on 5 August 1946 as the 951st Antiaircraft Automatic Weapons Battalion. The battalion was consolidated with the 250th Artillery on 1 May 1959.

967th Antiaircraft Artillery Missile Battalion

967th AAAMBn A. 1 Mar 56, Fort Hancock, NJ

I. 1 Sept 58

A	BR-17 Milford	/56-9/58	to A/3/56th
B	BR-65 Fairfield	/56- /57	to B/741st
	BR-04 Ansonia	/57-9/58	to B/3/56th
C	BR-73 Westport	/56- /57	to C/741st
	BR-15 Westhaven	/57-9/58	to C/3/56th

Fort Hancock ( ) West Haven

First constituted 25 February 1943 as the 967th Antiaircraft Artillery Gun Battalion Semimobile; activated 1 November 1943 on Guadalcanal. Replaced in the Bridgeport Defense Area by 3/56th Artillery.

979th Antiaircraft Artillery Missile Battalion (Nike)

979th FABn FR. 30 Jan 50, Detroit, MI; rd AAABn (90mm Gun) 1 Feb 55; rd AAAMBn (Nike) 1 Mar 58

Cons. 15 Mar 59

Detroit Artillery Armory

Not operational with Nike

Consolidated 15 March 1949 with the 177th Artillery; replaced in the Detroit Defense Area by 2/177th Artillery.

A.	activated
AA	antiaircraft
AAABn	Antiaircraft Artillery Battalion
AAAAWBn	Antiaircraft Artillery Automatic Weapons Battalion
AAAGBn	Antiaircraft Artillery Gun Battalion
AAAGMBn	Antiaircraft Artillery Guided Missile Battalion
AAAMBn	Antiaircraft Artillery Missile Battalion
AAASLBn	Antiaircraft Artillery Searchlight Battalion
ArNG	Army National Guard
AW	automatic weapons
B/U	broken up
CARS	Combat Arms Regimental System
CZ	Canal Zone
Db.	disbanded
FA	Field Artillery Battalion
FR.	federally recognized
GMBn	Guided Missile Battalion
HB	Headquarters Battery
HHB	Headquarters & Headquarters Battery
I.	inactivated
MP Bn	MP Battalion
Org.	organized
Rd.	redesignated
SP	self-propelled
TH	Territory of Hawaii

The ARADCOM CARS Battalions

On 1 September 1958 the Army reorganized and redesignated its individual combat arms battalions into battalions assigned to parent regiments under the Combat Arms Regimental System (CARS). The Regular Army antiaircraft battalions became missile or gun battalions assigned to numbered artillery regiments with the guard battalions following on 1 May 1959.

Battalions active on 20 December 1965 were redesignated as battalions assigned to parent regiments—Guard units redesignated on 1 January 1966—and on 1 September 1971 they became battalions assigned to regiments of Air Defense Artillery, with the Guard battalions following on 1 April 1972. On 13 September 1986 the Army withdrew the units from CARS and instead reorganized them under the US Army Regimental System.

1st Air Defense Artillery Regiment

Originally constituted in the Regular Army on 1 June 1821 as the 1st Regiment of Artillery and organized with headquarters at Fort Independence, Boston, MA.

3/1st ADA

C/1st AAAMBn cons. with C/1st Field Artillery, Rd. HHB 3/1st 1 Sept 58

I. 30 Aug 74

A	PI-25 Murrysville	9/58- /60	
B	PI-37 Cowansburg	9/58-3/74	
C	PI-36 Irwin	9/58-12/68	
D	PI-42 Elizabeth	9/58-4/60	to C/2/176th
	PI-43 Elrama	7/60-3/74	
	Irwin		

Originally organized in 1815 as Captain Stribling's Company of Light Artillery at Plattsburgh Barracks, NY. Replaced the 1st AAAMBn in the Pittsburgh Defense Area.

4/1st ADA

A. 15 Sept 58, Army Chemical Center, Edgewood, MD

I. 1 Aug 74

A	BA-03 Phoenix	9/58-12/62	to D/1/70th
	W-92 Rockville	/65-4/74	
B	BA-92 Cronhardt	9/58-9/59	to D/2/70th
	BA-79 Granite	8/60-12/62	to B/1/70th
	W-25 Davidsonville	/65-11/68	to A/1/70th
	N-25 Ft Story	6/71-4/74	
C	BA-18 Edgewood Arsenal	9/58-4/74	
D	BA-09 Fork	9/58-9/59	to D/1/70th
	BA-30 Tolchester Beach	12/62-4/74	
	Edgewood Arsenal		

Originally organized in 1815 as Captain Peyton's Company of Light Artillery at Fort Adams, RI. Replaced the 54th AAAMBn in the Baltimore Defense Area.

2nd Air Defense Artillery Regiment

Originally constituted in the Regular Army on 1 June 1821 as the 2nd Regiment of Artillery and organized with headquarters at Baltimore, MD.

6/2nd Artillery

6/2nd A. 20 Apr 60, Walker AFB, NM

    I. 25 Jun 60

    A   WA-10 Roswell

    B   WA-50 Hagerman

    Walker AFB

Originally organized in September 1812 as Captain Thomas Stockton's Company, 3rd Regiment. The unit never achieved operational status with Nike Hercules.

3rd Air Defense Artillery

Originally constituted in the Regular Army on 1 June 1821 as the 3rd Regiment of Artillery and organized with headquarters at Fort Washington, MD.

2/3rd ADA

2/3rd A. 13 Sept 72, Selfridge AFB, MI

    I. 30 Sept 74

    C   D-87 Commerce   9/72-4/74

    Selfridge AFB

Originally organized in July 1812 as Captain Roger Jones' Company, 3rd Regiment of Artillery at Sacketts Harbor, NY. Replaced the 3/517th ADA in the Detroit Defense Area.

4/3rd Artillery

4/3rd A. 1 Sept 58, Franklin, MI

    I. 22 Dec 60

A	D-69 River Rouge	9/58-11/59	to B/1/177th
B	D-86 Franklin	9/58-10/60	to A/2/177th
C	D-87 Commerce	9/58-12/60	to C/3/517th
D	D-97 Auburn Heights	9/58-11/59	to C/2/177th

    Franklin

Originally organized in July 1812 as Captain Michael Kalteisen's 3rd Company, 4th Battalion, Corps of Artillerists and Engineers at West Point, NY. Replaced the 18th AAAMBn in the Detroit Defense Area.

5/3rd Artillery

5/3rd A. 1 Sept 58, Pittsburgh, PA

I. 18 Oct 63

A	PI-93 Westview	9/58-10/63	to A/2/176th
B	PI-92 Bryant	9/58-8/59	to A/1/176th
	prob PI-71 Coraopolis	7/60-10/63	to B/2/176th
C	PI-03 Dorseyville	9/58-10/63	to C/2/176th
D	PI-02 Rural Ridge	9/58-4/60	to D/1/176th

Westview (12/61) Oakdale AADB

Originally organized in August 1794 as Captain Donald Mitchell's 4th Company, 2nd Battalion, Corps of Artillerists and Engineers at West Point, NY. Replaced the 74th AAAMBn in the Pittsburgh Defense Area.

6/3rd Artillery

6/3rd A. 1 Sept 58, Arlington Heights, IL

I. 1 Jun 65

A	C-80 Arlington Heights	9/58-6/60	
	C-49 Homewood	6/60-8/63	to A/1/202nd
	C-03 Montrose	8/63-6/65	
B	C-72 Addison	9/58-8/63	to B/1/202nd
	C-41 Jackson Park	8/63-6/65	to D/1/60th
C	C-84 Palatine	9/58-9/60	to B/1/202nd
	C-61 Lemont	12/61-4/64	to C/1/202nd
D	C-80 Arlington Heights	9/58-12/60	
	C-93 Northfield	12/60-4/64	to D/1/202nd

Arlington Heights (8/63) Montrose

Originally organized 1 October 1847 as Company M, 3rd Regiment of Artillery. Replaced the 86th AAAMBn in the Chicago Defense Area.

4th Air Defense Artillery

Originally constituted in the Regular Army on 1 June 1821 as the 4th Regiment of Artillery and organized with headquarters at Pensacola, FL.

1/4th ADA

1/4th A. 1 Sept 58, Fort Niagara, NY

I. 31 Mar 70

A	NF-03 Model City	9/58-7/60	to B/2/106th
	BU-18 Lancaster	12/61-4/63	to B/2/209th
B	NF-16 Sanborn	9/58-3/70	
C	NF-74 Grand Island	9/58-4/59	
	NF-41 Grand Island	4/59-4/63	to A/2/209th
D	NF-75 Grand Island	9/58-4/59	

Fort Niagara (6/62) Lockport AFS

1/4th A. 13 Sept 72, Fort Lawton, WA

I. 30 Jul 74

C	S-92 Kingston	9/72-7/74	

Fort Lawton

Originally constituted 20 October 1786 as Captain Henry Burbeck's Company of Artillery at West Point, NY. Replaced the 44th AAMBn in the Niagara Falls Defense Area and the 4/4th ADA in the Seattle Defense Area.

4/4th ADA

4/4th A. 1 Sept 58, Poulsbo, WA

I. 13 Sept 72

A	S-13 Redmond	4/59-10/64	to A/2/205th
B	S-61 Vashon Island	12/61-10/64	to B/2/205th
C	S-92 Kingston	9/58-9/72	to C/1/4th
D	S-81 Poulsbo	9/58-11/60	

Poulsbo (10/64) Fort Lawton

Originally organized in 1821 as Captain John Erving's Company of Artillery. Replaced the 513th AAAMBn in the Seattle Defense Area.

5th Air Defense Artillery

"Originally constituted in the Regular Army on 18 June 1861 as the 5th Regiment of Artillery and organized with headquarters at Fort Greble Pennsylvania." should be inserted after the "5th Air Defense Arillery" and before "1/5th ADA" like the other entries (See the one for the 4th Air Defense Artillery for example).

1/5th ADA

1/5th A. 13 Sept 72, Coventry, RI

I. 30 Oct 74

C	PR-38 Bristol	9/72-4/74	
D	B-05 Danvers	9/72-4/74	

Coventry

Originally constituted 18 June 1861 as Battery L, 5th Regiment of Artillery, Fort Greble, PA. Replaced 3/5th ADA in the New England Defense Area

3/5th ADA

3/5th A. 1 Sept 58, Bedford, MA

I. 13 Sept 72

A	B-73 South Lincoln	9/58-8/64	to A/1/241st
B	B-85 Bedford	9/58-12/61	
	B-36 Ft Duvall	12/61-8/64	to B/1/241st
C	B-84 Burlington	9/58-12/61	
	PR-38 Bristol	8/63-9/72	to C/1/5th
D	B-63 Needham	9/58-8/59	to B/1/241st
	B-05 Danvers	6/60-9/72	to D/1/5th

275

Bedford (/64) Rehoboth (6/71) Coventry

Originally organized 4 July 1861 as Battery B, 5th Coast Artillery Regiment, Fort Greble, PA. Replaced the 24th AAAMBn in the Boston Defense Area

4/5th Artillery
4/5th A. 1 Sept 58, Laytonville, MD
    I. Aug 60

A	BA-79 Granite	9/58-8/60	to B/4/1st
B	W-93 Laytonville	9/58-8/60	
C	W-94 Gaithersburg	9/58-6/60	to C/2/70th
D	W-92 Rockville	9/58-8/60	to D/1/71st

    Laytonville

Originally constituted 18 June 1861 as Battery G, 5th Regiment of Artillery and organized 4 July 1861 at Fort Greble, PA. Replaced the 602nd AAAMBn in the Baltimore/Washington Defense Area.

6th Air Defense Artillery
Originally constituted on 8 March 1898 as the 6th Regiment of Artillery and organized 23 March 1898 at Fort McHenry, MD.

6/6th Artillery
6/6th A. 1 Sept 58, Finleyville, PA
    I. 26 Jul 60

A	PI-71 Coraopolis	9/58-7/60	to B/5/3rd
B	PI-62 Bridgeville	9/58-8/59	to B/2/176th
C	PI-52 Finleyville	9/58-7/60	
D	PI-43 Elrama	9/58-7/60	to D/3/1st

    Finleyville

Originally organized 23 March 1898 as Battery F, 6th Regiment of Artillery, Fort McHenry, MD. Replaced the 509th AAAMBn in the Pittsburgh Defense Area

7th Air Defense Artillery
Originally constituted on 8 March 1898 as the 7th Regiment of Artillery and organized on 29 March at Fort Slocum, NY.

4/7th Artillery
4/7th A. 1 Sept 58, Savannah River Project, SC
    I. 20 Jan 60

    Savannah River Project

4/7th A. 19 Apr 60, Bergstrom AFB, TX
    I. 25 Jun 66

A	BG-40 Elroy	
B	BG-80 Austin	

    Bergstrom AFB

Originally organized 31 March 1898 as Battery D, 7th Regiment of Artillery, Fort Slocum, NY. The 4/7th replaced the 245th AAABn in the Savannah River Defense Area as a gun unit and then returned to service as a Hercules battalion at Bergstrom AFB.

5/7th Artillery

5/7th A. 1 Sept 58, Tappan, NY
I. 30 Nov 68

A	NY-03 Orangeburg	9/58-6/64	to C/1/244th
B	NY-94 Ramsey	9/58-11/68	to D/7/112th
C	NY-99 Spring Valley	9/58-6/60	to A/1/112th
	NY-80 Livingston	7/60-4/63	to B/7/112th

Tappan

Originally organized 31 March 1898 as Battery E, 7th Regiment of Artillery, Fort Slocum, NY. Replaced the 737th AAAMBn in the New York Defense Area

8/7th ADA (HAWK)

8/7th A. 1 Sept 71, Fort Bliss, TX
I. 13 Sept 72

Fort Bliss

Originally constituted 8 March 1898 as Battery H, 7th Regiment of Artillery, Fort Slocum, NY.

15th Artillery

Originally constituted on 3 June 1916 at Syracuse, NY and organized on 1 June 1917. The 15th is historically a field artillery unit; the 8th battalion was the only component to serve as air defense artillery.

8/15th Artillery (Hawk) 13

8/15th A. 19 Apr 61, Fort Bliss, TX
I. 1 Sept 71

A	HM-12 Miami	10/62-9/71	to A/3/68th
B		10/62-3/65	
	HM-39 Miami	3/65-9/71	to B/3/68th
C	HM-84 Miami	10/62-9/71	to C/3/68th
D	HM-60 Miami	10/62-6/65	
	HM-59 Miami	6/65-9/71	to D/3/68th

Ft Bliss (10/62) Naranja ( ) Homestead AFB

Originally constituted 1 July 1916 as Headquarters and Headquarters Detachment, 2nd Battalion, 15th Field Artillery. Organized 1 June 1917 at Syracuse, NY; replaced by 3/68th Artillery in the Homestead-Miami Defense Area and reverted to field artillery.

43rd Air Defense Artillery

Originally constituted 29 June 1918 as the 43rd Artillery (Coast Artillery Corps) at Haussimont, France and organized on 7 August 1918.

1/43rd ADA

1/43rd A. 1 Sept 58, Fairchild AFB, WA

    I. 25 Mar 66

A	F-07 Spokane	9/58-6/60	
B	F-37 Cheney	9/58-6/60	
C	F-45 Medical Lake	9/58-3/66	
D	F-87 Deep Creek	9/58-3/66	

    Fairchild AFB

1/43rd A. 13 Sept 72, Fort Richardson, AK

    I. 31 Jul 79

A	Site Point	9/72-5/79
B	Site Summit	9/72-5/79
C	Site Bay	9/72-5/79

    Fort Richardson

Originally organized 19 August 1901 as 107th Company, Coast Artillery Corps. Replaced the 10th AAAMBn in the Fairchild Defense Area; replaced 4/43rd ADA in the Anchorage Defense Area.

2/43rd Artillery

2/43rd A. 1 Sept 58, Redmond, WA

    I. 25 Mar 66

A	S-13 Redmond	9/58-4/59	to A/4/4th
	TU-28 Willingsham	11/60-3/66	
B	S-20 Cougar Mountain	9/58-6/59	to B/2/205th
	TU-79 Armena	11/60-3/66	
C	S-03 Kenmore	9/58-6/59	to A/2/205th
D	S-13 Redmond	9/58-4/59	

    Redmond (7/59) Turner AFB

Originally organized August 1907 as 138th Company, Coast Artillery Corps, Fort Mott, NJ. Replaced the 28th AAAMBn in the Seattle Defense Area prior to its transfer to the Robins Defense Area.

3/43rd ADA

3/43rd A. 1 Sept 58, Lumberton, PA

    I. 30 Sept 74

A	PH-41 Berlin	9/58-4/74	
B	PH-49 Pittman	9/58-10/60	to C/2/254th
	PH-58 Swedesboro	10/64-4/74	
C	PH-25 Lumberton	9/58-10/63	to A/7/112th
	PH-75 Edgemont	10/64-11/68	
D	PH-32 Marlton	9/58-10/60	to A/2/254th
	NY-49 Ft Tilden	6/74-4/74	

Lumberton (10/63) Pedricktown AADB (9/66) Edgemont

Originally organized 5 August 1916 as Fort Command Company, Fort Mills, Philippines. Replaced the 738th AAAMBn in the Philadelphia Defense Area

4/43rd ADA

4/43rd A. 15 Sept 58, Fort Richardson, TA
    I. 13 Sept 72

A	Site Point	4/59-9/72	to A/1/43rd
B	Site Summit	4/59-9/72	to B/1/43rd
C	Site Bay	4/59-9/72	to C/1/43rd

Fort Richardson

Originally organized 11 January 1918 as C Battery, 57th Artillery, Coast Artillery Corps, Fort Hancock, NJ. Replaced the 96th AAABn in the Anchorage Defense Area; replaced by 1/43rd ADA

6/43rd ADA

6/43rd A. 24 Jun 60, Offutt AFB, NE
    I. 25 Jun 66

A	OF-10 Council Bluffs	6/60-6/66
B	OF-60 Cedar Creek	6/60-6/66
C	LI-50 Crete	6/60-6/66
D	LI-01 Ceresco	6/60-6/66

Offutt AFB (/60) Omaha AFS

Originally organized 14 April 1917 as 5th Company, Coast Artillery Corps, Fort McKinley, ME.

44th Air Defense Artillery

Originally organized on 26 March 1918 in France as the Howitzer Regiment, 30th Brigade, Coast Artillery Corps. Redesignated 7 August 1918 as the 44th Artillery (Coast Artillery Corps).

3/44th Artillery

3/44th A. 1 Sept 58, Fairfield, CT
    I. 24 Mar 61

A	BR-94 Shelton	9/58-3/61	
B	BR-65 Fairfield	9/58-3/61	
C	BR-73 Westport	9/58-1/61	to B/1/242nd
D	HA-67 Plainville	9/58-3/61	

Fairfield

Originally organized 5 August 1907 as 151st Company, Coast Artillery Corps, Fort Revere, MA. Replaced the 741st AAAMBn in the Bridgeport Defense Area

5/44th Artillery

5/44th A. 18 Apr 60, Schilling AFB, KS

I. 26 Jun 60

SC-01 Schilling AFB	4/60-6/66	
SC-50 Schilling AFB	4/60-6/66	

Schilling AFB

Originally organized 5 July 1917 as 21st Company, Fort Mills, Philippines; not operational with Nike Hercules.

51st Air Defense Artillery

Originally constituted on 6 July 1917 as the 6th Provisional Company, Coast Artillery Corps and organized 21 July at Fort Adams, Rhode Island.

1/51st Artillery

1/51st A. 1 Sept 58, Plainville, CT

I. 25 Mar 61

A	HA-85 Avon	9/58-1/61	to B/1/192nd
B	HA-67 Plainville	9/58-3/61	to D/3/44th
C	HA-48 Cromwell	9/58-3/61	to D/2/55th

Plainville

2/51st A. 13 Sept 72, Highlands AADB, NJ

I. 4 Jun 73

B	NY-49 Ft Tilden	(9/72-6/73)	to D/3/43rd

Highlands AADB

Originally organized in 1808 as Captain Joseph Chandler's Company of Light Artillery, Fort Preble, MA. Replaced the 34th AAMBn in the Hartford Defense Area, replaced the 3/51st ADA in the New York Defense Area and was replaced by the 3/43rd ADA under combined New York-Philadelphia Defense Area.

2/51st Artillery

2/51st A. 1 Sept 58, San Francisco, CA 22

I. 30 Jun 71

A	SF-88 Ft Barry	9/58-6/71	to B/1/61st
B	SF-87 Ft Cronkhite	9/58-6/71	
C	SF-93 San Rafael	9/58-6/71	
D	SF-91 Angel Island	9/58-7/59	
	SF-51 Milagra	7/59-6/63	to A/1/250th

San Francisco () Fort Baker

Originally organized 3 September 1901 as 109th Company, Coast Artillery Corps, Fort Greble, PA. Replaced the 9th AAAMBn in the San Francisco Defense Area; replaced by 1/61st Artillery in consolidation of the San Francisco and Travis Defense Areas.

3/51st ADA

3/51st A. 1 Sept 58, Fort Tilden, NY

I. 13 Sept 72

A	NY-24 Amityville	9/58-6/64	to A/1/244th
	NY-58 South Amboy	6/64-11/68	
B	NY-49 Ft Tilden	9/58-9/72	to B/1/51st
C	NY-29 Lido Beach	9/58-12/60	to C/1/244th
	NY-56 Ft Hancock	6/64-6/71	
D	NY-25 Rocky Point	9/58-6/64	to B/1/244th
	NY-54 Holmdel	6/64-11/68	

Fort Tilden (6/64) Fort Hancock (11/68) Highlands AADB

Originally organized 22 August 1091 as 114th Company, Coast Artillery Corps, Fort Slocum, NY. Replaced the 505th AAAMBn in the New York Defense Area and was in turn replaced by the 1/51st.

4/51st Artillery

4/51st A. 1 Sept 58, Fort Monroe, VA

I. 26 Jul 60

A	N-02 Fox Hill	9/58-3/60	to B/5/111th
B	N-93 Hampton	9/58-3/60	to C/5/111th
C	N-85 Denbigh	9/58-7/60	to C/4/59th
D	N-75 Smithfield	9/58-7/60	to A/4/59th

Fort Monroe

Originally organized in 1907 as the 153rd Company (Coast Artillery Corps), Fort Andrews, MD. Replaced the 56th AAAMBn in the Norfolk Defense Area

6/51st Artillery

Designated for assignment to the Mountain Home Defense Area, not activated.

52nd Air Defense Artillery

Originally organized on 22 July 1917 at Fort Adams, Rhode Island as the 7th Provisional Regiment, Coast Artillery Corps. Redesignated as the 52nd Artillery (Coast Artillery Corps) on 5 February 1918.

1/52nd Artillery

1/52nd A. 1 Sept 58, Camp Hanford, WA

I. 21 Dec 60

A	H-06 Saddle Mountain	9/58-12/60
B	H-12 Othello	9/58-12/58
C	H-52 Rattlesnake Mountain	9/58-12/58
D	H-83 Priest Rapids	9/58-12/58

Camp Hanford

Originally organized in 1907 as 134th Company, Coast Artillery Corps, Fort Mitchie, NY. Replaced the 83rd AAAMBn in the Hanford Defense Area

2/52nd ADA

2/52nd A. 15 Apr 59, Fort Bliss, TX

    I. 15 Mar 83

A	HM-69 Florida City	6/65-6/79
B	HM-66 Florida City	10/62-6/65
	HM-40 Key Largo	6/65-6/79
C	HM-03 Opa Locka	10/62-6/79
D	HM-95 Southwest Miami	10/62-6/79

    Fort Bliss (10/62) West Homestead ( ) Homestead AFB (6/79) Fort Bliss

Originally organized 1 April 1917 as 6th Company, Fort Terry, NY. Replaced 6/43rd ADA at Fort Bliss; this was the last Nike Hercules battalion in the United States.

3/52nd Artillery

3/52nd A. 1 Sept 58, Quincy, MA

    I. 15 Dec 61

A	B-38 Cohasset	9/58-12/61	
B	B-55 Blue Hills	9/58-8/59	to A/1/241st
C	B-37 Squantum	9/58-12/61	
D	B-36 Ft Duvall	9/58-12/61	to B/3/5th

    Quincy

Originally organized in 1901 as 88th Company, Coast Artillery Corps, Fort Trumbull, MA. Replaced the 514th AAAMBn in the Boston Defense Area

4/52nd Artillery

4/52nd A. 1 Sept 58, Hegewisch, IL

    I. 24 Jun 60

A	C-49 Homewood	9/58-6/60	to A/6/3rd
B	C-44 Hegewisch	9/58-12/59	
C	C-46 Munster	9/58-6/60	to C/1/60th
D	C-44 Hegewisch	9/58-12/59	

    Hegewisch

Originally organized 1 April 1917 as 6th Company, Fort H.G. Wright, NY. Replaced the 49th AAAMBn in the Chicago Defense Area

---

55th Air Defense Artillery

Originally constituted on 1 December 1917 as the 55th Artillery (Coast Artillery Corps) and organized at Boston, MA.

1/55th Artillery

1/55th A. 1 Sept 58, Fort Totten, NY

    I. 26 Jul 60

A	NY-20 Lloyd Harbor	9/58-6/60	to A/1/245th
B	NY-09 Kensico	9/58-6/60	to B/1/212th
C	NY-23 Hicksville	9/58-6/60	to B/1/245th
D	NY-15 Ft Slocum	9/58-6/60	

Fort Totten

Originally organized 6 April 1901 as 83rd Company, Coast Artillery Corps, Fort Hamilton, NY. Replaced the 66th AAAMBn in the New York Defense Area

2/55th Artillery

2/55th A. 1 Sept 58, Manchester, CT
I. 28 Dec 64

B	HA-36 Portland	9/58-1/61	to A/1/192nd
	BR-04 Ansonia	9/61-8/64	to D/1/192nd
C	HA-25 Manchester	9/58-1/61	
D	HA-48 Cromwell	3/61-8/64	to B/1/192nd

Manchester (/61) New Britain

Originally organized 13 June 1901 as 96th Company, Coast Artillery Corps, Fort Warren, MA. Replaced the 11th AAAMBn in the Hartford Defense Area

3/55th Artillery

3/55th A. 1 Sept 58, Fort Wayne, MI
I. 23 Dec 60

A	D-23 Detroit City Airport	9/58-12/60	
B	D-26 Ft Wayne	9/58-12/60	to D/3/517th
C	D-54 Riverview	9/58-10/60	to C&A/1/177th
D	D-26 Ft Wayne	9/58	

Fort Wayne

Originally organized in February 1919 as Battery B, 55th Artillery, Coast Artillery Corps, Fort Winfield Scott, CA. Replaced the 85th AAAMBn in the Detroit Defense Area

4/55th Artillery

4/55th A. 1 Sept 58, Thule AB, GN
I. 20 Dec 65

Bty 01	9/58-10/65
Bty 13	9/58-10/65
Bty 40	9/58-10/65
Bty 60	9/58-10/65

Thule AB (10/65) Fort Totten

Originally organized February 1919 as Battery D, 55th Artillery (Coast Artillery Corps), Fort Winfield Scott, CA. Replaced the 65th AAGBn in the Thule Defense Area

5/55th Artillery

5/55th A. 1 Jun 59, Kansas City, MO

    I. 10 Feb 69

A	KC-10 Lawson	11/59-2/64	to A/3/128th
B	KC-30 Pleasant Hill	11/59-2/64	to B/3/128th
C	KC-60 Gardner	11/59-2/69	
D	KC-80 Ft Leavenworth	11/59-2/69	

    Kansas City (/59) NAS Olathe

Originally organized in February 1919 as Battery E, 55th Artillery (Coast Artillery Corps), Fort Winfield Scott, CA.

56th Air Defense Artillery

Originally constituted on 29 July 1921 in the Organized Reserves as the 506th Artillery (Antiaircraft) and organized in August 1922 at LaCross, WI. Redesignated as the 506th Coast Artillery on 20 February 1924; redesignated as the 56th Coast Artillery on 16 December 1940.

1/56th Artillery

1/56th A. 1 Sept 58, Pasadena, CA

    I. 12 Dec 68

A	LA-29 Brea	9/58-4/64	to C/4/251st
B	LA-09 Mt Disappointment	9/58-/61	
C	LA-14 South El Monte	9/58-/59	
D	LA-04 Mt Gleason	9/58-12/68	to A/4/65th

    Pasadena Army Support Center (6/64) Lang Station

    Current 1/56th ADA, 6th ADA Brigade, Ft Bliss, TX

Originally organized in August 1922 as Battery A, 506th Coast Artillery (Antiaircraft), in Wisconsin. Replaced the 933d AAAMBn in the Los Angeles Defense Area

3/56th Artillery

3/56th A. 1 Sept 58, West Haven, CT

    I. 1 Sept 61

A	BR-17 Milford	9/58-1/61	to A/1/242nd
B	BR-04 Ansonia	9/58-9/61	
C	BR-15 Westhaven	9/58-9/61	

    West Haven

Originally organized August 1922 as Battery C, 506th Artillery (Antiaircraft), in Wisconsin. Replaced the 967th AAAMBn in the Bridgeport Defense Area

4/56th Arty

4/56th A. 1 Sept 58, Bristol, MA

I. 26 Aug 63

A	PR-19 Rehoboth	9/58-6/59	
B	PR-29 Swansea	9/58-6/59	
C	PR-38 Bristol	9/58-8/63	to C/3/5th
D	PR-99 North Smithfield	12/61-8/63	to B/2/243rd

Bristol (8/60) Rehoboth

4/56th A. 20 May 67, Fort Bliss, TX

I. 31 Mar 70

Fort Bliss

Originally organized in August 1922 as Battery D, 506th Artillery (Antiaircraft) in Wisconsin. Replaced the 739th AAAMBn in the Providence Defense Area. Reactivated at Fort Bliss as a Hawk battalion.

5/56th Artillery

5/56th A. 15 Jun 59, Cincinnati, OH

I. 30 Mar 70

A	CD-27 Wilmington		
B	CD-46 Felicity	4/60-4/65	to A/1/137th
C	CD-63 Dillsboro		
D	CD-78 Oxford	3/60-4/65	to B/1/137th

Cincinnati (/60) Wilmington

Originally organized in August 1922 as Battery E, 506th Artillery (Antiaircraft) in Wisconsin.

57th Air Defense Artillery

Originally constituted 1 November 1917 as the 57th Artillery (Coast Artillery Corps) and organized at Fort Hancock, NJ on 11 January 1918.

1/57th Artillery

1/57th A. 1 Sept 58, Fort Banks, MA

I. 25 Jun 60

A	B-15 Beverly	9/58-8/59	to C/2/241st
B	B-05 Danvers	9/58-6/60	to D/3/5th
C	B-17 Nahant	9/58-6/60	
D	B-03 Reading	9/58-8/59	to D/2/241st

Fort Banks (/59) Nahant

Originally organized 11 January 1918 as Battery A, 57th Artillery, Coast Artillery Corps, Fort Hancock, NJ. Replaced the 605th AAAMBn in the Boston Defense Area.

2/57th Artillery

2/57th A. 1 Sept 58, Montrose, IL

I. 23 Aug 63

A	C-03 Montrose	9/58-8/63	to A/6/3rd

B	C-40 Burnham Park	9/58-8/63	
C	C-41 Jackson Park	9/58-8/63	to B/6/3rd
D	C-03 Montrose	9/58-5/59	

*Montrose

Originally organized in February 1919 as Company B, 57th Artillery, Coast Artillery Corps, Fort Winfield Scott, CA. Replaced the 485th AAAMBn in the Chicago Defense Area.

3/57th Artillery
3/57th A. 1 Sept 58, Fort MacArthur, CA
    I. 23 Apr 64

A	LA-32 Garden Grove	9/58-6/63	to A/4/251st
B	LA-78 Malibu	9/58-4/64	to B/4/65th
C	LA-43 Ft MacArthur	9/58-6/63	to D/4/251st
D	LA-55 Point Vicente	9/58-4/64	to B/4/251st

*Fort MacArthur

Originally activated 3 January 1941 as Battery C, 57th Coast Artillery, Fort Monroe, VA. Replaced the 554th AAAMBn in the Los Angeles Defense Area.

59th Air Defense Artillery
    Originally constituted on 1 December 1959 as the 59th Artillery (Coast Artillery Corps) and organized at Fort Hamilton, NY on 1 January 1918.

2/59th Artillery
2/59th A. 1 Sept 58, Edgemont, PA
    I. 9 Oct 64

A	PH-82 Paoli	9/58-4/60	to B/3/166th
B	PH-75 Edgemont	9/58-10/64	to C/3/43rd
C	PH-67 Chester	9/58-4/60	to C/3/166th
D	PH-58 Swedesboro	9/58-10/64	

*Edgemont

Originally organized in February 1919 as Battery B, 59th Artillery (Coast Artillery Corps), Fort Winfield Scott, CA. Replaced the 176th AAAMBn in the Philadelphia Defense Area.

3/59th Artillery
3/59th A. 1 Sept 58, Milwaukee, WI
    I. 30 Jun 71

A	M-02 Milwaukee	9/58-6/71	
B	M-20 Milwaukee	9/58-6/71	
C	M-86 Lannon	9/58- /60	
	M-74 Waukesha	8/61-6/64	to B/2/126th
D	M-96 Milwaukee	9/58-3/61	to B/1/126th

*Milwaukee

Originally organized in February 1919 as Battery C, 59th Coast Artillery (Coast Artillery Corps), Fort Winfield Scott, CA. Replaced the 852nd AAAMBn in the Milwaukee Defense Area.

4/59th Artillery

4/59th A. 1 Sept 58, Norfolk, VA
    I. 30 Jun 71

A	N-63 Nansemond	9/58-9/59	to B/4/111th
	N-75 Smithfield	7/60-6/61	
B	N-52 Deep Creek	9/58-12/64	to B/4/111th
C	N-36 Kempsville	9/58-9/59	to C/4/111th
	N-85 Denbigh	7/60-12/64	to C/4/111th
D	N-25 Ft Story	9/58-6/71	to B/4/1st

    * Ballentine School, Norfolk (/59) Craddock Branch (12/61) Hampton Roads Army Terminal (12/63) Fort Story

Originally organized in February 1919 as Battery D, 59th Artillery (Coast Artillery Corps), Fort Winfield Scott, CA. Replaced the 38th AAAMBn in the Norfolk Defense Area.

60th Air Defense Artillery

Originally constituted on 23 December as the 60th Artillery (Coast Artillery Corps) and organized at Fort Monroe, VA.

1/60th ADA

1/60th A. 1 Sept 58, Gary Municipal Airport, IN
    I. 30 Sept 74

A	C-47 Hobart	9/58-4/74
B	C-32 Porter	9/58-4/74
C	C-45 Gary	9/58-6/60
	C-46 Munster	6/60-11/68
D	C-48 South Gary	9/58-6/60
	C-41 Jackson Park	6/65-6/71

    *Gary Municipal (11/68) Munster

Originally organized 29 March 1898 as Battery G, 7th Regiment of Artillery, Fort Slocum, NY. Replaced the 79th AAAMBn in the Chicago Defense Area

2/60th Artillery

2/60th A. 1 Sept 58, Orland Park, IL
    I. 15 Dec 61

A	C-70 Naperville	9/58-12/59	to B/2/202nd
B	C-54 Orland Park	9/58-12/61	
C	C-51 Worth	9/58-12/59	
D	C-61 Lemont	9/58-12/61	to C/6/3rd

*Orland Park

Originally organized 29 March 1898 as Battery K, 7th Regiment of Artillery, Fort Slocum, NY. Replaced the 13th AAAMBn in the Chicago Defense Area.

3/60th Artillery

3/60th A. 1 Sept 58, Eureka, PA
I. 1 Sept 61

A	PH-91 Worchester	9/58-4/60	to A/2/166th
B	PH-99 Warrington	9/58-9/61	to A/2/59th
C	PH-07 Richboro	9/58-9/61	
D	PH-15 Newportville	9/58-4/60	to B/2/166th

*Eureka

Originally organized in 1907 as 128th Company (Coast Artillery Corps), Fort McHenry, MD. Replaced the 506th AAAMBn in the Philadelphia Defense Area

4/60th Artillery

4/60th A. 1 Scpt 58, Midway, WA
I. 15 Dec 61

A	S-61 Vashon Island	9/58-12/61	to B/4/4th
B	S-33 Lake Youngs	9/58-12/61	
C	S-32 Lake Youngs	9/58-12/61	
D	S-43 Kent	9/58-6/59	to B/3/205th

*Midway (7/59) Redmond

Originally activated 1 April 1929 as Battery F, 60th Coast Artillery, Fort Mills, Philippines. Replaced the 433rd AAAMBn in the Seattle Defense Area.

61st Air Defense Artillery

Originally constituted on 9 March 1918 as the 61st Artillery (Coast Artillery Corps) and organized at Fort Moultrie, SC.

1/61st ADA

1/61st A. 1 Sept 58, Travis AFB, CA
I. 30 Aug 74

A	T-10 Elmira	9/58-3/74	
B	T-53 Potrero Hills	9/58-1/59	
	SF-88 Ft Barry	6/71-3/74	
C	T-86 Fairfield	9/58-6/71	
D	T-33 Dixon	9/58-1/59	

*Travis AFB (/58) Elmira (6/71) Fort Baker

Originally organized in 1803 as Captain Nathan Eastbrook's Company of Light Artillery. Replaced the 436th AAMBn in the Travis Defense Area and the 2/51st Artillery in the San Francisco-Travis Defense Area.

3/61st Artillery

3/61st A. 1 Sept 58, Loring AFB, ME

    I. 25 Jun 66

A	L-13 Caswell	9/58-6/66
B	L-31 Limestone	9/58-6/60
C	L-58 Caribou	9/58-6/66
D	L-85 Conner	9/58-6/66

    Loring AFB

Originally activated 18 November 1939 as Battery D, 61st Coast Artillery, Fort Sheridan, IL. Replaced the 548th AAAMBn in the Loring Defense Area.

4/61st Artillery

4/61st A. 1 Sept 58, San Francisco, CA

    I. 25 Mar 66

A	SF-59 Ft Funston	9/58-7/59	to D/2/250th
	R-28 Jeffersonville	11/60-3/66	
B	SF-89 Ft Winfield Scott	9/58-7/59	to B/2/250th
	R-88 Byron	11/60-3/66	
C	SF-51 Milagra	9/58-7/59	to D/2/51st
D	SF-37 Coyote Hills	9/58-7/59	to C/1/250th

    Presidio of San Francisco (7/59) Robins AFB

Originally organized 20 November 1907 as 168th Company (Coast Artillery Corps), Fort Monroe, VA. Replaced the 740th AAAMBn in the San Francisco Defense Area prior to transferring to the Robins Defense Area.

62nd Air Defense Artillery

Originally constituted on 1 August 1921 as the 2nd Antiaircraft Battalion and organized at Fort Totten, NY on 4 September 1921. Redesignated the 62nd Artillery Battalion (Antiaircraft) on 1 June 1922 and as the 62nd Artillery (Antiaircraft)(Coast Artillery Corps) on 14 September 1922.

1/62nd Artillery

1/62nd AWBn A. 1 Jun 59, St Louis, MO; Rd. MBn 20 Dec 65

    I. 15 Jan 69

A	SL-10 Marine
B	SL-40 Hecker
C	SL-60 Pacific
D	SL-90 Alton

    St Louis (/59) Scott AFB

Originally organized in 1798 as Captain Callender Irvine's Company, 2nd Regiment of Artillerists and Engineers, Philadelphia, PA.

2/62nd Artillery

2/62nd A. 1 Sept 58, Lancaster, NY

I. 15 Dec 61

A	BU-09 Ransom Creek	9/58-12/61	
B	BU-18 Lancaster	9/58-12/61	to A/1/4th
C	BU-34 Orchard Park	9/58-8/60	to A&D/2/106th
D	BU-52 Hamburg	9/58-12/61	

Lancaster

Originally organized in 1808 as Captain George Peters' Company of Light Artillery. Replaced the 465th AAAMBn in the Buffalo Defense Area

4/62nd ADA

4/62nd A. 1 Sept 58, Fort MacArthur, CA

I. 30 Sept 59

A	LA-70 Hyperion	1-13 Sept 58	to C/720th
B	LA-73 Playa del Rey	1-13 Sept 58	to D/720th
C	LA-40 Long Beach	1-13 Sept 58	to A/720th
D	LA-57 Redondo Beach	1-13 Sept 58	to B/720th

Fort MacArthur (9/58) Fort Bliss

Originally organized in August 1838 as Company K, 3rd Regiment of Artillery, Fort Monroe, VA. Replaced the 865th AAAMBn in the Los Angeles Defense Area

65th Air Defense Artillery

Originally constituted on 26 December 1917 as the 65th Artillery (Coast Artillery Corps) and organized at Fort Stevens, OR.

1/65th ADA (Hawk)

1/65th A. 13 Sept 72, NAS Key West, FL

I. 79

A	KW-80 Fleming Key	9/72-/79	
B	KW-65 Key West	9/72-/79	
C	KW-24 Geiger Key	9/72-/79	
D	KW-10 Fleming Key	9/72-/79	

NAS Key West

Originally organized 17 August 1901 as 116th Company, Coast Artillery, Fort Screven, GA. Replaced the 6/65th ADA in the Key West Defense Area

2/65th ADA

2/65th A. 1 Sept 58, Camp Kilmer, NJ

I. 26 Jul 60

A	NY-73 Summit	9/58-9/59	to B/1/254th
B	NY-65 South Plainfield	9/58-7/60	to B/4/71st
C	NY-80 Livingston	9/58-7/60	to C/5/7th
D	NY-88 Mountain View	9/58-9/59	to D/1/254th

*Camp Kilmer

2/65th A. 13 Sept 72, Van Nuys, CA
I. 30 Sept 74

A	LA-04 Mt Gleason	9/72-3/74	
B	LA-78 Malibu	9/72-3/74	
C	LA-88 Chatsworth	9/72-3/74	

*Van Nuys

Originally organized in 1901 as 87th Company, Coast Artillery, Fort Slocum, NY. Replaced the 483rd AAAMBn in the New York Defense Area and the 4/65th ADA in the Los Angeles Defense Area.

3/65th Artillery

3/65th A. 1 Sept 58, Bratenahl, OH;
I. 30 Jun 71

A	CL-11 Painesville		
B	CL-34 Warrensville	9/58-1/61	to C/1/137th
C	CL-13 Willowick	9/58-6/61	to A/1/137th
	CL-69 Lordstown	8/61-2/63	to C/1/137th
D	CL-02 Bratenahl		

*Bratenahl (/59) Warrensville

Originally organized 15 October 1901 as 124th Company, Coast Artillery Corps, Fort Wadsworth, NY. Replaced the 508th AAAMBn in the Cleveland Defense Area

4/65th ADA

4/65th A. 1 Sept 58, Van Nuys, CA
I. 13 Sept 72

A	LA-94 Los Pinetos	9/58-11/68	
	LA-04 Mt Gleason	12/68-9/72	to A/2/65th
B	LA-98 Magic Mountain	9/58-/63	
	LA-78 Malibu	4/64-9/72	to B/2/65th
C	LA-88 Chatsworth	9/58-9/72	to C/2/65th
D	LA-96 Van Nuys	9/58-6/71	

*Birmingham Army Hospital, Van Nuys (/64) Van Nuys

Originally organized 5 April 1901 as the 89th Company, Coast Artillery, Fort Banks, MA. Replaced the 551st AAAMBn in the Los Angeles Defense Area and was replaced by 2/65th ADA.

6/65th ADA (Hawk)

6/65th A. 22 Dec 61, Fort Bliss, TX

    I. 13 Sept 72

A	KW-80 Fleming Key	10/62-9/72	to A/1/65th
B	KW-65 Key West	10/62-9/72	to B/1/65th
C	KW-24 Geiger Key	10/62-9/72	to C/1/65th
D	KW-10 Fleming Key	10/62-9/72	to A/1/65th

    Fort Bliss (10/62) NAS Key West

Originally organized 1 June 1917 as 7th Company, Fort Grant, Canal Zone. Replaced by 1/65th ADA.

67th Air Defense Artillery

Originally constituted on 2 May 1918 as the 67th Artillery (Coast Artillery Corps) and organized at Fort Winfield Scott, CA on 21 May 1918.

2/67th Artillery

2/67th A. 1 Sept 58, Ellsworth AFB, SD

    I. 25 Aug 61

A	Ellsworth AFB	9/58-1/61
B	Ellsworth AFB	9/58-10/58
C	Ellsworth AFB	9/58-10/58
D	Ellsworth AFB	9/58-10/58

    Ellsworth AFB

Originally activated 1 July 1940, Fort Bragg, NC. Replaced the 531st AAAMBn in the Ellsworth Defense Area.

3/67th Artillery

3/67th A. 1 Sept 58, Hales Corners, WI

    I. 25 Aug 61

A	M-64 Muskegon	9/58-2/61	to A/1/126th
B	M-42 Cudahy	9/58-8/61	
C	M-54 Hales Corners	9/58-8/61	
D	M-74 Waukesha	9/58-8/61	to C/3/59th

    Hales Corners

Originally organized in December 1917 as 45th Company, Coast Defenses of San Francisco, Presidio of San Francisco, CA. Replaced the 401st AAAMBn in the Milwaukee Defense Area.

4/67th Artillery

4/67th A. 1 Sept 58, San Pablo Ridge, CA

    I. 28 Jun 63

A	SF-31 Lake Chabot	9/58-6/63	to B/1/250th
B	SF-25 Rocky Ridge	9/58-7/59	
C	SF-08 San Pablo Ridge	9/58-7/59	to A/1/250th
D	SF-09 San Pablo Ridge	9/58-7/59	

*San Pablo Ridge

Originally activated 10 February 1941 as Battery Delta, 67th Coast Artillery, Fort Bragg, NC; replaced the 441st AAMBn in the San Francisco Defense Area.

68th Air Defense Artillery

Originally constituted on 1 June 1918 as the 68th Artillery (Coast Artillery Corps) and organized at Fort Terry, Long Island, NY.

1/68th Artillery

1/68th A. 1 Sept 58, Parma, OH

I. 25 Aug 61

A	CL-48 Garfield Heights	9/58-8/61	
B	CL-59 Parma	9/58-8/61	
C	CL-67 Lakefront	9/58-1/61	to B/1/137th
D	CL-69 Lordstown	9/58-8/61	to C/3/65th

*Parma

Originally organized 1 June 1918 as Battery A, 68th Artillery, Coast Artillery Corps, Fort Terry, NY. Replaced the 351st AAAMBn in the Cleveland Defense Area

2/68th Artillery (75mm)

2/68th A. 1 Sept 58, Camp Lucas, MI

I. Jun 60

*Camp Lucas

Replaced the 8th AAABn in the Sault Ste Marie Defense Area. The 2/68th was the last operational gun battalion in Army Air Defense Command.

3/68th ADA

3/68th A. 1 Jun 59, Minneapolis, MN

I. 30 Jun 71

A	MS-20 Roberts	10/59-6/71
B	MS-40 Farmington	10/59-6/71
C	MS-70 St Bonifacius	10/59-6/71
D	MS-90 Bethel	10/59-6/71

*Minneapolis (/59) Snelling AFS

3/68th A. 1 Sept 71, Homestead AFB, FL   Hawk

I.   79

A	HM-12 Miami	9/71-/79
B	HM-39 Miami	9/71-/79
C	HM-84 Miami	9/71-/79
D	HM-59 Miami	9/71-/79

Homestead AFB

Originally organized 1 June 1918 as Battery C, 68th Artillery (Coast Artillery Corps), Fort Terry, NY; replaced 8/15th Artillery in the Homestead-Miami Defense Area.

4/68th Artillery

4/68th A. 1 Sept 58, Coventry, RI
I. 15 Dec 61

A	PR-58 North Kingston	9/58-12/60	to A/2/243rd
B	PR-69 Coventry	9/58-12/60	to B/2/243rd
C	PR-79 Foster Center	9/58-12/60	to D/2/243rd
D	PR-99 North Smithfield	9/58-12/61	to B/2/243rd

Coventry

Originally organized 1 June 1918 as Battery D, 68th Artillery (Coast Artillery Corps), Fort Terry, NY. Replaced the 751st AAMBn in the Providence Defense Area

---

70th Air Defense Artillery   MDArNG

Organized 1 June 1959 through consolidation of the 683rd, 684th and 686th Antiaircraft Artillery Missile Battalions with the regiment assuming the lineage and emblem of the 683rd AAA Battalion; apparently the regiment had no connection with the Army's 70th Coast Artillery Regiment which later became the 562nd Air Defense Artillery. The 70th Regiment (Leadership) at Camp Fretterd Military Reservation in Reisterstown, MD, now holds the emblem and number of the 70th Artillery.

1/70th ADA

1/70th Org. 1 Jun 59, Fort Smallwood, MD
I. 30 Sept 74

A	BA-43 Jacobsville	3/60-12/62
	W-26 Annapolis	12/62-11/68
	W-25 Davidsonville	11/68-4/74
B	BA-79 Granite	12/62-4/74
C	W-44 Mattawoman	3/63-6/71
D	BA-09 Fork	9/59-12/62
	BA-03 Phoenix	12/62-4/74

Fort Smallwood (6/59) Towson (10/62) Granite

The 1/70th replaced the 683rd AAAMBn in the Baltimore Defense Area.

2/70th Artillery

2/70th A. 1 Jun 59, Towson, MD
I. 1 Mar 63

A	BA-79 Granite	3/60-3/63
C	W-94 Gaithersburg	6/60-3/63

| D | BA-92 Cronhardt | 9/59-9/63 | |

Towson (/59) Owings Mills

The 2/70th replaced the 684th AAAMBn in the Baltimore Defense Area.

3/70th Artillery
3/70th Org. 1 May 59, Accokeek, MD
I. 1 Mar 63

A	W-44 Mattawoman	12/61-3/63	to C/1/70th
B	W-35 Croom	6/60-3/63	
C	W-45 Accokeek	6/60-12/61	

Accokeek

The 3/70th replaced the 686th AAAMBn in the Washington Defense Area.

71st Air Defense Artillery
Originally constituted on 2 May 1918 as the 71st Artillery (Coast Artillery Corps) and organized at Fort Strong, MA on 12 May 1918. ARADCOM created the 1st and 4th battalions through the redesignation of existing Nike Ajax batteries.

1/71st Artillery
1/71st A. 1 Sept 58, Fort Belvoir, VA
I. 1965

A	W-25 Davidsonville	12/62- /65	to B/4/1st
B	W-83 Herndon	9/58-11/62	
C	W-64 Lorton	9/58-8/63	to A/4/111th
D	W-74 Fairfax	9/58-9/59	to B/1/280th
	W-92 Rockville	8/60- /65	to A/4/1st

Fort Bliss (/53) Fort Belvoir (/55) Rockville (9/58) Fort Belvoir (3/63) Suitland

The battalion was originally constituted on 2 May 1918 as Battery A, 71st Artillery (Coast Artillery Corps) and organized on 12 May 1918 at Fort Strong, MA; it replaced the 71st AAAMBn in the Washington Defense Area.

4/71st Artillery
4/71st A. 1 Sept 58, Fort Hancock, NJ
I. 19 Jun 64

A	NY-58 South Amboy	9/58-6/64	to A/3/51st
B	NY-53 Leonardo	9/58-6/60	to C/1/245th
	NY-65 South Plainfield	7/60-4/63	to C/7/112th
C	NY-56 Ft Hancock	9/58-6/64	to C/3/51st
D	NY-54 Holmdel	9/58-6/64	to D/3/51st

South Amboy (9/58) Fort Hancock

The battalion originally organized on 12 May 1918 as Battery D, 71st Artillery at Fort Andrews, MD; it replaced the 526th AAMBn in the New York Defense Area.

106th Artillery   NYArNG

Originally constituted 23 July 1940 as the 1st Battalion, 209th Coast Artillery (Antiaircraft) with the headquarters receiving its Federal recognition in Buffalo on 14 October 1940. On 16 March 1959 the state consolidated the 106th Antiaircraft Artillery Missile Battalion with the 106th Artillery under CARS. The only unit currently with the 106 designation in the New York National Guard is the 106th Regional Training Institute at Camp Smith, Cortlandt Manor. It draws its lineage from the 106th Infantry and the World War II–era 186th Field Artillery.

2/106th Artillery

2/106th Org. 1 Jun 59, Buffalo, NY

    I. 1 Mar 63

A	BU-34 Orchard Park	8/60-3/63
B	NF-03 Model City	7/60-3/63
D	BU-34 Orchard Park	8/60-3/63

    Buffalo

The 2/106th replaced the 106th AAAMBn in the Buffalo Defense Area; it was replaced in turn by the 2/209th Artillery.

111th Air Defense Artillery   VAArNG

Originally constituted on 2 July 1946 in the Virginia National Guard as the 691st Antiaircraft Artillery Automatic Weapons Battalion and organized in Virginia, with the headquarters and headquarters battery receiving its Federal recognition in Portsmouth on 13 December 1946. Reorganized on 1 June 1959 through consolidation of the 111th Field Artillery and the 125th, 129th (former 691st), 615th and 710th Antiaircraft Artillery Battalions. The regiment is currently inactive; the last component, the 3/111th ADA, inactivated in February 2006 and reorganized as the 2/183rd Cavalry.

4/111th ADA

4/111th Org. 1 Jun 59, Reidsville, VA

    Db. 1 Aug 74

A	W-64 Lorton	8/63-4/74
B	N-63 Nansemond	9/59-11/64
	N-52 Deep Creek	12/64-4/74
C	N-36 Kempsville	9/59-/64
	N-85 Denbigh	12/64-4/74

    Reidsville (/64) Deep Creek

The 4/111th replaced the 615th in the Norfolk Defense Area. In 1963 it expanded to replace the 1/280th in the Washington–Baltimore Defense Area.

5/111th Artillery

5/111th Org. 1 Jun 59, Newport News, VA

> Db. 1 Mar 63

B	N-02 Fox Hill	3/60-3/63	
C	N-93 Hampton	3/60-3/63	

> *Newport News*

The 5/111th replaced the 710th AAAMBn in the Norfolk Defense Area.

112th Artillery   NJArNG

The New Jersey Army National Guard created the 112th Artillery on 1 March 1959 through the consolidation of the 157th, 199th, 228th, 286th, 695th and 696th Armored Field Artillery Battalions. The reorganization yielded the 1st, 2nd and 3rd Howitzer Battalions, 5th Rocket Howitzer Battalion and the 6th and 7th Howitzer Battalions.

   The regiment reorganized as the 112th Field Artillery on 1 May 1972. The current operational unit of the regiment is the 3/112th FA in Morristown, assigned to the 50th Infantry Brigade, NYArNG 42nd Infantry Division.

7/112th Artillery

7/112th Org. 1 Mar 63, Livingston, NJ

> Db. 1 Dec 71

A	PH-25 Lumberton	10/63-6/71	to A/1/254th
B	NY-80 Livingston	4/63-6/71	to B/1/254th
C	NY-65 South Plainfield	4/63-6/71	
D	NY-93 Ramsey	11/68-6/71	

> *Livingston*

The 7/112th replaced the 1/254th Artillery in the New York Defense Area and was in turn replaced by the 1/254th in June 1971. It formed during a 1 March 1963 reorganization of the 112th Artillery, which saw the 7/112th reorganize at Livingston from an existing field artillery battalion. In June 1971 the 7/112th turned two of its four Nike Hercules sites to the reformed 1/254th Artillery; the battalion disbanded on 1 April 1972.

126th Artillery   WIArNG

Originally organized on 6 April 1880 in Milwaukee as the Light Horse Squadron, Wisconsin National Guard. Reorganized as the 126th Field Artillery on 1 October 1959 and reorganized again on 15 February 1959 through consolidation of the 126th Field Artillery and 132nd Antiaircraft Artillery Battalions. The 1/126th Field Artillery currently serves in Kenosha.

1/126th Artillery

1/126th Org. 15 Feb 59, Milwaukee, WI

Rd. 5 Nov 63

A	M-64 Muskegon	2/61-3/63	rd A/1/126th FA
B	M-96 Milwaukee	3/61-3/63	rd B/1/126th FA

Milwaukee

2/126th Artillery
2/126th Org. 1 Mar 63, Milwaukee, WI

I. 30 Jun 71

B	M-74 Waukesha	6/64-6/71	

Milwaukee

The 2/126th replaced the 1/126th Artillery in the Milwaukee Defense Area as part of a mission and equipment reorganization.

128th Artillery   MOArNG
The regiment was first constituted and organized as the 1st Field Artillery in St Louis, MO on 29 June 1917. A reorganization of 22 May 1962 created the 1st and 2nd Howitzer Battalions and the 3rd Missile Battalion, 128th Artillery.

As a side note, A/1/128th Field Artillery drew its lineage to 1812 as a battery of artillery commanded by Capt Charles Choteau. At the time of its reorganization as a transportation company in late 2005 at Jefferson Barracks, Battery A, 1/128th FA was the oldest unit in the Missouri Army National Guard and the oldest Army combat organization west of the Mississippi River. The regiment is currently inactive.

3/128th Artillery
3/128th Org. 1 Mar 63, Pleasant Hill, MO

Db. Feb 69

A	KC-10 Lawson	2/64-2/69	
B	KC-30 Pleasant Hill	2/64-2/69	

Pleasant Hill

132nd Artillery   TXArNG
Originally formed in 1880 as the 1st Cavalry, Texas Volunteer Guard. On 16 March 1959 the Texas Army National Guard consolidated the 558th, 646th and 961st Armored Field Artillery Battalions into the 132nd Artillery creating the 1st and 2nd Howitzer and 3rd Rocket Howitzer Battalions. The regiment is currently inactive.

4/132nd Artillery
4/132nd Org. 10 Aug 62, Duncanville AFS, TX

I. Oct 68

A	DF-01 Denton	2/64-10/68	
B	DF-20 Terrell	2/64-10/68	

Duncanville AFS

137th Artillery   OHArNG

On 1 September 1959 the State of Ohio consolidated the 177th and 182nd Antiaircraft Artillery Battalions and the 179th Antiaircraft Artillery Missile Battalion to form the 137th Artillery under CARS. The regiment is currently inactive.

1/137th Artillery

1/137th FR. 1 Sept 59, Shaker Heights, OH

Db. Mar 71

A	CL-13 Willowick	6/61-2/63
	CD-46 Felicity	4/65-3/70
B	CL-65 Lakefront	1/61-2/63
	CD-78 Oxford	4/65-3/70
C	CL-34 Warrensville	1/61-2/63
	CL-69 Lordstown	2/63-6/71

Shaker Heights (/64) Wilmington

The 1/137th initially replaced the 179th AAAMBn in the Cleveland Defense Area; it subsequently manned two sites in the Cincinnati-Dayton Defense Area.

166th Artillery   PAArNG

Prior 166th Field Artillery, reorganized on 1 June 1959 as the 166th Artillery under CARS including the consolidation of the 707th and 709th Antiaircraft Artillery Missile Battalions. The 166th Regiment at Fort Indiantown Gap carries on the number and emblems through the 1/166th (Armor), 2/166th (Eastern Aviation Training Site), 3/166th (NCO Academy) and 4/166th (OCS/MOS).

2/166th Artillery

2/166th Org. 1 Jun 59, Worchester, PA

Db. 15 Jun 71

A	PH-91 Worchester	4/60- /63
	PH-99 Warrington	10/64-11/68
B	PH-15 Newportville	4/60- /63
	PH-99 Warrington	10/64-6/71
C	PH-67 Chester	4/60- /63

Worchester (/64) Warrington

Replaced the 707th AAAMBn in the Philadelphia Defense Area.

3/166th Artillery

3/166th Org. 1 Jun 59, Paoli, PA

Db. 1 Mar 63

B	PH-82 Paoli	4/60-3/63
C	PH-67 Chester	4/60-3/63

Paoli

Replaced the 709th AAAMBn in the Philadelphia Defense Area.

176th Air Defense Artillery   PAArNG

Originally organized in Pittsburgh on 5 September 1831 as the Duquesne Greys, subsequently became the 18th Infantry, Pennsylvania National Guard. On 1 June 1959 the Pennsylvania Army National Guard consolidated the 708th and 724th Antiaircraft Artillery Missile Battalions with the 176th Field Artillery to create the 176th Artillery under CARS. The 128th Forward Support Battalion currently holds the lineage and honors of the 724th AAAMBn and the 176th ADA Regiment with headquarters in Pittsburgh.

1/176th Artillery

1/176th Org. 1 Jun 59, Rural Ridge, PA

Db. 1 Apr 63

A	PI-92 Bryant	8/59-4/63
D	PI-02 Rural Ridge	4/60-4/63

*Rural Ridge

The 1/176th replaced the 708th AAAMBn in the Pittsburgh Defense Area.

2/176th ADA

Org. 1 Jun 59, Carnegie, PA

Db. 1 Jul 74

A	PI-93 Westview	10/63-6/71
B	PI-62 Bridgeville	8/59-4/63
	PI-71 Coraopolis	10/63-3/74
C	PI-42 Elizabeth	4/60-4/63
	PI-03 Dorseyville	10/63-3/74

*Logan Armory, Carnegie (4/63) Westview

The 2/176th replaced the 724th AAAMBn in the Pittsburgh Defense Area and continued the honors and lineage of the original Duquesne Greys following the regiment's reorganization on 1 April 1963.

177th Air Defense Artillery   MIArNG

The current unit with the numerical designation in the Michigan Army National Guard is the 177th MP Brigade at Taylor. Its assigned units are the 1/182nd FA (MLRS), 210th MP Battalion and 156th Signal Battalion; notably, the 182nd FA incorporates the former 177th Field Artillery Battalion, which consolidated into the 182nd Artillery on 1 June 1959.

1/177th ADA

1/177th FR. 1 Jun 59, Detroit, MI

Db. Apr 74

A	D-54 Riverview	10/60-2/63
	D-06 Utica	2/63-4/74
B	D-69 River Rouge	11/59-2/63
	D-61 Romulus	2/63-6/71
C	D-54 Riverview	11/59-2/63
	D-58 Carleton	2/63-4/74
D	D-17 Algonac	11/59-2/63

Detroit Artillery Armory

Replaced the 227th AAAMBn in the Detroit Defense Area.

2/177th Artillery

2/177th Org. 1 Jun 59, Detroit, MI

    Db. Feb 63

A	D-86 Franklin	10/60-2/63
C	D-97 Auburn Heights	11/59-2/63

Detroit Artillery Armory (/59) Dearborn

Replaced the 979th AAAMBn in the Detroit Defense Area.

192nd Artillery   CTArNG

Originally established in 1642 at Stamford as a company of militia under Capt John Underhill. On 1 May 1959 the Connecticut Army National Guard reorganized the 192nd Field Artillery to form the 192nd Artillery under CARS. The currently active battalion is the 2/192nd Field Artillery in Westbrook with a detachment in Ansonia and batteries in Norwich, Stratford and Naugatuck; it descends from the Regiment of Fairfield County, formed in 1672.

1/192nd Artillery

1/192nd Org. 1 May 59, West Hartford, CT

    Db. 21 Jun 71

A	HA-36 Portland	1/61- /63
B	HA-85 Avon	1/61- /63
	HA-48 Cromwell	8/64-11/68
D	BR-04 Ansonia	8/64-6/71

West Hartford

The 1/192nd replaced the 238th AAABn in the Hartford Defense Area.

202nd Air Defense Artillery   ILArNG

Originally constituted on 1 July 1897 in the Illinois National Guard as a Squadron of Cavalry. Reorganized on 1 March 1959 through consolidation of the 248th and 698th Antiaircraft Artillery Missile Battalions; notably, the two missile battalions of the 202nd were created through redesignation vice the standard activation/inactivation method.

1/202nd ADA

698th AAAMBn Rd.1/202nd 1 Mar 59, Arlington Heights, IL; Rd.1/202nd ADA 1 Apr 72

    Db. 30 Sept 74

A	C-92 Mundelein	8/60-8/63
	C-49 Homewood	8/63-4/74
B	C-84 Palatine	9/60-8/63
	C-72 Addison	8/63-8/74

C	C-94 Libertyville	8/60-8/63
	C-61 Lemont	4/64-11/68
D	C-98 Ft Sheridan	8/60-8/63
	C-93 Northfield	4/64-4/74

Arlington Heights

The 1/202nd replaced the 698th AAAMBn in the Chicago Defense Area. The battalion took the ARAD-COM Commander's Trophy in 1959.

2/202nd Artillery
248th AAAMBn Rd. 1 Mar 59, Chicago, IL

Db. 8 Oct 63

A	C-44 Hegewisch	12/59-3/63
B	C-70 Naperville	12/59-3/63
C	C-51 Worth	12/59-3/63
D	C-44 Hegewisch	12/59-3/63

Chicago

The 2/202nd replaced the 248th ΛAAMBn in the Chicago Defense Area. It received the 1963 ARAD-COM Commander's Trophy as the top Nike Ajax unit in the command.

205th Air Defense Artillery   WAArNG
The 1st Battalion, 205th Coast Artillery (Antiaircraft) received its Federal recognition as a unit of the Washington National Guard in Seattle on 30 November 1939. The state formed the 205th Artillery on 15 April 1959 through the consolidation of the 240th and 770th Antiaircraft Artillery Missile Battalions and the 286th and 420th Antiaircraft Artillery Battalions. The unit currently holding the number is the 205th Regiment (Leadership) at Camp Murray, WA.

2/205th ADA
2/205th Org. 15 Apr 59, Phantom Lake, WA

Db. 1 Jul 74

A	S-03 Kenmore	6/59-3/64
	S-13 Redmond	10/64-3/74
B	S-20 Cougar Mountain	6/59-3/64
	S-61 Vashon Island	10/64-3/74

Phantom Lake (6/60) Cougar Mountain (3/64) Redmond

The 2/205th replaced the 770th AAAMBn in the Seattle Defense Area.

3/205th Artillery
3/205th Org. 15 Apr 59, O'Brien, WA

Db. 25 Feb 63

A		to A/241st Signal Bn
B	S-43 Kent	6/59-2/63

C   S-62 Ollala   6/59-2/63

O'Brien (6/59) Midway

Replaced the 240th AAAMBn in the Seattle Defense Area.

209th Artillery

Originally constituted on 23 July 1940 in the New York National Guard as the 2/209th Coast Artillery (Antiaircraft) and Federally recognized in Rochester on 10 February 1941. On 16 March 1959 the unit—at the time designated the 102nd Antiaircraft Artillery Battalion in Niagara Falls—was reorganized and redesignated the 209th Artillery. The regiment is currently inactive.

2/209th Artillery

2/209th Org.   63, Lancaster, NY
    Db. Mar 70
      A   NF-41 Grand Island   4/63-3/70
      B   BU-18 Lancaster   4/63-3/70
    Lancaster

The 2/209th replaced the 2/106thAAAMBn in the Buffalo–Niagara Falls Defense Area for Nike Hercules operations.

212th Artillery

Originally organized as companies of the 1st Battalion, 12th Regiment in the National Guard, State of New York with Companies A and B forming in New York City on 16 November 1859. On 16 March 1959 the state formed the 212th Artillery through consolidation and reorganization of the 773rd Antiaircraft Artillery Battalion. The regiment is currently inactive.

1/212th Artillery

1/212th Org. 16 Mar 59, White Plains, NY
    Db. 1 Mar 63
      A   NY-99 Spring Valley   6/60-3/63
      B   NY-09 Kensico   6/60-3/63
    White Plains

The 1/212th replaced the 773rd AAAMBn in the New York Defense Area.

241st Air Defense Artillery

Originally constituted in the Massachusetts National Guard as the 1st Battalion, 1st Coast Defense Command, Coast Artillery Corps and Federally recognized at Medford on 14 March 1921. On 1 May 1959 the State of Massachusetts consolidated the 704th and 772nd Antiaircraft Artillery Missile Battalions with the 972nd Antiaircraft Artillery Battalion to create the 241st Artillery. The regiment is currently inactive.

1/241st ADA

Org. 1 May 59, Natick, MA; Rd.1/241st ADA 1 April 1972

Cons. 14 Sept 74			
HHB	Natic		to HHB 1/241st FA
A	B-55 Blue Hills	8/59-3/63	to A/1/241st FA
	B-73 South Lincoln	8/64-4/74	
B	B-63 Needham	8/59-3/63	to B/1/241st FA
	B-36 Ft Duvall	8/64-4/74	
C	(training)		to C/1/241st FA
D	(training)		to D/1/241st FA

Natick

The 1/241st replaced the 704th AAAMBn in the Boston Defense Area. On 14 September 1974 it consolidated with the 3/101st Field Artillery as 1/241st FA and equipped with the Honest John artillery rocket. On 1 December 1975 1/241st FA consolidated with the 1/101st Field Artillery. Through its various consolidations, the 1/241st draws its lineage from the 13 December 1636 formation of the South Regiment in Boston, Dorchester, Roxbury, Weymouth and Hingham, which made it one of the four oldest units in the National Guard.

2/241st Artillery

Org. 1 May 59, Chelsea, MA

I. 1 Mar 63			
HHB	Chelsea		to HHD 164th Trans Bn
A	(training)		to 721st Ord Co
B	(training)		to 721st Ord Co
C	B-15 Beverly	8/59-3/63	to 1059th Trans Co
D	B-03 Reading	8/59-3/63	to 1058th Trans Co

Chelsea

The 2/241st replaced the 772nd AAAMBn in the Boston Defense Area. On 1 March 1963 its elements consolidated into the 1st Battalion with the batteries redesignating into other missions. Through its various consolidations, the 2/241st drew its lineage from the 13 December 1636 formation of the South Regiment in Boston, Dorchester, Roxbury, Weymouth, and Hingham, which made it one of the four oldest units in the National Guard.

242nd Air Defense Artillery   CTArNG

Originally constituted as the 242nd Coast Artillery, Connecticut National Guard. On 1 May 1959 the state consolidated the 211th Antiaircraft Artillery Missile Battalion and the 283rd Antiaircraft Artillery Battalion as the 242nd Artillery under CARS. The current CTArNG unit carrying the number is the 242nd Engineer Battalion in Stratford, which draws its lineage and honors from the 283rd AAABn.

1/242nd Artillery

1/242nd Org. 1 May 59, Bridgeport, CT

I.	63		
A	BR-17 Milford	1/61-/63	
B	BR-73 Westport	1/61-/63	

*Bridgeport

Replaced the 211th AAAMBn in the Bridgeport Defense.

243rd Artillery   RIArNG

Originally constituted as the 1st Battalion, 243rd Artillery, Coast Artillery Corps with headquarters
receiving its Federal recognition in Providence on 1 October 1923; Batteries A and B dated their lineage to
the 11 May 1818 organization of the 1st Light Infantry Company, 2nd Regiment, Rhode Island Militia. On
1 April 1959 the state consolidated the 243rd Antiaircraft Artillery Missile Battalion and the 705th
Antiaircraft Artillery Battalion to form the 243rd Artillery. The 243rd Regiment (Regional Training
Institute) at Camp Varnum in Narrangansett preserves the number and heraldry of the 243rd Artillery.

2/243rd Artillery

2/243rd Org. 1 Apr 59, Providence, RI

    Db. 1 Jun 71

A	PR-58 North Kingston	12/60-6/63
B	PR-69 Coventry	12/60-6/63
	PR-99 North Smithfield	8/63-6/71
D	PR-79 Foster center	10/60-6/63

    *Providence

Replaced the 243rd AAAMBn in the Providence Defense Area.

244th Air Defense Artillery   NYArNG

Originally constituted as the 3rd Battalion, 9th Coast Defense Command, Coast Artillery Corps with
headquarters receiving its Federal recognition in New York City on 10 December 1920. On 16 March
1959 the state redesignated the 259th Antiaircraft Artillery Missile Battalion as the 244th Artillery under
CARS. The regiment is currently inactive.

1/244th ADA

1/244th Org. 16 Mar 59, Roslyn AFS, NY; Rd.1/244th ADA 1 Sept 72

    Db. 1 Sept 74

A	NY-24 Amityville	6/64-4/74
B	NY-25 Rocky Point	6/64-6/71
C	NY-29 Lido Beach	12/60- /63
	NY-03 Orangeburg	6/64-4/74
D	NY-29 Lido Beach	12/60- /63

    *Roslyn AFS

The 1/244th replaced the 259th AAAMBn in the New York Defense Area.

245th Artillery   NYArNG

Originally constituted as the 13th Regiment, New York State Militia and organized in Brooklyn on 5 July

1847. On 16 March 1959 the state redesignated the 245th Antiaircraft Artillery Missile Battalion as the 245th Artillery under CARS. The regiment is currently inactive.

1/245th Artillery

1/245th Org. 16 Mar 59, Lloyd Harbor, NY

Db. 30 Apr 63

A	NY-20 Lloyd Harbor	6/60-4/63
B	NY-23 Hicksville	6/60-4/63

Lloyd Harbor

Replaced the 245th AAAMBn in the New York Defense Area.

250th Air Defense Artillery   CAArNG

First organized on 8 May 1861 in San Francisco as the 1st Infantry Regiment, California Militia, subsequently—following several reorganizations—the 1st Coast Defense Command, Coast Artillery Corps and 25th Coast Artillery. On 1 May 1959 the state consolidated the 271st and 728th Antiaircraft Artillery Missile Battalions with the 951st Antiaircraft Artillery Battalion to form the 250th Artillery.

1/250th ADA

1/250th Org. 1 May 59, Presidio of San Francisco, CA

Db. 1 Jul 74

A	SF-08 San Pablo Ridge	7/59-3/63
	SF-51 Milagra	6/63-3/74
B	SF-31 Lake Chabot	6/63-3/74
C	SF-37 Coyote Hills	7/59-3/63

Presidio of San Francisco

Replaced the 271st AAAMBn in the San Francisco Defense Area.

2/250th Artillery

2/250th Org. 1 May 59, Berkeley, CA

Db. 1 Mar 63

B	SF-89 Ft Winfield Scott	7/59-3/63	to C/3/250th (105mm)
D	SF-59 Ft Funston	7/59-3/63	to C/3/250th (105mm)

Berkeley

Replaced the 728th AAAMBn in the San Francisco Defense Area.

251st Air Defense Artillery   CAArNG

Originally organized in San Diego on 12 October 1887 as Company B, 1st Infantry Regiment, California Militia; and as 8th Company, 1st Coast Defense Command, Coast Artillery Corps in San Diego on 11 May 1901. After multiple reorganizations the two components became batteries of the 2nd Battalion, 250th Coast Artillery (Harbor Defense), which reorganized as the 251st Coast Artillery (Harbor Defense) on 1 November 1924.

On 1 May 1959 the California Army National Guard consolidated the 720th Antiaircraft Artillery Missile Battalion and 746th and 951st Antiaircraft Artillery Battalion as the 251st Artillery under CARS. The regiment is currently inactive.

4/251st ADA

4/251st Org. 1 May 59, Long Beach, CA

    I. 1 Jul 74

A	LA-40 Long Beach	5/59-6/63
	LA-32 Garden Grove	6/63-3/74
B	LA-57 Redondo Beach	5/59-6/63
	LA-55 Point Vicente	4/64-3/74
C	LA-70 Hyperion	5/59-6/63
	LA-29 Brea	4/64-6/71
D	LA-73 Playa del Rey	5/59-6/63
	LA-43 Ft MacArthur	6/63-3/74

    Long Beach

The 4/251st replaced the 720th AAAMBn in the Los Angeles Defense Area. The battalion took the ARADCOM Commander's Trophy in 1960.

254th Air Defense Artillery   NJArNG

On 1 March 1959 the New Jersey Army National Guard consolidated the 109th and 116th Antiaircraft Artillery Missile Battalions as the 254th Artillery. The current unit designated in the New Jersey Army National Guard is the 254th Regiment (Combat Arms) at Sea Girt, under assignment to 57th Troop Command.

1/254th ADA

1/254th Org. 1 Mar 59, Summit, NJ

    Db. 1 Apr 63

B	NY-73 Summit	9/59-4/63
C	NY-53 Leonardo	6/60-4/63
D	NY-88 Mountain View	9/59-4/63

    Summit

1/254th Org. 1 Jun 71, Livingston, NJ

    Db. 1 Sept 74

A	PH-25 Lumberton	6/71-4/74
B	NY-80 Livingston	6/71-4/74

    Livingston

The 1/254th replaced the 109th AAAMBn in the New York Defense Area, was replaced by 7/112th Artillery for the conversion to Nike Hercules...and in turn replaced the 7/112th Artillery in the New York-Philadelphia Defense Area.

2/254th Artillery

2/254th Org. 1 Mar 59, Bellmawr, NJ

    Db. 1 Mar 63

A	PH-32 Marlton	10/60-3/63
C	PH-49 Pittman	10/60-3/63

    Bellmawr

The 2/254th replaced the 116th AAAMBn in the Philadelphia Defense Area.

280th Artillery   VAArNG

On 1 June 1959 the Virginia Army National Guard consolidated the 125th Antiaircraft Artillery Missile Battalion with the 280th Artillery. The regiment is currently inactive.

1/280th Artillery

1/280th Org. 1 Jun 59, Vienna, VA

    Db. 1 Mar 63

A	W-64 Lorton	9/59-3/63
B	W-74 Fairfax	9/59-3/63

    Vienna

The 1/280th replaced the 125th AAAMBn in the Washington Defense Area and was replaced by the 4/111th.

298th Artillery   TH/HIArNG

Originally organized between 1893 and 1895 as the 1st Regiment, National Guard of Hawaii. On 1 May 1959 the 158th and 297th Antiaircraft Artillery Missile Battalions were reorganized as battalions assigned to the 298th Antiaircraft Artillery Group. The group and battalion emblems and numbers are preserved by the 298th Regional Training Institute, Bellows Air Force Station, Waimanalo, HI.

1/298th Artillery

1/298th Org. 1 May 59, Fort Ruger, HI

    Db. Mar 70

B	OA-17 Kauka	1/61-3/70
C	OA-32 Bellows AFS	3/61-3/70
D	OA-32 Bellows AFS	3/61-3/70

    Fort Ruger

The 1/298th replaced the 158th Antiaircraft Artillery Missile Battalion in the Oahu Defense Area.

2/298th Artillery

2/298th Org. 1 May 59, Wahiawa, HI

    Db. Mar 70

B	OA-63 Ewa	1/61-3/70
C	OA-84 Waialua	1/61-3/70
D	OA-63 Ewa	1/61-3/70

*Fort Ruger

The 2/298th replaced the 297th Antiaircraft Artillery Missile Battalion in the Oahu Defense Area.

517th Air Defense Artillery

Originally constituted in the Organized Reserves in July 1917 as the 517th Coast Artillery; organized August 1925.

1/517th Artillery

1/517th A. 1 Sept 58, Mundelein, IL

    I. 23 Dec 60

A	C-92 Mundelein	(9/58-8/60	to A/1/202nd
B	C-94 Libertyville	9/58-8/60	to C/1/202nd
C	C-98 Ft Sheridan	9/58-8/60	to D/1/202nd
D	C-93 Northfield	9/58-12/60	to D/6/3rd

    *Mundelein

Originally organized in August 1925 as Battery A, 517th Coast Artillery; replaced the 78th AAAMBn in the Chicago Defense Area.

2/517th Artillery

2/517th A. 1 Sept 58, Carleton, MI

    I. 8 Feb 63

A	D-51 NAS Grosse Isle	9/58-2/63	
B	D-57 Carleton	9/58-2/63	
C	D-61 Romulus	9/58-2/63	to C/1/177th
D	D-58 Carleton	9/58-2/63	

    *Carleton

Originally organized in August 1925 as Battery B, 517th Coast Artillery; replaced the 504th AAAMBn in the Detroit Defense Area.

3/517th ADA

3/517th A. 1 Sept 58, Selfridge AFB, MI

    I. 13 Sept 72

A	D-16 Selfridge	9/58-6/71	
B	D-06 Utica	9/58-2/63	to A/1/177th
C	D-14 Selfridge	9/58-7/59	to B/2/177th
	D-87 Commerce	12/60-9/72	to C/2/3rd
D	D-17 Algonac	9/58-11/59	to D/2/177th

    *Selfridge AFB

Originally organized in August 1925 as Battery C, 517th Coast Artillery; replaced the 516th AAAMBn in the Detroit Defense Area; replaced by 2/3rd ADA

5/517th Artillery

5/517th A. 15 Mar 60, Dyess AFB, TX

I. 24 Jun 66

A	DY-10 Ft Phantom Hill	10/60-6/66
B	DY-50 Camp Barkeley	10/60-6/66

Dyess AFB

Originally organized in August 1925 as Battery E, 517th Coast Artillery.

562nd Air Defense Artillery

Originally constituted in the Organized Reserves on 5 September 1928 as the 562nd Coast Artillery.

1/562nd Artillery

1/562nd A. 1 Sept 58, Fort George G. Meade, MD

I. 11 Dec 62

A	W-26 Annapolis	9/58-12/62	to A/1/70th
B	W-25 Davidsonville	9/58-12/62	to B/1/71st
C	BA-43 Jacobsville	9/58-3/60	to A/1/70th
D	BA-30 Tolchester Beach	9/58-12/62	to D/4/1st

Fort George G. Meade

Originally constituted 5 September 1928 as Battery A, 562nd Coast Artillery, in Virginia; replaced the 36th AAAMBn in the Baltimore–Washington Defense Area.

2/562nd Artillery

2/562nd A. 15 Sept 58, Eielson AFB, AK

I. 30 Jun 71

A	Site Tare	3/59-4/71
B	Site Peter	3/59-4/71
C	Site Mike	3/59-4/70
D	Site Jig	3/59-4/70
E	Site Love	3/59-4/71

Eielson AFB

Originally constituted 5 September 1928 as Battery B, 562nd Coast Artillery, in Virginia; replaced the 502nd AAABn in the Fairbanks Defense Area.

3/562nd Artillery

3/562nd A. 1 Sept 58, Croom, MD

I. 15 Dec 61

A	W-45 Accokeek	9/58-6/60	to C/3/70th
B	W-35 Croom	9/58-6/60	to B/3/70th
C	W-44 Mattawoman	9/58-12/61	to A/1/71st
D	W-36 Brandywine	9/58-12/61	

* Croom (/59) Suitland

Originally constituted 5 September 1928 as Battery C, 562nd Coast Artillery, in Virginia; replaced the 75th AAAMBn in the Washington Defense Area.

4/562nd Artillery

4/562nd A. 15 Jun 59, Dallas, TX

I. 10 Feb 69

A	DF-01 Denton	9/60-2/64	to A/4/132d
B	DF-20 Terrell	8/60-2/64	to B/4/132d
C	DF-50 Alvarado	8/60-10/68	
D	DF-70 Ft Wolters	9/60-10/68	

Dallas (/59) Duncanville AFS

Originally constituted 5 September 1928 as Company D, 562nd Coast Artillery, in Virginia.

5/562nd Artillery

5/562nd A. 17 Mar 60, Barksdale AFB, LA

I. 25 Mar 66

A	BD-10 Bellevue	11/60-3/66
B	BD-50 Stonewall	11/60-3/66

Barksdale AFB (/60) Louisiana Army Ammunition Plant

Originally constituted 5 September 1928 as Battery E, 562nd Artillery, in Virginia.

A.	activated
Cons.	consolidated
Db.	disbanded
I.	inactivated
Org.	organized
Rd.	redesignated

PART III: DISTINCTIVE INSIGNIA OF ARAACOM AND ARADCOM UNITS

Heraldry of the Air Defense Artillery

The adoption of arms and badges for organizations of the Army was formally approved towards the end of 1919. Regimental arms were used on the colors in place of the arms of the United States, the retention of the eagle showed the Federal nature of the organization, but the remainder of the design applied only to that particular unit which reflected the traditions, ideals, wars, battles, and other incidents connected to that unit's history. In addition a distinctive insignia was developed from an element of the arms for use as a marker and an emblem to be worn on the uniform.

A coat of arms, in the ordinary acceptation of the phrase, consists essentially of a **shield**, with the most important accessories being the **crest** and **motto**. The **shield** consists of a base metal (gold or silver) and one or more solid colors on which are placed designs to illustrate the history of the unit. The crest was formerly worn on the helmet and, whenever practicable, was so shown. Due to the manner in which the arms and crest were placed on the regimental color, the helmet was often omitted, but on drawings, stationery, etc., it was used to support the crest, thus avoiding the appearance of a crest suspended in midair. The heraldic wreath typified the torse of cloth or silk formerly used to fasten the crest to the helmet, and was always shown. It was placed between the helmet and the crest, or as the support of the crest if the helmet was omitted. The mantling was an accessory of the helmet. It symbolized the mantle formerly worn over the knight's armor, and was always the principal color of the shield, lined with the principal metal; and the same rule holds true for the wreath. The **motto** was placed on a scroll or ribbon, usually below the shield, but occasionally elsewhere, there being no fixed rule about its placement or color.

Artillery units developed and adopted insignia from 1920s through the 1950s. Coat of arms were initially established for regiments. Later as the number of units escalated during the WW II years, the development of full coats of arms was generally abandoned and only the shield/crest with or without a motto was designed for use as a distinctive unit insignia and for the regimental flag. As the artillery regiments were converted to independent battalions, these battalions adopted insignia as well from the 1940s through the mid 1950s, as well as insignia for group and brigade level units.

In 1957 the Combat Arms Regimental System (CARS) was established as the independent artillery battalions were being reorganized into administrative regiments again. Generally historic artillery, coast artillery, and antiaircraft artillery regiments were reestablished and the original insignia/coat of arms were used for the CARS regiments, although there were many acceptations, modifications, and inaccuracies in this process.

The unit insignia were used for flags, medals, seals, decorations, marks, emblems, guidons, buckles, streamers, etc. upon request of and approval by the Quartermaster Department. After 1960 this responsibility was assigned to the Institute of Heraldry, headquartered in Virginia. The most commonly seen heraldic items are the distinctive unit insignia pins that were worn on the dress uniform lapels and service caps, which are shown in this book. For further information please consult these references:

Coast Artillery, Antiaircraft Artillery, Air Defense Artillery Distinctive Insignia Catalog, compiled by the American Society of Military Insignia Collectors (ASMIC), 526 Lafayette Avenue, Palmerton, PA 18071-1621.

Sawicki, James P., *Antiaircraft Battalions of the U.S. Army, Volumes 1 & 2*, Wyvern Publications, Dumphries, VA, 1991.

Coat of Arms of the Third Artillery Regiment

Text adapted from Sawicki, James P., Antiaircraft Battalions of the U.S. Army, Wyvern Publications, Dumphries, VA, 1991; see this reference for definitions of heraldic terms.

Shield: *Or,* on a chevron *gules* above an imperial Chinese dragon of the like armed *azure* three mullets argent, on a chief of the second two pallets of the fourth an arrow in fess counterchanged.

Crest: Out of a mural crown *or* masoned *gules* a garland—the dexter branch cactus, the sinister palm—proper encircling a sun in spendor argent.

Motto: *Non Cedo Ferio* (Yield Not, Strike).

Symbolism: Scarlett is used for artillery. The two white stripes on the scarlett chief, the colors of the campaign streamers for the War of 1812, commemorating the participation of several companies of the regiment. The arrow alludes to the Indian wars. The chevron and stars indicate service in the Civil War. The stars also refer to the numerical designation of the regiment. The dragon represents service in China; the claws and teeth are blue to indicate that elements of the regiment served in the China Relief Expedition as infantry. The mural crown, cactus, and palm signify the regiment's participation in the Mexican War and elements of the regiment in the Philippine Insurrection. The sun in its glory commemorates the laurels earned by the regiment during its days of glory.

Distinctive Insignia: An adaption of the crest and motto of the coat of arms.

Distinctive Insignia of the Army Antiaircraft Artillery/ Air Defense Commands

Distinctive insignia pins from the collections of Mark Berhow, Charles Bogart, Bob Capistrano, Greg Hagge, Mark Morgan, Ron Parshall, Jim Rutherford, and Tom Vaughn. Pins photographed by Robert Stewart, Artseed Studio, http://www.artseed.org.

ARAACOM

ARADCOM

Air Defense School

Insignia of ARAACOM Separate Battalions (1950-1959)

AA Battalions that served at antiaircraft gun (75 mm, 90 mm, 120 mm) sites in the USA 1950-1959. (M) indicates battalions that were redesignated antiaircraft missile battalions assigned to Nike sites 1954-1958.

Army National Guard battalions are indicated by a two letter state abbreviation.

Units which did not receive insignia are not shown in this table.

1st AA (M)

2nd AA

8th AA

9th AA (M)

10th AA (M)

11th AA

12th AA

13th AA (M)

14th AA

16th AA

18th AA (M)

19th AA

20th AA

24th AA (M)

27th AA

28th AA (M)

33rd AA

34th AA (M)

35th AA

36th AA (M)

38th AA (M)

41st AA

44th AA (M)

49th AA(M)

51st AA

52nd AA

54th AA (M)

56th AA (M)

66th AA (M)

69th AA

70th AA

71st AA (M)

74th AA (M)

75th AA (M)

77th AA

78th AA (M)

79th AA (M)

83rd AA (M)

85th AA (M)

86th AA (M)

89th AA

90th AA

93rd AA

95th AA (M)

96th AA

98th AA

102nd AA NY

109th AA (M) NJ

114th AA TN

116th AA (M) NJ

120th AA NM

137th AA OH

150th AA NC

156th AA DE

158th AA (M) HI

168th AA (M)

175th AA (M)

177th AA OH

179th AA (M) OH

180th AA OH

202nd AA IL

203rd AA MO

211th AA (M) CT

213th AA PA

227th AA (M) MI

238th AA (M) CT

243rd AA (M) RI

245th AA (M) NY

248th AA (M) IL

250th AA GA

257th AA MN

259th AA (M) NY

260th AA DC

271st AA (M) CA

283rd AA CT

336th AA NY

337th AA PA

340th AA (M) DC

351st AA (M)

369th AA NY

380th AA (M) DC

401st AA (M)

425th AA

433rd AA (M)

436th AA (M)

441st AA (M)

450th AA

464th AA

465th AA (M)

466th AA

483rd AA (M)

485th AA (M)

495th AA (M)

501st AA

502nd AA

504th AA (M)

505th AA (M)

506th AA (M)

509th AA (M)

513th AA (M)

514th AA(M)

516th AA (M)

517th AA (M)

518th AA

519th AA

526th AA (M)

527th AA LA

531st AA (M)

546th AA

548th AA (M)

549th AA (M)

550th AA

551st AA (M)

554th AA (M)

598th AA MN

601st AA

602nd AA (M)

605th AA (M)

606th AA

633rd AA NY

682nd AA CA

689th AA (M) PA

698th AA (M) IL

701st AA

703rd AA ME

704th AA (M) MA

705th AA RI

707th AA (M) PA

708th AA (M) PA

709th AA (M) PA

717th AA NM

718th AA CA

719th AA CA

720th AA (M) CA

724th AA (M) PA

726th AA NM

728th AA (M) CA

730th AA CA

734th AA

736th AA DE

737th AA (M)

738th AA (M)

739th AA (M)

740th AA (M)

741st AA (M)

746th AA CA

749th AA

751st AA (M)

752nd AA

768th AA IL

770th AA (M) WA

772nd AA (M) MA

852nd AA (M)

865th AA (M)

867th AA

933rd AA (M) IL

967th AA (M)

979th AA (M) MI

The following battalions had approved insignia, but were NOT photographed:

99th AA

101st AA GA

106th AA (M) NY

115th AA MS

132nd AA WI

182nd AA OH

201st AA MO

210th AA NH

278th AA AL

300th AA MI

308th AA NJ

341st AA AL

398th AA

451st AA

478th AA

496th AA (M)

508th AA (M)

615th AA (M) VA

684th AA (M) MD

711th AA AL

712th AA

715th AA NY

716th AA NM

744th AA NH

745th AA CT

771st AA NY

951st AA CA

Insignia of ARADCOM Air Defense Artillery Regiments (1958-1972)

Regiments with battalions that served at Nike missile sites in North America and Hawaii.
Army National Guard battalions are indicated by a two letter state abbreviation.
Units which did not receive insignia are not shown in this table.

1st ADA

2nd ADA

3rd ADA

4th ADA

4th ADA

5th ADA

5th ADA

6th ADA

6th ADA

7th ADA

7th ADA

15th ADA

43rd ADA

44th ADA

51st ADA

52nd ADA

55th ADA

56th ADA

57th ADA

59th ADA

60th ADA

61st ADA

62nd ADA

65th ADA

65th ADA

67th ADA

68th ADA

70th ADA MD NG

71st ADA

106th ADA NY NG

111th ADA VA NG

137th ADA OH NG

166th ADA PA NG

176th ADA PA NG

177th ADA MI NG

202nd ADA IL NG

205th ADA WA NG

209th ADA NY NG

212th ADA NY NG

241st ADA NY NG

242nd ADA CT NG

243rd ADA RI NG

244th ADA NY NG

245th ADA NY NG

250th ADA CA NG

251st ADA CA NG

254th ADA NJ NG

265th ADA FL NG

517th ADA

562nd ADA

The following ADA regiments had insignia, but were NOT photographed:

112th ADA NJ NG

126th ADA WI NG

128th ADA MO NG

132nd ADA TX NG

182nd ADA MI NG

298th ADA HI NG

Bibliography

Bibliography

Alaska Office of History and Archaeology, *Site Summit, Nike-Hercules Missile Installation*, Anchorage, AK: Alaska Department of Natural Resources, 1996.

American Society of Military Insignia Collectors, *Anti-Aircraft Coast Artillery Corps Distinctive Insignia*. Pamphlet, series 20, n.d.

Arkin, William M., and Richard W. Fieldhouse, *Nuclear Battlefields*. Cambridge, MA: Ballinger Publishing Company, 1985.

Barnard, LCOL Roy S., *The History of ARADCOM: Vol I, The Gun Era 1950-1955*. Historical Project ARAD 5M-1. Ent AFB, CO: HQ, Army Air Defense Command, n.d. (reprinted by the Fort MacArthur Military Press, 1995, San Pedro, CA)

Bearss, Edwin C., *Historical Resources Study: Fort Hancock, 1948-1974*, Denver: Denver Service Center, National Park Service, n.d.

Berhow, Mark A., and Chris Taylor, *US Strategic and Defensive Missile Systems 1950–2004*. New York: Osprey Publishing Limited, 2005. Fortress 36, edited by Marcus Cooper and Nickolai Bagdanovic

Bright, Christopher, "The Quiver of Zeus: Nike Anti-Aircraft Missiles in Fairfax County," *Fairfax Chronicles*, Vol. XIX, No. 1, (1996) 1-11.

Bruce-Briggs, B., *The Shield of Faith: Strategic Defense from Zeppelins to Star Wars*. New York: Simon & Shuster, Inc., 1988.

Cagle, Mary T., *Development, Production, and Deployment of the Nike-Ajax Weapon System 1945-1959*, Redstone Arsenal, AL: US Army Ordnance Missile Command, 30 June 1959.

Cagle, Mary T., *History of the Nike-Hercules Weapon System*. Redstone Arsenal, AL: U.S. Army Missile Command, 1973.

Carlson, Christina M., and Robert Lyon, *Last Line of Defense: Nike Missile Sites in Illinois*, Denver, CO: National Park Service, Rocky Mountain System Support Office, 1996. PDF version available at http://www.fas.org/nuke/guide/usa/airdef/index.html.

Chun, Clayton K.S., "Winged Interceptor: Politics and Strategy in the Development of the BOMARC missile." *Air Power History*, Winter 1998, 44-59.

Cole, Merle T., "W-25: The Davidsonville Site and Maryland Air Defense, 1950-1974," *Maryland Historical Magazine*, Vol. 80, No. 3, Fall 1985, 240-260. Comeaux, Mike, "Nuclear Missile Sites Once Dotted Southland," San Fernando, CA, *Daily News*, 3 October 1993, 1, 8-9.

Denfield, D. Colt, "Nike Becomes History," *Air Defense Artillery*, November-December 1987, 35-37.

_____. *Nike Missile Defenses in Alaska: 1958-1979*. Historic American Engineering Record. Anchorage, AK: U.S. Army Corps of Engineers, Alaska District, January 1988.

Department of the Army, FM 44-82: Procedures and Drills for Nike-Hercules Missile Battery, November 1968.

_____. *Preventative Maintenance Guide for Commanders: Nike-Hercules and Improved Nike-Hercules Air Defense Guided Missile System*. Washington, DC: Department of the Army, August 1965.

_____. Section "Air Defense," *Statistical Yearbook, FY 1960*, Washington, DC: Office, Deputy Chief of Staff for Military Operations, GPO, 1961.

Department of Energy, *Atmospheric Nuclear Weapons Testing 1951-1963*, September 2006.

DS, GS, and Depot Maintenance Manual: *Intercept-Aerial Guided Missile Ammunition Items (Nike-Hercules and Improved Nike-Hercules Air Defense Guided Missile System)*, Technical Manual, TM 9-1410-206- 35. Washington, DC: Department of the Army, April 1963.

Fagen, M.D., ed., *A History of Engineering and Science in the Bell System: National Service In War and Peace, 1925-1975*. Murray Hill, NJ: Bell Telephone Laboratories, Inc., 1978.

Flanagan, R. J., *Comments on the Use of Parachute Recovery of Air-Defense Warheads to Prevent Plutonium Contamination*, Sandia National Laboratory, 15 October 1956.

Friedman, Norman, *US Naval Weapons*. Annapolis: U.S. Naval Institute Press, 1985.

Gaddis, John L., *The United States and the Origin of the Cold War*, New York: Columbia University Press, 1972.

Gibson, James N., *The History of the U.S. Nuclear Arsenal*. Greenwich, CT: Brompton Books Corp., 1989.

Groueff, Stephane, *Manhattan Project: The Untold Story of Making of the Atomic Bomb*, iUniverse, 2000.

Gunston, Bill, *The Illustrated Encyclopedia of the World's Rockets and Missiles*. London: Leisure Books, Ltd., 1979.

Haller, Stephen A., and John A. Martini, *The Last Missile Site: An Operational and Physical History of Nike Site SF-88, Fort Barry, California*. Bodega Bay, CA: Hole in the Head Press, 2009.

Hansen, Chuck, *Swords of Armageddon* (Version 2.0), Chukelea Publications, Sunnyvale, CA 2007 (CD).

_____. *U.S. Nuclear Weapons—The Secret History*. Aerofax, Inc., Arlington, TX: Aerofax, New York, NY, 1988.

Hatheway, Roger, and Stephen van Wormer, *Historical Cultural Resources Survey and Evaluation of Nike Missile Sites in the Angeles National Forest, Los Angeles County, California*. San Diego: Westec Services, Inc., February 1987. (reprinted by the Fort MacArthur Military Press, 1993, San Pedro, CA)

Hatheway, Roger, and Stephen van Wormer, *Historical Cultural Resources Survey and Evaluation of Nike Missile Site at White Point, Fort MacArthur, Los Angeles County, California*. San Diego: Westec Services, Inc., February 1987. (reprinted by the Fort MacArthur Military Press, 1993, San Pedro, CA)

Henry, Lisa B., ed., *1993 Air Defense Artillery Yearbook*. Fort Bliss, TX: Air Defense Artillery Association, 1993.

_____. *1994 Air Defense Artillery Yearbook*. Fort Bliss, TX: Air Defense Artillery Association, 1994.

Hollinger, Kristi, *Nike Hercules Operations in Alaska, 1959-1979*, Conservation Branch Directorate of Public Works, U.S. Army Garrison of Alaska, July 2004. On-line version at

Kelley, Robert L., *Historical Study No. 4, Army Antiaircraft in Air Defense 1946 to 1954*, Colorado Springs, CO: United States Army, Directorate of Historical Services, Headquarters ADC, 30 June 1954.

Kitchens, James H. III, *A History of the Huntsville Division 15 October 1967–31 December 1976* (construction of the Sentinel & Safeguard sites), USACE, Huntsville, AL, Sept. 1978.

Koker, Hubert L., ed., *Air Defense Artillery Regimental Handbook*. Fort Bliss, TX: U.S. Army Air Defense Artillery School, 1992.

Lonnquest, John C., and David F. Winkler, *To Defend and Deter: The Legacy of the United States Cold War Missile Program*, USACERL Special Report 97/01, U.S. Army Construction Engineering Research Laboratories, Champaign, IL. Rock Island, IL: Defense Publishing Service, November 1996. Web and PDF versions available at http://www.af.mil/.

Loop, James W., "AAA Gun Unit Data." Draft working paper, Rev. 2. San Diego, CA: by author, 1993.

_____. "Non ARAACOM/ARADCOM Units." Draft working paper. San Diego, CA: by author, n.d.

_____. "Random Thoughts On Nike Sites." Notes for lecture presented at the 10th Annual Meeting of the Coast Defense Study Group, San Diego, CA, August 1992.

_____. "Units Assigned to ARAACOM/ARADCOM 1951-1979." San Diego, CA: by author, 26 November 1993.

Martini, John A., and Stephen A. Haller, *What We Have We Shall Defend: An Interim History and Preservation Plan for Nike Site SF-88L, Fort Barry, California*, San Francisco: National Park Service, Golden Gate Recreation Area, Feb. 1998.

McKenney, Janice, compiler, *Air Defense Artillery*. Washington, DC: Center of Military History, 1985.

McMaster, B.N., et al., *Historical Overview of the Nike Missile System*. Gainesville, FL: Environmental Science and Engineering, Inc., December 1984 (reprinted by the Fort MacArthur Military Press, 1993, San Pedro, CA).

McMullen, Richard F., *ADC Historical Study No. 14: History of Air Defense Weapons, 1946-1962*. Ent AFB, CO: Headquarters, Air Defense Command, n.d.

Millett, Allan R., and Pete Maslowski, *For the Common Defense—A Military History of the United States* (revised and expanded). New York: The Free Press, McMillan, Inc., 1994.

Moeller, Stephen P., "Vigilant and Invincible, United States Army Air Defense Command." *Air Defense Artillery* HQDA PB 44-95-3, May-June 1995, 2-42. Web versions available at http://www.redstone.army.mil/history/vigilant/

Murphey, Joseph, *Supplement to the Reconnaissance Survey of Cold War Properties, McGuire Air Defense Missile Site, New Egypt, New Jersey, McGuire Air Force Base* (BOMARC), for United States Air Force Air Mobility Command, Scott Air Force Base, Illinois, United States Air Force Air Mobility Command Cold War Series, Report of Investigations, Number 8-A, U.S. Army Corps of Engineers, Fort Worth District, January 1998.

Newhouse, John, *War and Peace in the Nuclear Age*, New York: Alfred A. Knopf Co., 1989.

Nike-Hercules System, Albuquerque: Sandia Base, Nuclear Training Directorate Field Command, 1 April 1969.

"Nike Missile Site SF88L—Fort Barry," Interpretive folder. Sausalito, CA: Marine Headlands District, Golden Gate National Recreation Area, National Park Service, n.d.

"Nike Missile System Orientation," Redstone Arsenal, AL: U.S. Army Missile and Munitions Center and School, June 1971, revised February 1976.

Olson, L.D. and C.L. Kassensm, Sandia document SCDR-221-59 *Report of Test Flight No. 7.8-24 WX-7/Nike-Hercules Warhead Installation*, November 1959.

Osato, Timothy, "Militia Missilemen: The Army National Guard in Air Defense 1951–1967." ARADCOM Historical Monograph ARAD 3 M, Headquarters US Army Air Defense Command, Ent Air Force Base, Colorado Spring, CO: Office of the Chief of Military History, Washington, DC: Dept. of the Army, 1968.

Peter, Joel, "The Nike Missile System," Pamphlet. Oakland, CA: East Bay Regional Park District, April 1976.

Rolbein, Seth, "Nukes in the Neighborhood," *Boston Magazine*, February 1995, 39-45.

Sandia National Laboratory, Memo Re: Static Test of XW-31 from Mr. A.W. Fite to Mr. P.R. Owens, 19 October 1955.

Sawicki, James A., *Antiaircraft Battalions of the US Army* (2 volumes), Dumfries, VA: Wyvern Publications, 1991.

Schaffel, Kenneth, *The Emerging Shield: The Air Force and the Evolution of Continental Air Defense, 1945-1960*. Washington, DC: Office of Air Force History, 1991.

Standish, Robert Norris, et al., "United States Nuclear Tests, July 1945 to 31 December 1992," Nuclear Weapons Databook Working Paper NWD 94-1, Natural Resources Defense Council, Washington, D.C., 1994.

Sunderlin, Richard N., *U.S. Army Air Defense Command Annual Report of Major Activities 1 Jan 1974–31 December 1974*, (RCS CSHIS-6 Z [R2]) ENT AFB, CO: Headquarters, USARADCOM, 1974.

Thompson, Erwin N., *Pacific Ocean Engineers: History of the U.S. Army Corps of Engineers in the Pacific 1905-1980*, USACE Office of History, GPO, Washington, DC, 1982.

Torres, Louis, *Historical Structure Report: Historical Data Section of Fort Tilden.* Denver: Denver Service Center, National Park Service, n.d.

United States Army, *American Military History.* Washington, DC: Center of Military History, 1989.

_____. "80th Anniversary of Fort MacArthur & Guide to Fort MacArthur." pamphlet, San Pedro, CA: U.S. Army, 1968.

_____. FM 44-1-2 ADM Reference Handbook

United States Army Air Defense Artillery Museum, *A Pocket History of Air Defense Artillery*, Fort Bliss, TX: n.d.

U.S. Army Picatinny Arsenal, Cartridge Assembly & Instructor's Control Panel Assembly, Nike-Hercules Trainer, M-74, MIL-C-48832 (PA) 9 June 1975.

U.S. Army Picatinny Arsenal, Warhead Section Assembly Nike-Hercules Trainer M-74, MIL-C-48829 (PA), 9 June 1975

Walker, James A., Frances Martin, and Sharon S. Watkins. *Strategic Defense: Four Decades of Progress*, Huntsville, AL: Historical Office, U.S. Army Space and Strategic Command, 1995.

Walker, James A., Frances Martin, Sharon Watkins, Mark E. Hubbs, and James E. Zielinski. *Historic American Engineering Record Documentation for the Stanley R. Mickelson Safeguard Complex* (HAER Number ND-9), Volumes 1 and 2. Washington, DC: National Park Service, September 1996.

Walker, Martin, *The Cold War—A History.* New York: Henry Holt & Co., 1994.

Watson, A.O., DRSMI-SH, "Congressional Testimony," memorandum to DRSMI-LL, 19 May 1983.

Winkler, David F., *Searching the Skies: The Legacy of the United States Cold War Defense Radar Program*, United States Air Force Combat Command, Langley AFB, VA, US Army Construction Engineering Research Laboratories, Champaign, IL, June 1997. Web and PDF versions available at http://www.fas.org/nuke/guide/usa/airdef/searching_the_skies.htm.

Yanarella, Ernest J., *The Missile Defense Controversy—Strategy, Technology, and Politics, 1955-1972*, Lexington KY: Univ. of Kentucky Press, 1977.

Internet Resource Sites

An increasing number of web sites on the Nike missile program can be found by using a search engine and the key words "Nike missile." A search using these words found over 1,380,000 web pages in October 2009.

Here are a few key web sites on the Nike air defense missile system. These sites have extensive information, photographs, document resources, and site links, making them a good starting point for web-based Nike research.

The US Army Redstone Arsenal Nike Site
http://www.redstone.army.mil/history/nikesite/welcome.html

Ed Thelen's Nike Missile Web Site
http://ed-thelen.org

Donald Bender's Nike Missiles & Missile Sites
http://alpha.fdu.edu/~bender/nike.html

The Nike Missile System (the official Site SF-88L web site)
http://www.nikemissile.org

The Stanley R. Mickleson Safeguard Complex
http://www.srmsc.org

The FAS United States Nuclear Forces Guide (has a number of documents on Cold War missile programs)
http://www.fas.org/nuke/guide/usa/

The Environmental Analysis Branch-ACC/CEVP (provides a number of historical studies in downloadable PDF format under: Cultural Resources, Cold War Related Studies, context studies: Cold War era)
http://www.cevp.com

Andreas Parsch's Directory of U.S. Military Rockets and Missiles
http://www.designation-systems.net/dusrm/index.html

Air Force Radar and the Army Nike Missile Air-Defense System, part of The Online Air-Defense Radar Museum
http://www.radomes.org/museum/nikeinfo.php

Selected Nike-Ajax & Nike-Hercules Manuals

TM 9-1100-200/250-40-2 15 Sep 1975
(CRD) General Support Maintenance (Assembly, Test, and Storage Procedures) (SUPPLEMENT) For M22 and M97 Warhead Sections, M21 Training Warhead Section (Nike-Hercules): M27, M47, and M48 Warhead Sections, M49 and M72 Training Warhead Sections (Honest John) (U) [DOE-DNA TP W31 8-18])

TM 9-1100-200-250-40-3 31 Jul 1978
(CRD) General Support Maintenance (Assembly, Test and Storage Procedures) (Supplement) For M22 and M97 Warhead Sections, M21 Training Warhead Section (Nike-Hercules): M27, M47, and M48 Warhead Sections (U) [DOE-DNA TP W31 8-1Z]

TM 9-1100-250-10   31 Jan 1984
Operator's Manual for M22 and M97 Nuclear Weapons Sections (Nike-Hercules Air Defense Guided Missile System)

TM 9-1100-250-12-2   30 Mar 1984
(CRD) Operator and Organizational Maintenance: M22 and M97 Atomic Warhead Sections (Nike-Hercules Air Defense Guided Missile System) (U)

TM 9-1100-250-20   31 Jan 1984
(C) Organizational Maintenance for Nike-Hercules Air Defense Missile System, M22 and M97 Nuclear Weapons System (U)

TM 9-1100-250-20P   07 Oct 1970
Organizational Maintenance Repair Parts and Special Tools List (Illustrated Parts Breakdown) M22 and M97 Atomic Warhead Sections [DNA TP W31 8-4A]

TM 9-1100-251-12   30 Jun 1977
Operator and Organizational Maintenance: M74 Training Warhead Section (Nike-Hercules Air Defense Guided Missile System)

TM 9-111-251-35   15 Oct 1964
Field and Depot Maintenance Warhead Section Forward Body Section Atomic Training (Nike-Hercules Air Defense Guided Missile System)

TM 9-1100-251-45P   29 May 1970
GS and Depot Maintenance Repair Parts and Special Tool Lists (Illustrated Parts Breakdown) M74 Training Atomic Warhead Section technical manual. Washington, DC: Department of the Army, November 1967.

TM 9-1400-250-10/2   29 Dec 1960
(C) Operator's Manual: Overall System Description (Improved Nike-Hercules Air Defense Guided Missile System and Nike-Hercules Anti-Tactical Ballistic Missile (ATBM) System (U)

TM 9-1400-250-15/2   21 Jul 1965
Organizational, Direct Support, General Support, and Depot Maintenance Manual: Destruction to Prevent Enemy Use (Nike-Ajax, Nike-Hercules and Improved Nike-Hercules Air Defense Guided Missile Systems and Nike-Hercules Anti-Tactical Ballistic Missile Systems) (24X Microfiche)

TM 9-1400-250-15/3   12 Mar 1968
Operator's Organizational, Direct Support, General Support, and Depot Maintenance Manual: General and Preventive Maintenance Services (Nike-Hercules and Improved Nike-Hercules Air Defense Guided Missile Systems and Nike-Hercules Anti-Tactical Ballistic Missile System)

TM 9-1410-250-35   02 Apr 1963
Direct Support, General Support, and Depot Maintenance Manual: Intercept-Aerial, Guide Missile Ammunition Items (Nike-Hercules and Improved Nike-Hercules Air Defense Guided Missile Systems)

TM 9-1410-250-12/1   Nov 1967
Operator and Organizational Maintenance Manual: Intercept-Aerial Guided Missile MIM-14A, MIM-14B, and MIM-14C (Nike-Hercules and Improved Nike-Hercules Air Defense Guided Missile Systems)

TM 9-1410-250-12/2 **27 Nov 1967**
(C) Operator and Organizational Maintenance
Manual: Theory and Functional Schematics for
Intercept-Aerial Guided Missile MIM-14A and
MIM-14B (Nike-Hercules and Improved Nike-
Hercules Air Defense Guided Missile Systems) (U)

TM 9-1410-250-24P-1-1 **22 Jul 1982**
Organizational, Direct Support, and General
Support Maintenance Repair Parts and Special
Tools List (Including Depot Maintenance Repair
Parts and Special Tools) For Guided Missile, Air
Defense, MIM-14B and MIM-14C (Improved Nike-
Hercules Air Defense Missile System)

TM 9-1410-250-24P-1-2 **13 Jul 1982**
Organizational, Direct Support and General
Support Maintenance Repair Parts and Special Tool
Lists (Including Deport Maintenance Repair Parts
and Special Tools) Illustration Supplement for
Guided Missile Intercept-Aerial, MIM-14B and
MIM-14C (Improved Nike-Hercules Air Defense
Guided Missile System)

TM 9-1410-250-24P-2-1 **22 May 1981**
Organizational, Direct Support, and General
Support Maintenance Repair Parts and Special
Tools List (Including Depot Maintenance Repair
Parts and Special Tools) for Simulator, Guided
Missile Flight, OA-1643C/M (NSN 4935-00-084-
2972): Missile Guidance Set, AN/DPW-17A or
AN/DPW-17B, AN/DPW-18A or AN/DPW-21
(Improved Nike-Hercules Air Defense Guided
Missile System)

TM 9-1410-250-24P-2-2 **01 Jun 1978**
Organizational, Direct Support, and General
Support Maintenance Repair Parts and Special
Tools List (Including Depot Maintenance Repair
Parts and Special Tools) for Simulator, Guided
Missile Flight, OA-1643C/M (NSN 4935-00-084-
2972): Missile Guidance Set, AN/DPW-17A or
AN/DPW-17B, AN/DPW-18A or AN/DPW-21
(Improved Nike-Hercules Air Defense Guided
Missile System)

TM 9-1410-250-34 **01 Dec 1965**
Direct Support and General Support, and Depot
Maintenance Manual: The Nike-Hercules Guided
Missile (Less the Missile Guidance Set) (Nike-
Hercules and Improved Nike-Hercules Air Defense
Guided Missile Systems)

TM 9-1410-250-35/2 **03 Dec 1965**
Direct Support and General Support, and Depot
Maintenance Manual: Test Procedures for Guided
Missile (Nike-Hercules and Improved Nike-
Hercules Air Defense Guided Missile Systems)

TM 9-1410-250-35-3 **30 Jun 1976**
(C) Direct Support and General Support, and Depot
Maintenance Manual: Units of Transponder
Control Group and Flight Simulator Group Tested
at RF and Pulse Test Set, AN/TSM-36 (Nike-
Hercules and Improved Nike-Hercules Air Defense
Guided Missile Systems)

TM 9-1410-250-35-4 **30 Jun 1976**
(C) Direct Support and General Support, and Depot
Maintenance Manual: Transponder-Control Groups
Tested at Transponder Test Set (AN/TSM-35)
(Nike-Hercules Air Defense Guided Missile
Systems) (U)

TM 9-1410-250-35-5 **24 Jun 1976**
Direct Support and General Support, and Depot
Maintenance Manual: Units of Missile Guidance
Set Group Tested at AF Power Test Set (AN/TSM-
37) (Nike-Hercules and Improved Nike-Hercules
Air Defense Guided Missile Systems)

TM 9-1410-251-34 **19 Feb 1959**
Field Maintenance: Missile Guidance Sets,
AN/DPW-10 and AN/DPW-11 Tested at Guidance
Set Group Test Equipment (Nike-Ajax/Hercules
Guided Missile Systems) (24X Microfiche)

TM 9-1410-251-35 **03 Mar 1959**
Field and Depot Maintenance: Theory and General
Maintenance For Missile Guidance Sets, AN/DPW-
10 and AN/DPW-11 and Flight Simulator
AN/MPM-28, AN/MPM-28A and AN/MPM-28B
Tested at Guidance Set Group Test Equipment
(Nike-Ajax/Hercules Guided Missile Systems) (24X
Microfiche)

TM 9-1410-251-50   **18 Sep 1961**
(C) Depot Maintenance Manual: Units of Missile
Guidance Set and Guided Missile Flight Simulator
Tested at Radio Set Position of Depot Maintenance
Test Equipment (Nike-Hercules Air Defense
Guided Missile System) (U)

TM 9-1410-252-50   **07 Sep 1961**
Depot Maintenance Manual For Units of Missile
Guidance Set and Guided Missile Flight Simulator
Tested at Fail Safe Position of Depot Maintenance
Test Equipment (Nike-Hercules Air Defense
Guided Missile System) (24X Microfiche)

TM 9-1410-253-50   **02 Oct 1961**
(C) Depot Maintenance Manual: Units of Missile
Guidance Set and Guided Missile Flight Simulator
Tested at Radio Set Position of Depot Maintenance
Test Equipment (Nike-Hercules Air Defense
Guided Missile System) (U)

TM 9-1410-255-50   **29 Aug 1961**
Depot Maintenance Manual: For Units of Missile
Guidance Set and Guided Missile Flight Simulator
Tested at Driver Detector Position of Depot
Maintenance Test Equipment (Nike-Hercules Air
Defense Guided Missile System) (24Xmicrofiche)

TM 9-1410-261-50   **12 Sep 1961**
Depot Maintenance Manual: Units of Missile
Guidance Set and Flight Simulator Tested at
Amplifier-Decoder Position of Depot Maintenance
Test Equipment (Nike-Ajax and Nike-Hercules Air
Defense Guided Missile Systems) (24X Microfiche)

TM 9-1410-262-50   **14 Sep 1961**
Depot Maintenance Manual: For Units of Missile
Guidance Set and Flight Simulator Tested at
Modulator Position of Depot Maintenance Test
Equipment (Nike-Ajax and Nike-Hercules Air
Defense Guided Missile Systems) (24X Microfiche)

TM 9-1410-263-50   **04 Oct 1961**
Depot Maintenance Manual: Units of Missile
Guidance Set and Flight Simulator Tested at
Control Servo Position of Depot Maintenance Test
Equipment (Nike-Ajax and Nike-Hercules Air
Defense Guided Missile Systems) (24X Microfiche)

TM 9-1410-264-50   **05 Oct 1961**
Depot Maintenance Manual: Units of Missile
Guidance Set and Flight Simulator Tested at Power
Supply Position of Depot Maintenance Test
Equipment (Nike-Ajax and Nike-Hercules Air
Defense Guided Missile Systems) (24X Microfiche)

TM 9-1410-256-50   **23 Oct 1961**
Depot Maintenance Manual: For Units of Missile
Guidance Set and Flight Simulator Tested at
Amplifier Position of Depot Maintenance Test
Equipment (Nike-Ajax and Nike-Hercules Air
Defense Guided Missile Systems) (24X Microfiche)

TM 9-1410-266-50   **15 Sep 1961**
Depot Maintenance Manual: For Units of Missile
Guidance Set and Flight Simulator Tested at Input
Networks Position of Depot Maintenance Test
Equipment (Nike-Ajax and Nike-Hercules Air
Defense Guided Missile Systems) (24X Microfiche)

TM 9-1425-250-12/1   **25 Mar 1968**
Operator and Organizational Maintenance Manual:
Voice Communications System (Nike-Hercules and
Improved Nike-Hercules Air Defense Guided
Missile Systems and Nike-Hercules Anti-Tactical
Ballistic Missile (ATBM) System

TM 9-1425-250-24P   **01 Feb 1982**
Organizational, Direct Support, General Support
and GSSB Essential Repair Parts Stockage List
(Improved Nike-Hercules Air Defense Guided
Missile System)

TM 9-1425-250-34-1-1   **18 Jul 1977**
Direct Support and General Support Maintenance
Manual for Units of Nike-Hercules, and Improved
Nike-Hercules Air Defense Guided Missile Systems
Tested at Position 1 of Trailer-Mounted Electronics
Shop 1 (24X Microfiche W/C1 Thru 3, Order Basic
Only)

TM 9-1425-250-34-1-2   **25 Jul 1977**
Direct Support and General Support Maintenance
Manual for Units of Nike-Hercules, and Improved
Nike-Hercules Air Defense Guided Missile Systems
Tested at Position 1 of Trailer-Mounted Electronics
Shop 1 (24X Microfiche W/C1 Thru 4, Order Basic
Only)

TM 9-1425-250-34-1-3　　　　**22 Jul 1977**
Direct Support and General Support Maintenance
Manual for Units of Nike-Hercules, and Improved
Nike-Hercules Air Defense Guided Missile Systems
Tested at Position 1 of Trailer-Mounted Electronics
Shop 1 (24X Microfiche W/C1 Thru 3, Order Basic
Only)

TM 9-1425-250-34-1-4　　　　**26 Aug 1977**
(C) Direct Support and General Support
Maintenance Manual for Units of Nike-Hercules
and Improved Nike-Hercules Air Defense Guided
Missile Systems Tested at Position 1 of Trailer-
Mounted Electronic Shop 1 (U)

TM 9-1425-250-L　　　　**25 Oct 1978**
List of Applicable Publications (LOAP) for Nike-
Hercules and Improved Nike-Hercules Air Defense
Guided Missile Systems

TM 9-1430-250-10/3　　　　**09 Jan 1976**
(C) Operator's Manual: Electronic Counter-
Countermeasures, Radar Course Directing Central
(Nike-Ajax, Nike-Hercules, and Improved Nike-
Hercules Air Defense Guided Missile Systems and
Nike-Hercules Anti-Tactical Ballistic Missile
System) (U)

TM 9-1430-250-14P-9-2　　　　**28 Jan 1976**
Operator's Organizational, Direct Support, and
General Support Maintenance Repair Parts and
Special Tools List (Including Depot Maintenance
Repair Parts and Special Tools) Illustration
Supplement for Director Station Guided Missile,
Trailer Mounted AN/MSQ-96 (NSN 1430-00-433-
9147) and AN/MSQ-100 (1430-00-403-5580)
(Improved Nike-Hercules Air Defense Guided
Missile System) (24X Microfiche W/C1)

TM 9-1430-250-14P-11-1　　　　**21 Feb 1975**
Operator's Organizational, Direct Support, and
General Support Maintenance Repair Parts and
Special Tools List (Including Depot Maintenance
Repair Parts and Special Tools) for Radar Course
Directing Central Antenna Receiver-Transmitter
Group, Acquisition (HIPAR) (NSN 1430-00-086-
6861) (Improved Nike-Hercules Air Defense Guided
Missile System)

TM 9-1430-250-14P-11-2　　　　**31 Dec 1975**
Operator's Organizational, Direct Support and
General Support Maintenance Repair Parts and
Special Tools Lists (Including Depot Maintenance
Repair Parts and Special Tools) Illustration
Supplement for Antenna Receiver-Transmitter
Group, Acquisition (HIPAR) (NSN 1430-00-086-
6861) (Improved Nike-Hercules Air Defense Guided
Missile System)

TM 9-1430-250-20/3　　　　**09 Jun 1960**
(C) Organizational Maintenance Manual: Theory
for Radar Course Directing Central Computer
System and Recording Devices (Nike-Hercules and
Improved Nike-Hercules Anti-Tactical Ballistic
Missile (ATBM) Systems) (U)

TM 9-1430-250-20/5　　　　**17 Jan 1961**
(C) Organizational Maintenance Manual: Theory,
Radar Course Directing Central (Less HIPAR) Low-
Power Acquisition Radar System (Improved Nike-
Hercules Air Defense Guided Missile System) (U)

TM 9-1430-250-20/6　　　　**23 Feb 1961**
(C) Organizational Maintenance Manual: Theory
for Target Tracking, Target Ranging and Missile
Tracking Radar Systems and Radar Test Set Group
(Improved Nike-Hercules Air Defense Guided
Missile System and Nike-Hercules Anti-Tactical
Ballistic Missile System) (U)

TM 9-1430-250-20/7　　　　**17 Jan 1961**
(C) Organizational Maintenance Manual: Theory
Radar Course Directing Central: Tactical Control
and Power Distribution System (Improved Nike-
Hercules Air Defense Guided Missile System) (U)

TM 9-1430-251-10　　　　**06 Jan 1959**
(C) Operator's Manual: Assembly and Emplacement
Radar Course Directing Central (Nike-Hercules and
Improved Nike-Hercules Air Defense Guided
Missile Systems and Nike-Hercules Anti-Tactical
Ballistic Missile (ATBM) System (U)

TM 9-1430-251-10/2　　　　**29 Dec 1960**
(C) Operator's Manual: Sitting Requirements for
Radar Course Directing Central (Improved Nike-
Hercules Air Defense Guided Missile System) (U)

TM 9-1430-251-12/1 20 Aug 1964
(C) Operator and Organizational Maintenance
Manual: Check Procedures for Computer System
and Multichannel Data Recorder (Nike-Hercules
and Improved Nike-Hercules Air Defense Guided
Missile Systems) (U)

TM 9-1430-253-24P-1-1 30 Sep 1983
Organizational, Direct Support and General
Support Maintenance Repair Parts and Special
Tools list (Including Depot Maintenance Repair
Parts and Special Tools) *Illustration Supplement* for
Antenna-Receiver Transmitter Group, Acquisition
(EFS-HIPAR) (NSN 1430-00-973-0393) (EFS/ATBM-
HIPAR) (1430-00-973-0394) (German EFS-HIPAR)
(NSN-1430-01-061-1932) and (Belgium and
Netherlands EFS-HIPAR) (1430-01-061-5319)
(Improved Nike-Hercules Air Defense Guided
Missile System)

TM 9-1430-253-24P-2-1 28 Jan 1983
Organizational, Direct Support and General
Support Maintenance Repair Parts and Special
Tools list (Including Depot Maintenance Repair
Parts and Special Tools) for Director Station,
Guided Missile, Trailer Mounted AN/MSQ-97
(NSN 1430-00-433-9142) and AN/MSQ-101 (1430-
00-403-5561) (Improved Nike-Hercules Air Defense
Guided Missile System)

TM 9-1430-253-34 22 Jan 1960
Direct Support and General Support Maintenance
Manual: Target-Tracking, Target Ranging and
Missile Tracking Antenna-Receiver-Transmitter
Group and Radar Test Set Group (Nike-Hercules
and Improved Hike-Hercules Air Defense Guided
Missile Systems and Nike-Hercules Anti-Tactical
Ballistic Missile System)

TM 9-1430-254-12/3 18 Aug 1966
Operator and Organizational Maintenance Manual:
Assembly and Emplacement Radar Set AN/MPQ-
43 (Improved Nike-Hercules Air Defense Guided
Missile System and Nike-Hercules Anti-Tactical
Ballistic Missile System)

TM 9-1430-254-12/4 17 Jun 1969
(C) Operator and Organizational Maintenance
Manual: Anti-Jam (Improvements High-Power
Acquisition Radar (Systems 538 through 594)
(Nike-Hercules Air Defense Guided Missile System
and Nike-Hercules ATBM System) (U)

TM 9-1430-254-12-5 31 May 1974
(C) Operator and Organizational Maintenance
Manual: Check Procedures for Anti-Jam
Improvements, High-Power Acquisition Radar
(Systems 538 through 594 and 801 and above)
Improved Nike-Hercules Air Defense Guided
Missile System and Nike-Hercules ATBM System)
(U)

TM 9-1430-254-12-6 23 May 1969
(C) Operator's and Organizational Maintenance
Manual Unit Schematic Diagrams for Anti-Jam
Improvements, High-Power Acquisition Radar
(Systems 538 through 594 and 801 and above)
Improved Nike-Hercules Air Defense Guided Missile
System and Nike-Hercules ATBM System (U)

TM 9-1430-254-12-7 12 Jun 1969
(C) Operator and Organizational Maintenance
Manual: Functional Schematic Diagrams, Anti-Jam
Improvements, High-Power Acquisition Radar (All
Systems) (Improved Nike-Hercules Air Defense
Guided Missile System and Nike-Hercules ATBM
Systems) (U)

TM 9-1430-254-12-8 12 Jun 1969
(C) Operator and Organizational Maintenance
Manual: Theory for Anti-Jam Improvements, High-
Power Acquisition Radar (Systems 538 through 594
and 801 and above) (Improved Nike-Hercules Air
Defense Guided Missile System and Nike-Hercules
ATBM System) (U)

TM 9-1430-254-12-9 12 Jun 1969
(C) Operator and Organizational Maintenance
Manual: Anti-Jam Improvements, High-Power
Acquisition Radar (Systems 801 and above) (Improved
Nike-Hercules Air Defense Guided Missile System
and Nike-Hercules ATBM System) (U)

TM 9-1430-254-20/2 **01 Mar 1061**
(C) Organizational Maintenance Manual Functional Schematic Diagrams for Low Power Acquisition Radar and Tactical Control System (Less HIPAR) Improved Nike-Hercules Air Defense Guided Missile System (U)

TM 9-1430-254-20/6 **23 Apr 1963**
(C) Organizational Maintenance Manual Functional Schematic Diagrams for Low Power Acquisition Radar and Tactical Control Circuits (ATBM) (Nike-Hercules Anti-Tactical Ballistic Missile System) (U)

TM 9-1430-254-24P-1 **03 Oct 1983**
Organizational, Direct Support and General Support Maintenance Repair Parts and Special Tools List (Including Depot Maintenance Repair Parts and Special Tools) for Radar Set AN/MPQ-43 (Mobile HIPAR) (NSN 1430-00-909-6959) and Radar Set (German Mobile HIPAR) (1430-01-145-9814) (Improved Nike-Hercules Air Defense Guided Missile System)

TM 9-1430-254-24P-2 **03 Oct 1983**
Organizational, Direct Support and General Support Maintenance Repair Parts and Special Tools List (Including Depot Maintenance Repair Parts and Special Tools) *Illustration Supplement* for Radar Set AN/MPQ-43 (Mobile HIPAR) (NSN 1430-00-909-6959) and Radar Set (German Mobile HIPAR) (1430-01-145-9814) (Improved Nike-Hercules Air Defense Guided Missile System)

TM 9-1430-254-24P-3 **17 Sept 1979**
Organizational, Direct Support, and General Support Maintenance Repair Parts and Special Tools List (Including Depot Maintenance Repair Parts and Special Tools) for Anti-Jam Improvements modification (AJI) (HIPAR) (Improved Nike-Hercules Air Defense Guided Missile System) (24X Microfiche)

TM 9-1430-254-24P-4 **17 Sept 1979**
Organizational, Direct Support, and General Support Maintenance Repair Parts and Special Tools List (Including Depot Maintenance Repair Parts and Special Tools) *Illustration Supplement* for Anti-Jam Improvements modification (AJI) (HIPAR) (Improved Nike-Hercules Air Defense Guided Missile System) (24X Microfiche)

TM 9-1430-254-34 **22 Dec 1959**
Direct Support and Field Maintenance Acquisition Antenna-Receiver-Transmitter Group (Nike-Hercules and Improved Nike-Hercules Air Defense Guided Missile System and Nike-Hercules Anti-Ballistic Missile System)

TM 9-1440-250-10/1 **29 Nov 1986**
Operator's Manual: Guided Missile Launching Set (Nike-Hercules and Improved Nike-Hercules Air Defense Guided Missile Systems)

TM 9-1440-250-12/1 **28 Jun 1965**
Operators and Organizational Maintenance Manual: Daily, Weekly, Monthly and Quarterly Check Procedures for Guided Missile Launching Set (Nike-Hercules and Improved Nike-Hercules Air Defense Guided Missile Systems)

TM 9-1440-250-12/2 **29 Aug 1966**
Operation and Organizational Maintenance Manual: Assembly and Emplacement for Launching Set (Nike-Hercules, Improved Nike-Hercules Air Defense Guided Missile Systems)

TM 9-1440-250-12/3 **09 Mar 1962**
Operation and Organizational Maintenance Manual: Daily, Weekly and Monthly Check Procedures: Guided Missile Launching Set with Nike-Ajax Missile (Nike-Hercules Air Defense Guided Missile System)

TM 9-1440-250-20/1 **22 Mar 1965**
Organizational Maintenance Manual: Guided Missile Launching Set (Nike-Hercules and Improved Nike-Hercules Guided Missile Systems)

TM 9-1440-250-20/2 **09 Apr 1965**
(C) Organizational Maintenance: Schematics and Theory, Guided Missile Launching Set (Nike-Hercules and Improved Nike-Hercules Air Defense Guided Missile Systems) (U)

TM 9-1440-250-24/2 **05 Jan 1970**
Organizational, Direct Support and General Support Maintenance Manual for Technical Evaluation Procedures to Determine Maintenance Requirements for the Launcher Area Equipment (Nike-Hercules and Improved Nike-Hercules Air Defense Guided Missile Systems)

TM 9-1440-250-24P-1-1   **22 Feb 1982**
Organizational, Direct Support and General Support Maintenance Repair Parts and Special Tools List (Including Depot Maintenance Repair Parts and Special Tools) Illustration Supplement for Launcher, Monorail, Guided Missile, M36E1 (NSN 1440-00-620-9266); Control Indicator C4820/TSW (1440-00-078-4865); Side Truss, Loading Rack, Guided Missile, M1 (1440-0-587-3361); Rack, Loading, Guided Missile, M10 (1440-00-587-3362); Modification Kit, Guided Missile Launching Section, M141 (1440-00-705-0404); Winterization Kit, Guided Missile Launcher, M164 (1440-00-708-2804);Winterization Kit, Guided Missile Launching Section M150 (1440-00-708-2803); Shield, Guided Missile Launcher, M2A1 (1440-00-790-7442); Modification Kit, Guided Missile Launcher, M150 (1440-00-664-1084); Accessory Kit, Mobile Unit (1440-00-875-9782); Modification Kit, Guided Missile Launching Area (1440-00-073-3810) (Improved Nike-Hercules Air Defense Guided Missile System)

TM 9-1440-250-24P-1-2   **17 Feb 1982**
Organizational, Direct Support and General Support Maintenance Repair Parts and Special Tools List (Including Depot Maintenance Repair Parts and Special Tools) *Illustration Supplement* for Launcher, Monorail, Guided Missile, M36E1 (NSN 1440-00-620-9266); Control Indicator C4820/TSW (1440-00-078-4865); Side Truss, Loading Rack, Guided Missile, M1 (1440-0-587-3361); Rack, Loading, Guided Missile, M10 (1440-00-587-3362); Modification Kit, Guided Missile Launching Section, M141 (1440-00-705-0404); Winterization Kit, Guided Missile Launcher, M164 (1440-00-708-2804);Winterization Kit, Guided Missile Launching Section M150 (1440-00-708-2803); Shield, Guided Missile Launcher, M2A1 (1440-00-790-7442); Modification Kit, Guided Missile Launcher, M150 (1440-00-664-1084); Accessory Kit, Mobile Unit (1440-00-875-9782); Modification Kit, Guided Missile Launching Area (1440-00-073-3810) (Improved Nike-Hercules Air Defense Guided Missile System)

TM 9-1440-250-24P-2-1   **28 Dec 1983**
Organizational, Direct Support and General Support Maintenance Repair Parts and Special Tools List (Including Depot Maintenance Repair Parts and Special Tools) for Launcher Control Group, Guided Missile, Trailer Mounted AN/MSW-4 (NSN 1440-00-586-6024) (Improved Nike-Hercules Air Defense Guided Missile System)

TM 9- 1440-250-24P-2-2   **28 Dec 1983**
Organizational, Direct Support and General Support Maintenance Repair Parts and Special Tools List (Including Depot Maintenance Repair Parts and Special Tools), *Illustration Supplement* for Launcher Control Group, Guided Missile, Trailer Mounted AN/MSW-4 (NSN 1440-00-586-6024) (Improved Nike-Hercules Air Defense Guided Missile System)

TM 9-1440-250-24P-3-1   **29 Jan 1984**
Organizational, Direct Support and General Support Maintenance Repair Parts and Special Tools List (Including Depot Maintenance Repair Parts and Special Tools) for Control-Indicators, C-7590/TSW and C-7590A/TSW (NSN 1440-00-880-3166 and 1440-00-880-3165) (Improved Nike-Hercules Air Defense Guided Missile System)

TM 9-1440-250-24P-3-2   **29 Jan 1984**
Organizational, Direct Support and General Support Maintenance Repair Parts and Special Tools List (Including Depot Maintenance Repair Parts and Special Tools) *Illustration Supplement* for Control-Indicators, C-7590/TSW and C-7590A/TSW (NSN 1440-00-880-3166 and 1440-00-880-3165) (Improved Nike-Hercules Air Defense Guided Missile System

TM 9-1440-250-24P-4-1   **05 Apr 1984**
Organizational, Direct Support and General Support Maintenance Repair Parts and Special Tools List (Including Depot Maintenance Repair Parts and Special Tools) for Simulator Group, OH-10/MSW-4 (NSN 6929-00-880-2217) (Improved Nike-Hercules Air Defense Guided Missile System)

TM 9-1440-250-24P-4-1   **05 Apr 1984**
Organizational, Direct Support and General Support Maintenance Repair Parts and Special Tools List (Including Depot Maintenance Repair Parts and Special Tools) *Illustration Supplement* for Simulator Group, OH-10/MSW-4 (NSN 6929-00-880-2217) (Improved Nike-Hercules Air Defense Guided Missile System)

TM 9-1440-250-24P-5-1   **29 Jan 1984**
Organizational, Direct Support and General Support Maintenance Repair Parts and Special Tools List (Including Depot Maintenance Repair Parts and Special Tools) for Rail, Launching-Handling, Guided Missile M3A1 (NSN-1450-00-474-0717) (Improved Nike-Hercules Air Defense Guided Missile System)

TM 9-1440-250-24P-5-2   **29 Jan 1984**
Organizational, Direct Support and General Support Maintenance Repair Parts and Special Tools List (Including Depot Maintenance Repair Parts and Special Tools) *Illustration Supplement* for Rail, Launching-Handling, Guided Missile M3A1 (NSN-1450-00-474-0717) (Improved Nike-Hercules Air Defense Guided Missile System)

TM 9-1440-250-34   **25 Jan 1961**
Direct Support and General Support Maintenance Manual: Control-Indicator C-2620B/TSW and Simulator Group OA-2080/MSW-4 (Nike-Hercules and Improved Nike Hercules Air Defense Guided Missile Systems) and Control-Indicator C-1488/MSE-2 and Simulator Group OA-758/MSE-2 (Nike-Ajax Air Defense Guided Missile System)

TM 9-1440-250-35/1   **07 Dec 1969**
Direct Support, General Support and Depot Maintenance Manual: Wiring Lists Guided Missile Launching Set (Nike-Hercules and Improved Nike-Hercules Air Defense Guided Missile Systems)

TM 9-1440-252-34   **05 Aug 1960**
Direct Support and General Support Maintenance Manual: Monorail Launcher, Launching-Handling Rail, Side Tress, Loading Rack Support, Modification Kit and Launcher Basic Accessory Kit (Nike-Hercules and Improved Nike-Hercules Air Defense Guided Missile Systems)

TM 9-1440-253-35   **04 May 1960**
Direct Support, General Support, and Depot Maintenance: Launcher Control-Indicator C-2699/TSW (Nike-Hercules Air Defense Guided Missile System)

TM 9-1450-250-12   **26 May 1964**
Operator and Organizational Maintenance Manual: Assembly and Emplacement Servicing and Handling Equipment (Nike-Hercules and Improved Nike-Hercules Air Defense Guided Missile Systems)

TM 9-1450-250-24P-3-1   **15 Jun 1981**
Organizational, Direct Support and General Support Maintenance Repair Parts and Special Tool Lists (Including Depot Maintenance Repair Parts and Special Tools) for Truck, Guided Missile Body Section, M473 (NSN-1450-00-609-4079); Truck, Guided Missile Rocket Motor, M442 (1450-00-588-5011); Adapter, Adjustable Trailer to Guided Missile Component M36 (1450-00-586-5016); Ring Handling, Guided Missile (1450-00-602-7949); Truck, Guided Missile Nose Section, M489 (1450-00-604-0694); Truck, Guided Missile Test Set, M451 and M451A1 (4935-00-586-5017 and 4935-00-857-1441) (Improved Nike-Hercules Air Defense Guided Missile System)

TM 9-1450-250-24P-3-2   **15 Jun 1981**
Organizational, Direct Support and General Support Maintenance Repair Parts and Special Tool Lists (Including Deport Maintenance Repair Parts and Special Tools) *Illustration Supplement* for Truck, Guided Missile Body Section, M473 (NSN-1450-00-609-4079); Truck, Guided Missile Rocket Motor, M442 (1450-00-586-5016); Adapter, Adjustable, Trailer to Guided Missile Component, M36 (1450-00-586-5011); Ring, Handling, Guided Missile (1450-00-602-7949); Truck, Guided Missile Nose Section, M489 (1450-00-604-0694); Truck, Guided Missile Test Set, M451 and M451A1 (4935-00-586-5017 and 4935-00-857-1447) (Improved Nike-Hercules Air Defense Guided Missile System)

TM 9-1450-250-24P-4-1　　　　03 May 1982

Organizational, Direct Support and General Support Maintenance Repair Parts and Special Tools List (Including Depot Maintenance Repair Parts and Special Tools) for Sling, Multiple Leg, M20 (NSN 1450-00-474-6385) Bean, Hoisting, Guided Missile (8003042) (1450-00-388-9652); Hoisting Unit, Portable, Guided Missile, M26A1 (1450-00-593-9477); Beam, Hoisting, Guided Missile, M8 (1450-00-593-9473), M7A2 (1450-00-897-5442) and Modification Kit, Guided Missile Assembly Area (145-00-973-3920) (Improved Nike-Hercules Air Defense Guided Missile System)

TM 9-1450-250-24P-4-2　　　　03 May 1982

Organizational, Direct Support and General Support Maintenance Repair Parts and Special Tools List (Including Depot Maintenance Repair Parts and Special Tools) *Illustration Supplement* for Sling, Multiple Leg, M20 (NSN 1450-00-474-6385) Bean, Hoisting, Guided Missile (8003042) (1450-00-388-9652); Hoisting Unit, Portable, Guided Missile, M26A1 (1450-00-593-9477); Beam, Hoisting, Guided Missile, M8 (1450-00-593-9473), M7A2 (1450-00-897-5442) and Modification Kit, Guided Missile Assembly Area (145-00-973-3920) (Improved Nike-Hercules Air Defense Guided Missile System)

TM 9-1450-250-34P-6-1　　　　15 Jul 1982

Direct Support and General Support Maintenance Repair Parts and Special Tools List (Including Depot Maintenance Repair Parts and Special Tools) for Panel Assembly, Air Control (NSN-4935-00-591-7184); Valve Angle (4935-00-856-0411); Tester, Guidance Section Air Leakage (4935-00-564-9980); Fixture Assembly, Nose Section (4935-00-776-8888); Test Set, Resistor, AN/PSM-12 (4935-00-646-8391); Fixture Assembly, Actuator Centering (4935-00-897-7229): Fixture Assembly, Hydraulic Valve, Dynamic Test (4935-00-646-8387); Fixture Assembly, Auxiliary Power Supply Mounting (4935-00-677-8197); Truck, Guided Missile Body Section, M490 (1450-00-593-9478); Rack Assembly, Fin Holding (4935-00-677-8286); Fixture, Position Control, Fin (4935-00-677-8184) (Improved Nike-Hercules Air Defense Guided Missile System)

TM 9-1450-250-34P-6-2　　　　15 Jul 1982

Direct Support and General Support Maintenance Repair Parts and Special Tools List (Including Depot Maintenance Repair Parts and Special Tools) *Illustration Supplement* for Panel Assembly, Air Control (NSN-4935-00-591-7184); Valve Angle (4935-00-856-0411); Tester, Guidance Section Air Leakage (4935-00-564-9980); Fixture Assembly, Nose Section (4935-00-776-8888); Test Set, Resistor, AN/PSM-12 (4935-00-646-8391); Fixture Assembly, Actuator Centering (4935-00-897-7229): Fixture Assembly, Hydraulic Valve, Dynamic Test (4935-00-646-8387); Fixture Assembly, Auxiliary Power Supply Mounting (4935-00-677-8197); Truck, Guided Missile Body Section, M490 (1450-00-593-9478); Rack Assembly, Fin Holding (4935-00-677-8286); Fixture, Position Control, Fin (4935-00-677-8184) (Improved Nike-Hercules Air Defense Guided Missile System)

TM 9-1450-250-35　　　　19 Nov 1965

Direct Support, General Support, and Depot Maintenance Manual: Handling and Servicing Equipment (Nike-Hercules and Improved Nike-Hercules Air Defense Guided Missile System)

ORD 9 SNL J737-1-2　　　　29 June 1962

Group J. List of All Service Parts of Test Set, Computer AN/PM-45 (8514390) and Test Set, Computer (9983983) (Nike-Ajax, Nike-Hercules, and Improved Nike-Hercules Air Defense Guided Missile System)

ORD 9 SNL Y4-2-8　　　　31 July 1959

Group Y. List of All Service Parts of Fan, Centrifugal HD-167 (XN-1)/M (Equipment Cooling) (8010350) Cabinet (Equipment Cooling) (8007298); and Cabinet Electrical Equipment (8158225) (Nike-Ajax Antiaircraft Guided Missile System)

ORD 9 SNL Y5　　　　06 Nov 1957

Group Y. List of All Service Parts of Launcher-Loader Assembly Guided Missile, M26A2, M26A3 and Underground Launcher-Loader (8166450 and 8166570) Nike-Ajax Antiaircraft Guided Missile

General Index

A

acquisition radar (ACQR), **13**, 18-19, 40, 42, 63, 64, 74, 80, 123, 144, 203

Administration area, 12; buildings, **20**, 73, 204

Advanced Research Projects Agency (ARPA), 64

Air Defense Artillery (ADA), 3, 121, 272; battalions, 45-46; home of, 121; school, 121-122

Air Defense Artillery Battalions, 1958-1972 (by unit):

3/1st, 171, 172, 214, 272, 276

4/1st, 83, 84, 85, 159, 199, 202, 221, 272, 276, 295, 310

6/2nd, 196, 197, 273

2/3rd, 111, 113, 114, 273, 309

4/3rd, 113, 114, 217, 273

5/3rd, 170, 171, 172, 173, 222-223, 273-274, 276

6/3rd, 97, 99, 100, 101, 102, 224, 225, 274, 282, 285-286, 287, 309

1/4th, 46, 95, 156, 157, 192, 220, 274, 275, 290

4/4th, 189, 191, 192, 248, 275, 278, 288

1/5th, 89, 175, 275

3/5th, 89, 90, 91, 92, 126, 174, 175, 218, 275, 282, 285

4/5th, 46, 84, 202, 203, 252, 276

6/6th, 172, 173, 247, 276

4/7th, 87, 276, 277

5/7th, 150, 155, 262, 277, 291

8/7th, 277

8/15th, 128, 129, 130, 277, 294

1/43rd, 68, 216, 278, 279

2/43rd, 122, 218, 278

3/43rd, 122, 262, 263, 278, 280, 286

4/43rd, 226, 278, 279

6/43rd, 279, 282

3/44th, 92, 93, 94, 127, 263, 279, 280

5/44th, 187

1/51st, 127, 152, 153, 218, 219, 280, 281

2/51st, 182, 183, 185, 215, 280, 288, 289

3/51st, 151, 152, 153, 154, 246, 247, 280, 295

4/51st, 158

1/52nd, 224, 281

2/52nd, 68, 282

3/52nd, 248, 282

4/52nd, 220, 282

1/55th, 150, 151, 165, 221, 222, 282

2/55th, 45, 93, 126, 127, 168, 169, 216

3/55th, 111, 112, 224, 283

4/55th, 250, 283

5/55th, 132, 133, 146, 284

1/56th, 122, 139, 140, 143, 268, 284

3/56th, 93, 268, 284

4/56th, 174, 175, 176, 188, 263, 284, 285

5/56th, 104, 105, 118, 285

1/57th, 88, 89, 252, 285

2/57th, 97, 245, 285

3/57th, 140, 141, 142, 251, 286,

2/59th, 167, 168, 169, 231, 286, 288

3/59th, 145, 267, 286, 292,

4/59th, 159, 160, 161, 220, 281, 287

1/60th, 97, 98, 99, 224, 274, 282, 287

2/60th, 99, 100, 216, 287

3/60th, 166, 169, 247, 288

4/60th, 190, 242

1/61st, 183, 194, 195, 242, 280, 288

3/61st, 137, 221, 250, 289

4/61st, 177, 182, 184, 263, 289

1/62nd, 289

2/62nd, 94, 244, 290

4/62nd, 68, 267, 290

1/65th, 68, 134, 290, 292

2/65th, 46, 139, 142, 143, 154, 155, 244, 245, 290, 291

3/65th, 106, 107, 247, 291, 293

4/65th, 46, 139, 142, 143, 251, 284, 286, 291

6/65th, 133, 134, 290, 291, 292

2/67th, 116, 117, 249, 292

3/67th, 145, 146, 241, 292

4/67th, 181, 182, 242, 243, 292, 293

1/68th, 107, 240, 293

2/68th, 185, 186, 215, 293

3/68th, 68, 129, 130, 147, 148, 277, 293

4/68th, 175, 176, 265, 294

1/70th MDArNG, 83, 84, 199, 200, 254, 272, 294, 295, 300

2/70ᵗʰ MDArNG, 84, 85, 203, 254, 272, 276, 294, 295, 300

3/70ᵗʰ MDArNG, 200, 201, 294, 295, 310

1/71ˢᵗ, 199, 200, 201, 202, 222, 249, 276, 295, 310

4/71ˢᵗ, 152, 153, 154, 249, 291, 295

Air Defense Command (ADC), vii, 9, 49-50, 117, 123, 144, 147, 178, 191, 193, 293; Headquarters, 144, reorganization, 50

Air Force (USAF), 8, 9, 43, 46-47, 48, 49, 50, 54, 58, 62, 74, 80, 86, 96, 104, 110, 123, 144, 165, 185, 188, 193, 194, 195, 196

Air Force bases (AFB):
Barksdale (LA), 53, 86; Beale (CA), 53, 180; Bergstorm (TX), 53, 87, 227; Biggs (TX), 245; Carswell (TX), 4, 9; Castle (CA), 4; Charleston (SC), 56; Clinton County (OH), 104; Columbus (MI), 108; Dow (ME), 55, 56; Duluth (MN), 56; Dyess (TX), 53, 114, 115; Edwards (CA), 76; Eglin (FL), 32; Eielson (AK), 25, 118, 119; Ellsworth (SD), 9, 11, 116-117; Elmendorf (AK), 25, 82; England (LA), 86; Ent (CO), 9, 117; Fairbanks (WA), 4, 25, 120; Fairchild (WA), 4, 53, 120; Francis E. Warren (WY), 65, 66, 67, 123; Glasgow (MT), 56; Grand Forks (ND), 52, 65, 66, 67, 123-124; Griffiss (NY), 50; Gunter (MO), 52; Hamilton (CA), 50, 53; Hanscom (MA), 88; Hickman (HI), 162; Holloman (NM), 121; Homestead (FL), 68, 128, 131; Hurlbert (FL), 53, 56; KI Sawyer (MI), 53, 185; Kincheloe (MI), 55, 56; Ladd (AK), 118, 119; Langley (VA), 55, 56; Larson (WA), 53, 120; Lincoln (NE), 53, 135, 164; Little Rock (AK), 136; Loring (ME), 9, 11, 52, 137; Luke (AZ), 50, 53, 180; Malmstorm (MT), 53, 56, 65, 66, 67, 144, 148, 193; March (CA), 4, 50; McChord (WA), 49, 52, 53, 120, 188, 190-191; McGuire (NJ), 48, 52, 55, 56, 165; Minot (ND), 53, 56; Montgomery (AL), 177; Mountain Home (ID), 148, 193; Norton (CA), 53, 138, 180; Offutt (NE), 53, 164; Otis (MA), 55; Paine Field (WA), 56, 188; Parks (CA), 181; Rapid City (IA), 4; Richards-Gebaur (MO), 49, 50, 52, 53, 131; Robins (GA), 52, 177; Schilling (KS), 187; Scott (IL), 178; Selfridge (MI), 110-111; Sheppard (TX), 193; Stead (NV), 53; Stewart (NY), 52, 149, 170; Suffolk County (NY), 56; Tinker (OK), 49; Travis (CA), 4, 9, 53, 56, 180, 194, 195; Turner (GA), 52, 195-196; Tyndall (FL), 50; Vandenberg (CA), 56; Walker (NM), 196, 197; Wheeler (HI), 162; Whiteman (MO), 65, 66, 67, 203; Wright-Patterson (OH), 104

Air Force radar sites, 86, 110, 165, 170

Air Force Reserves, 87

Air Force stations (AFS):
Adair (OR), 53, 56, 180; Belleville, (IL), 179; Bellows (HI), 162, 163, 308; Blaine (WA), 188; Cape Charles (DE), 158; Caribou (ME), 136; Caswell (ME), 136; Custer (MI), 52, 110, 170; Duncanville (TX), 108, 109; Eufala (AL), 195; Fairfield (CA), 194; Fire Island, Cook Inlet (AK), 82; Fort Lee (VA), 50, 52, 158, 170, 198; Gibbsboro (NJ), 165; Highlands (NJ), 149, 153; Lockport (NY), 94, 156, 157; Mill Valley (CA), 180, 184; Moorestown (NJ), 165; Murphy Dome (), 119; Mt Kaala (HI), 162; Oklahoma City (OK), 49, 50, 53; Olathe (KS), 131; Omaha (NE), 53, 135, 164; Osceola (WI), 147; Richmond (FL), 128, 129; San Clemente Island (CA), 138; San Pedro Hill (CA), 138, 141; Snelling (MN), 147; Sweetwater (TX), 53, 114, 115; Texarkana (AR), 86; Topsham (ME), 52, 136

Ajax—*see* Nike-Ajax

alternate battery acquisition radar (ABAR), 40, 80, 84, 91, 93, 95, 97, 98, 100, 105, 109, 110, 112, 113, 129, 130, 132, 133, 135, 140, 141, 143, 147, 153, 154, 155, 160, 166, 167, 168, 172, 173, 176, 178, 179, 183, 185, 189, 195, 199, 200

annual service practice (ASP), 82, 122

antiaircraft artillery (AAA), 4, 8, 9, 45, 46, 186; and Guided Missile Center, 121

Antiaircraft Battalions, 1950-1958 (by unit), 214-269

antiaircraft guns:
40mm, 2, **4**, 5, 6, 9
75mm (Skysweeper), 2, **3**, **5**, **6**, 9, 186, 204, 245, 316
90mm, 2, **5**, 6, 9, 186, 204, 316
120mm, 2, 5, 6, **7**, 9, 124, 204, 316

antiaircraft missile battalions (AAAMBn)—*see* air defense artillery battalions

antiballistic missile (ABM), vii, 55, 62-69, 73, 74, 88, 123, 144

Anti-Ballistic Missile Treaty, 67, 73, 74, 144

Anti-Ballistic Missile Treaty, 67, 73, 74, 144

Army (USA), 3-5, 6, 8—*see also* specific units, commands, programs

Army Air Defense Brigades:

31st, 68, 122, 129, 131, 147, 157, 172, 190, 191, 192

35th, 50, 122, 156, 198, 199

40th, 183

45th, 101, 102, 103, 136, 225

47th, 129, 131, 141, 183

52nd, 68, 122, 150, 154, 282

53rd, 107

56th, 89, 91, 93, 97, 104, 105, 122, 139, 140, 158, 159, 160, 161, 174, 175, 176

102nd, 150

104th, 89

107th, 160

114th, 183

115th, 189

Army Air Defense Groups:

2nd, 156, 157

3rd, 160

5th, 125

7th, 150

11th, 174

12th, 139

13th, 129, 130, 131, 147, 184

15th, 90, 91

16th, 102, 103, 153

17th, 84, 160

18th, 157, 172

19th, 19, 141, 153, 202

22nd, 99, 103

24th, 166, 168, 169, 175

26th, 192

28th, 102, 111

29th, 195

30th, 184

40th, 106, 184

47th, 141

49th, 192

50th, 147

53rd, 178

61st, 103, 146

62nd, 178

63rd, 127

64th, 109

67th, 106

74th, 132

80th, 154

87th, 119

88th, 104

90th, 106

100th, 160

101st, 157

108th, 141

191st, 106

202nd, 101

209th, 95

233rd, 183

234th, 140

240th, 150

244th, 150

254th, 153, 208

298th, 163

691st, 83

Army Air Defense Command (ARADCOM), 9, 16, 24, 26, 43, **44**, 45-46, 49, 52-53, 57, 58, 64, 65, 67-68, 73, 75, 80, 96, 103, 105, 110, 116, 117, 121, 123-124, 128, 131, 133, 144, 149. 156, 158, 178, 180, 185, 186, 191, 193, 214, 219

Army Air Defense Command Post (AADCP), 41, 42, 43, 44, 46, 47, 49, 52, 53, 80, 82, 83, 86, 94, 96, 103, 105, 110, 114, 126, 131, 135, 144, 147, 149, 156, 158, 162, 164, 165, 170, 174, 177, 178, 180, 185, 188, 195, 198

Army Air Defense Command Regions: 44, 45, 68, 110, 149, 180

Army Air Defense Units (1950-58), 6

Army Air Forces (AAF), 3-4, 5, 7, 8

Army Alaska (USARAL), 82, 118, 119

Army Antiaircraft Command (ARAACOM), 2, 3-4, 9, 105, 117, 214-215

Army National Guard—*see* National Guard

Army Reorganization Act (1950), 9

Atlas, 62, 63, 114, 120, 135, 164, 187—*see also* intercontinental ballistic missiles (ICBMs)

Atomic Energy Commission (AEC), 9, 29, 32, 34, 36, 58, 186

B

Ballistic Missile Defense Center (BMDC), 64, 72

Battalions, Army (AA, ADA)—see Antiaircraft Battalions and Air Defense Artillery Battalions

Battery Control Area Cable System, 20

battery integration and radar display equipment (BIRDIE), 41, 42, 43, 44, 46, 80, 86, 87, 104, 106, 109, 115, 117, 121, 129, 132, 147, 160, 164, 175, 177, 188, 192, 195, 196

Bell Labs/ Bell Telephone Company, 5, 62

Boeing Aircraft Company, 54

BOMARC missile (US Air Force missile): display, **55**; program, vii, 23, 54-56, 123, 144, 156, 158, 165, 185, 188

BOMARC sites—see "Index of Nike/BOMARC Missile Sites"

Brigades—see Army Air Defense Brigades

bombers, Soviet (TU-4 "BULL"), 8

Bush Administration, 74

C

Canadian Air Defence Command, 9

Canadian Artillery Units, Royal, 185

Canadian BOMARC sites, 55

Chicago-Milwaukee Radar Ring, 103

China, People's Republic of, 67, 315

Clinton Administration, 74

Coast Artillery Corps, xi, 3, 4, 5, 7, 9

combat centers, SAGE, 46, 49-50, 53

Command Structure (US Army Air Defenses), 45-46

Continental Air Defense Command (CONAD), 9, 46, 49, 50, 117

Cuban Missile Crisis, 57, 128, 133

D

data processing system (DPS), 64, 69, 72

defense acquisition radar (DAR), 42, 80

defense areas (ARAACOM, ARADCOM), 26, 45, 52, 64, 82-203—see also Air Force Bases

     Anchorage (AK), 82

     Baltimore (BA), 83

     Boston (B), 88-92

     Bridgeport (BR), 92-94

     Buffalo (BU), 94-95

Chicago (C), 96-103

Cincinnati-Dayton (CD), 104-105

Cleveland (CL), 105-107

Columbus (CX), 108

Dallas-Fort Worth (DF), 108-109

Detroit (D), 110-114

Dyess (DY), 114-115

Ellsworth AFB (E), 116-117

Ent AFB, 117

Fairbanks, Alaska, 118-119

Fairchild AFB (F), 120-121

Fort Bliss 121-122

Francis E. Warren AFB, 123

Grand Forks AFB, 123-124

Hanford (H), 124-125

Hartford (HA), 126-127

Homestead-Miami (HM), 128-131

Kansas City (KC), 131-133

Key West (KW), 133-134

Lincoln (LI), 135

Little Rock (LR), 136

Loring (L), 136-137

Los Angeles (LA), 138-143

Malmstrom AFB, 144

Milwaukee (M), 144-146

Minneapolis-St Paul (MS), 147-148

Mountain Home (MH), 148

New York (NY), 149-155

Niagara Falls (NF), 156-157

Norfolk (N), 158-161

Oahu (OA), Hawaii, 162-163

Offutt (O), 164-165

Philadelphia (PH), 165-169

Pittsburgh (P), 170-173

Providence (PR), 174-176

Robins (R), 177

St Louis (SL), 178-179

San Francisco (SF), 180-185

Sault Ste Marie, 185

Savannah River, 186

Schilling (SC), 187

Seattle (S), 188-192

Sheppard (SH), 193

Thule, 193

Travis (T), 194-195

Turner (TU), 195-196
Walker (WA), 196-197
Washington, DC (W), 198-203
Whiteman AFB, 203
defense center, SAGE, 48, 121,
**Defense Environmental Restoration Program
(DERP)**, 75
discrimination radar (DR), 63
distinctive insignia, 314-327
**Douglas Aircraft Company (McDonnell-Douglas
Astronautics)**, 5, 29, 34, 62, 64

E
Eisenhower Administration, 63
Ent, Major General Uzal G., 117

F
Federal Aviation Administration (FAA) radars, 50,
80, 162, 184
fire coordination center (FCC), 64
FOIA (Freedom of Information Act), 27
formerly used defense site (FUDS), 75
Forts: Banks (MA), 88; Bliss (TX), 4, 8, 32, 43, 57, 68,
76, 121; Cronkhite, 7; Devens (MA), 88; Eustis (VA),
4; George C. Meade (MD), 10, 41, 83; MacArthur
(CA), 41; Richardson (AK), 68; Sheridan (IL), 4;
Snelling (MN), 147

G
General Services Administration (GSA), 75
Groups—*see* Army Air Defense Groups

H
Halsey, Milton B. "Bud", 76
HAWK (US Army missile), 56-57, 60, **61**, 67, 68, 80,
128, 129, 130, 133, 134, 277, 285, 290, 293
Hercules—*see* Nike-Hercules
high-power acquisition radar (HIPAR), **17, 21, 40,
42,** 80, 82, 83, 84, 86, 87, 89, 90, 97, 98, 99, 100,
102, 104, 105, 106, 107, 108, 109, 111, 113, 114,
115, 116, 118, 119, 120, 124, 126, 127, 128, 129,
130, 131, 132, 135, 136, 138, 139, 140, 141, 142,
143, 144, 145, 146, 147, 148, 149, 150, 151, 152,
153, 155, 156, 157, 158, 159, 160, 162, 164, 165,
167, 169, 170, 171, 173, 174, 175, 177, 178, 179,
180, 180, 182, 183, 188, 191, 192, 194, 195, 198,
199, 201, 202

I
intercontinental ballistic missile (ICBM), 55, 62-63,
65, 66, 67, 116, 123, 136; Soviet and Chinese
ICBMs, 62, 67
integrated fire control (IFC), 12, 18, **20**, 26, 27, 36,
40, 49, 80
insignia, distinctive, 314-327

J
Johnson Administration, 64-65
Joint Surveillance System, 50, 119, 134

K
Kennedy Administration, 63
Korean War, 9, 10
Kwajalein Atoll test facility, 63

L
Launcher area (L), **10**, 12
low-power acquisition radar (LOPAR), **12, 17, 21,
40-41**, 76, 80, 121, 137, 145

M
magazines (Nike), 14, 26-27, 75, 81
Marines—*see* US Marines
Martin Company (Martin-Marietta), 41, 64, 83
**McDonnell-Douglas Astronautics (Douglas Aircraft
Company)**, 5, 29, 34, 62, 64
McNamara, Robert S., 63, 64, 65,
Minuteman, 67, 116, 123, 203—*see also* intercontinental ballistic missiles
missile assembly building,
Missile Master, 41, 42, 43, 44, 46, 80, 88, 101, 111,
126, 149, 165, 188, 192
Missile Mentor, 42, 43, 46, 80, 88, 101, 111, 134,
174
Missile Minder, 44, 80
missile site radar (MSR), 64, 65, 66, 69-70, 71, 72,
73, 74, 123, 124, 144
missile sites—*see* "Index of Nike/BOMARC
Missile Sites"
missile-tracking radar (MTR), **12, 13, 17**, 18, **19, 21,**
36, **40**, 63, 76, 80
multifunction array radar (MAR), 64

N

National Guard, Air, 104, 136

National Guard, Army, 9, 19, 25, 45, 57, 67, 75, 138, 158, 162, 170, 177, 188, 204, 214, 225-230, 232-238, 240-242, 249, 251, 253, 254-261, 264-268, 296-298, 300-304, 308

National Guard Special Security Force, 124

National Park Service , 76, 180

National Security Act (1947), 8

Navy (USN), 8, 48, 54, 58-59, 195

Nike missile sites—*see* "Index of Nike/BOMARC Missile Sites"

Nike program, origins of, xi, 5, 7, 8, 9

Nike-Ajax, i, viii, 2, 7, 8, 9, 10-18, 20, 22, **23**, 24, 25, 26, 27, 28, 39, 40, 42, 45, 58, **61**, 67, 80, 81, 110, 120, 121, 122, 124, 138, 149, 158, 177, 185, 186, 198, 204, 215, 219, 224, 225, 227, 245, 253, 254, 258, 260, 295, 302

Nike-B (Nike-Hercules), 23, 29, 34, 36, 62

Nike-Hercules, viii, x, 14, 22, 23-30, 32-35, 38-41, **43**, 54, 55, 56, 58, **61**, 62, 64, 65, 80, 81, 82, 86, 92, 104, 108, 116, 118, 120, 121, 122, 124, 128, 136, 144, 147, 148, 149, 160, 162, 174, 178, 188, 193, 194, 195, 204, 219, 230, 238, 245, 263, 273, 277, 280, 282, 297, 303, 307; decline of, 67-68, 74

Nike-II (Nike-Zeus), 62

Nike-X, 64

Nike-Zeus, 60, **61**, 62-63, 64, 67, 123

Nixon Administration, 66

North American Air/Aerospace Defense Command (NORAD), 9, 42, 43, 44, 46, 49, 50, 53, 110,117,120, 156, 185

North Korea, 74

O

Operation *Snodgrass*, 32-33,

Operation *Hardtack*, 34

Operation *Greenhouse*, 36

Operation *Roller Coaster*, 38

P

perimeter acquisition radar (PAR)—*also* PARCS, 64, 65, 66, 69, 72, **73**, 74, 80, 123, 124, 144, 203

Project Wizard (USAF), 62

R

radar, 5, 6, 17, 18, 19, 20, 21, 27, 28, 32, 40-41, 42, 46, 47, 48, 50, 54, 56, 58, 62, 64, 66, 67, 69, 70, 71, 72, 73, 74, 76, 80—*see also specific radars*

radar vans, 76

Reagan Administration, 68, 74

remote radar integration station (RRIS), 42, 80, 89, 106, 143, 146, 152, 159, 167, 168

remote Sprint launch site (RSL), 69, 73, 74, 123, 124, 203

regions (Air Defense) (ARADCOM), 44, 45, 68, 110, 149, 180

Russia—*see* Union of Soviet Socialist Republics

Royal Canadian Artillery Units, 185

S

Safeguard, 66-67, 69, 72, 73, 74, 80, 88, 123, 124, 144, 203

Safeguard Systems Command (SAFSCOM), 73

SALT I treaty, 123

seacoast fortifications, xi

secondary master fire unit (SMFU), 42, 80, 83, 84, 89, 97, 104, 105, 114, 128, 129, 133, 138, 143, 144, 147, 149, 152, 158, 159, 165, 167, 170, 171, 188, 189, 194

sector directional centers (SDC) (USAF), 42

Semi-automatic Ground Environment (SAGE), 42-43, 44, 46-51, 52, 53, 54, 96, 101, 110, 111, 120, 123, 131, 136, 138, 144, 147, 149, 153, 156, 158, 164, 165, 168, 170, 173, 177, 178, 179, 180, 188, 190, 198

Sentinel, 64-67, 88, 123

short-notice annual practice (SNAP), 43, 122

sites—*see* "Index of Nike/BOMARC Missile Sites"

Skysweeper—*see* antiaircraft guns, 75 mm

Soviets, 8, 62, 65, 66, 67, 164

Soviet ICBMs, 62, 63, 65, 67

Spartan (XLIM-49A), 60, **61**, **62**, 64, 65, 69, 70, 72, 73, 124

Sprint, 60, **61**, 64, 65, 69, 70, 72, 73, 123, 124, 144, 203

Stanley R. Mickleson Safeguard Complex (SRMSC), 69-70, 73, 123

Strategic Air Command (SAC) (USAF), 8, 24, 26, 27, 43, 47, 49, 58, 67, 881, 2, 87, 104, 108, 114, 123,

135, 136, 144, 148, 164, 177, 187, 193, 194, 195
Strategic Defense Initiative (SDI) "Star Wars", 68

T
Talos (US Navy missile), 33, **58**, 60, **61**,
target-ranging radar (TRR), 17, 21, 40, 80
target-tracking radar (TTR), 12, 17, 18, 21, 40, 63, 80
Terrier, ground-based (US Navy missile), 58-**59**, 60, **61**
Testing, nuclear weapons, 30-33, 36, **37**-39
Titan, 62, 116, 136, 148
Tu-4 "Bull" (Soviet bomber), 8

U
Union of Soviet Socialist Republics (USSR, Russia), 8, 65—*see also* Soviets
US Air Force (USAF—*see* Air Force
US Army (USA)—*see* Army
US Army Alaska (USARAL)—*see* Army Alaska
US Navy (USN)—*see* Navy

W
warhead tests, 30-33, 36, **37**-39
Western Electric Company, 5, 62
White Sands Missile Range (Proving Grounds), **10**, 23, **25**, 32, 33, **43**, 63, 121, 215

Z
Zeus—*see* Nike-Zeus
Zeus acquisition radar (ZAR), **63**, 64

Index of Nike/BOMARC Missile Sites

ALASKA

BAY Site "C" 82
Eielson AFB...119
Fire Island AFS AADCP 82
Fort Richardson 82
Fort Wainwright 119
FOX 118
JIG...119
LOVE 119
MIKE 119
Murphy Dome AFS 119
PETER 118
POINT Site "A" 82
SUGAR..118
SUMMIT Site "B" 82
TARE...119

ARKANSAS

Cabot LR-10..136
Conway LR-80 136

CALIFORNIA

Angel Island SF-91 185
Barley Flats LA-09 139
Benecia 181
Berkeley..181
Berkeley SF-09 181
Birmingham Army Hospital 143
Brea LA-29..140
Castro Valley SF-31 182
Cement Hills 195

Chatsworth LA-88 143
Coyote Hills SF-37 182
Elmira T-10 194
Dixon T-33 194
Fairfield T-86 195
Fort Baker SF-81 183
Fort Barry 184
Fort Barry SF-88 183
Fort Cronkhite SF-87.........................183
Fort Funston SF-59 182
Fort MacArthur LA-43 141
Fort MacArthur LA-45 141
Fountain Valley..................................140
Garden Grove LA-32 140
Hyperion LA-70 142
Lake Chabot SF-31 182
Lakewood LA-40.................................140
Lambie T-33 194
Lang LA-98 143
Long Beach LA-41..............................140
Long Beach Airport LA-40 140
Los Angeles Airport LA-73 142
Los Pinetos LA-94 143
Magic Mountain 143
Malibu LA-78......................................142
Milagra SF-51 182
Mill Valley AFS SF-90DC 184
Mt Disappointment LA-09 139
Mt Gleason LA-04 139
Mt San Bruno SF-59...........................182
Mt Sutro SF-89...................................184

Newark SF-37 182

Newhall LA-94 143

Oat Mountain LA-88 143

Pacifica SF-51 182

Palmdale LA-04 139

Parks AFB T-25 181

Pasadena Army Support Ctr 139

Playa del Rey LA-70 142

Playa del Rey LA-73 142

Point Vicente LA-55 141

Potrero Hills T-53 194

Presidio of San Fran SF-77 183

Presidio of San Fran SF-78 183

Presidio of San Fran SF-89 184

Presidio of San Fran T-89 184

Puente Hills LA-29 140

Redondo Beach LA-57 142

Rocky Ridge SF-25 181

San Pablo Ridge SF-08 181

San Pablo Ridge SF-09 181

San Pedro Hill AFS RP-39 141

San Rafael SF-93 185

Saugus LA-98 143

Sausalito SF-87 183

Sausalito SF-88 183

Sepulveda LA-96 143

Signal Hill LA-41 140

South El Monte LA-14 139

Torrance LA-57 142

Travis AFB 195

Van Nuys LA-96 143

CONNECTICUT

Ansonia BR-04 93

Avon HA-85 127

Bridgeport 94

Cromwell HA-48 127

East Windsor HA-08 126

Fairfield BR-65 93

Manchester HA-25 126

Milford BR-17 93

New Britain 127

Plainville HA-67 127

Portland HA-36 127

Shelton BR-94 94

Simsbury HA-85 127

Warehouse Point HA-08 126

West Hartford 127

Westhaven BR-15 93

Westport BR-73 93

FLORIDA

Boca Chica Key KW-10 133

Carol City HM-03 129

Fleming Key KW-80 130

Florida City HM-69 130

Florida City HM-65 130

Florida City HM-66 130

Geiger Key KW-24 134

Goulds HM-05 129

Homestead AFB HM-98 131

Key Largo HM-40 129

Key West KW-65 134

Key West KW-95 134

Miami HM-12 129

Miami HM-39 129

Miami HM-59 129

Miami HM-60 130

Miami HM-80 130

Miami HM-84 130

Naranja HM-82 130

NAS Key West KW-19DC 134

Opa Locka HM-01 128

Opa Locka HM-03 129

Richmond AFS HM-01DC 129

South Miami Heights HM-85 130

Southwest Miami HM-95 130

Sugarloaf Key KW-15 133

West Homestead HM-97 131

West Homestead HM-99 131

GEORGIA

Armena TU-79 196

Byron R-88 177

Jeffersonville R-28 177

Robins AFB R-44DC.................................177

Sasser TU-79 196

Savannah River Plant 186

Sylvester TU-28 196

Turner AFB TU-01 196

Willingsham TU-28 196

HAWAII

Bellows AFS OA-32 163

Dillingham OA-84 163

Ewa OA-63 163

Fort Ruger 163

Kahuku OA-17 162

Kauka OA-17 162

Makakilo OA-63 163

Wahiawa 163

Waialua OA-84 163

Waimanalo OA-32 163

IDAHO

Mountain Home MH-05 148

Mountain Home MH-79 148

ILLINOIS

Addison C-72 100

Alton SL-90 179

Arlington Heights C-81.................................101

Arlington Heights C-80 100

Arlington Heights C-80DC.................................101

Belleville AFS SL-47DC 179

Belmont C-03.................................97

Burnham Park C-40 97

Chesterton C-32 97

Chicago 102

Dixon, IL CM-62R.................................103

Fort Sheridan C-98 102

Hecker SL-40 179

Hegewisch C-44 98

Homewood C-50 99

Homewood C-50R.................................99

Jackson Park C-41 97

La Grange C-51 99

Lemont C-61 100

Libertyville C-94 102

Marine SL-10 178

Montrose C-03.................................97

Mundelein C-92 101

Museum of Science & Industry 97

Naperville C-70 100

Northfield C-93 102

Orland Park C-54.................................99

Palatine C-84 101

Palos Heights C-51 99

Pere Marquette SL-90 179

Porter C-32 97

Rossville, IL CM-50R 103

Scott AFB SL-20 178

Skokie C-93.....................................102

Wenona, IL CM-55R 103

Wolf Lake C-44 98

Worth C-51 99

INDIANA

Dillsboro CD-63 105

Gary Municipal Airport C-45 98

Hobart C-47 98

Logansport CM-43R 103

Munster C-46....................................98

South Gary C-48................................99

Wheeler C-47 98

IOWA

Council Bluffs OF-10 164

KANSAS

Fort Leavenworth KC-80.....................133

Gardner KC-60..................................132

Kansas City 132

NAS Olathe KC-65DC 132

Schilling AFB 187

Schilling AFB SC-01 187

Schilling AFB SC-50 187

LOUISIANA

Bellevue BD-10 86

Louisiana Army, Ammunition Plant 86

Stonewall BD-50...................................86

MAINE

Caribou L-58 137

Caswell L-13 137

Conner L-85 137

Limestone L-31 137

Loring AFB 137

MARYLAND

Aberdeen Proving Ground BA-14 84

Accokeek W-45 201

Annapolis W-26 199

Army Chemical Center BA-14 84

Bay Bridge W-26 199

Brandywine W-36 200

Chestertown BA-30/31 84

Cronhardt BA-92.................................85

Croom W-35......................................200

Davidsonville W-25 199

Derwood W-93...................................202

Edgewood Arsenal BA-18 84

Edgewood Arsenal BA-14 84

Fork BA-09 83

Fort George G. Meade W-13 DC 199

Fort George G. Meade W-13 199

Fort Smallwood...................................84

Gaithersburg W-94 203

Granite BA-79 84

Jacobsville BA-43 84

La Plata W-44....................................200

Laytonville W-93 202
Marlboro W-35 200
Mattawoman W-44 200
Naylor W-36............200
Owings Mills 85
Pamonkey W-54 201
Phoenix BA-03 83
Rockville W-92 202
Skidmore W-26 199
Suitland W-34 200
Sweet Air BA-03 83
Tolchester Beach BA-30/31 84
Towson............83
Waldorf W-44 200

MASSACHUSETTS

Bedford B-85 92
Beverly B-15 89
Blue Hills B-55 90
Burlington B-84 91
Chelsea 89
Cohasset B-38 90
Danvers B-05............89
Fort Banks B-21DC 89
Fort Devens B-82 91
Fort Heath B-21R 89
Fort Strong B-75R 91
Ft. Duvall B-36............90
Hingham B-38 90
Hull B-36............90
Long Island B-35R............89
Nahant B-17 89
Natick B-71 91
Needham B-63 91

Quincy B-37 90
Quincy B-40 90
Reading B-03 88
Rehoboth PR-19 174
South Lincoln B-73 91
Squantum B-37 90
Swansea PR-29............175

MICHIGAN

Adamsville, MI CM-30R 103
Algonac D-17 111
Auburn Heights D-97 114
Bingham D-86 113
Camp Lucas 185
Carleton D-57 112
Carleton D-58 113
Commerce D-87 114
Dearborn D-61 113
Detroit Artillery Armory 111
Detroit City Airport D-23 111
Detroit City Airport D-26 112
Fort Wayne D-26............112
Franklin D-86 113
Grandhaven, MI CM-21R 103
Kercheval D-23 111
Ludington, MI CM-48R............103
Marine City D-17 111
NAS Grosse Isle D-51 112
Newport D-58 113
River Rouge Park, Detroit D-69 113
Riverview D-54 112
Romulus D-61 113
Selfridge AFB D-14 110

Selfridge AFB D-15DC 111
Selfridge AFB D-16 111
Union Lake D-87 114
Utica D-06 110
Wyandotte D-54 112

MINNESOTA

Bethel MS-90 148
Farmington MS-40 147
Ishanti MS-90...............................148
Snelling AFB MS-48DC 147
St Bonifacius MS-70 148

MISSISSIPPI

Columbus Cx-15 108
Columbus Cx-60...............................108

MISSOURI

Lawson KC-10...............................132
Pacific SL-60 179
Pleasant Hill KC-30...............................132
Cedar Creek OF-60 165
Ceresco LI-01 135
Crete LI-50 135
Davey LI-01...............................135
Omaha AFS 164

NEW JERSEY

Belford NY-53 152
Bell Mawr 167
Berlin PH-41/43 167
Camp Kilmer 154
Clementon PH-41/43 167
Darlington NY-93/94 155

East Hannover NY-80 155
Essex Fells NY-80 155
Fort Dix 167
Fort Hancock NY-56 153
Fort Mott 167
Hazlet NY-54 153
Highlands NY-55DC 153
Homdel NY-54 153
Leonardo NY-53 152
Livingston NY-80 155
Lumberton PH-23/25...............................166
Mahwah NY-93/94 155
Marlton PH-32 166
Morristown NY-80R...............................155
Mount Nebo NY-03/04 150
Mountain View NY-88 155
Orangeburg NY-03/04 150
Orangeburg Section No. 2 NY-04R 150
Packanack Lakes NY-88...............................155
Pedricktown PH-64DC...............................168
Pittman PH-49 167
Ramapo NY-99...............................155
Ramsey NY-93/94 155
South Amboy NY-58/60...............................154
South Amboy Section No. 1 NY-60R 154
South Plainfield NY-65 154
Spring Valley NY-99 155
Summit NY-73 154
Swedesboro PH-58 167
Tappan NY-01 150
Watchung NY-73 154
Wayne NY-88 155

NEW MEXICO

Hagerman WA-50 197
Roswell WA-10 197
Walker AFB 197

NEW YORK

Brookhaven NY-25 152
Buffalo 95
Cambria NF-16 157
Cambria NF-16R...156
Farmingdale NY-24 151
Fort Niagara 156
Fort Slocum NY-15 151
Fort Tilden NY-49 152
Fort Totten 150
Fort Wadsworth 154
Grand Island NF-41 157
Grand Island NF-74 157
Grand Island NF-75 157
Hamburg BU-52 95
Harrison NY-09 150
Hicksville NY-23 151
Huntington NY-20 151
Kensico NY-09 150
Lancaster BU-18...95
Lido Beach NY-29/30...152
Lloyd Harbor NY-20 151
Lockport AFS NF-17DC...157
Milgrove BU-18...95
Millersport BU-09...95
Model City NF-03 156
North Amityville NY-24 151
Orchard Park BU-34/35...95
Oyster Bay NY-23 151

Ransom Creek BU-09...95
Rocky Point NY-25 152
Roslyn ANGS 151
Sanborn NF-16 157
White Plains NY-09 150

NORTH DAKOTA

Cavalier 124
Concrete...124
Nekoma...124

OHIO

Bratenahl CL-02...106
Cleveland 107
Fairview Park CL-69...107
Felicity CD-46 104
Garfield Heights CL-48 107
Highland Hills CL-34 106
Highland Hills CL-34 DC 106
Lakefront Airport CL-67 107
Lordstown Military Reservation CL-69 107
Midpark Station CL-59 107
Oxford CD-78 105
Painesville CL-11...106
Parma CL-59 107
Shaker Heights Armory 106
Warrensville CL-34 106
Warrensville CL-34 DC 106
Willowick CL-13 106
Wilmington CD-27 DC 104
Wilmington CD-27 104

PENNSYLVANIA

Beacon PI-71 173
Blawnox 171
Bridgeville PI-62 172
Bryant PI-92 173
Carnegie 172
Center Square PH-91 169
Chester PH-67 168
Coraopolis PI-71 173
Corydon PH-15 166
Cowansburg PI-37 171
Delaware City PH-75 168
Dorseyville PI-03 171
Edgemont PH-75 168
Elizabeth PI-42 172
Elrama PI-43 172
Eureka PH-97R 169
Eureka PH-99 169
Finleyville PI-52 172
Herminie PI-37 171
Hickman PI-62 172
Indianola PI-03 171
Irwin PI-36 171
Logan Armory 172
Media PH-67 168
Monroe PI-25 171
Moon Run 173
Murrysville PI-25 171
Newportville PH-15 166
North Park PI-92 173
Oakdale AADB PI-70 172
Paoli PH-82 169
Richboro PH-07 166

Rural Ridge PI-02 171
Swarthmore 168
Valley Forge PH-82 169
Village Green PH-67 168
Warrington PH-99 169
Westview PI-93 173
Worchester PH-91 169

RHODE ISLAND

Bristol PR-38 175
Coventry PR-69 176
Coventry PR-69DC 175
Davisville PR-58 175
Foster Center PR-79 176
Foster PR-99 176
North Kingston PR-58 175
NorthSmithfield PR-99 176
Woonsocket PR-79 176

SOUTH DAKOTA

Ellsworth AFB 117
Ellsworth AFB E-01 116
Ellsworth AFB E-20 116
Ellsworth AFB E-40 117
Ellsworth AFB E-70 117

TEXAS

Abilene DY-10 115
Abilene DY-50 115
Alvarado DF-50 109
Austin BG-80 87
Bergstrom AFB 87
Burkburnett SH-70 193

Camp Barkeley DY-50 115
Dallas 109
Denton DF-01 109
Duncanville AFS DF-30DC 109
Dyess AFB 115
Elroy BG-40..87
Fort Bliss 121
Fort Phantom Hill DY-10 115
Fort Wolters DF-70 109
Petrolia SH-20....................................193
Sweetwater AFS 115
Terrell DF-20 109

VIRGINIA

Alexandria 201
Ballentine School 159
Camp Patrick N-85 161
Carrollton N-75 160
Craddock Branch 160
Deep Creek N-52 160
Denbigh N-85 160
Dranesville W-83 202
Fairfax W-74 202
Fort Belvoir 201
Fort Monroe N-08 159
Fort Myer 202
Fort Story N-25..................................159
Fox Hill N-02 158
Hampton N-93 161
Hampton Roads Army Terminal N-55DC........160
Herndon W-83 202
Kempsville N-36 159
Lorton W-64 201
Nansemond N-63 160
Newport News 161

Ocean View N-20 159
Patrick Henry N-85 161
Pohick W-74 202
Portsmouth 160
Portsmouth N-52 160
Reidsville 159
Smithfield N-75 160
South Norfolk 159
Spiegelville N-93 161
Suffolk N-63......................................160
Vienna 202

WASHINGTON

Bainbridge Island S-82........................191
Camp Hanford 125
Cheney F-37 120
Cougar Mountain S-20 189
Deep Creek F-87 121
Fairchild AFB 120
Fort Lawton S-90 192
Fort Lawton S-90DC 192
Fort Worden S-93R 192
Issaquah S-20 190
Kenmore S-03....................................189
Kent S-43 190
Kent S-45 190
Kingston S-92 192
Lake Youngs S-32 190
Lake Youngs S-33 190
McChord AFB 190
Medical Lake F-45 120
Midway S-43 190
O'Brien S-41 190
Ollala S-62 191
Othello H-12 125

Phantom Lake S-12 189

Poulsbo S-81 191

Priest Rapids H-83............................125

Rattlesnake Mountain H-52 125

Redmond S-13............................189

Redmond S-14............................189

Renton S-33 190

Saddle Mountain H-06 125

Seattle Artillery Armory 190

Spokane F-07 120

Vashon Island S-61 191

Winslow S-82............................191

WISCONSIN

Argyle, WI CM-71R 103

Cudahy M-42 145

Hales Corners M-54 145

Lannon M-86 146

Milwaukee............................146

Milwaukee M-02 145

Milwaukee M-20 145

Milwaukee M-96 146

Muskegon M-64 145

Paynesville M-54 145

Princeton, WI CM-97R............................103

Prospect M-64 145

Roberts MS-20 147

Tisch Mills, WI CM-10R............................103

Waukesha M-74 146

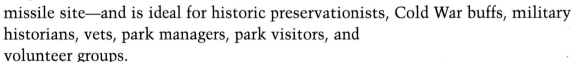